METAPHYSICS

'Informative, accessible, and fun to read – this is an excellent reference guide for undergraduates and anyone wanting an introduction to the fundamental issues of metaphysics. I know of no other resource like it'.

Meghan Griffith, *Davidson College, USA*

'Marvellous! This book provides the very best place to start for students wanting to take the first step into understanding metaphysics. Undergraduates would do well to buy it and consult it regularly. The quality and clarity of the material are consistently high'.

Chris Daly, *University of Manchester, UK*

Ever wondered about Gunk, Brains in a Vat or Frankfurt's Nefarious Neurosurgeon?

With complete explanations of these terms and more, *Metaphysics: The Key Concepts* is an accessible and engaging introduction to the most widely studied and challenging concepts in metaphysics. The authors clearly and lucidly define and discuss key terms and concepts, under the themes of:

- Time
- Particulars and universals
- Realism and anti-realism
- Free will
- Personal identity
- Causation and laws

Arranged in an easy-to-use A–Z format, each concept is explored and illustrated with engaging and memorable examples, and accompanied by an up-to-date guide to further reading. Fully cross-referenced throughout, this remarkable reference guide is essential reading for students of philosophy and all those interested in the nature of reality.

Helen Beebee is a Professor of Philosophy at the University of Birmingham, UK. She is the author of *Hume on Causation*, published by Routledge.

Nikk Effingham is a Lecturer in Philosophy at the University of Birmingham, UK.

Philip Goff is currently Research Fellow with the AHRC project 'Phenomenal Qualities' at the University of Hertfordshire, UK.

ALSO AVAILABLE FROM ROUTLEDGE

Eastern Philosophy: Key Readings
Oliver Leaman
978–0–415–17358–2

Key Concepts in Eastern Philosophy
Oliver Leaman
978–0–415–17363–6

Nietzsche: The Key Concepts
Peter R. Sedgwick
978–0–415–26377–1

Fifty Major Philosophers
Kathryn Plant and Diane Collinson
978–0–415–34609–2

METAPHYSICS

The Key Concepts

Helen Beebee, Nikk Effingham and Philip Goff

Routledge
Taylor & Francis Group

LONDON AND NEW YORK

First published 2011
by Routledge
2 Park Square, Milton Park, Abingdon, Oxon OX14 4RN

Simultaneously published in the USA and Canada
by Routledge
711 Third Avenue, New York, NY 10017

Routledge is an imprint of the Taylor & Francis Group, an informa business

Typeset in Bembo by
Book Now Ltd

British Library Cataloguing in Publication Data
A catalogue record for this book is available from the British Library

Library of Congress Cataloguing in Publication Data
Beebee, Helen.
Metaphysics: the key concepts/By Helen Beebee, Nikk Effingham, and Philip Goff.
p. cm.
Includes bibliographical references and index.
1. Metaphysics–Dictionaries. I. Effingham, Nikk. II. Goff, Philip. III. Title.
BD111.B33 2011
110—dc22   2010024258

ISBN13: 978–0–415–55927–0 (hbk)
ISBN13: 978–0–415–55928–7 (pbk)
ISBN13: 978–0–203–83525–8 (ebk)

CONTENTS

ACKNOWLEDGEMENTS

We would like to thank Chris Daly, Dan Korman and an anonymous reader from Routledge for very helpful and detailed comments on an earlier draft and also Sophie Thomson at Routledge for her help and patience. We also thank the Leverhulme Trust for their generous support.

LIST OF CONCEPTS

Abstract vs Concrete
Agent Causation
Aleph
Analysis
Analytic vs Synthetic Truths
Ancestral Relation
Animalism
Anti-Criterialism
Anti-Realism
A Posteriori
A Priori / A Posteriori
Aristotle
Armstrong, David
A-Theory
Austere Nominalism

Backwards Causation
Being
Berkeley, George
Bilking Argument
Bodily Continuity
Bradley's Regress
Brains in a Vat
B-Theory
Bundle Theory of the Self or
  Person
Bundle Theory vs Substance-
  Attribute Theory

Canberra Plan
Carving Nature at its Joints
Categorical and Dispositional
  Properties

Causal Relata
Causation and Laws
Causation by Absence
Chance
Class
Class Nominalism
Common Sense
Compatibilism
Concept
Conceptual Analysis
Conceptual Scheme
Conceptual vs Logical Truths
Concrete
Consequence Argument
Contingent Truths
Counterfactual Conditional
Counterfactual Theory of
  Causation
Criterion of Ontological
  Commitment

Determinables and Determinates
Determinism
Diachronic Identity
Direction of Time
Dispositional Properties
Dretske-Tooley-Armstrong View
  of Laws

Empiricism
Endurantism
Essence
Eternalism

Singleton
Singular Causal Sentences
Singularism
Soft Determinism
Sortals
Source Incompatibilism
Sparse Property
Special Composition Question
Split Brain Case
States of Affairs
Subsistence
Substance
Substance-Attribute Theory
Substratum
Sum
Supertask
Supervenience
Survival
Synchronic Identity
Synthetic Truths

Temporal Parts
Temporary Intrinsics
Tensed and Tenseless Theories of
    Time

Theoretical Virtues
Thought Experiment
Time
Time Travel
Token
Token-Level Causation
Transitive Closure
Transitive Relation
Trope Theory
Trumping
Truth
Truthbearers
Truth Conditions
Truthmakers
Type-Level Causation
Type and Tokens

Universalism
Universals
Unreality of Time
Unrestricted Mereological
    Composition

Zeno

INTRODUCTION

What is metaphysics?

Broadly speaking (although this, like most other things in metaphysics, is controversial), we can take metaphysics to be the philosophical study of the nature of reality. The 'philosophical' part of 'philosophical study' is important, because of course, plenty of other people study the nature of reality, for example, physicists, biologists, sociologists and archaeologists. The *philosophical* study of the nature of reality is distinctive in two related ways.

First, metaphysicians study questions that do not appear to be answerable – or at least, not fully answerable – by physicists or biologists or sociologists. Take the question, 'do we have **free will**?'. This is a question about the nature of reality, for it is a question about whether human beings, or perhaps persons, have a particular feature or capacity (the capacity for acting freely). However, it is a question that is not (or at least not fully) answered by considering facts about physics or even neuroscience or psychology (see **neuroscience and free will**). One reason for this is that whether or not we have free will depends, in part, on what it *means* to attribute free will to someone. For example, must it be genuinely undetermined, right up until you make a decision, which decision you will make, for you to decide freely?, or is freedom of the will merely a matter of you having a certain kind of control over your decisions, where the kind of control that is required is compatible with your decisions being fully determined well before you actually make them? These questions are *conceptual* questions – questions about what 'free will' *means* – and answering them requires distinctively philosophical investigation (which goes under the broad heading of **conceptual analysis**): we need to consider why the concept of free will is important, we need to disentangle various senses in which someone might be 'in control' of his or her decisions and actions and what kind of circumstances might deprive him or her of that control, and so on. These are not questions that can be answered by investigations in physics or neuroscience or psychology.

Similarly – to draw on some other examples explored further in this book – although physicists and biologists might have views about what is

necessary or what is **possible** (e.g. the view that it is impossible for something to travel faster than the speed of light), it is neither part of their job to try and articulate what it *is* for something to be necessary or possible, coming up with a 'theory of **modality**' (a theory of necessity and possibility) is not part of their remit, nor part of their remit to figure out what it means to say that one thing **causes** another or to ascribe **truth** to a sentence.

Second, and relatedly, physicists (well, some of them), biologists and psychologists study the nature of reality by going out and taking a look: they run experiments, dissect insects, observe breeding patterns, and so on. Their method, in other words, is a scientific one: they come up with theories and test them against the evidence thrown up by their observations and experiments. Metaphysics, by contrast, is done, as it is sometimes put, 'from the armchair'. We have already seen one reason why this is so; metaphysicians ask questions about our *concepts*, and these questions cannot be answered by running a physics experiment. Many metaphysicians, however, insist that metaphysics is not *merely* restricted to answering conceptual questions. After all, metaphysics is supposed to be concerned with the nature of *reality* and not just the nature of our concepts. For example, we are interested not merely in what it *means* to say that one thing causes another but in *what causation is* (see the section on **metametaphysics** for more on this).

This gets us into the business of **ontology**: considering what there is, and what it is like. For example, do **numbers** really exist? Are there, in addition to particular objects such as cats and chairs and subatomic particles, **universals** – features (such as *being furry* or *having positive charge*) that are genuinely shared by different particular objects? Again, it seems that scientific investigation is not going to furnish us with answers to these questions; so again, a distinctively philosophical investigation is required. In the case of numbers, for example, we need to ask questions such as the following: Does the fact that claims such as 'there are infinitely many prime numbers' are true, just by itself, give us good reason to believe in numbers?, what kind of thing is a number anyway? Are numbers somehow creations of the human mind, or do they exist independently of us? and does the fact that numbers do not have spatio-temporal location and are not directly observable create problems for this latter option? (How, for example, can we be sure that the number 537,582,201.8 really exists?) Again, it is not in the job description of mathematicians to come up with answers to these kinds of question; if we want to find out the answers, we need to engage in metaphysics.

How to use this book?

We hope that this book can be used in two different ways. First of all, it can be used as a quick reference guide: if you come across a term in metaphysics that you have not heard before, or whose meaning is not clear, you may well find a definition of it in this book. It is extremely important in metaphysics, and indeed in philosophy in general, to be very clear about exactly what you mean when you use a particular expression, and a philosophical debate will go badly wrong if the parties to the dispute are using a key term to mean different things. Unfortunately, a lot of terms in metaphysics are used by different authors to mean different things. In such cases, we have tried to explain the different meanings that are normally intended, but it is impossible to be completely exhaustive.

Second, although some of the entries are quite short entries that seek to do little more than define a term and explain its relevance to various philosophical debates, many entries go into quite a lot of detail about a particular philosophical dispute, discussing the major alternative positions and their various strengths and weaknesses. They often also cross-refer to other entries, so that you can really go into a topic in quite a lot of detail if you follow up all the cross-references. Hence, we hope that the book can also be used as a kind of basic crash course in various topics in metaphysics. The major topics (designated by entries with section headings) are free will, personal identity, particulars and universals, realism and anti-realism, time, and causation and laws. Of course, a traditional introductory textbook on metaphysics may also help. Each of Blackburn (1999), Conee and Sider (2007) and Carroll and Markosian (2010) covers many of the topics in this book.

Many entries have a 'Further reading' section. Where possible, we have only listed as further reading articles, book chapters or internet sources that are reasonably accessible to an undergraduate audience, both in an intellectual sense (they are not too technical or difficult) and in a practical sense (they should be available in most university libraries, either in print or online, or are available from open-access internet sites). The *Further reading* titles are often themselves general overviews aimed at undergraduate students but go into more detail than is possible in this book. References to other works are also often included in the text of the entries, so that you can follow up a specific issue in detail. (These works are sometimes less accessible in both senses.)

METAPHYSICS

The Key Concepts

ABSTRACT VS CONCRETE

Concrete objects ('concreta') are not, as you might expect, those that are mainly made of cement. In metaphysics, the concrete things include tables, chairs, mountains, cars, stars, you and me (although it does, also, include those things that are made mainly of cement). In other words, material objects are said to be concrete. However, other things are usually said to be concrete as well: if there are *immaterial* objects (ghosts, angels, souls, God, etc.) they, too, are concrete; **events** (such as Second World War or your lunch yesterday) are often labelled as being concrete; **immanent universals** are concrete; **tropes** are usually said to be concrete; and for those who believe in them, **holes** are concrete objects. Roughly, then, the things in space and time are concrete (with exceptions made for angels and God, which are not in space and time – but that is why we used the word 'roughly').

Concreta are to be contrasted with *abstract* objects ('abstracta'). Examples of abstracta include platonic **universals**, **numbers** and **classes** (see the entry on **platonism** for more examples). The received wisdom is that such things are not to be found anywhere in space and time – that is, you would not find the number six lurking around somewhere in Liverpool, nor will you accidentally trip over the property *redness* any time soon. There are some dissenters, so again the rough characterisation of the abstract objects not being in space and time is not to be taken as the last word.

There are two main parts to the debate concerning abstract and concrete objects. First, whether there are any abstract objects. For instance, whether properties, numbers and so on exist is the crux of the debate concerning whether **platonism** is true or not and a major issue in the contemporary debate over **ontology**. Second, what exactly the correct definitions of 'abstract' and 'concrete' are. As the rough sketch above adequately demonstrates, it is a bit tricky to pin down exactly what it takes to be abstract or concrete. A lot of ink has been spilt trying to get the correct necessary and sufficient conditions for both of those terms, and doubtless more ink will be spilt in the future (see Lewis 1986a: 81–6; Rosenkrantz 1995).

Further reading: Swoyer (2008)

AGENT CAUSATION

Some philosophers hold that it is only by being an 'uncaused cause' of one's actions that an agent can truly be said to be ultimately responsible

3

for their actions and hence to act freely and be morally responsible (see **free will** and **moral responsibility**). Such philosophers hold that the relation between the agent and her free actions (normally thought to be her intentions or, in more old-fashioned terms, her 'acts of will' or 'willings') is that of 'agent causation'.

Most contemporary philosophers hold that the **causal relata** – the entities that stand in causal relations to one another – are spatiotemporally located entities, such as events (or facts or states of affairs). Thus, when we say the short circuit caused the fire, we are saying that the causal relation obtains between two events: the short circuit and the fire. In the mental case, the events in question will be mental events: for example, someone is having a particular belief or desire at a particular time. Hence, for instance, Jane's *being hungry at time* t_1 caused her *decision to order a pizza at time* t_2. Agent causation (if it exists) is a different kind of relation, because in this case, the cause is not an event (or fact or state of affairs) but the agent herself, conceived as a **substance**. *Jane herself* – and not the event of her being hungry at t_1 or the fact that she was hungry at t_1 – agent causes her intention or decision to order pizza.

Agent causation is sometimes thought to require the falsity of **determinism**, that is, the truth of **indeterminism**. For, it is claimed, it must be the case both that the agent is not causally determined to bring about her act (a decision, let us say) by any preceding state of the world (hence 'uncaused cause') and that the decision itself is not determined by the **laws of nature** plus facts about the past. If Jane's causing her decision to order pizza – or the decision itself – was itself fully determined by past facts (about Jane's level of hunger, liking for pizza, knowledge of the local pizza delivery number, etc.), this would not count as genuine agent causation. However, some agent-causalists (e.g. Markosian 1999) are **compatibilists**: they think that agent causation is compatible with determinism.

Criticisms of agent causation

Agent-causal views have come in for a lot of criticism. One criticism focuses on the fact that to act rationally, an agent must somehow or other act on the basis of reasons. (Jane orders the pizza *because* she is hungry and thinks that pizza will satisfy her hunger.) According to a standard non-agent-causal story, this requirement is easy to satisfy: the agent's *reasons* are also *causes* of her action, and it is in this causal sense that an agent acts 'on the basis of' reasons. An agent-causal view, however, would seem to preclude this explanation of the agent's rationality: it is the agent herself, and not her reasons, that cause her intention, so in what sense does she act on the basis of reasons? Some recent accounts of agent causation have attempted to show that, in fact, agent causation is not incompatible with allowing reasons to play a causal role in intentions and decisions (see Clarke 1993). Another criticism is that it is mysterious what agent causation really is. What is it about agents – and agents alone – that give them (as opposed to, say, their mental states) this ability to cause things? After all, on the standard view of causal relata, other objects (e.g. rocks and dogs) do not, strictly speaking, cause anything; rather, events or states of affairs involving them, or perhaps their properties, are what do the causing. (Hence, when a dog fetches a ball, it is features of the dog, including, presumably, mental or at least quasi-mental features, that do the causing: its seeing the ball, its wanting to fetch it, its running in the ball's direction, etc.) How is it that agents get to have this special causal status? One answer to this question is that the mind of a genuine agent, capable of free action, is an immaterial substance; hence, on this view, dualism is required for agent causation. This would of course deliver a salient difference between free agents on one hand and dogs and rocks on the other (both of which lack immaterial minds). However, not all agent-causalists hold that dualism is required for agent causation.

Further reading: Clarke (1993, 2008, §§ 3–4)

ALEPH

Aleph-zero, Aleph-one, Aleph-two and so on are names of the different sizes of **infinity**.

ANALYSIS

See **conceptual analysis**.

ANALYTIC VS SYNTHETIC TRUTHS

Analytic truths are true merely in virtue of the meaning of words (e.g. 'all bachelors are unmarried'), whereas synthetic truths are all the rest (e.g. 'some bachelors are tall').

Intuitively – and according to some philosophers – the analytic truths are just those truths that we can know *a priori*, whereas the truth of synthetic truths can only be known *a posteriori* (i.e. through empirical investigation). However, **Immanuel Kant** (who is responsible for the terms 'analytic' and 'synthetic') famously held that some truths (e.g. the truths of mathematics) are synthetic and yet knowable *a priori*. More recently, **W. V. Quine** (1951) famously argued that there is no genuine distinction to be drawn between the analytic and the synthetic (see also **conceptual vs logical truths** and **metametaphysics**).

A second related distinction is that between *necessary truths* (see **necessity**) and **contingent truths**: a necessary truth *has* to be true (it is, as it is sometimes put, true in all **possible worlds**), whereas a contingent truth *might have been* false (there is at least one possible world where it is false). Whether the distinction between necessary and contingent truths lines up neatly with the distinction (if there is one!) between analytic and synthetic truths is a matter of dispute; in particular, **Saul Kripke** argues, in effect, that there are some necessary truths that are not analytic and so cannot be known *a priori* (see **necessary a posteriori truths**).

Further reading: Quine (1951); Grice and Strawson (1957)

ANCESTRAL RELATION

Take any relation of your choosing and call it R. If x_1 is R related to x_2, and x_2 is R related to x_3, x_3 is R related to x_4 and so on, then, although x_1 may not be R related to anything else in that chain other than x_2, we *can* say that x_1 stands in the relation of being in a *chain* of R relations to such things. Call *that* relation – the relation of being in a chain of R relations – the *ancestral* relation of R. This is sometimes called the *transitive closure* of R: **transitive** because ancestral relations are always transitive.

Here is an example (indeed, this example is responsible for the term's name). My father stands in the *parent of* relation to me, my grandfather stands in the *parent of* relation to my father, my great-grandfather stands in the *parent of* relation to my grandfather and so on. In that example, only my father stands in the *parent of* relation to me, but my grandfather, great-grandfather, great-great-grandfather and so on are all in a chain of parents that connects, ultimately, to me. Hence, they all stand to me in the ancestral relation of *parent of*. That ancestral relation is, funnily enough, the *ancestor of* relation (i.e. my father, grandfather, great-grandfather, etc. are all my ancestors). Note that the *parent of* relation is intransitive, if *a* is a parent of *b*, and *b* is a parent of *c*, one would very much hope that *a* is not a parent of *c*. However, the *ancestor of* relation is transitive: if *a* is an ancestor of *b* and *b* is an ancestor of *c*, then *a* must be an ancestor of *c*.

Another example: If I am touching you and you are touching someone else who I am not touching, then I do not stand in the *touches* relation to them. However, there is a chain of people who touch one another, and both they and I are part of that chain. Hence, we all stand in the ancestral of the *touches* relation – call it the 'connected relation'. So, even though I do not touch everyone in the chain, I am connected to them, that is, stand in the *connected* relation to them.

Ancestral relations are sometimes appealed to in metaphysical theories. In particular, in the **counterfactual theory of causation**, the (transitive) relation of causation is defined as the ancestral of the (intransitive) relation of 'causal dependence'. In addition, in the **psychological continuity** theory of personal identity, psychological continuity is defined as the ancestral of 'psychological connectedness'. In each case, the point of defining an ancestral relation is to deliver a transitive relation; for example, because identity (and hence personal identity) is transitive (if *a* = *b* and *b* = *c*, then *a* = *c*), personal identity cannot be defined just in terms of the intransitive relation of psychological connectedness.

ANIMALISM

Animalist theories of **personal identity** are perhaps the most popular rival to **psychological continuity** theories of personal identity (see also **bodily continuity**). Whereas psychological continuity theories ground personal identity in *psychological* facts, animalists ground personal identity in *biological* facts.

Animalists claim that, as matter of contingent fact, each and every person on this planet is identical to a human animal (we could easily alter this slightly if we wished to allow that some higher animals should be counted as persons, but we shall ignore this complication in what follows). For Old Jack to be one and the same person as Wee Johnny is for Old Jack to be one and the same human animal as Wee Johnny. In general, for person *x* at time t_1 to be identical with person *y* at t_2 is for *x* and *y* to be the same human animal. In this way, the **diachronic identity** (i.e. the identity over time) of persons (on this planet) is explained in terms of the diachronic identity of human animals. Of course, this leaves us with the remaining challenge of giving an account of the diachronic identity of human animals, but arguably, progress has been made by reducing a deeply puzzling issue to a more tractable one.

Animalism does not entail that, necessarily, all persons are human animals. It allows for the possibility of other planets being populated with persons identical to animals of other biological species, or of the future containing persons identical with machines. The view is merely that all the persons on this planet at this time are human animals.

Nor does animalism entail that all human animals are persons. A foetus is clearly a human animal, as is an individual in a permanent vegetative state, but most animalists would not want to claim that these things are persons. Animalist Eric Olson explains the view in the following way: the word 'person' is a *phase sortal*, that is, a word that picks out a period in a thing's existence. Just as the phase sortal, 'child' denotes one phase of a human animal's existence, so the phase sortal 'person' denotes another, usually longer, period of a human animal's existence.

Relatedly, the animalist denies that we (persons, every one of us) are *essentially* persons (see **essence**) and claims that this has the advantage of fitting with much of pre-theoretical **common sense**. Outside the philosophy seminar room, the average woman believes that she was once a foetus, and that an accident might render her a vegetable. However, neither a foetus nor a vegetable is a person, assuming that by 'person' we mean a thinking, reflective being. Therefore, if the average woman is essentially a person, then her common-sense belief that *she* was once a foetus and one day might become a vegetable must be false; something that is essentially a person cannot have been, and cannot become, something that is not a person. Indeed, given that we cannot assume from the off that you and I are essentially persons, Olson thinks that starting off discussion asking about the diachronic identity of *persons* is a rather limiting enterprise: better to start by asking what kind of thing you and I are (for the sake of simplicity, however, I will continue to discuss animalism as an account of the diachronic identity of persons).

Animalism also deals easily with what is sometimes called the 'too-many-thinkers problem'. Consider yourself: the person currently reading this book. That person is a conscious, thinking thing. However, it is difficult to deny that there is a human animal reading this article, and that that human animal is a thinking conscious thing. On the assumption that you are not identical with an animal, it seems that there are right now, sat on your chair, two thinking conscious things reading this article: you and the animal. That seems weird.

This is a closely related epistemological worry. If there are two thinkers, a person and an animal, reading this article right now, how do you know which one you are? Is what it is like to be the person different to what it is like to be the animal? A philosophical opponent of animalism claims that she is not an animal, but if there is an animal under her skin, thinking the same thoughts, feeling the same feelings, how can she be so sure that she is not that animal? Of course, animalists are untouched by either of these worries. If you are identical to the animal reading this article, then there is no need to think that there is more than one thinker reading the article.

The biggest objection to animalism, which also constitutes an important argument for psychological continuity theories, is the lack of ease it has accommodating our intuitions concerning brain transplant cases. Suppose Barack Obama's brain is removed from his body and hooked up to David Cameron's body (whose brain has been scooped out and disposed of), such that Obama's body is left in a vegetative state, whereas the resulting person with Cameron's body is psychologically continuous with Obama. It is extremely intuitive to describe this as a situation where Obama – the person – now occupies Cameron's body: call this the 'person transplant intuition'.

There is strong pressure for the animalist to deny the person transplant intuition. It looks as though the body of Obama, and the body of Cameron, still constitute (or are identical with) the same living human animals as before the brains were removed. Because of this it is hard for the animalist not to describe this as a situation in which Obama becomes a vegetable, whereas Cameron gains a whole host of delusory beliefs, for example, that he is the president of the United States and has a wife called Michelle.

Having said that, there is just about room in logical space for animalists to accept the person transplant intuition. A minority of animalists describe the above situation as one in which the human animal that is Obama is 'whittled down' to the size of a brain and then built up again to the size a human animal normally is, and in this way make sense of Obama coming to occupy the body Cameron used to occupy (presumably the animal that was Cameron is destroyed in the process).

Alternatively, the animalist might try to explain why we are tempted to accept the person transplant intuition even though it is false. Although Olson is an animalist, he follows Parfit in holding that it is '**survival**' (in Parfit's sense of the word), not literal identity, that is intrinsically important. As an animalist, Olson describes the above situation as one in which the animal that is Obama is reduced to a vegetative state by having its brain removed. However, because survival is what is important – according to Olson – Obama ought not to be concerned that he will be reduced to a vegetative state, given that he will 'survive' in the distinct person of Cameron. Olson even thinks that if Obama-pre-brain-removal committed a crime, it would be just to punish Cameron-with-Obama's-brain for it, even though these two people are not identical. It is because we tend to think (falsely) that these normative matters are more closely associated with identity, Olson argues, that we falsely assume that Obama-pre-brain-removal and Cameron-with-Obama's-brain are identical.

Further reading: Noonan (1989, Chapter 11); Olson (1997, 2008); Snowdon (1991); van Inwagen (1990, Chapters 15 and 16)

ANTI-CRITERIALISM

Anti-criterialism is another word for the **simple view of personal identity**.

ANTI-REALISM

See **realism and anti-realism**.

A POSTERIORI

See ***a priori / a posteriori***.

A PRIORI/A POSTERIORI

These terms refer to two kinds of knowledge that we can have. A claim is knowable *a priori* if our justification for believing the claim need not rely on experience in any way. For example, one can prove that there are infinitely many prime numbers by deriving it from some basic mathematical and logical principles, themselves knowable *a priori*. Note that something can be knowable *a priori* even though someone, in fact, comes to learn it through sensory experience (e.g. a child might learn that 2 + 5 =7 by getting a group of two objects and another group of five objects and counting how many objects they have altogether). Also, something can be know*able* *a priori* even if a particular person's justification for it comes from sensory experience. For example, if a clever and trustworthy mathematician tells you that there are infinitely many prime numbers, then that is a good reason for you to believe that there are indeed infinitely many primes – but your *justification* for believing it rests on your having heard a trustworthy person tell you. Nonetheless, *someone* (perhaps the same person who told you) can justify the claim without relying on sensory experience (by deriving it from axioms) and that is enough for the claim to be knowable *a priori*.

A claim is knowable (only) *a posteriori* if it can be justified but only by appeal to experience. Most of our knowledge is *a posteriori*: the belief that kettles tend to heat up water, that Canberra is the capital of Australia, and so on, can only be justified by appealing to information gained from our senses.

According to **empiricists**, *all* our knowledge of the external world is *a posteriori*: although we might be able to know the truths of mathematics and logic *a priori* (though some empiricists hold that this knowledge is *a posteriori* too), we can know nothing about the external world without appealing to our sensory experience (see also **analytic vs synthetic truths**).

ARISTOTLE

Aristotle (384 BC–322 BC) is one of the most influential and important figures in metaphysics. He was taught by Plato, and his metaphysics can be seen as a 'bringing down to Earth' of Plato's theory of Forms (see **platonism**). Although Plato took **universals** to exist outside space and time, Aristotle believed that a universal is wholly present in the object that instantiates it. Although Plato believed that ultimate reality lies outside the observable realm, Aristotle believed that the basic **substances** that constitute reality are ordinary observable organisms, such as people, animals and plants.

Western philosophy in the thirteenth and fifteenth centuries was dominated by the 'Scholastic tradition': roughly, Aristotle's views mixed with Christianity (one of the most important figures in this tradition being Thomas Aquinas). The early modern period of philosophy, beginning with Descartes in the seventeenth century, marked a move away from this tradition.

Further reading: Barnes (1992)

ARMSTRONG, DAVID

David Armstrong, born in Melbourne in 1926, is a contemporary Australian metaphysician who spent most of his career at the University of Sydney. His work is very much in the realist (see **realism and anti-realism (global)**), naturalist tradition of Australian philosophy, which sees metaphysics as continuous with natural science. Much of early twentieth-century philosophy was characterised by suspicion of metaphysics, and a belief that philosophical puzzles were to be solved by linguistic analysis (this movement in philosophy is often referred to as the '**linguistic turn**'). Armstrong was one of the leading figures in re-popularising metaphysics, making it okay for philosophers in the Anglo-Saxon tradition to enquire into the nature of reality rather than the nature of language.

Armstrong is best known for his defence of **immanent realism** about **universals**, and his novel theory of **laws of nature** as contingent relations between universals (see **Dretske-Tooley-Armstrong view of laws**). He is also one of the pioneers of the Australian brand of materialism about the mind. According to this tradition, the concept of a mental state is the concept of a state which is *apt to be the cause of certain effects or apt to be the effect of certain causes*, for example, the concept of pain is the concept of a state that is apt to be caused by bodily damage and apt to cause avoidance behaviour. As it happens, thinks Armstrong, it is physical brain states that have these causal profiles, and hence, mental states are just physical brain states (see **Canberra Plan**).

Armstrong advocates an ontology according to which the basic constituents of reality are **states of affairs**. He has come to be a strong believer in **truthmakers**, seeing the 'truthmaker principle' as the best way of cashing out global realism (see **realism and anti-realism (global)**).

Armstrong is also famous for the combinatorial theory of **modality**, which he advanced in the 1980s, according to which all possible states of affairs are recombinations of actual entities, and as such are useful fictions. However, later in life he came to reject this theory.

Further reading: Mumford (2007)

A-THEORY

See **tensed and tenseless theories of time**.

AUSTERE NOMINALISM

Realists about **universals** postulate universals in the explanation of resemblance: the telephone box and the Coke can are both red in virtue of the fact that they both instantiate the universal of redness. In opposition to this, the **nominalist** – the philosopher who denies the existence of universals – has two options. First, he or she can offer some more fundamental metaphysical explanation of what it is for both the telephone box and the Coke can to be red, which does not involve a universal. The **class nominalist**, for example, might explain this fact in terms of the telephone box and the Coke can both being in the class of red things. The **trope theorist** explains this fact in terms of the Coke can and the telephone box having resembling red tropes.

Alternatively, she can deny that the fact that both the Coke can and the telephone box are red requires any deeper explanation. The Coke can is red. The telephone box is red. There is no deeper metaphysical account of what is going on here. As Wittgenstein said, explanation has to end somewhere, and, with respect to explaining resemblance, the austere nominalist stops at the start.

This second strategy, most famously defended by **W. V. Quine**, was mockingly dubbed 'ostrich nominalism' by **David Armstrong**. For Armstrong, this kind of nominalist, rather than attempting to give a metaphysical account of resemblance, just sticks her in the head in the sand and says nothing. She refuses, as Armstrong (1980: 161–2) puts it 'to answer a compulsory question on the examination paper'.

The issue is closely connected with Quine's criterion of **ontological commitment**. For Quine, we are ontologically committed to, and only to, those entities that are the values of our bound variables. Suppose I assert, 'There is something that is a telephone box and is red'. According to Quine, this assertion commits me to the existence of a red telephone box, but it does not commit me to the existence of either *redness* or *telephone box-ness*. My use of predicates, such as 'is red' and 'is a telephone box', does not oblige me to believe in the existence of attributes corresponding to those predicates (indeed the mere fact that we use predicates does not commit us to the existence of anything, given that we are only committed to the values of our bound variables).

Armstrong claims that this Quinean criterion of ontological commitment does not take predicates ontologically seriously. The predicate does not have some purely formal role in the sentence, such as is arguably had by the word 'and'. It contributes to what the sentence says about reality, and this, according to Armstrong, ought to be reflected in what accepting the sentence as true ontologically commits us to. Armstrong's rejection of the Quinean criterion is connected with his support for **truthmaker** theory. On the assumption that for an entity *e* to be truthmaker for a proposition *p*, the mere existence of *e* must necessitate the truth of *p*, the telephone box is not sufficient truthmaker for 'the telephone box is red'. For the telephone box might have existed and yet the sentence 'the telephone box is red' be false (e.g. if the telephone box was green).

Even if we accept the Quinean theory of ontological commitment, austere nominalism still faces problems accounting for the truth of sentences that appear to have bound variables ranging over properties. For example, the sentence, 'Wisdom is a virtue', is most straightforwardly analysed as 'There is something that is wisdom and is a virtue', and the truth of this sentence, according to Quinean criterion, commits us to the existence of wisdom. Quine advocates offering a **paraphrase** of such a sentence that (i) does not contain bound variables ranging over properties and (ii) can be reasonably claimed to capture the *true logical form* of the original sentence. In this way, the austere nominalist can claim that 'Wisdom is a virtue' is merely a loose manner of speaking, the true meaning of which is given by the paraphrase.

The trouble is that such paraphrases are hard to come by. A first stab at paraphrasing 'Wisdom is a virtue' might be 'All wise things are virtuous things' (note that the bound variables in this sentence only range over particular things, hence the sentence is nominalistically kosher). However, this cannot be right as some wise people are not virtuous due to having a vice ridden character in many other respects, for example, being selfish and greedy. We recommend having a go yourself at paraphrasing 'Wisdom is a virtue' in a way that does not contain bound variables ranging over properties. It is not easy!

Further reading: Armstrong (1980); Devitt (1980); Loux (2006, Chapter 2)

BACKWARDS CAUSATION

Backwards causation takes place if a cause of an event takes place *after* that event takes place. For instance, imagine that in the year 2010, Marty kisses his girlfriend goodbye before using his time machine to travel to 1955. Unfortunately, his girlfriend had a cold virus, so in 1955, Marty develops a cough and a sore throat. Hence, there is an event in 1955 (Marty's coughing) that is caused by an event in 2010 (Marty's kissing his girlfriend) – the cause is later than the effect, and so we have a case of backwards causation. Clearly, this is related to **time travel**, although backwards causation should be distinguished from time travel in general, for it is at least (allegedly) conceivable that backwards causation could take place without any object travelling through time. For instance, it is conceivable that there could be a magic button such that, if you pressed it, someone in 1955 would spontaneously catch a cold without sending any viruses back through time – there would then be backwards causation even though nothing went through time.

The *bilking argument*, due to Black (1956), aims to show that backwards causation is impossible. The basic idea is that no matter what happens, you can never have evidence for thinking that backwards causation has taken place. For instance, Dummett (1964) imagines that a hunting party comes back after a successful hunt, at which point the shaman does a dance to *cause* the hunt to have been successful. According to the bilking argument, it is more reasonable to think that successful hunts cause the shaman to dance than to believe that there is backwards causation whereby the shaman's dance causes the hunt to succeed.

Another problem is that, as backwards causation is so closely related to time travel, problems for time travel are often problems for the possibility of backwards causation, for example, the grandfather paradox (see **time travel**) is just as threatening even if nothing travels through time, but backwards causation is permitted. Imagine a magic button, such that if Marty pressed it, then his grandfather dies back in 1901 – clearly, even though nothing travels through time we end up with the same sorts of paradoxes of how Marty could exist to press the button if his grandfather died at the turn of the previous century.

Finally, the possibility of backwards causation looks inconsistent with proposed analyses of causation that include as a criterion that the cause comes before the effect (such as the **regularity theory of causation**). Whether or not this bodes ill for the proposed analysis or for the possibility of backwards causation is an open question.

Further reading: Faye (2010)

BEING

It is sometimes thought that metaphysics is all about *being*. Most metaphysicians, however, are not at all sure what 'being' is supposed to be, and by and large avoid the term.

Having said that, there are two particular places in metaphysics where the notion of being does still, sometimes, crop up. First, being is taken to be the same as **subsistence**, which (on some views) is different to *existence*. Relatedly, 'being' is sometimes taken to be what **non-existent objects** have (again, obviously non-existent objects – if there are any – do not *exist*).

Second, being is sometimes mentioned in discussions of **essence**. John **Locke** famously defined essence as 'the being of a thing, whereby it is what it is', and the essence of a thing is thus sometimes taken to be the 'being of a thing': meaning not that the thing exists (or subsists), but that it has some special nature, in virtue of which it is *that* thing and not something else.

By and large, though, most metaphysicians hold that the notions of *existence* and *essence* are the only comprehensible and useful notions we need. First, the idea that, say, unicorns have being but lack existence is regarded as an **ontological commitment** that we can do without (i.e., it violates Ockham's razor – see **theoretical virtues**). Furthermore, second, the idea that we can define the notion of essence in terms of the notion of being is often regarded as being rather unilluminating, because the notion of 'the being of a thing, whereby it is what it is' is less clear than the notion of essence it is being used to define.

BERKELEY, GEORGE

The Irish philosopher George Berkeley (1685–1753) – often referred to as 'Bishop Berkeley' because he was Bishop of Cloyne as well as a philosopher – was the second of the three great British Empiricists, sandwiched between **John Locke** and **David Hume**. His most famous philosophical works are *A Treatise Concerning the Principles of Human Knowledge* (1710) and *Three Dialogues between Hylas and Philonous* (1713), and he is best known for defending idealism (see **phenomenalism and idealism**), his criticisms of Locke's distinction between **primary and secondary qualities** and his arguments for the existence of God. He also had what is now quite a famous university campus in the United States named after him.

Further reading: Berkeley's *Principles* and *Three Dialogues* are freely available online from various sources. 'Translations' of them into contemporary English can be found on Jonathan Bennett's Early Modern Texts website (www.earlymoderntexts. com/f_berkeley.html)

BILKING ARGUMENT

See **backwards causation.**

BODILY CONTINUITY

Bodily continuity theories identify persons with their bodies (or sometimes with their brains), and in doing so ground **personal identity** in facts about the **diachronic identity** (i.e. identity over time) of bodies (or of brains): for grey-haired Old Jack in 2010 to be one and the same person as Wee Johnny, who ran in the 1952 Olympics in Helsinki, is for Old Jack and Wee Johnny to be identical to one and the same body (or brain). That Old Jack and Wee Johnny have the same body does not entail that they have exactly the same atoms. Most theories of the diachronic identity of physical objects such as bodies allow that a physical object can change its parts while remaining the same object, as long as such changes are reasonably gradual (usually causal continuity, perhaps a specific kind of causal continuity, is also required).

It is not clear whether bodily continuity theories that identify the person with the whole body (as opposed to just the brain) are distinct from **animalist** theories of personal identity, which identify each person with a human animal. It would be a little strange to hold that my living body is distinct from the human animal that is co-located with it, such that one could outlive the other. If living body and human animal are identified, then 'bodily continuity theory' and 'animalism' are just different names for the same theory. Even if the two theories remain in some sense distinct, many of the same advantages and disadvantages will accrue to each (see **animalism**).

The other option for the bodily continuity theorist is to identify the person with their brain. This might appear to be an unstable halfway house between full-body continuity theories and psychological continuity theories. Why would one want to identify the person with the brain, rather than the feet or the liver? Surely, the answer is that the brain is the ground of thought and consciousness, in principle capable of facilitating psychological continuity in the absence of the rest of the body, for example, if it were removed and kept alive in a vat. However, then it seems to go against this motivation to claim that a person ceases to exist when there is psychological continuity in the absence of brain continuity. A human being can survive with only one of its two brain hemispheres intact. If one is inclined to think that a person can continue to exist as a brain in a vat, then one is probably going to be inclined to think that a person can continue to exist as a brain hemisphere in a vat (provided there is sufficient psychological continuity). However, allowing a person to survive with only *part* of their brain seems to go against the view that a person is identical with its brain.

Further reading: Noonan (1989, Chapters 1 and 11); Parfit (1984, Chapter 10); Williams (1970); Olson (2008)

BRADLEY'S REGRESS

Substance-attribute realists (see **bundle theory vs substance–attribute theory**) about **universals** explain the fact *that Plato is wise* in terms of a particular object, that is, Plato (or more precisely Plato's substratum, but let us overlook that subtlety) and the universal of wisdom. However, the mere existence of Plato and of wisdom cannot be enough to explain this, for the existence of these two things does not imply that Plato is wise. In a possible world where Socrates and Plato exist, but only the former is wise, both Plato and wisdom exist without it being the case that Plato is wise.

What we require is not only that both Plato and wisdom exists but also that Plato (or his substratum) *instantiates* wisdom. It seems then that we need to invest in an **instantiation relation**. (Note that if there is such a thing as an instantiation relation, it appears to be a universal, something that is present wherever a thing instantiates properties.) However, even when we add an instantiation relation, we still do not have enough entities to guarantee that Plato is wise. In the possible world described earlier, Plato and wisdom exist but so does the relation of instantiation (relating Socrates to wisdom).

What we require is not only that Plato and wisdom and the instantiation relation exist, but also that Plato *instantiates* the instantiation relation that relates him to wisdom. It seems then that we need a second instantiation relation, call it instantiation★, which relates particular objects to the instantiation relation we started out with. However, the mere existence of Plato, wisdom, instantiation and instantiation★ is not sufficient to guarantee that Plato is wise, for in the possible world described earlier Plato, wisdom, instantiation and instantiation★ (relating Socrates to instantiation that relates him to wisdom) may all exist without it being the case that Plato is wise.

It might look like what we need is instantiation★★ to relate Plato to instantiation★ to relate him to instantiation to relate him to wisdom, but of course, similar reasoning will show that this collection of entities will not be sufficient to guarantee that Plato is wise. This is Bradley's regress (Bradley 1930: 17–18), and many philosophers take it to be a serious problem for substance-attribute realism about universals (we can probably create a version to threaten trope versions of substance-attribute theory too). It seems to be a vicious regress that threatens the attempt to explain property possession in terms of the instantiation of universals, because at each stage of the explanation, the explanation seems incomplete; we have not postulated enough universals to explain the fact that the object has the relevant property.

It might be thought that the substance-attribute theory realist about universals can simply stop the regress before it begins, by denying that instantiation is a genuine relation, and just taking it as a primitive fact that Plato instantiates wisdom, something that cannot be explained in more fundamental terms. However, if it is legitimate to take it as just a primitive fact that Plato instantiates wisdom, then one may wonder why we do not stop explanation a stage earlier, as the **austere nominalist** does, and just take it as a primitive fact that Plato is wise (remember, the realist about universals explains the fact that Plato is wise in terms of the fact that Plato instantiates wisdom). It may seem *ad hoc* for the realist about universals to demand an explanation of the fact that Plato is wise but not to demand an explanation of the fact that Plato instantiates wisdom.

Perhaps the most well-known response to these difficulties is to hold that the fundamental constituents of reality are not particular things and universals, such that we then have the problem of how we stick these things together in such a way as to avoid Bradley's regress. Rather, the fundamental constituents of reality are irreducibly unified wholes of *particular-things-having-universals* (see **reductionism** for what 'irreducibly' means here). Hence, instantiation is not really a *relation* at all: it is, to use P. F. Strawson's (1959, Chapter 5) expression, a 'non-relational tie'. In our thinking, we can consider in isolation the particular thing that has the universals on one hand and the universals on the other, but in reality, these 'two things' are inseparable aspects of the fundamental unified reality of *the-particular-thing-having-universals*. Armstrong presents this strategy as equivalent to the belief that reality is ultimately made up of **states of affairs** rather than things.

Because they do not believe in substrata, bundle theorists (see **bundle theory vs substance attribute theory**) obviously do not have the challenge of explaining how a substratum and its properties are bound together. However, they may face a similar challenge explaining how a given group of properties are 'bundled up' into an object. Suppose that *redness* and *sphericity* stand in relation R, in virtue of which they form a red ball. Presumably, the mere existence of *redness*, *sphericity* and R is not sufficient to explain the existence of the red ball, for all these things would exist in a possible world where there was a green ball (constituted by *greeness* and *sphericity* standing in relation R) and a red cube (constituted by *redness* and *cuboid-hood* standing in relation R). Perhaps it might be supposed that we need to postulate a further relation $R^\star$, which relates properties to R, to explain why R is related to *redness* and *sphericity*. However, of course, this is not going to do the trick, as the possible world described earlier presumably also contains $R^\star$ (relating *greenness* and *sphericity* to R, and relating *redness* and *cuboid-hood* to *R*). It should be clear that this difficulty is analogous to the difficulty faced by the substance-attribute theorist described earlier.

Further reading: Martin (1980); T. Wetzel (2008)

BRAINS IN A VAT

The 'brains in a vat' hypothesis (henceforth 'BIV') is Putnam's (1981: Chapter 1) contemporary take on René Descartes' 'evil demon' or 'malicious demon' hypothesis (see **scepticism**) and is relevant to the debate about **realism and anti-realism (global)**. The possibility that Putnam asks us to imagine is that we are really disembodied brains, kept alive in vats of nutrients. According to BIV, we (our brains) are hooked up to a giant computer that feeds us with electrical impulses that cause us to have sensory experiences that are exactly the same as the ones we actually have: sensory experiences that, in turn, cause us to have exactly the beliefs that we actually have, for example, the belief that there are elephants and chairs and planets, and – crucially – the belief that we are *not* brains in vats. (This 'sceptical scenario' bears a striking resemblance to the situation depicted in the 1999 film *The Matrix* – except that in the film it is the whole body that is envatted and not just the brain, and also some people get set free from their vats and discover what the world is really like.)

Sceptical scenarios such as BIV are normally invented to show that we really do not know – indeed, we have no reason to believe – the things about the external world that we do believe. Because I cannot distinguish between the situation I believe to be real (e.g. that I am currently sitting at a table, typing on a keyboard) and the sceptical scenario (I am a disembodied brain; there is no table and no keyboard, and I do not have hands), I really have no reason to think that I am sitting at a table, as opposed to being a brain in a vat. Putnam's aim, however, is very different. He argues that the claim, 'I am a brain in a vat' is a 'self-refuting hypothesis', so it cannot possibly be true. Hence, there is no problem of external-world scepticism after all.

Here is a very quick summary of Putnam's argument. Envatted people (or rather, envatted brains) lack the conceptual resources to refer to things such as brains and vats because they are not causally connected to any such things (or at least, not in the way they think they are): when they learn the meaning of 'vat' by 'seeing' a vat and being told 'that is a vat', they are not really seeing a *vat* at all, but only an image or a simulation of a vat, produced by the computer. Hence, they cannot refer to vats (or brains, for that matter), and so do not mean by 'vat' and 'brain' what we mean, and so simply cannot express the thought that we express in English by the sentence 'I am a brain in a vat'. Indeed, the thought they express by the equivalent sentence of vat-English is false, as uttered by them, just as the sentence in English is false as uttered by us (assuming we aren't brains in vats). Hence the conclusion that 'I am a brain in a vat' could not possibly be true.

Putnam's (1981: 50) view seems to be that the coherence of the claim that we *could* be BIV 'assumes a God's Eye point of view', that is, there must be (for the above claim to be coherent) some perspective external to our own perspective, from the point of view of which we could truly be judged to have conceptual resources that are incapable of reflecting our own, envatted predicament. However, – at least if we remove the evil scientist out of the story, who presumably *would* have such a perspective – there *is* no such external perspective: there is no such thing as a '**God's eye view**'.

Thus, Putnam offers us a kind of anti-realist response to the problem of scepticism (see **realism and anti-realism (global)** and **scepticism**). The intelligibility of sceptical scenarios presupposes a distinction between how things *really* are, independent of our perception, theories, language or whatever, and how they are *according to* our perception, theories, language or whatever, and then the sceptic gets a hold by pointing out that the latter might be radically different from the former. Putnam, in effect, denies that the first part of the sceptical strategy is coherent: the nature of reality is *constrained* by what our best theory says about the nature of reality. Perhaps, we have not hit on our 'best' theory yet, but whatever our best theory turns out to be, it will certainly not be one that somehow steps outside our **conceptual scheme** and reveals reality for what it 'really is'; that is a trick that simply cannot, in principle, be turned.

Further reading: Putnam (1981, Chapter 1); Brueckner (2008); Chalmers (undated)

B-THEORY

See **tensed and tenseless theories of time**.

BUNDLE THEORY OF THE SELF OR PERSON

Most philosophical interest in **personal identity** concerns the **diachronic identity** of a person: the identity of a person over time. However, debates between bundle theorists and their opponents concern synchronic facts about a person: facts about a person at a time. Specifically, the issue is whether the self is an *irreducibly* unified thing (see **reductionism**). It is a plain fact that introspection at a given moment reveals diversity: a huge variety of thoughts, feelings and sensory impressions are introspectively available at a given moment. However, many philosophers claim to also find in introspection a strong unity binding this diversity together, such that all these varied phenomena are just different aspects of the fundamentally unified thing I refer to with the personal pronoun 'I'. Bundle theorists deny that the self exemplifies such irreducible unity.

Bundle theory comes in a strong or a mild form. In its strong form, most famously defended in the Western philosophical tradition by **David Hume**, it simply denies the existence of the self. Hume famously claimed, when introspecting, to be unable to find an experience of the self:

> For my part, when I enter most intimately into what I call *myself*, I always stumble on some particular perception or other, of heat, or cold, light or shade, love or hatred, pain or pleasure. I never can catch *myself* at any time without a perception, and never can observe anything but the perception.
>
> Hume (1739–40: 252)

The more moderate version of the bundle theory, defended by Derek Parfit, does not deny that the self exists, but denies its irreducible unity. Parfit explains this by analogy with a nation (following Hume who compared the self with a republic). According to Parfit, a nation exists: it is a single thing. However, the existence of the nation is nothing over and above the existence of its citizens and the various relations between them. In the same way, the self exists, is a singular thing, but is nothing over and above various mental events standing in certain relations to each other. (This view is similar to, but not to be confused with, the bundle theory of objects, see **bundle theory vs substance–attribute theory**.)

There is an interesting overlap between the thinking of Western bundle theorists and Buddhist philosophy. It is arguable that Buddhist doctrine involves a commitment to a bundle theory of the self. Consider the following extract from Buddhist scripture:

> The mental and the material are really here,
> But here there is no human being to be found,
> For it is void and merely fashioned like a doll,
> Just suffering piled up like grass and sticks.
>
> The *Visuaddhimagga*, quoted in Collins (1982: 33)

Further reading: Collins (1982); Hume (1739–40, Book I, Part IV, § 6); Parfit (1984, Chapter 1)

BUNDLE THEORY VS SUBSTANCE-ATTRIBUTE THEORY

Consider an ordinary apple. Consider its characteristics – or as philosophers like to say, its **properties** – for example, its shape, colour and juiciness. Some philosophers think that all it is for an apple to have a given shape or colour is for it to be a member of a certain class (see **class nominalism**) or to bear a certain resemblance to other particular objects (see **resemblance nominalism**). Other philosophers believe that (at least some of) the properties of the apple, its size, shape and colour, are constituents of the apple in some sense.

Suppose we follow the latter camp of philosophers and take the properties of the apple to be constituents of the apple. We now face a pressing follow-up question: is there any other metaphysical constituent of the apple besides its properties? If we imaginatively strip away all the properties of the apple – its size, shape and juiciness – is there anything left? Those philosophers who answer 'no' to these questions are known as 'bundle theorists'. The bundle theorist believes that the apple – or any other particular object – is nothing more than a collection of properties, bound together by some relation, such as *compresence* or *co-location*. Those philosophers who answer 'yes' to this question are known as 'substance-attribute theorists'. The substance-attribute theorist believes that the apple is 'made up' of not only its properties but also its **substratum**: a thing that is not itself a property but that *bears* the properties of the apple.

The definition of 'bundle theory' leaves open whether properties are **universals** or **tropes**, but there is a significant difficulty facing the bundle theorist who takes properties to be universals. This is because the conjunction of **bundle theory** and realism about universals entails that two distinct objects cannot have all the same properties. If object x is just a bundle of its properties, object y is just a bundle of its properties, and the properties of x are numerically identical to the properties of y (being universals), it follows that x is numerically identical to y. However, it seems eminently possible for there to be two distinct objects with all the same properties; the world might have been such that only two electrons exist (this argument assumes that bundle theory is, if true, necessarily true). Bundle theorists who are also trope theorists avoid this difficulty.

Historically, empiricists have worried about the alleged unobservability of substrata: I can see the apple's colour and shape, but I cannot seem to see its substratum. However, the difficulty that has most occupied contemporary substance-attribute theorists is that of explaining how the substratum and the properties it bears are united together in such a way as to avoid **Bradley's regress**.

Proponents of both sides of this debate accuse the other side of making unintelligible claims. Substance-attribute theorists sometimes accuse bundle theorists of conceptual confusion in taking properties to be *parts* of objects. The top half and the bottom half of the apple are parts of the apple, but are the apple's shape and size also parts of it? Can we even make sense of properties existing without there being something, distinct from the properties, that literally has them?

Substance-attribute theories suffer from attacks on the coherence of substrata ('substrata' is the plural of 'substratum'). The substratum of the apple 'has properties' in the sense that it bears the properties of the apple. However, there is a further question as to whether the intrinsic nature of the substratum involves properties, or whether it is a *bare particular*, that is, an entity whose intrinsic nature does not involve properties. There is strong pressure to take substrata to be bare particulars. The properties of the apple are borne by the apple's substratum. If properties need bearers, and there are properties involved in the nature of the substratum, then it looks like we need to invest in something, a *sub-substratum*, to bear the properties of the substratum. However, if the being of the sub-substratum involves properties, then we need to invest in a sub-sub-substratum to bear the properties of the sub-substratum. The only way to stop this regress is to postulate a bearer of properties whose intrinsic nature does not involve properties, in other words a bare particular. However, if we are going to have to admit the existence of a bare particular at some point anyway, we might as well stop the regress from starting by holding that the apple's substratum is a bare particular.

However, it is not clear that we can make intelligible sense of a bare particular, of an object that *just is* in a way that does not involve properties. Moreover, it is difficult to deny that a substratum has a nature of some kind, for example, it is concrete particular (as opposed to an abstract object) and something that *bears* properties (as opposed to itself *being* a property). However, it is difficult to make sense of something's having an intrinsic nature in a way that does not involve the having of properties.

Some substance-attribute theorists try to avoid these difficulties by supposing that the fundamental constituents of reality are not substrata or properties, but some union of the two: the *substratum-having-properties*. Both the properties on one hand and the substratum on the other are aspects of this reality that we can consider in abstraction from the fundamental reality of the *substratum-having-properties*, but which are not separable from it. Consider again the apple. What we have here is a single thing: *substratum-having-redness-&-roundness-&-juiciness and so on*. When thinking about this reality, we may choose to focus on its roundness or its juiciness, or we may choose to consider it as a thing that *has* roundness of juiciness. However, when we do so, we are just focusing on different aspects of an irreducibly unified reality. (**David Armstrong** takes this approach, and sees it as involving a commitment to a world made up of **facts**, or **states of affairs**, rather than things.)

Further reading: Allaire (1963); Ayer (1954); Loux (2006, Chapter 3); Williams (1953)

CANBERRA PLAN

The Canberra Plan, so-called because of its association with philosophers at the Australian National University in Canberra, is a specific form of **conceptual analysis**. The basic idea is this. Suppose we want to come up with an analysis of concept 'C'. First, take a bunch of 'platitudes': the things that ordinary people take to be distinctive of Cs. This gives us the 'folk theory' of C (see also **common sense**). Hence, for example, we might hold that *pain* is the kind of thing that (according to the folk) is typically caused by certain kinds of bodily damage (touching a hot iron, being stuck with a pin and having a brick fall on your head) and in turn typically causes people to behave in certain ways (roll around clutching their head, saying 'ouch!' and moving their hand away from the iron very quickly).

Now we ask: what kind of thing in the world might (as it is sometimes put) 'play the pain role' – or, in other words, what kind of thing might *satisfy* the folk theory? A popular answer is that *physical* (or, more specifically, neurological) states can plausibly be thought to play that role: a particular state of your brain is the kind of thing that might plausibly be caused by (say) touching the hot iron and in turn causes you to say 'ouch!' and move your hand away. If all of this is correct (and of course this is a big 'if'), physicalism (the view that the mental **supervenes** on the physical) looks like a plausible position. At any rate, we have given an analysis of *one* mental concept ('pain') in such a way that it is plausible to think that that concept can be satisfied by physical events or states.

'Canberra planners' have advanced this kind of analysis for all kinds of things that metaphysicians have found troublesome. For example, Menzies

(1996) has applied the Canberra Plan to the case of **causation**. In this case, the 'platitudes' are things such as 'causes typically raise the chances of their effects' and 'causation is an **intrinsic** relation'. When we ask what kind of thing might satisfy this concept or 'play the causation role', the answer might, Menzies thinks, be something like 'energy transfer' (see **process theories of causation**).

Menzies' approach is appealing for two main reasons (which apply to Canberra Plan-style analyses in general; we are just using causation as an example here). First of all, the 'typically' part gets around the problem that some cases of causation appear *not* to be cases of chance-raising. This is a problem if we are attempting (as accounts of causation usually do) to provide a full-blown reductive analysis of causation, where sticking a 'typically' in here and there is not allowed (see **reductionism**).

Second, we now have an account of causation that is metaphysically unmysterious (we are **ontologically committed** to the existence and transfer of energy in any case if we believe our best physical theories – which we should). Of course, the same can arguably be said for the version of the process theory that simply says that causation is, *in fact*, energy transfer and stops there. However, the advantage of the Canberra Plan approach is that it explains, via the satisfaction of the 'folk theory of causation', *why* we should think that causation is, in fact, energy transfer, and what conditions a relation would have to satisfy to count as the causal relation in **possible worlds** where there is no such thing as energy transfer (see **process theories of causation**). (Interestingly, **David Lewis**, having more or less invented the Canberra Plan, argues that causation is one place where we should be doing old-school, reductionist conceptual analysis and resist Canberra planning (Lewis 2004).)

This example demonstrates some of the alleged virtues of the Canberra Plan, and why it became very popular. Another, related reason why it has been popular relates to fundamental questions about what metaphysics actually does: are we just analysing our concepts (in which case, we say nothing about the nature of reality), or are we attempting to actually uncover the nature of reality (in which case, how can we possibly claim to be able to do this without getting up from our armchairs and conducting some empirical investigation?). The Canberra Plan provides a neat middle way between these two extremes. The analysing of the 'folk concept' itself says nothing about the nature of the world: it just says what kind of 'role' something would have to play to count as pain, or causation or whatever. However, then we add an empirical hypothesis to the effect that some feature of reality (brain states, or energy transfer or whatever) really does play that role. This hypothesis is advanced from the armchair, admittedly – but the hope is that the empirical information we have about the world makes the hypothesis pretty plausible. Of course, if it turns out *not* to be an empirically plausible hypothesis, then it needs to be discarded, and we need to consider what other feature of reality might play the relevant role.

Further reading: Lewis (2004)

CARVING NATURE AT ITS JOINTS

It is uncontroversial that we can distinguish between true and false descriptions of reality. What is a lot more philosophical contentious is whether we can distinguish among the *true* descriptions a special class of descriptions that enjoy some special metaphysical privilege over and above truth.

Our language distinguishes between blue and green things. Imagine a language that does not contain the words 'green' and 'blue' but instead has the word 'grue' – which applies to green things if the time is before midday but to blue things if the time is after midday – and the word 'bleen', which applies to blue things if the time is before midday but to green things if the time is after midday (so an emerald is grue in the morning and bleen in the afternoon). Suppose that the speakers of this language speak the truth about as much as we do; they correctly or incorrectly apply the words 'grue' and 'bleen' to more or less the same degree we correctly or incorrectly apply the words 'green' and 'blue'. Is there nevertheless a sense in which our language, insofar as it distinguishes between green and blue rather than grue and bleen, better reflects the nature of reality?

Some philosophers think that the predicates 'blue' and 'green' are *more natural* than the predicates 'grue' and 'bleen', and that – insofar as we think of those predicates as corresponding to properties – the properties blue and green are *more natural* than the properties grue and bleen. The notion is difficult to get a handle on – some philosophers think it unintelligible – but roughly the idea is that, although *we* can artificially carve up the world into grue and bleen things, *the world itself* comes already carved up into blue and green things.

According to **David Lewis** (1983a), there are two ways of further characterising the difference between natural properties and properties that are not natural. (Terminological difficulty: the term 'non-natural property' is sometimes used to indicate a property that is not to be found in the natural world, e.g. G. E. Moore took *goodness* to be a 'non-natural' – in this sense – property. This is not the way we are using the term in the current context: the failure of grue to be a natural property does not entail that it is a property that exists outside the natural order.) First, the sharing of natural properties is said to constitute 'objective similarity' – similarity in reality itself – as opposed to the mere sharing of predicates: grass and leaves are objectively similar in that they both are green, whereas grass before midday and Smurfs after midday are not objectively similar in both being grue. Second, natural properties are said to be the properties involved in **causation** and **laws of nature**: the greenness of the grass causes my green experience when I look at the grass, whereas the grueness of grass in the morning does not cause anything.

Some see the distinction between natural and non-natural properties as all-or-nothing; others think that the distinction admits of degree: some properties are *perfectly* natural – they feature in fundamental laws and are such that two objects that share all and only the same perfectly natural properties perfectly resemble each other – whereas other properties are natural to a greater of lesser degree. We have been using blue and green as our examples of natural properties, but arguably the most plausible candidates for *perfectly* natural properties are those that feature in fundamental physics, for example, *mass* or *negative charge*. We can still, however, think of blue and green as being fairly natural, even if not perfectly natural, properties; we can suppose that blue and green are more natural than grue and bleen.

Some metaphysicians try to give a reductive (see **reductionism**) account of the naturalness of predicates or properties. One way to do this is to identify the perfectly naural properties with **universals**, whilst giving a **nominalist** account of the other properties, for example, identifying them with classes of objects (see **class nominalism** for an account of the nominalist strategy of identifying properties with classes of objects). It is difficult to see how this kind of view can account for naturalness admitting of degree; presumably, a predicate either does or does not correspond to a genuine universal. However, perhaps the realist about universals can make sense of quite, but less than perfectly, natural properties in terms of suitably related families of universals.

It is difficult to see how a **class nominalist** can give a *reductive* account of naturalness. However, a class nominalist may take it as a primitive fact that some classes of object are more natural than others, for example, that the class of negatively charged things is more natural than the class of green things, and the class of green things more natural than the class of grue things. Less austere forms of nominalism may provide a reductive account of the varying degrees of naturalness among classes. The **trope theorist** can explain the greater naturalness of the class of negatively charged things relative to the class of green things in terms of the greater degree of resemblance between negative charge tropes relative to greenness tropes. The **resemblance nominalist** can explain this fact in terms of the greater degree of resemblance between negatively charged things relative to green things.

The idea that some true descriptions might better reflect the nature of reality than others, that only a sub-class of true descriptions 'carve nature at the joints', goes back to Plato. However, it was brought back into prominence by Lewis (1983a) in his article, 'New work for a theory of universals'. Lewis argued for the distinction between natural and unnatural properties on the basis of its philosophical usefulness. Without such a commitment, Lewis claims, it becomes very difficult – perhaps even impossible – to give metaphysical accounts of a wide range of phenomena, for example: **intrinsic properties, laws of nature, causation** and **supervenience.**

A second place where the question of 'carving nature at its joints' arises is in the debate about **natural kinds** (see also **essence**). As with properties, the question is whether there is a 'natural' classification of things into kinds. We think of, say, *horse, magnesium, proton,* and so on, as 'natural' kinds of thing, whereas *object bigger than a car, raven-or-electron* and *spherical object* are not natural kinds. However, what distinguishes the natural from the non-natural kinds: which of the above categories carve nature at its joints?

It is important to note that the natural kind question is a distinct, additional question to the question we started out with, concerning properties. Imagine that we have some distinction between the natural and the unnatural properties. That, by itself, does not answer the natural kind question. After all, *being spherical* is probably going to come out as a natural property, and yet the class of spherical objects clearly does not constitute a natural kind: it includes, for example, tennis balls and planets and some lampshades (see **natural kinds** for some positive proposals).

Finally, if you want something a bit more difficult, there is an interesting contemporary debate in **metametaphysics** concerning whether some meanings of the *logical quantifiers* are more natural than others; the question here is whether, as Theodore Sider puts it, some quantifiers 'carve nature at the logical joints'. Sider (2001: Introduction) is the main proponent of this view, whereas Eli Hirsch (2005) is the main opponent (see **metametaphysics** for more discussion of this).

Further reading: Armstrong (1989) is structured around the need to give some account of the distinction between natural and non-natural classes. Chapter 1 argues for this need; later chapters describe various reductionist and non-reductionist accounts of the distinction. See also Lewis (1983a)

CATEGORICAL AND DISPOSITIONAL PROPERTIES

There is an important metaphysical distinction between two types of **property**: categorical properties and dispositional properties (the latter are sometimes called 'powers'). It is philosophically contentious how to characterise this distinction, so it is perhaps better to begin with reasonably uncontroversial examples. *Fragility* and *solubility* are generally taken to be dispositions. *Being square* and *having such and such a molecular structure* are generally taken to be categorical properties (at least for those who believe that there are categorical properties).

For an object to have a dispositional property is something to do with how it *would be* in certain circumstances, whereas for an object to have a categorical property is to do with how it *is*, here and now. To put this point in a slightly more technical way, each dispositional property has some kind of definitional connection with a certain subjunctive or **counterfactual conditional**. For example, by definition, if something is fragile then (all things being equal) if it were struck with a certain force it would break, and, by definition, if something is soluble then (all things being equal) if it were put into water it would dissolve. Categorical properties are properties that have no such definitional connection with a subjunctive conditional. Saying much more about the definition would get us into philosophically contentious territory.

Many philosophers claim that, when we look to the details of our fundamental sciences, we find that the properties dealt with (e.g. mass, charge and spin – all properties of elementary particles) are characterised dispositionally. Some philosophers are comfortable with at least some of the fundamental properties of the physical world being dispositions. Others – many of them believers in **Humean supervenience** – hold that dispositional properties must be grounded in categorical properties. They point to the definitional connection between dispositions and counterfactual conditionals, and go on to claim that the truth conditions for counterfactual conditionals can be given in terms of facts about the closest **possible world** – facts that do not (so they claim) themselves appeal to dispositions. Such philosophers are committed to the view that if science characterises reality only in dispositional terms, then it leaves us ignorant of reality's underlying categorical nature.

Further reading: Fara (2009)

CAUSAL RELATA

There is a question for both **type-level causation** and **token-level causation** as to what the **relata** involved in the causal relation are meant to be. In the case of type-level causation (as in 'smoking causes cancer'), it is relatively uncontentious that the relata are **properties** (such as *smokes* and *has cancer*). The debate heats up, though, when we consider token-level causation, as in 'the brick I threw smashed the window'.

The most popular option is that the relata are **events**, such as my throw of the brick and the smashing of the window. (This option is endorsed by **David Lewis** (1986c), Kim (1973) and Davidson (1969), among others.) Another popular option is that the causal relata are **facts**. According to Mellor (1995), for example, the basic logical form of a causal claim is '*E* because *C*' (the window broke because I threw the brick), where *E* and *C* are facts and not '*c* caused *e*' (my throw of the brick caused the smashing of the window), in which *c* and *e* are events.

Facts, rather than events, have a plus side when it comes to **causation by absence**. For instance, take the sentence 'the lack of oxygen caused Joe to fall unconscious'. It seems that that there is a fact, a **negative fact**, that there is no oxygen in a particular place (i.e. wherever Joe is) which causes another fact (the fact that Joe loses consciousness). Trying to account for such causation by absence with events can be tricky, because there is widespread reluctance to believe that there are negative *events* (such as the event of there *not* being enough oxygen). Events seem to involve something happening, not the lack of something happening (although negative facts are also viewed with some suspicion, so they themselves may not get off the hook entirely).

Even if facts do have the upper hand when it comes to causation by absence, however, there are other reasons why events seem better suited to being causal relata. For instance, events are located in space and time (they are **concrete**) whereas facts do not seem to be so located (they seem to be **abstract**). Consider: when the judge asks the witnesses to my heinous brick throwing where said event took place, and on what date, they are picking out the spatial and temporal location of an event; but it seems odd to ask where and when is the *fact* that I threw the brick. That such things, located outside space and time, are the fundamental relata of causation strikes some people as odd. Causation, they say, intuitively holds between physical, concrete things – it is something that goes on between items within the physical realm, not objects in **Platonic Heaven**. Finally, facts run into problems with Davidson's 'slingshot argument', which allegedly demonstrates that, given some supposedly uncontentious assumptions concerning logic and reference, if facts were the causal relata, then *every* fact that obtained would cause *every other* fact that obtained (see Lowe 2002: 167–73 for more on this).

Facts and events are not the only candidates for being the relata of causation. Others say it is **states of affairs** or **tropes** or categories of entities not covered in this book (such as 'descriptions' or 'situations'). In addition, there is a debate about whether a 'unified' account of causal relata is required (see Menzies 1989), that is, whether we should think that all causal relata are of the same kind (e.g. that all causal relata are events). Dissenters from the unified approach include believers in **agent causation**: those who believe that agents cause their own actions in a way that is not reducible to causal relations between events or facts (such as their beliefs and desires on one hand and their actions on the other).

Further reading: Menzies (1989); Lowe (2002, Chapter 9); Schaffer (2008, § 1)

CAUSATION AND LAWS

The modern debate about the metaphysics of causation and laws of nature finds its roots in the work of **David Hume**, the Humean line being that there is no **natural necessity** in the world (see also **Humean supervenience**). Given this denial, the Humeans have to account for causation and the laws of nature without relying on such natural necessity: for instance, what is it for one thing to cause another if it is not the case that the former *necessitates* the latter in some sense? In modern times, the Humean arguments have been spearheaded by **David Lewis**, whereas philosophers such as **David Armstrong** have toed the anti-Humean line.

Laws of nature, such as the law that nothing can accelerate at the speed of light, or that electrons are negatively charged, have to be reduced by the Humean down to something not involving natural necessity (see **reductionism**). For instance the **regularity theory of laws** says that laws are just regularities – if something regularly happens, that is just what it is to be a law of nature. Worried by the possibility of 'accidental regularities' (i.e. that something regular might happen by chance when it is, intuitively, not a law), more sophisticated Humean theories have been advanced, the most widely accepted of which is the **Ramsey–Lewis view of laws**. On the side of the anti-Humeans, we find the **Dretske-Tooley-Armstrong view of laws** arguing that there *is* some form of natural necessity required to adequately account for the laws of nature.

In the case of causation, we have to account for the truth of sentences such as 'Jim's bad driving caused the car to crash'. Again, the Humean has a **regularity theory** of causation – that one thing causes another thing if and only if things of the same kind as the former thing are regularly followed by things of the same kind as the latter thing. That, too, receives more sophisticated treatments, such as the introduction of **INUS conditions** and the **counterfactual theory of causation** (although those theories have problems of their own, such as with **pre-emption, overdetermination** and **causation by absence**). Anti-Humean treatments of causation include **singularism**. Connected with this debate is a debate about whether causation is really susceptible to a **reductionist** analysis at all. Unsurprisingly, anti-Humeans think not; but some Humeans are also suspicious, for example, Menzies (1996), who suggests a **Canberra Plan**-style analysis.

There are other topics that intersect with the philosophy of causation and laws. One is **indeterminism**: if what happens is not causally *determined* to happen, can there still be such a thing as causation? Most philosophers think so, and some have developed **probabilistic theories of causation**. Similarly, the leading accounts of laws of nature have probabilistic versions. There are also questions about what 'things' are the **relata** of the causation relation (see **causal relata**), for instance, whether it is **events** or **facts** that cause one another. Finally, causation and laws crop up in the debate about **free will**. Some philosophers have argued that **incompatibilism** – the view that free will and determinism are incompatible – can be avoided if we adopt a Humean account of laws (see Beebee and Mele 2001). Furthermore, some argue that free will requires **agent causation**: the causation of actions by agents and not merely by their beliefs, desires, and so on.

Further reading: Armstrong (1983); Carroll and Markosian (2010, Chapters 2 and 4)

CAUSATION BY ABSENCE

Sometimes we seem to assert that absences cause things to happen: 'the lack of oxygen caused Joe to fall unconscious'; 'the lack of sleep caused him to crash his car'; 'he didn't have any savings, which caused him to rob the bank'; 'the absence of light caused the plant to die'; 'not having any love in the relationship caused the marriage to fail' and so on.

This is a problem for certain theories of causation. For instance, most theories take **events** to be the **causal relata**. However, that seems to indicate that some event of *not having enough oxygen* caused Joe to fall unconscious (or what have you). Such 'negative events' are repudiated by most metaphysicians – there is an event of oxygen going into one's lungs, but not an event of oxygen not being there at all. To see how odd negative events would be, consider the following examples: are you currently caught up in the event of Doctor Who not fighting Daleks in the room where you are? Or has the Earth been continually participating in the event of not being made of 99 per cent arsenic? When you sleep are you engaged in the event of not spontaneously combusting? Or not purring like a kitten? Or not doing aerobics? Or . . . well, you get the picture. That there are scads of such negative events that everything is continually participating in seems just plain strange.

There are a few alternatives at this stage. One might try and offer an explanation whereby such causation can take place but where there are no causal relata (Lewis 2004), or one might take facts, namely negative facts, to be the causal relata. That it is a *fact* that Doctor Who is not fighting the Daleks, or a *fact* that Earth is not made of 99 per cent arsenic, and so on, seems far less strange than 'negative events'. Even negative facts, however, are not without their critics. Moreover, a version of the above problem remains: if the *fact* that there is no oxygen is a cause of Joe's falling unconscious, is not the fact that no oxygen-producing machine has been teleported into the room equally a cause? (See Beebee 2004 and McGrath 2005 for an attempt to avoid this problem.)

Further reading: Beebee (2004); Lewis (2004)

CHANCE

Chance is generally thought to be a very specific kind of **probability**. (Chance is sometimes known as 'propensity', but not everyone means the same thing by 'propensity', so beware. In fact, not everyone means the same thing by 'chance', for example, some philosophers use 'chance' just to mean 'probability'. We are using it in a much more restrictive sense in this section.) Like all probabilities, chances are measured on a scale of 0–1. The crucial thing about chances, though, is that they only get values *between* 0 and 1 if **indeterminism** is true. (As we just said, though, not all philosophers use 'chance' in this way.) Chances are 'rock-bottom' probabilities – or, as it is sometimes put, 'single-case' probabilities – such as the probability of a strontium-90 atom decaying in the next 15 years, as opposed to the probability that the next card you turn up from the deck will be an ace: in this latter case, the *chance* that it is an ace is (arguably) 1 or 0, because the card is right there, and either it is an ace or it is not (see **indeterminism** for more on this).

In the rest of this section, we will assume that indeterminism is true – not because we think it is, but because if it is not, chance is not a very interesting topic. A second caveat: we are making the numbers up! Given that chances are rock-bottom probabilities, we (or rather quantum physicists) have a good idea of what the chances of some quantum-level events are (as with the strontium-90 atom). Unfortunately, we have no idea at all, really, what the chances of John McCain winning the US election were just before polling day.

Note that this technical sense of 'chance' is not at all like the common sense notion we deploy when we say things such as 'there's a good chance the next card will be an ace', or 'chances are, David Cameron won't still be Prime Minister come 2015'. By philosophers' lights, claims such as these are best interpreted as claims about probabilities: it makes perfectly good sense to say that the *probability* that the next card is an ace is high, because probabilities generally need not be 'rock-bottom' probabilities: they can be relative to how much information you have, or to how the 'reference class' is described, or whatever (see **probability** for a bit more on this).

An interesting feature of chances is that they can 'evolve' or change over time, eventually becoming 0 or 1. The chance that John McCain won the 2008 US election is now 0: it did not happen (whereas the chance that Obama won is now 1). At the start of election day, McCain's chance of winning was (remembering the second caveat above!) above 0 but not by much; there was still, at that time, some chance that people who ended up voting for Obama would vote for McCain in sufficient numbers for him to win. When the election campaign was going well for McCain, it was quite high. When McCain was 10 years old, and had not even decided to enter politics, the chance of him winning the election was correspondingly lower. Before the human race even existed, the chance was vanishingly small. And so on.

From a metaphysical point of view, the obvious question is what *are* chances? (See Mellor 1971 for a detailed discussion of this question.) This is a question that particularly worries Humeans (see **Humean superve-nience**), because chances look rather like they must be irreducible potentialities or powers (or *propensities*): a kind of probabilistic version of **natural necessity** (see **probability** for a bit more on this). Thus, some Humeans think of chances as a sort of ideal level of 'credence' or 'degree of belief': roughly, if you knew everything there was to know about the past and the **laws of nature**, what would be the most rational degree of belief for you to adopt with respect to the proposition that the next card will be an ace, or that the coin you are about to toss will land heads-up or that this strontium-90 atom will decay in the next 15 years? Others think of chances as 'relative frequencies' (see **probability**), but where the 'reference class' is fully specified. Hence, for example, take our deck of cards. Relative to just specifying that it is a normal deck of cards, the probability that the top card is an ace is 1/13: if you kept on getting decks of cards and turning up the top one, you would get an ace, on average, once in every 13 attempts. However, if we got a huge series of decks of cards that were all arranged in exactly the same way, so that the top card was the same every time, we would either *always* turn up an ace (probability 1) or we *never* would (probability 0). Hence, we can equate the *chance* of the card's being an ace with the relative frequency in this fully specified reference class.

Further reading: Hájek (2010, § 3.4); Gillies (2000, Chapter 6)

CLASS

Often used interchangeably with '**set**'. Classes are a technical device introduced by mathematicians and are such that given some things, you have a class of those things (which are called 'members' of the class). For instance, there is a class of all men, a class of all women, a class of all goats and so on. Nor are the classes limited to resembling things: there is a class with just myself and Brad Pitt's left arm, a class with ten random atoms of hydrogen and the right toes of the entire cast of *Dallas* and so on. Two classes are identical if and only if they have the same members (so, for instance, the class of all men is distinct from the class of all women, and the class of all men is distinct from the class {Rowan Williams, the Moon} even though they have a member in common). That something is a member of a class is expressed as $o \in A$ where o is the member and A is the class.

Classes are represented by placing 'curly' brackets (i.e. '{ }') around the members of that class. Hence, if there are three things, a, b and c, we represent the class of all three of them as:

$$\{a, b, c\}$$

Note that membership is not a **transitive** relation. For example, a is a member of $\{a, b\}$, and $\{a, b\}$ in turn is a member of $\{\{a, b\}, \{c, d\}\}$. However, a is not a member of this latter class, because this latter class's members are $\{a, b\}$ and $\{c, d\}$.

Notably, there is a class with *no* members: the 'empty set'. This is represented as either { } or Ø. Also, classes can have other classes as members. Hence, if there is a class $\{a, b, c\}$, then there is also the class:

$$\{\{a, b, c\}\}$$

Furthermore, given that class exists, there is also the class:

$$\{\{\{a, b, c\}\}\}$$

As you can see, this process can keep on going. Each of the above classes is distinct, because their members are different. For instance, $\{a, b, c\}$ has three members, a, b and c, whereas $\{\{a, b, c\}\}$ has but one member, namely $\{a, b, c\}$. Hence, when we have one class, the rules governing what further classes there are immediately generate an infinite number of them.

Usually, classes are taken to be **abstract** objects, outside space and time. Hence, the orthodox line is that when you are talking about the class of all men you are *not* talking about 'all men' but about a single, abstract entity the *class* of those things. This makes some people think classes are strange entities. Given both this and the resistance many philosophers have to including abstract objects in their **ontology**, you might imagine they would be unpopular entities. However, as classes play a crucial role in mathematics, many metaphysicians (such as **W.V. Quine** and **David Lewis**) are happy to include them in their ontology, while repudiating the existence of other abstract objects (or effecting an ontological reduction by identifying other abstract objects with the classes; for instance see **class nominalism**).

Nomenclature

Further to the curly brackets, there are some other common words and symbols that are used:

$$o \in A =_{df} o \text{ is a member of class } A.$$
$$A \subset B =_{df} A \text{ is a subset of } B.$$

Every class is a subset of itself (just like every object is an **improper part** of itself), and the empty set is a subset of every class (including itself). Furthermore, if every member of A is a member of B, then A is a subset of B. For instance, $\{a\}$ and $\{b, c\}$ are just two of the eight subsets that $\{a, b, c\}$ has (we leave the identity of the others as an exercise for the interested reader).

$$A \subseteq B =_{df} A \text{ is a proper subset of } B.$$

(Note that sometimes the symbol '$\subset$' is used instead of '$\subseteq$' for subset.) The only difference between a *proper* subset and a subset is that although every class is a subset of itself, it is not a proper subset of itself (in the same way that an object might be a **part** of itself but not a **proper part**). With that small difference in mind, if someone is not clear about whether they mean proper subset or subset, it almost certainly does not matter.

$$A \cup B =_{df} \text{the union of } A \text{ and } B.$$

Hence, '$A \cup B$' denotes one single class. It is the class that has all and only the members of A and B combined, so the union of $\{a\}$ and $\{b\}$ is $\{a, b\}$.

$$A \cap B =_{df} \text{the intersection of } A \text{ and } B.$$

Again, it denotes a single class. It is the class that has only members that appear in *both* A and B. Hence, $\{a, b\}$ and $\{b, c\}$ have, as a union, $\{b\}$, whereas $\{a\}$ and $\{b\}$ do not have any members in common, so have the empty set $\{\ \}$ as their intersection.

$\{x : Fx\}$ denotes the class that has, as members, everything that is F. For instance, the class $\{x : x$ is a prime number $\}$ is the class of all prime numbers whereas $\{x : x$ is a man$\}$ is the class of all men.

Further reading: The above will probably suffice, as most discussions of set theory became quite complicated. If needed, however, you might wish to refer to Jech (2009)

CLASS NOMINALISM

(It is probably better to read the general entry on **nominalism** before reading this entry.) Class nominalists explain property possession and resemblance in terms of **classes** (or, equivalently, **sets**) of particular objects. An object is red in virtue of being a member of the class of red things. Two objects resemble one another in virtue of being members of the same class.

The class nominalist may be an anti-realist about **properties** (redness, say), which usually involves trying to offer a **paraphrase** of sentences containing terms that look like they refer to properties, for example, 'wisdom is a virtue'. However, they are more likely to *identify* properties with classes of particular objects: redness just is the class of red things – so they are **realists** about properties but offer a reductive analysis of them (see **reductionism**).

Class nominalism faces difficulties with co-extensive properties, that is, properties possessed by all and only the same objects, for example the property of *having-a-heart* and the property of *having-kidneys*. The class of things with kidneys is identical to the class of things with a heart (because two classes that have all and only the same members are identical), so the class nominalist is obliged to identify the property of *having-a-heart* (which is identical to the class of things with a heart) with the property of *having-kidneys* (which is identical to the class of things with kidneys), and yet these seem like distinct properties.

David Lewis avoids this difficulty by embracing *genuine modal realism* (see **modal realism** and **possible worlds**), that is, by believing in the existence of non-actual possible things as well as actual things. For Lewis, the property of *having-a-heart* is identical to the class of things *in all possible worlds* that have a heart, and the property of *having-kidneys* is identical to the class of things *in all possible worlds* that have kidneys. These two classes are not identical, as there is a possible world where there is a strange kind of animal that has a heart but no kidneys and vice versa, so there is no pressure for Lewis to say these two properties are identical, that is, one and the same property.

There are also a number of more intuitive difficulties with class nominalism. It involves a strange order of explanation, explaining the fact that the ball is round in terms of its being a member of the class of round things, when intuitively the explanation goes the other way round. Also, there is a worry that, on the class nominalist view of things, an object has no nature in and of itself; the ball's *being round* consists solely in its relationship with a huge, possibly infinite class (the class of round things).

Further reading: Armstrong (1989, Chapter 2); Loux (2006, Chapter 2)

COMMON SENSE

There are a number of propositions concerning the nature of reality which the average Joe is implicitly, but deeply, committed to: that there exists an external world that we can experience with our senses and that is not merely a figment of our collective imagination, that mammals are conscious but tables are not, that we are (in some specific but difficult to clarify sense) moving towards the future and away from the past, and so on. Call these propositions 'common sense'. To what degree, if at all, are metaphysicians obliged to produce theories that respect common sense?

We can distinguish three positions on this issue. *Strong conservatives* hold that any metaphysical theory that entails the falsity of any proposition of common sense ought to be rejected. *Mild conservatives* hold that it is a **theoretical virtue** of a metaphysical theory that it entails the truth of a proposition of common sense, and a theoretical vice of a theory that it entails the falsity of a proposition of common sense (but because there are other theoretical virtues, abiding by common sense is just one of the factors by which a metaphysical theory should be judged). *Anti-conservatives* hold that both mild and strong conservatives are wrong: the metaphysician has no obligation to respect common sense.

Mild conservativism, the view defended by **David Lewis** (actually, Lewis goes slightly further and suggests that a theory that rejects too much of common sense is not to be taken seriously), is probably the most common of these positions in contemporary metaphysics. Lewis argues that there is a theory implicit in common sense, and that this theory is our starting point for metaphysical theorising. We are entitled to make changes to that theory only to the extent that doing so makes it more theoretically virtuous. Perhaps ironically, many of the theories Lewis ends up with, such as **perdurantism**, **universalism** and genuine **modal realism**, would seem to be a million miles away from common sense. On the other hand, it rather depends which propositions one takes to be part of common sense. For example, one argument of Lewis's for genuine modal realism is that it is common sense that there are *ways the world might have been*, but an opponent might claim that it is equally common sense that there are not infinitely many concrete possible worlds.

It is not clear, however, whether or to what extent taking common sense seriously in metaphysics can be justified: why should the fact that most people have a very strong conviction that *p* constitute a reason for believing *p*?

Which of these views philosophers are drawn to is in general a reflection of how much faith they have in the methods of metaphysics. It tends to be those who are hostile to metaphysics, or at least to metaphysics conceived as a way of finding out the nature of mind-independent reality (see **metametaphysics** for various forms of this kind of 'metaphobia'), who are attracted to conservativism. In contrast, those who take metaphysical enquiry to be a powerful tool for finding out what the mind-independent world is like tend to be open to metaphysics, just like science, telling us odd things about the nature of reality. In between, David Lewis defends mild-conservatism as 'the only sensible policy for theorists of limited powers' (Lewis 1986a: 134).

Further reading: Lewis (1986a, 133–5) discusses his attitude to common sense. A strong attack on the tendency of metaphysicians to value what is 'intuitive' is found in Chapter 1 of Ladyman *et al.* (2007)

COMPATIBILISM

Compatibilists hold that **free will** (and so **moral responsibility**) is compatible with **determinism**. If it turned out that everything we do was determined by the laws of nature and facts about the past, then that would be no bar to doing what we do freely. A powerful objection to compatibilism comes from the **consequence argument**, according to which (a) *being able to do otherwise* is a requirement on acting freely (this is the **Principle of Alternate Possibilities** or PAP) and (b) that ability is incompatible with determinism. (Compatibilist responses to this problem are dealt with in the section on the **Principle of Alternate Possibilities**.)

Of course, even if there is an adequate compatibilist response to this challenge, that does not amount to a full-blown compatibilist theory of free will: to explain why the existence of free will does not require determinism is not to provide a theory of what free will and moral responsibility *do* require. Compatibilists are typically pretty permissive when it comes to what is required for free will. **David Hume** famously said:

> By liberty, then, we can only mean a power of acting or not acting, according to the determinations of the will; this is, if we choose to remain at rest, we may; if we choose to move, we also may. Now this hypothetical liberty is universally allowed to belong to every one who is not a prisoner and in chains
>
> Hume (1748/51, § 8)

Thus, he subscribes to what is sometimes called the 'conditional analysis' of the ability to do otherwise (see **Principle of Alternate Possibilities**).

Hume here limits the ability to act freely to beings that are capable of *choice* and then notes that this ability is further restricted to those who are not prisoners or in chains (because people in those situations lack 'hypothetical liberty': even if the prisoner chooses to leave her cell, she will find that she cannot do so). The first requirement, or something like it, restricts freedom to beings that have certain sorts of *mental* capacities – we might add to the ability to choose the ability to *think* about the *desirability* of various possible options and decide, on the basis of *reasoning*, which option to go for.

Frankfurt's compatibilism

The above conception of free will is rather crude, and some compatibilists have developed more sophisticated accounts of what is required. Frankfurt (1971), for example, makes a distinction between 'first-order' and 'second-order' desires. Examples of first-order desires would be the desire for coffee or a cigarette or a beer or the desire to go to the gym today. Second-order desires, by contrast, are desires *for first-order desires*, for example, the desire to *want* to go to the gym or the desire to not want to have another drink or cigarette. (That these two can come apart should be pretty obvious, unless you are very unusual. I might not want to go to the gym, but I would *like* to want to go to the gym, because then I would probably actually go to the gym, and that would be good for me.)

Armed with this distinction, Frankfurt distinguishes between freedom of action and freedom of the will. Freedom of action requires only that one is able to do what one wants to do; so to be capable of acting freely, one needs only to have first-order desires. Thus a dog, on Frankfurt's view, is perfectly capable of acting freely. It is only beings that have second-order desires, however, that enjoy freedom of the will and are, thus, capable of moral responsibility (hence, although dogs can act freely, they are not morally responsible for what they do).

Consider someone who wants, and because of that desire has, a drink. They *act* freely. However, whether their *will* is free depends on the relationship between their first- and second-order desires. We might characterise *addiction* as a condition whereby one's first-order desires are insensitive to one's second-order desires: the alcoholic is someone who wants a drink no matter what their second-order desires are with respect to wanting a drink (they might be a 'willing' or an 'unwilling' addict). The non-addict is someone whose first-order desires are sensitive to their second-order desires (i.e. their second-order desires are 'effective'): if the non-addict does not want to want a drink, then he or she would not want a drink, and if he or she does want to want a drink, then she *will* want a drink. Hence, with respect to drinking, the non-addict's will is free but the addict's is not.

Frankfurt's account is a compatibilist one, because the effectiveness of our desires, according to Frankfurt, in no way depends on the falsity of determinism: the distinction between the addict and the non-addict, for example, does not rest on the thought that the addict could not have done otherwise, whereas the non-addict could have done otherwise.

One objection to Frankfurt's account is that it is susceptible to counter-examples. We can all agree that someone whose first-order desires are being controlled by some external agent – perhaps because they have been brainwashed or are being controlled by clever alien puppet-masters – does not enjoy freedom of the will. However, what if the brainwashing or manipulation by the alien puppet-masters affects the person's second-order desires as well as their first-order desires, so that they meet Frankfurt's condition that their second-order desires are effective? It looks as though such a person does not enjoy freedom of the will, because the source of their second-order desires is external to them. This kind of case places the onus of responsibility on the compatibilist to distinguish between 'internal' and 'external' sources of second-order desires, so that only desires arising from 'internal' sources deliver freedom of the will. However, it is hard to see how this might be done, and this might lead us towards incompatibilism, on the grounds that, if determinism is true, the ultimate source of *all* our thoughts, desires and actions is external to us (see **incompatibilism** and **agent causation**).

Dennett's compatibilism

Another staunch defender of compatibilism is Daniel Dennett. In his 1984 book *Elbow Room*, he argues that the ability to do otherwise is not required for moral responsibility (see **Principle of Alternate Possibilities** and Dennett 1984, Chapter 6), and that determinism does not rob us of *control* over our actions either (Dennett 1984: Chapter 4). He notes that our everyday notion of control, according to which thermostats control temperature and someone can learn to control the movements of a remote-control model plane, is compatible with determinism and argues, in effect, that the notion of control relevant to freedom and moral responsibility *is* just this notion of control. What distinguishes us from thermostats is not that we have some metaphysically distinctive *kind* of control over our actions (e.g. we **agent cause** our acts, or we have 'regulative control' over them – see later), but rather that there are perfectly straightforward and unmysterious differences between the two cases. For example, we are vastly more complex and sophisticated than a thermostat and can exercise control over a huge range of actions in response to a huge range of situations, whereas a thermostat can respond to exactly one kind of stimulus (whether it is hotter or colder than whatever temperature T it has been set at) in exactly one way (turn the heating on if it is colder than T, and turn it off if it is hotter than T).

Fischer's semicompatibilism

A more recent version of compatibilism – or at least something in that ballpark – is John Martin Fischer's 'semicompatibilism' (see e.g. Fischer 2007). This is the view that determinism is compatible with moral responsibility, even if it is incompatible with free will, at least in some sense of 'free will'. A central distinction that Fischer makes is the distinction between what he calls 'regulative control' and 'guidance control'. Guidance control is pretty much the same as Dennett's notion of control, and, in common with Dennett, Fischer thinks it is guidance control that is required for moral responsibility. Regulative control, by contrast, requires access to alternative possibilities and is required for acting freely. (Fischer is neutral on whether determinism undermines regulative control.) That these are two distinct notions of control is demonstrated, Fischer thinks, by **Frankfurt's nefarious neurosurgeon**. Jones, who decides to kill Smith 'on his own' but would have been forced to make the same decision by Black if he had been about to decide *not* to kill Smith, has guidance control over his decision (he did it 'on his own') but not regulative control (there were no available alternative possibilities). Thus, on Fischer's view, Jones is morally responsible for killing Smith, even if he did not do it freely.

Further reading: McKenna (2009); Dennett (1984)

CONCEPT

Concepts, roughly speaking, are the ingredients of thought. Needless to say, it is a hotly contested issue what exactly concepts *are*. The early modern philosophers, such as **Locke**, **Berkeley** and **Hume**, called (what we would now call) concepts 'ideas', which they mostly thought of as visual mental images, so that to think of the Queen of England, say, would be to have an image of the Queen come before one's mind. Correspondingly, to *have the concept or idea* of the Queen would be for that image to somehow be filed away in one's mind, so that one could then get it out and take a look as required.

This view has fallen by the wayside, however, not least because there are so many concepts for which visual images would seem not to be available (e.g. what would a visual image of a poltergeist be? Or God? Or a magnetic field?). Nonetheless, what seems (to many philosophers) right about the early moderns' view is that concepts are *mental representations*. A real portrait of the Queen wearing a crown is a *representation* of the Queen wearing a crown, and so is a mental image of the Queen wearing a crown. However, so is the thought *that the Queen is wearing a crown*. The early moderns took it for granted that language represents the world *because* we 'associate' words with ideas, which are themselves non-linguistic items (images, in fact). Many contemporary philosophers hold that concepts *are* just linguistic items – they do not inherit their ability to represent the world from some separate, non-linguistic mental entity.

Other philosophers take concepts to be **abstract** objects rather than entities that literally exist in our heads – often taking their lead from the German philosopher Gottlob Frege (1848–1925, also often known as the father of modern logic), who argued against 'psychologism' in general. 'Psychologism' is a charge levelled at philosophical views that, roughly, take the 'laws' of logic and mathematics to be facts about the workings of the human mind – so, for example, there is no more to necessity and possibility (see **modality**) than the fact that we find some things conceivable and others inconceivable. (Hence, 'necessarily, *P*' just means 'not-*P* is inconceivable' and 'possibly, *P*' just means '*P* is conceivable.)

The view that concepts are abstract objects connects with the view that **propositions** are abstract objects: because concepts are taken to be constituents or ingredients of propositions, concepts had better be abstract too. Hence, on this view, when you have the thought that the Queen is wearing a crown, this is a matter of your standing in a relation to a proposition, and your having the relevant concepts – *Queen, crown, wearing* – is also a matter of you standing in some sort of relation to an abstract object, namely a concept. Of course, one difficulty here is that of explaining what this relation is, and how it is that we can stand in this relation to abstract objects. Philosophers sometimes talk of 'grasping' concepts and propositions, but what does this amount to? Grasping an abstract object is not at all like grasping a rope!

Further reading: Margolis and Laurence (2008)

CONCEPTUAL ANALYSIS

Conceptual analysis was thought to be the primary aim of metaphysics (and indeed philosophy in general) throughout much of the twentieth century. To *analyse* a concept (such as the concept of **causation** or **free will** or **time** or **law of nature**) is, basically, to provide a definition of it. For example, to analyse the concept of free action would be to fill in the '*X*' in 'an agent *S* performs act *A* freely if and only if *X*'. Hence, as a first pass, we might try making '*X*' something like '*S* could have done otherwise than *A*', or '*S* was not coerced into doing *A*' or 'if *S* had chosen not to do *A*, then she would not have done *A*' or whatever. According to such a definition, then, any agent that satisfies '*X*' acts freely (i.e. satisfying *X* is *sufficient* for acting freely), and in addition, anyone who acts freely satisfies '*X*' (satisfying *X* is *necessary* for acting freely). Definitions or conceptual analyses are, thus, supposed to provide 'necessary and sufficient conditions' for – in this case – acting freely.

Such conceptual analyses are normally taken to be satisfactory only if they are true necessarily (or 'in all **possible worlds**'). Hence, it needs to be the case (sticking with our example) not only that all and only the *actual* free actions satisfy the definition, but also that all and only *possible* free actions do so.

A fair amount of metaphysics consists in people proposing an analysis of a given concept, and other people trying to come up with counter-examples. For example, let us imagine that someone proposes a conceptual analysis of acting freely that says, '*S* performs *A* freely if and only if *S* could have done otherwise than *A*'. One kind of counter-example would claim that the ability to do otherwise is not *necessary* for acting freely; this is exactly what some philosophers claim is demonstrated by **Frankfurt's nefarious neurosurgeon** case, which is allegedly a possible case of someone acting freely despite lacking the ability to do otherwise. The other kind of counter-example would claim that the ability to do otherwise is not *sufficient* for acting freely. Hence, for example, one might argue that someone who merely performs an act randomly is not acting freely, even though they could have done otherwise (see **problem of luck**).

In the face of an alleged counter-example to our favoured analysis, we can either try to modify the analysis or else try to argue that the alleged counter-example is not really a counter-example at all (e.g. that the agent in Frankfurt's nefarious neurosurgeon case does not, *pace* Frankfurt, act freely after all). In some areas, a good proportion of philosophical discussion consists in a cycle of proposing an analysis, thinking of a counter-example, coming up with an amended analysis that deals with the counter-example, thinking of a new counter-example to the new analysis, and so on. (A lot of the literature on the **counterfactual theory of causation**, for example, takes this form.) One specific form of conceptual analysis – the **Canberra Plan** – is rather less demanding than the kind outlined earlier and so may be less susceptible to counter-examples.

Sometimes, it is argued that our ordinary concept (of free will, say, or causation) is actually ambiguous or confused or internally incoherent or misguided in some way. In such cases, a conceptual analysis offers a 'revisionary' analysis: one that does not seek to define the ordinary concept that is deployed by people in everyday life, but instead seeks to define a better, refined concept, shorn of ambiguity or internal incoherence (see **common sense**).

What is the point of conceptual analysis?

Some philosophers (particularly those influenced by the so-called 'linguistic turn' in the mid-twentieth century – see **metametaphysics**) have thought that *all* metaphysics can do is delineate the meanings of our concepts; hence, conceptual analysis is really the only job that a metaphysician can legitimately perform. Others hold that conceptual analysis can go at least part of the way towards actually telling us something about the nature of reality. For example, if we can analyse 'cause' in terms that do not themselves appeal to causation (e.g. if we can analyse causal claims just by appealing to regularities), then that tells us, at the very least, that we have no good reason to think that there is any '**natural necessity**' in the world. Such a view of the analysis of a given concept (causation, say) fits well with **reductionism**, so that a regularity theorist about the *concept* of causation will also typically be a reductionist about causation itself: causation is nothing over an above the obtaining of a regularity. Still other philosophers, however, are more sceptical about the role of conceptual analysis; see **metametaphysics**.

CONCEPTUAL SCHEME

The notion of a 'conceptual scheme' is sometimes used in the debate about **realism and anti-realism (global)**, with anti-realists – those who deny that our talk and thought can describe reality 'as it is in itself' – sometimes claiming that all we can talk and think about is reality *as constrained by* our conceptual scheme.

We would not try to *define* a conceptual scheme – any definition we gave would be controversial in any case – but, as a first pass, think of it as the entire stock of concepts that you use to think about the world. This does not just mean all the *words* that you use to describe reality, because you do not automatically get two distinct conceptual schemes just because you have got two different languages; the concept German speakers express by 'Schnee' is the very same concept that we express by 'snow'. Davidson (1974), in a well-known but difficult article, 'On the very idea of a conceptual scheme', defines *distinct* conceptual schemes as *mutually untranslatable* languages – so German and English would count as a single conceptual scheme (or perhaps expressions of a single conceptual scheme) because German and English are mutually translatable. (Davidson goes on to argue that it is, in fact, impossible for there to be distinct conceptual schemes, see later.) The idea is that speakers of mutually translatable languages can coherently be seen as agreeing or disagreeing with each other: if a German speaker says 'heute ist Montag' and their English companion says 'today is Tuesday', they are just having a straightforward disagreement about what day of the week it is. If, however, speakers of two mutually untranslatable languages tried to have a conversation, they would, of course, not be able to understand each other, and there would be no sense in which they could be said to agree or disagree about anything. (It is worth noting that the standard metaphysical account of **propositions** is not going to be one that the believer in different conceptual schemes is going to approve of. In fact, the same goes for quite a lot of metaphysical theories.)

One way to articulate and motivate the idea that the nature of the reality we describe is constrained by the very conceptual scheme we use to describe it – popular among anti-realists – is to cast the realist as someone who upholds the 'correspondence theory of truth' (see **truth**): the view that a sentence is true just in case it 'corresponds' to reality. Now, when we talk and think about the world, we cannot help but categorise it in various ways. Every time we use a noun ('tiger', 'chair', 'person' and 'planet') or adjective ('red', 'weighs 3 kg' and 'deciduous'), we are in effect bundling a collection of objects together and distinguishing them from other objects. However (so the argument goes), the correspondence theory of truth – at least when endorsed by a realist – requires the world *itself* to come pre-packaged into those very categories. So the categories (tigers, planets, and so on) exist independently of our classificatory system, and we are merely attaching our own labels to them.

The anti-realist points out, however, that what we just called 'bundling a collection of objects together' is something that *we* do, in a way that reflects our own cognitive and perceptual resources and interests. Hence, for example, one might say that when we categorise someone's behaviour as 'chivalrous' or 'gentlemanly' or 'disgusting', we are imposing our 'value system' onto that behaviour. The claim that someone is chivalrous, for instance, only makes sense from the perspective of a rich and complex web of values – one that some cultures possess but other cultures might lack entirely, having instead a completely different set of values from the perspective of which the notion of chivalry has no place at all.

The anti-realist takes this point about the concept of chivalry to apply across the board to *all* our concepts. The concept 'planet', for example, picks out the celestial bodies it does only given the context of a particular system of astronomical classification that human beings have devised for the purpose of predicting and explaining various phenomena. We might have devised a completely different system of classification that would have been just as effective at prediction and explanation, or some alien race with very different sensory and cognitive capacities might, again, have carved things up very differently. In other words, the very existence of planets is constrained by, or dependent on, our conceptual scheme.

Thus – argues the anti-realist – the correspondence theory of truth is a non-starter and so is the more general view that there is such a thing as **carving nature at its joints** and, even more generally, the view that we can as much as conceive 'mind-independent reality' at all. Planets, of course, were not created by us: we did not fashion them out of big bits of rock and fire them out into the solar system. However, when we talk about planets (for instance, when we assert that planets exist, or that they orbit the sun), we are talking about a world as classified, or conceptualised, by us and not the world as it is in itself (i.e. as it is independently of our conceptual scheme). Other kinds of being (or perhaps just other cultures or people from the same culture in a different historical period) might have a radically different conceptual scheme, 'incommensurable' with our own – that is to say, the language of their 'scheme' cannot be translated into the language of ours – in which case, the world *they* describe is, quite literally, a different world from the world we describe.

There are, of course, claims that the realist might dispute here. The claim that there are, or could be, different, incommensurable conceptual schemes is disputed by Davidson (1974). His argument, in a nutshell, is that we can only recognise a being that is making noises or inscribing squiggles on a piece of paper as *speaking a language* at all insofar as we conceive them as saying or writing things that could be true or false. However, we can only conceive *that* insofar as we take what they say to be translatable, in principle, into our own language and – once translated – evaluable as true or false. Furthermore, if that is right, distinct 'incommensurable' conceptual schemes are just impossible: if the language of another alleged conceptual scheme cannot be translated into the language of our conceptual scheme, then we cannot recognise it as a language – a way of *describing* the world – at all.

Nagel (1986: Chapter 6), however, disputes the anti-realist's claim (which, in fact, Davidson seems to agree with) that we can only conceive reality-as-conceptualised-by-us and not of reality as it is independently of us. The mere fact that we can only describe or represent the world by *using* a language – language is the 'vehicle of thought' – does not entail that what we thereby describe or represent – the *content* of thought – is itself infected by our language or conceptual scheme. (Think of the analogy of picturing a tree in your mind's eye. What you are picturing is a *tree* and not a *picture* of a tree.)

Further reading: Abridged versions of Davidson (1974) and Nagel (1986, Chapter 6), along with some commentary and explanation, are to be found in Beebee and Dodd (2006, Chapter 3). See also Kirk (1999, Chapter 2)

CONCEPTUAL VS LOGICAL TRUTHS

A *conceptual truth* is a statement or proposition that is true merely in virtue of the meanings of its constituent **concepts**. A well-worn example is 'all bachelors are unmarried': the definition of 'bachelor' is 'unmarried man', so it follows just from the definition of 'bachelor' that all bachelors are unmarried.

A *logical truth* is a statement or proposition that is true merely in virtue of its 'logical form', for example, 'if snow is white, then snow is white' (which has the logical form 'if P then P'), or 'either unicorns exist or unicorns do not exist' ('either P or not-P'). The idea here is that no matter what sentence you substituted for 'P', the resulting statement or proposition would be true ('if grass is green, then grass is green', etc.). Note that this is not the case for conceptual truths: 'all bachelors are unmarried' has the logical form 'all As are Bs', and there are plenty of substitutions for 'A' and 'B' that would render the resulting proposition false (e.g. 'all cats are dogs').

Because conceptual and logical truths are true merely in virtue of meaning and/or logical form, they are all *necessary* truths – they *could not* have been false (see **modality**). They are also knowable *a priori*: you do not need to do any empirical investigation to know that all bachelors are unmarried – you just need to know what 'bachelor' means. It would be tempting to conclude from this that (a) the realm of necessary truths *is* just the realm of conceptual and logical truths, and hence (b) the realm of necessary truths *is* just the realm of truths that are knowable *a priori*. However, **Saul Kripke** famously argued that there is another class of necessary truths that are not logical or conceptual truths and that cannot be known *a priori* (see **necessary *a posteriori***).

A note of caution is in order about the very notion of a conceptual truth. What we have defined as the class of conceptual and logical truths is the class of truths that are sometimes known as 'analytic' truths (as opposed to 'synthetic' truths); and **W. V. Quine** (1951) famously argued that no hard and fast distinction can be drawn between the analytic and the synthetic truths (see **analytic vs synthetic truths**).

CONCRETE

See **abstract vs concrete**.

CONSEQUENCE ARGUMENT

The 'Consequence Argument' for **incompatibilism** is the argument advanced by van Inwagen (1975) in his classic article, 'The incompatibility of **free will** and **determinism**' (though the view that free will and determinism are incompatible had been around for a long time before 1975). The argument is so-called because it trades on the fact that if determinism is true, then all our actions are the logical *consequences* of facts about the past and facts about the **laws of nature**.

van Inwagen's article is quite technical, but the Consequence Argument itself is not so difficult; here is a summary of it.

The argument assumes that acting freely requires the ability to do otherwise: if an act *A* (including a mental act such as deciding to do something) of an agent *J* is to be free, it must be the case that *J* could have done *otherwise*. (This assumption is explored in detail in the section on the **Principle of Alternate Possibilities**.) van Inwagen characterises the ability to do otherwise as the ability to *render some proposition false*, where the proposition in question is a proposition about something you have done or will do in the future. Hence, for example, imagine that Jane made a cup of tea at eight o'clock in the morning on 1 January 2009 (call this time t_1). The claim that Jane could have done otherwise amounts to the claim that Jane could have rendered false the proposition, 'Jane makes a cup of tea at t_1'. Call this proposition *P*. Of course, Jane cannot *now* – after 1 January 2009, that is, after t_1 – render *P* false; the tea is long made and drunk, and Jane cannot do anything about that. However – or so one might think – Jane could have rendered *P* false *before* t_1. For example, perhaps just before t_1, Jane was wondering whether to make tea or coffee and decided on tea. She *could*, one might think, have decided on coffee and, therefore, made coffee instead, and if she had done that, *P* – that is, the proposition 'Jane makes a cup of tea at t_1' – would have been false. However, the Consequence Argument purports to show that if determinism is true, then this cannot be so: Jane could not, at the time when she was consciously considering whether to make tea or coffee – or indeed at any other time – have rendered *P* false.

Here is why. Let P_0 be a statement that describes the exact state of the whole Universe at a particular time t_0, and let *L* be a statement that describes all the laws of nature. The thesis of **determinism** states that P_0 & *L* logically entail a statement that describes the exact state of the Universe at any other time. Hence – to use our example – let time t_0 be, say, midnight on 15 December 2008 (though we might just as well pick a time two seconds before t_1, or for that matter 826 BC; the argument will work just the same). P_0 is then a statement that describes the exact state of the whole Universe at t_0 (including, of course, plenty of facts about Jane, unless we have picked a time before she was even born). Assuming that determinism is true, P_0 & *L* logically entail a statement that describes the exact state of the Universe at any other time, so, in particular, it entails that

Jane had a cup of tea at eight o'clock on the morning of 1 January 2009. In other words, P_0 & L entail our proposition P.

Given this, could Jane really have rendered P false – could she really have done otherwise than make a cup of tea at t_1? According to van Inwagen, no, she could not. He argues for this by appealing to a general principle, as follows: suppose some proposition A entails some other proposition B (so that if A is true, B is guaranteed to be true too). Then, if someone (Jane, say) cannot render A false, they cannot render B false either. Hence, according to the principle, *if* Jane cannot render P_0 & L false, then she cannot render P false, because (assuming determinism) the former entails the latter.

It would seem that Jane, when she was deliberating about whether to make tea or coffee just before t_1, could not render P_0 & L false. She could not render P_0 false, because she could not, on 1 January 2009, render false any proposition about what happened a fortnight earlier, on 15 December 2008. Furthermore, she could not render L false, because nobody can render false a true proposition about what the laws of nature are. You cannot render false the proposition that nothing travels faster than the speed of light, or the proposition that people who have an uninterrupted fall from the top of the Empire State Building onto the street below all die. Hence – still assuming determinism – Jane could not, in fact, have rendered P false, because she could not render P_0 & L false, which is to say that she could not, in fact, have done otherwise than make the cup of tea.

The upshot of the Consequence Argument – to put it in a nutshell – is that one cannot do otherwise if what one does is determined by facts about the past and the laws. Therefore, given our initial assumption that acting freely requires that one *can* do otherwise, free will is incompatible with determinism.

Whether the Consequence Argument really is a sound argument has been the subject of a huge amount of philosophical debate; see the sections on **incompatibilism** and the **Principle of Alternate Possibilities**.

Further reading: van Inwagen (1975); Vihvelin (2008); Fischer (1995, Chapters 1–4)

CONTINGENT TRUTHS

A contingent truth is a sentence or **proposition** that is (a) true and (b) not *necessarily* true (see **necessity**). For example, 'Barack Obama won the

2008 US presidential election' is true, but not necessary – it *might* have been false. Hence, it is a contingent truth.

COUNTERFACTUAL CONDITIONAL

A counterfactual conditional (or 'counterfactual' for short) is a special case of the subjunctive conditional, which uses what is known in grammar as the 'subjunctive mood'. A counterfactual conditional has the form 'if P had been the case, then Q would have been the case' – for example, 'if I'd got up an hour earlier this morning, I would have got more work done'. This is normally represented by the 'box-arrow': $P \,\square\!\!\rightarrow\, Q$. The antecedent (P) must actually be false ('contrary to fact') for the conditional to be a genuine counterfactual.

What the **truth conditions** of counterfactuals are is a difficult question to answer. The standard analysis is due to **David Lewis**, who uses the machinery of **possible worlds**. Roughly, the counterfactual '$P \,\square\!\!\rightarrow\, Q$' is true if and only if Q is true at the 'closest' possible world at which P is true (where 'closest' means 'most similar to the actual world'). Hence, the truth conditions for 'if I'd got up an hour earlier this morning, I would have got more work done' go like this. First, find the possible world that is as similar to the actual world as it can be, but at which I got up an hour earlier. Call this world *w*. Hence, if I actually got up at 8 am, then *w* will be a world at which I got up at 7 am. However, in most other respects – and in virtually all respects before 7 am this morning – it will be the same as the actual world: *w* will not be a world at which, as well as getting up at 7 am, I was driving a cab all night, or my house burns down at 7.05 am (because neither of these things happened in the actual world). Now, having alighted on the closest possible world *w* (or in the event of a tie, all the equally close closest worlds), do I get more work done at *w*? If yes, then the counterfactual is true; and if no, it is not.

Of course, it is one thing to say what the truth conditions are, and quite another to figure out whether or not they obtain in any given case. However (or at least this is what is hoped), at least some cases are reasonably straightforward. Normally, let us suppose, I do get more work done when I get up at 7 am than when I get up at 8 am, and today is no different in relevant respects to those days where I do get up earlier and do more work. Hence, it is fairly safe to suppose that if I had got up an hour earlier, I would indeed have got more work done.

It is not always plain sailing, though. Take a common-or-garden football match. Arsenal score an early goal, Chelsea equalise just after half time and the game ends in the draw Chelsea needed to win the title. Is it true that if Chelsea had not scored, Arsenal would have won? You might think so – after all, surely the score would have been 1-0 and not 1-1. However (both intuitively and according to the possible-world analysis of counterfactuals), it is not so clear. Imagine that Chelsea did not score that goal. What would have happened next? They would have been losing and so would have been trying really hard in the second half to equalise. Arguably, they just would not have played in the remainder of the game in anything like the way they actually played, when they were at 1-1 and only needed to draw to win the title. Hence, it is not at all clear whether our counterfactual is true.

One of the major uses of counterfactuals in metaphysics is in the **counterfactual theory of causation**. Another is in the analysis of dispositions (see **dispositional and categorical properties**).

COUNTERFACTUAL THEORY OF CAUSATION

The counterfactual theory is intended, like the **regularity theory**, to be a reductive analysis of causation (see **reductionism**). The most basic version of the counterfactual theory endorses the following:

> c is a cause of e if and only if c and e occur, and if c had not occurred, e would not have occurred (or, in other words, if and only if e counterfactually depends on c).

In other words, the truth of a causal claim depends just on the truth of a particular **counterfactual conditional**. Hence, for instance, if you shoot me with a gun, it is true that if you had not pulled the trigger, I would not be bleeding. Thus, given the analysis, it is true (as it should be) that you cause me to bleed.

Unfortunately, the above analysis pretty obviously needs improving because of the phenomenon of **pre-emption**. Imagine that there was a second shooter getting ready to fire at me. They saw you fire and so desisted – but if you had not fired, they would have fired, and doubtless, if they had done so, I would still be bleeding. The presence of the second shooter (or 'back-up cause') does not make you any less of a cause of my bleeding, but it does stop my bleeding counterfactually depend on your firing – I would have been bleeding anyway even if you had not fired. Lewis' solution to this problem is to take the above as the definition of 'causal dependence' and then to define causation as the **ancestral** of causal dependence (see **pre-emption** for more on this). Unfortunately, the problems do not stop there. In particular, there are trickier pre-emption cases (such as 'trumping pre-emption' and 'late pre-emption'; again, see **pre-emption**), and there is also **overdetermination** to worry about. (Pre-emption and overdetermination are sometimes collectively known as 'redundant causation'). The upshot has been numerous counterfactual theories, each more complex than the last, each trying to solve a different alleged counter-example, and each of them going beyond the very basic analysis given earlier. There is a veritable cottage industry of published philosophy detailing scenarios where a counterfactual theory gets it wrong and a competing industry detailing how to tweak the analyses to avoid these problems.

The main advocate of the counterfactual theory is **David Lewis**, with his original theory detailed in his article (Lewis 1973a). His last version of the theory (Lewis 2000), which was a lot more complex than the original, was introduced to deal with a wide variety of counter-examples that affected the 1973 version. Lewis' reasons for favouring the counterfactual theory are that (a) he upholds the thesis of **Humean supervenience** and (b) he does not see any other way of doing it (because the other main contender, the regularity theory, is hopelessly inadequate). Needless to say, many philosophers who see no need to uphold Humean supervenience have taken the increasing complexity of counterfactual theories and the apparently limitless supply of counter-examples to be a sign that counterfactual analyses are doomed.

Further reading: Lewis (1973a, 2000); Menzies (2008); Psillos (2002, Chapter 3)

CRITERION OF ONTOLOGICAL COMMITMENT

See **ontological commitment**.

DETERMINABLES AND DETERMINATES

The **property** of *being square* and the property of *being round* are determinates of the property of *being shaped*; the property of *being shaped* is a determinable of the properties of *being square* and *round*. The property of *being six* *foot two inches tall* is a determinate of the property of *being tall*; the property of *being tall* is a determinable of the property of *being six foot two inches*. The property of *being scarlet* is a determinate of the property of *being red*, which is in turn a determinate of *being coloured*; the property of *being coloured* is a determinable of the property of *being red*, which is in turn a determinable of the property of *being scarlet*. In general, property x is a determinate of property y if and only if having x is a specific way of having y; *being square* is a specific way of *being shaped*, and *being scarlet* is a specific way of *being red*, which in turn is a specific way of *being coloured*. If property x is a determinate of property y, then property y is a determinable of property x.

Some philosophers, out of respect for economy as a **theoretical virtue**, think that facts about the determinable properties a given object instantiates are reducible (see **reductionism**) to facts about that object's instantiating specific determinates of those determinables. For example, the fact that the baseball is shaped is reducible to the fact that the baseball is spherical: all there is to being shaped is to be spherical or cubical or pyramid shaped or . . ., and so on.

Further reading: Sanford (2008)

DETERMINISM

Imagine watching a game of pool. You can see the player hit the cue ball – reasonably hard, say, and dead centre. You can see that the cue ball is directly in line with a red, which itself is directly in line with the centre pocket. You know that it is a normal pool table, and the balls are normal, there is nobody around to pluck the red off the table and you have a lot of experience of pool, so you know how pool balls behave in normal circumstances. It seems fairly reasonable to say that if you really knew all of this, you could predict with certainty that the red will go in the pocket.

Suppose you *can*, in principle, predict this with certainty. The thesis of determinism is, very roughly, the thesis that the entire Universe is just like the pool example just given – except, of course, that the Universe is a vastly bigger and more complex place than a pool table.

Rather less roughly, determinism is the thesis that the precise state of the Universe at any moment (a billion years ago, or five seconds ago or whatever), together with the **laws of nature**, determines the precise state of the Universe at any other time (999 million years ago, in one second's time or in another 999 million years' time). To put it even more precisely, let

P_t be a statement that describes the exact state of the whole Universe at a particular time t, and let L be a statement that describes all the laws of nature. Then P_t & L logically *entail* a statement that describes the exact state of the Universe at any other time (compare **indeterminism**). Hence, *if* someone knew all the facts about the state of the Universe at a given moment, *and* they knew all the laws of nature, then they would be able to predict with certainty what the state of the Universe will be in, say, ten seconds' time. (Note that this is a very big 'if'!)

Determinism is an empirical thesis: it is not up to philosophers to take a stand on whether or not the Universe is really deterministic. All we can do is appeal to the best available science, which, unfortunately, does not settle the issue (see **indeterminism**).

Determinism is relevant to the topics of **free will** and **causation and laws**. In the case of free will, many philosophers – **incompatibilists** – have held that if determinism is true, then we never act freely (one argument for this is the **Consequence Argument**). In the case of causation, most philosophers used to subscribe to the view that causes are sufficient conditions for, or determine, their effects (indeed 'determinism' is often called 'causal determinism'). Nowadays, however, most philosophers agree that indeterministic causation is possible (see **probabilistic theories of causation**).

Further reading: Hoefer (2008); Salmon (1998, Chapter 2); Earman (1986, Chapters 1 and 2)

DIACHRONIC IDENTITY

See **identity** *and* **identity over time**.

DIRECTION OF TIME

Events occur in an order of the earliest events to the latest. For instance, take three events: the American Revolution, the Battle of Hastings and the Boer War. They have a natural ordering:

The Battle of Hastings → the American Revolution → the Boer War

That order is, of course, from the earliest event to the most recent event. This is different from, say, a spatial ordering. Take three cities: Moscow, Paris and Beijing. They can be ordered from west to east (Paris, Moscow and Beijing) or east to west (Beijing, Moscow and Paris). Neither ordering is better than the other, so although both series, spatial and temporal, have an order, only time has a *direction*.

One interest in the philosophy of time is to find out what explains this direction of time. There are several explanations on offer. The *thermodynamic answer* (favoured by the physicist Boltzmann) says that the direction of time is fixed by entropy increasing. Entropy is a measure of how chaotic and disorganised a system is. Some systems, say the system of atoms composing you, are quite organised and have low entropy; other systems, such as a gas dispersing randomly across a room, are more chaotic and have comparatively high entropy. There can be, and often are, local decreases in entropy; for instance, when you build something you are making part of the world more organised. However, this *local* decrease expends energy, which results in an *overall* increase of entropy throughout the universe. Indeed, the Second Law of Thermodynamics says that, over time, overall entropy tends to increase. In light of this, Boltzmann said that the rise in overall entropy actually fixes the direction of time itself. The problem here is that overall entropy may *tend* to increase, but it need not always – it is possible that it randomly decreases at some point. We can easily imagine random decreases in local entropy, for instance, if, by chance, the dispersed gas suddenly coalesced in the centre of the room in a particularly organised fashion. This is not *likely* to happen, but it *could*, consistent with the **laws of nature**. If such events occurred all over the universe (which is *really* unlikely but still not impossible), then the overall entropy would decrease. However, if we sided with Boltzmann, then we would have to say that time had then gone backwards, which does not sound right at all.

The psychological answer fixes the direction of time by making it dependent on psychological features. What we remember has an order to it. At one time we remember some set of things, at another time we can remember yet more things (as our memories accumulate), and this applies for everyone – accidents and amnesia aside, the direction of the accumulation of memories is universally the same. We might, then, want to say that time goes in the same direction as this psychological arrow. There are problems here, particularly in that by fixing the direction of time to matters of psychology we seem to make it somehow mind dependent – something not everyone will be happy with.

One final popular way to fix the direction of time is to fix it in the direction of causation. Events are later than earlier events just *because* it is the earlier events that cause the later ones, rather than *vice versa*. Obviously, unless one wishes to get caught up in circularity, this move is only open to those theorists who do not, even partially, analyse the causal relation in terms of temporal relations (so it rules out the **regularity theory of causation**, which stipulates that the cause must come before the effect). There are also other problems, such as what to do in a world where very little causation takes place, and what happens in worlds where **backwards causation** is possible (for in such worlds causes can precede their effects).

Further reading. Dainton (2001, Chapter 4); Le Poidevin (2003, Chapter 12)

DISPOSITIONAL PROPERTIES

See **categorical vs dispositional properties**.

DRETSKE-TOOLEY-ARMSTRONG VIEW OF LAWS

Dretske (1977), Tooley (1977) and Armstrong (1983) all independently came up with a view of the laws of nature now often called the Dretske-Tooley-Armstrong view (DTA), and sometimes referred to simply as 'Armstrong's view'. DTA holds that a proposition is a law of nature when **universals** stand in a certain, special, relation: 'contingent necessitation' (sometimes known as **natural necessitation**). 'All humans are mortal' states a law of nature (though admittedly not a very interesting one) just because the universal *being human* stands in the natural necessitation relation to the universal *being mortal* (Armstrong writes this as '$N(F,G)$' where F and G are universals, here *being human* and *being mortal*, and N is the necessitation relation). Hence, the thinking goes, this is why all humans are mortal: because the first universal necessitates the second, such that anything instantiating the first *must* instantiate the second. N is 'contingent' necessitation because it is a contingent matter *which* universals (if any) are related by N: there are **possible worlds** where the laws of nature are different and indeed worlds where there are no laws at all (i.e. worlds where N does not exist).

One major benefit of DTA is that it avoids problems that the **regularity view of laws** encounters. In particular, the regularity view mistakenly counts accidental regularities as laws of nature. For instance, there is a rare metal called lutetium. Like most other metals it is solid at room temperature but can be melted down (or even vapourised) at high temperatures.

Imagine that, as it happened, all of the lutetium – past, present and future – was located in very hot places and so was in a liquid state. Given the regularity view of laws, it would then be a *law of nature* that lutetium is a liquid, rather than just being a mere accidental regularity. DTA avoids this unfortunate consequence, for although it is *true* that all lutetium is a liquid, there is no corresponding law of nature, because the universal *being made of lutetium* does not stand in the natural necessitation relation to the universal *being a liquid*. Similarly, DTA avoids issues that plague the **Ramsey–Lewis View of law**, which makes use of problematic epistemic notions like 'simplicity'. DTA does not include any such problematic epistemic notions and so has no difficulty there.

Some problems for DTA

Uninstantiated laws: One might think that there could be uninstantiated laws of nature. For instance, it is a law of nature that force equals mass multiplied by acceleration, so it is a law of nature that an object weighing 534.24 kilograms will accelerate at a speed (in metre per square) equal to the force applied to it (in Newtons), divided by 534.24. Hence, given DTA, there is a relation of natural necessitation between various universals, including the universal *weighing 524.24 kilograms*. However, that is not to say that any object actually *has* that mass (indeed, for some value of mass – even if not this one – there would not be anything with that mass). In that case, that universal must exist even though it has no instantiations. For a realist like Armstrong, who only believes in **immanent universals**, this poses a problem, because only universals that are instantiated exist (although it poses no problems for a **platonist** like Tooley – see Tooley 1987: Chapter 2).

What is contingent necessitation? **David Lewis** (1983a) worries what the natural necessitation relation is meant to be. Although the relation is labelled 'the necessitation relation', Lewis says that without more explication of what this relation is and how it does what it does, DTA does not end up *explaining* anything. Lewis even manages to sneak in one of metaphysics' best jokes (although we cannot promise you will laugh): saying that there is a relation that we call the 'necessitation' relation no more demands that one universal necessitates another than calling someone 'Armstrong' demands that he has mighty biceps, that is, the explanation of someone having mighty biceps involves more than simply saying he has got a certain name; why would *that* explain anything? Similarly, DTA does not explain anything unless and until we find out more about this 'contingent necessitation' relation: why and how does the fact that F and G stand in a relation we have conveniently called 'N' guarantee that all Fs are Gs?

Ontological worries: Obviously, DTA is only open to those who believe in universals. For an **ontology** that does not have them (i.e. any version of **nominalism**), DTA is not going to work. Whether this is a problem, of course, will depend on what you think of universals.

Further reading: Armstrong (1983); Psillos (2002, Chapter 6)

EMPIRICISM

Empiricism is, minimally, the view that all our knowledge of the external world is *a posteriori* and contrasts with **rationalism**. Classic empiricists include **John Locke**, **George Berkeley** and **David Hume** (they are often known as the 'British Empiricists'). Traditionally, empiricists (including the British Empiricists) also believed that all our 'ideas' (or **concepts**) come from experience, so that when you came into the world your mind was a blank slate or 'tabula rasa': you had no ideas at all until you started to experience the world around you. Thus, we have not only no 'innate knowledge' of the world (we are not born knowing anything at all, even implicitly) but also no 'innate ideas' either: we are not born with, but acquire through experience, the concepts that are the building blocks of thought.

This second form of empiricism sometimes (notably in Hume) takes the form of an even stronger thesis, sometimes known as *meaning-empiricism*. This is the thesis that if an alleged 'idea' or concept cannot be traced to some source in our direct sensory experience, then it is not really a genuine idea: when we attempt to deploy it in thought, we are not really thinking anything coherent at all. Hume (arguably) thought that the alleged ideas of **natural necessity** and the self fall into this category (see **realism and anti-realism** and **bundle theory of the person or self**).

Empiricism might be thought (and certainly was, by Hume) to be in serious tension with the very idea of metaphysics, conceived as an investigation into the nature of reality. For the metaphysician does not deploy 'empirical' methods – he or she does not conduct experiments or (mostly) consult the evidence of his or her senses, but rather comes to conclusions on the basis of 'armchair' reasoning. Hence, it looks as though the metaphysician is claiming that his or her conclusions about the nature of reality are knowable *a priori* – which of course conflicts with the empiricist claim that we can only have *a posteriori* knowledge of the external world. Moreover, meaning-empiricism in particular might be thought to put paid to some forms of metaphysical speculation; indeed, this was an explicit aim of Hume's. Speculation into the nature of the self, for example, will be completely worthless if we have no genuine idea of the self to start with.

Most contemporary philosophers reject meaning-empiricism, however, holding that we can perfectly well have legitimate concepts that we do not acquire through direct sensory experience of what they are concepts *of*. One motivation for this view comes from considering the higher reaches of theoretical physics. It is a brave person who accuses the physicist of deploying meaningless terms when they talk about superstrings or quarks or the Higgs boson, on the grounds that you cannot observe these things. On the other hand, the broader question of whether metaphysics actually does, or even aims to, generate *a priori* knowledge of the external world is one that metaphysicians still disagree with each other about (see also **metametaphysics** and **conceptual analysis**).

ENDURANTISM

Endurantism has had a hard time finding a good definition. Usually, it is said to be the view that objects are 'wholly present' at every time at which they exist, but there is some consternation over what that is supposed to mean. However, for most purposes you can take endurantism to simply be the denial of **perdurantism**, which is the view that objects have **temporal parts**, with different parts existing at different times (just as different parts of you – your nose, left foot, and so on – exist in different places). Hence, loosely speaking, endurantists do not believe that objects have **temporal parts** at every time at which they exist. Although they are, almost without exception, united in that regard, endurantists vary greatly over the specifics of their position.

One way they vary is over how they deal with the argument from temporary intrinsics (see **perdurantism** for more information). Another is how they deal with the *argument from coincidence*. Imagine that a lump of clay is shaped into a statue. Because the lump of clay has existed for longer than the statue, their properties are different. Because their properties are different, the objects must be distinct (by **Leibniz's Law**, or, more precisely, the 'indiscernibility of identicals'). However, that means there are *two* objects (the statue and the lump) in the same place at the same time (see also **identity**). This conclusion seems reprehensible.

Perdurantists are often thought to have an easy way out (see **perdurantism**), but endurantists think that they have ways out of this as well. Some endurantists bite the bullet and say that there *are* two objects in the same place at the same time, and that the lump of clay *constitutes* the statue. This is called the 'Standard Account' (for it was once the standard reply to this scenario). One alleged problem for the standard account is 'double counting': it just gets the number of objects that there are *wrong* (for surely there is only one thing there, not *two*!), and this is not a bullet that can be bit. Another problem concerns the properties of the objects. The properties of the lump and the statue are different, yet they are composed of exactly the same sub-atomic particles arranged in the same way. However, if we assume, as seems reasonable to most, that the properties of macroscopic objects **supervene** on the properties and arrangement of their sub-atomic particles, then both the statue and the lump should have the same properties (Burke 1992). As this is not the case, the Standard Account has a problem.

There are endurantist alternatives, but their palatability varies. What follows is just a sample of alternative theories. Some eliminate the statue or the lump or both. For instance, Burke (1994) believes that when you make a statue, the lump of clay is destroyed, so there is no lump to cause a problem. Alternatively, you might believe there are no statues at all, just lumps of matter (and, by parity of reasoning, no tables or chairs, and the universe consists only of material lumps). Finally, the *nihilists* believe that neither the statue nor the lump really exists, and the only material objects that really exist are sub-atomic particles (see **nihilism**).

Other alternatives include taking the statue and lump to be *temporarily* identical; identical only when the lump is shaped into a statue. At that time, as they are identical, there is only *one* thing, so the repugnant conclusion is avoided. At the earlier time, however, the lump *was not* identical to the statue. However, most people believe that 'temporary identity' is not a form of identity at all, or that if you *really* understand what it is to be the same thing as something else you see that temporary identity makes no sense.

Further reading: Olson (1996); Sider (2001, Chapter 5)

ESSENCE

The essence of a thing is (to quote **John Locke**) 'the being of a thing, whereby it is what it is'. We need to distinguish, however, between 'individual' and 'kind' essences. The *kind* essence of a thing — a horse, say — is whatever it is in virtue of which it is a member of that kind. (Philosophers of biology, and indeed biologists themselves, spend a lot of time arguing about whether the kind *horse* really has an essence, and, if it does, whether that essence is a matter of evolutionary history – this view is known as 'cladism' – or intrinsic features, e.g., some common feature of horses' DNA.) The *individual* essence of a thing is whatever makes it the *particular* thing it is: what makes Dobbin the horse not just *a* horse but this particular horse.

The notion of 'essence' is an extremely slippery one, because different philosophers mean different things by it (and that is only the ones who are clear about what they mean!). Hence, when a philosopher calls themself (or is accused of being) an 'essentialist', it is often not very clear exactly what they are committed to. Roughly speaking, though, we can think of accounts of essence as falling into two broad categories: 'modalist' and 'non-modalist'.

On a modalist view of essence, an account of essence can be given in modal terms, that is, facts about the individual or kind essence of a thing are analysable in terms of facts about **necessity** and **possibility** (see **modality**). For example, we might say that 'object *a* is essentially *F*' just means 'in every possible world at which *a* exists, *a* is *F*' (so to say that Philip is essentially human is just to say that at every world in which Philip exists, he is a human being; he is not a gorilla or a robot in any possible world. Even if there are possible worlds containing gorillas or robots that are a lot like Philip, they are not *Philip*). Similarly, to say '*K*s are essentially *F*' (where '*K*' picks out some kind, such as *human being* or *horse*) is just to say that at every possible world in which there are members of kind *K*, those objects are all *F*. (Hence, to say that human beings are essentially descended from apes just means that there are no possible worlds at which there are human beings that are *not* descended from apes.)

The modalist view naturally lends itself to quite a metaphysically 'thin' notion of essence, in the sense of not bringing any substantive **ontological commitments**. To see why, consider Locke's position. Locke is quite happy to speak about the (kind) essences of things. However, for Locke, the essence of a kind merely amounts to whatever features we happen to use as a basis for classification. If we classify something as a watch on the basis of its being reasonably portable and able to tell the time, then that is the essence (actually the 'nominal essence', from the Latin *nominare*, meaning 'to name') of a watch, which is just to say that nothing that is either not reasonably portable or unable to tell the time can be a watch. (Of course, any individual watch will have underlying features that explain why it satisfies these conditions – e.g. having cogs and other mechanical parts arranged in a certain way, and being a certain size – and these features constitute the watch's 'real essence'. However, the essence of a *watch* – what *makes* it a watch – is just its nominal essence. A mechanical watch and a digital watch have different underlying features in virtue of which they tell the time. However, they both are watches, because they both tell the time.) On a Lockean view of essences, we might say that the dispute in biology about the essences of species is one for which there is no fact of the matter about who is right: there are simply different species concepts and a different essence for each concept.

According to the anti-modalist conception, the connection between essence and modality runs in the other direction: it is *because* an object (or kind) has the essence it has that the relevant modal facts (facts about necessity and possibility) are true of it. The anti-modalist view is, thus, most naturally seen as a metaphysically 'thick' notion of essence. Such a 'thick' view is normally committed to one or more of three claims. First, not every concept corresponds to a kind essence: only kinds that **'carve nature at its joints'** have genuine essences (so chemical and physical kinds, such as *hydrogen*, *electron* and *gold*, and maybe biological kinds, such as *horse*, have essences; chairs, dominoes and watches, on the other hand, do not). Second, there is a mind- and language-independent fact of the matter about the essence of a given kind (or individual). Hence, for example, one side or other in the dispute about species essences is correct, and which is correct is determined solely by the nature of species themselves. Finally, the essence of a kind is only discoverable *a posteriori*. Thus, for example, the claim 'water is H_2O' is necessarily true (because it tells us what the essence of water is) but nonetheless can only be discovered by scientific investigation into the nature of water (see **necessary *a posteriori***).

Further reading: Locke (1690, Book III, Chapter 3)

ETERNALISM

Eternalism is one of the three main theories concerning the ontology of time. Unlike those who uphold **presentism** and **growing block theory**, eternalists believe that all times exist. Hence, the death of the dinosaurs, and the dinosaurs themselves, exist; the Big Bang that happened 15 billion years ago exists; similarly, should we ever colonise Mars then, even though that takes place in the future, the Martian outposts exist. This may sound very strange, but eternalists are quick to point out that they do not mean that these things exist *now*. In the same way that things exist on the other side of the planet from me even though they are not *here* – they are not spatially local to me – the Big Bang, dinosaurs and Martian outposts exist even though they are not *now* – they are not *temporally* local. This sense of existence is a 'tenseless' sense. In the same way that some people think **abstract** things like **numbers** or **universals** exist even though they are not in space and time *at all* (so it is misleading to say that such abstract things *presently* exist), eternalists think other times (and things at those times) exist but not presently. (If you have a hard time getting a grip on the notion of tenseless existence, then note that some people find the notion so unintelligible that they repudiate eternalism on that ground alone; see Crisp 2004a, 2004b and Ludlow 2004.)

Eternalism is almost always combined with a tenseless view of time (see **tensed and tenseless theories of time**; although see also the **moving spotlight**). Historically, it was also paired with **perdurantism**, but more recently, it has become popular to think eternalism is neutral with respect to which of perdurantism and **endurantism** is true.

Motivations

Many people accept eternalism because they believe that it succeeds in over-coming objections that presentism faces. For instance, presentism has prob-lems accounting for true **propositions** containing singular terms that refer to things that no longer exist, say <Ghenghis Khan was a warlord>. Classical logic allegedly then entails that Ghenghis Khan exists, and the presentist wants to say he does not. However, eternalism has no such problem, for given eternalism Ghenghis Khan *does* exist (just not now but back in the past). Where presentism has problems accounting for **relativity** (which seems to indicate that there is no privileged present moment) eternalism has no such difficulty. As long as the eternalist accepts the tenseless theory of time (which they invariably do), there *is not* a privileged present. Similarly, where pre-sentism has problems with the possibility of **time travel** – for how can one travel to another time if other times do not exist? – eternalism obviously has no such difficulty (for the other times *do* exist).

The same applies to **truthmaking** issues. Those who accept truthmak-ing have difficulty in seeing what makes true the proposition <dinosaurs existed in 1,000,000 BC> if you are a presentist. For the eternalist, it is easy. What makes the proposition true is that 1,000,000 BC exists, and dinosaurs exist, and there is a **state of affairs** of the dinosaurs being located at that time. It is that state of affairs that makes it true that dinosaurs existed in 1,000,000 BC.

Obviously this undermining of presentism only guarantees eternalism if it is the only alternative. Although little ink has been spilt defending eter-nalism against growing block theory, you can assume that most eternalists who do not mention it consider growing block theory to be false as well, leaving eternalism the only remaining genuine option.

Objections

Besides the problem concerning making sense of what 'tenseless existence' amounts to, most objections revolve around undermining the motivations. So where the eternalist says that they can handle truthmaking better than the presentist, the presentist demurs; where the eternalist says that presentism cannot handle relativity, the presentist offers reasons to reject that claim, and so on. Then, taking themselves to have undermined the motivations for eternalism, presentists add that, as it is more intuitive that the Big Bang, dinosaurs and Martian outposts do not exist (tenselessly or otherwise), we should not prefer eternalism to presentism.

Further reading: Rea (2003); Sider (2001, Chapter 2)

EVENT

Events are one of the commonly accepted ontological categories, corresponding roughly (but only very roughly, on some views) to the events that are recognised in ordinary language. Hence, examples of events would be the Battle of Hastings, your eighteenth birthday party, Barack Obama's inauguration, the extinction of the dinosaurs and the collapse of communism. Events can also be very short and insignificant (and here we start to part company with ordinary language). Every time my heart beats, that is a different event; if I trip over on the way to work, that is an event; a water molecule somewhere in the ocean moving half an inch is an event; and so on. They might not be *important* events, but they still count as events.

Events are particularly interesting when it comes to causation, because they are often taken to be the **causal relata**, and the philosophy of mind, where there has been a lot of debate concerning the relationship between mental events, such as being in pain, and physical events, such as certain neurons firing in your brain. More generally, whether they exist or not – and what they are like if they do – falls under the general remit of **ontology**.

Reasons to believe in events

First, events are often taken to be the relata of the causal relation. If that is right, then given that we know there is causal activity in the world, there must be events (however, see **causal relata** for objections). Second, people often endorse some form of **W. V. Quine**'s criterion of **ontological commitment**. Davidson argues that the underlying logical form of sentences such as 'Barack Obama slowly walked to the podium' includes quantification over events (the above sentence is equivalent to 'there is some event *e*, such that *e* was a walking in the direction of the podium by Barack Obama'). Hence (given that theory of ontological commitment), events exist (Davidson 1967: 1969). Finally, we might take events to be **truthmakers** for certain propositions (see Simons 2003: 363–4).

Other metaphysical issues

If events do exist, then there remain questions about them, and in particular, what they *are*? These questions are often answered on the basis of what events would have to be like to serve as the relata of causation. Lewis (1986c), for example, takes this approach, and for this reason claims that there are no such things as 'disjunctive' events: there is an event that is John's saying 'hello' but no event that is John's saying 'hello' or eating a banana. Similarly, events can be more or less 'fragile': John says 'hello' loudly. You might think that is just one event, but it is not: John's saying 'hello' is a different (but not wholly distinct) event from his saying 'hello' loudly. Lewis himself takes events to be **properties** of spatio-temporal regions. Others take events to be spatio-temporal regions themselves. Kim (1973) – also with an eye on the need for events to do work as the relata of causation – takes an event to be the exemplification of a property by a particular object at a time. And so on.

Another issue is whether events are entities in a category of their own (e.g. as Quine, Anscombe and Davidson hold), or whether they can be reduced to a different type of entity (see **reductionism**)? Various reductions have been offered, such as identifying them with **tropes**, **states of affairs** or a type of **class** (see Simons 2003: 365–9 for more on this).

Further reading: Lowe (2002, Chapter 12); Macdonald (2005, Chapter 5); Simons (2003); Casati and Varzi (2010)

EXEMPLIFICATION

See **instantiation relation**.

EXISTENCE

Because **ontology** concerns what exists, it is unsurprising that the concept of existence comes under scrutiny. There are three noteworthy features of that concept that are generally (but, as always, not universally) accepted within traditional analytic metaphysics. First, existence is all or nothing. You are either in or out: existence does not come in degrees. You might be a bit tall, or a bit bald or a bit boring, but you cannot exist just a bit.

Second, everything exists in the same way, so there is no sense to be made of saying that **concrete** objects exist but not in the same way that, say, **numbers** or **universals** do. One good reason for thinking this follows from **W. V. Quine**'s criterion of **ontological commitment**. For Quine, what exists is what the best theory quantifies over. However, so the argument goes, there is only one type of existential quantifier that is used to quantify over all existing things (namely '∃') so only one type of existence. Although commonly accepted, this is not uncontroversial. For instance, Aristotle had many different types of existence, Russell thought that **universals** and other **abstract** things do not exist but did **subsist**, and more recently McDaniel (2009), spurred on by the works of Heidegger, has claimed that there are multiple modes of existence. Third and finally, the existing things are all that there are, that is, there is not anything that does not exist (again, not everyone agrees with this; see **non-existent objects** and **being**).

There are other features of existence that are nowadays generally accepted, but to less of a degree than the above two features. For instance, it seems straightforward that everything that exists also actually exists – that is, there are no 'mere possibilia'. Not everyone agrees, for instance **David Lewis**'s version of **modal realism** asserts that things that exist at other worlds do not actually exist, as 'actually' is just an **indexical** term like 'here' (and things can exist which do not exist *here*). Another feature: since Kant, a lot of people have said that existence was not a predicate. (Although Kant himself never said exactly that – he thought it was a perfectly fine predicate, but it was not a *determining* predicate: that predicating it of a concept did not add anything to that concept). Others disagree, thinking that existence is, indeed, a predicate (and *does* add something to the concept it is predicated of). Hence, do be aware of these commonly accepted (though not totally uncontroversial) assumptions that most analytic metaphysicians make when they talk about existence.

Further reading: Daly (2009); van Inwagen (1998)

EXPERIMENTAL PHILOSOPHY

The term 'experimental philosophy' has two quite different meanings. First, during the enlightenment, it was used (along with 'natural philosophy') to refer to what we would now call science or the scientific method: the method of investigating the nature of reality by devising and testing hypotheses on the basis of experiment and observation, as opposed to *a priori* reasoning (or, less charitably, armchair speculation). Experimental philosophy (in this sense) and what we now think of as philosophy enjoyed something of a symbiotic relationship. On one hand, the philosophical work of Bacon (1561–1626) on scientific methodology – which focused on freeing the mind of untestable preconceptions and prejudices and promoting the inductive method – led directly to the formation of the Royal Society, which was originally a forum for natural philosophers, including Newton (1642–1727) and Boyle (1627–91), to discuss experiments and hypotheses (**John Locke** was also a member). On the other hand, the empiricist tradition in philosophy owes much to the success (particularly in the hands of Newton) of experimental philosophy; for example, the subtitle of **David Hume**'s *A Treatise of Human Nature* (1739–40) is 'an attempt to introduce the experimental method of reasoning into moral subjects'.

The second meaning of 'experimental philosophy' refers to a very recent method for approaching some kinds of philosophical question. At its most basic level, this involves testing people's intuitions, particularly (but not exclusively) concerning **thought experiments**. Philosophers, as you may have noticed, will often try to justify a position or a criticism on the basis of the fact that something is intuitively plausible. Experimental philosophy starts from the rather plausible assumption that what a particular professional philosopher – particularly one who already has a philosophical thesis they want to defend – finds intuitively plausible may well not be a very good guide to what people *generally* find intuitively plausible. If 'intuitively plausible' is supposed to mean 'what most people find intuitively plausible', then the only sensible way to find out what is and is not intuitively plausible is to ask people, and this is (part of) what experimental philosophers do. Experimental philosophers devise questionnaires, with philosophy undergraduates typically acting as their experimental subjects, which normally involve describing a scenario or thought experiment and asking questions. (Hence, e.g., this might involve describing a scenario where someone, Joe, robs a bank, say, but where their doing so is fully determined by facts about the distant past and the laws of nature, and then asking whether Joe is morally responsible for the bank robbery. The aim here is to elicit people's intuitions about whether **determinism** is compatible with

moral responsibility.) Eliciting people's intuitions in this way is important for a variety of related reasons; see **conceptual analysis, Canberra Plan, thought experiment** and **common sense**.

A more ambitious form of experimental philosophy is very close to psychology, and aims to *explain* why we have the intuitions that we do. For example, it turns out that sometimes you can get people's intuitions about a case to change by describing the case in different terms. For example, it seems to matter whether you describe the case in highly abstract terms or whether you make it more concrete and personal. If you are trying to elicit people's intuitions about determinism and moral responsibility, for instance, giving the perpetrator a name and having them do something really horrific is more likely to elicit the judgement that they are morally responsible than just asking whether deterministic agents are generally morally responsible for anything. Some experimental philosophers are interested in understanding the psychological processes at work here. For example, is it just that people find concrete, personal cases easier to understand, or does the personal example push their emotional buttons (this is not a technical term)? And, if the latter, should we think of this as distorting their judgement or instead as playing an important conceptual role in moral judgement?

Experimental philosophy is in its infancy and its legitimacy is questioned by some philosophers, some thinking that experimental philosophers tend to ignore alternative explanations of the data, and some having the more deep-seated concern that finding out what 'the folk' think just is not relevant to the philosophical enterprise. These worries raise interesting questions about the nature and purpose of metaphysical enquiry, and indeed philosophical enquiry more generally (see **metametaphysics**).

Further reading: Knobe and Nichols (2008, especially the Introduction)

EXTRINSIC PROPERTIES

See **intrinsic vs extrinsic properties**.

FACTS

When some philosophers talk about 'facts', they just mean something like 'true **propositions**' or 'true sentences'. Other philosophers take facts ontologically seriously and hold that facts are real constituents of nature (see also **states of affairs**). Ludwig Wittgenstein (or rather, the early Wittgenstein) seems to have held this view; indeed, the second sentence of his *Tractatus Logico-Philosophicus* says: 'The world is the totality of facts, not of things'.

Facts – considered as genuine entities – have been pressed into service in various ways by metaphysicians. For example, some hold that facts (and not, as many philosophers think, **events**) are the primary **causal relata**. Some argue that facts (or states of affairs) are the entities to which true propositions correspond (see **truth**) or are the **truthmakers** for true propositions.

Facts understood in this way are generally conceived as having both **particulars and universals** as constituents (see **states of affairs**), so that the fact that *a* is *F* (e.g. the fact that the apple is round) has as constituents both a particular – the apple – and a universal (roundness), or one might think that the fact that the apple is round has as constituents the apple and a round **trope** (which is itself a particular). Facts considered as genuine entities are, thus, generally thought to be off-limits for some nominalists. In particular, **austere nominalists** think that predicates do not denote real features of objects. Hence, for the austere nominalist, it can still be *true* both that the apple is red and that the apple is round, and hence still a fact that it is red and a (different) fact that it is round, in the metaphysically uninteresting sense of 'fact'. However, arguably, there are not two *entities* – the fact that the apple is round, and the fact that the apple is red, that make these two sentences true (see **truthmakers**).

FICTIONALISM

Fictionalism is a type of **anti-realism** about a certain category of entities. If one is a fictionalist about that category, then the entities are taken not to exist and are, instead, fictions. The analogy here is with literary fiction. It is, of course, literally false that Sherlock Holmes lived at 221b Baker Street. However, there seems to be *a* sense in which it is true (for instance, if asked during a pub quiz where Holmes lived, the only appropriate answer would be '221b Baker Street'). We can make sense of this by saying that 'Sherlock lived at 221b Baker Street' is 'true-in-a-fiction', that is to say, true *according to* the Sherlock Holmes novels.

The motivation behind fictionalism in metaphysics is, obviously, to remove certain entities from our **ontology**, either because removing the entities makes things simpler or because the entity's existing would be somehow reprehensible (see **theoretical virtue**). For instance, consider the sentence 'There is a prime number between 5 and 11'. Interpreted literally, it says that there exists a prime **number**, namely the number 7. However, such a thing would appear to be **abstract**, and we might abhor such abstract things. The fictionalist notes that, although there are no numbers, the **platonist** about numbers will say that there are. Thus, it is true *according to the fiction of platonism about numbers* that there is a number between 5 and 11. Furthermore, just as believing that, according to the fiction of *Independence Day*, the White House was destroyed by aliens does not commit me to the existence of aliens or to the White House being zapped by flying saucers, the above sentence about the platonist fiction does not commit one to numbers either: it is literally false that there is a prime number between 5 and 11, just as it is literally false the the White House was destroyed by aliens.

Fictionalists about numbers (e.g. Field 1980) deploy this strategy in various different ways to rid their ontology of undesirable elements. They might say that what our sentences really mean are these fictionalist translations – so the meaning of '2 + 2 = 4' is the proposition <according to the platonist fiction, 2 + 2 = 4> (this is called 'hermeneutic fictionalism'); that the sentence about platonist fiction is a **paraphrase** of the original sentence; that the fictionalist translation fixes the truth conditions of the original sentence, or that the original sentence is ontologically committed to the worrisome entities, so what we should be saying *instead* of the original sentence is the revised sentence about the platonist fiction (this is called 'revolutionary fictionalism').

Varieties of fictionalism

One can be a fictionalist about all sorts of undesirables, not just numbers. Another area that has received a fictionalist treatment is **possible worlds** (e.g. Rosen 1990). This theory has unfortunately been lumbered by the misnomer 'modal fictionalism' rather than 'possible worlds fictionalism'. It is a misnomer because modal sentences (such as 'I could have been a fisherman') are literally true according to the modal fictionalist. However, where the modal realist normally says that they are true if and only if the respective possible world translation is true (i.e. 'there is a possible world at which I am a fisherman'), the fictionalist disagrees. The possible world translations are false (i.e. for at least some translations, there is no such possible world), but the translations are true *according to the fiction* of possible worlds (i.e. 'according to the possible worlds fiction, there is a possible world at which I am a fisherman' is true). Hence, the modal fictionalist says, a modal sentence is true if and only if the respective translation is true according to the possible worlds fiction.

Modal fictionalists are faced with a few problems, not the least being *which* possible worlds fiction to go with. For instance, what is true according to **David Lewis**'s fiction of genuine modal realism is substantially different from what is true according to an ersatz theory (see **modal realism**). For example, Lewis does not believe that there are worlds containing disconnected space-times, whereas most ersatz theories do. Although most modal fictionalists endorse Lewis's theory as being the fiction to work with, there is a good question as to why that fiction in particular is so important.

Another problem is the 'Brock-Rosen objection'. So the argument goes, according to Lewis's theory of possible worlds, the possible worlds *have* to exist. No matter what possible world you are at, it is true that there are infinitely many concrete possible worlds. If it is true at every world, then (according to Lewis's genuine modal realism) it is necessarily true that there are infinitely many concrete possible worlds. However, if a modal sentence is true if and only if the respective translation is true according to Lewis's fiction, then the modal sentence 'Necessarily, there are infinitely many concrete possible worlds' turns out to be true. Because it is uncontroversial that if something is necessarily the case, then it is actually the case, the fictionalist seems to be committed to saying that possible worlds *do* exist.

One can be a fictionalist about all kinds of things, such as musical works (so we do not believe that there are any **abstract** works of music, such as Beethoven's symphonies, but the respective fictional sentences are true and metaphysically useful; see Kania 2008), composite objects (to resolve answering the **special composition question**, we might be fictionalists about material objects; see Rosen and Dorr 2002), **temporal parts** (Kroon 2001) or – most obviously – fictional characters (some people think that sentences such as 'Holmes lived at 221b Baker Street' demand that Holmes exists as a fictional, abstract object, but we could instead be fictionalists about Holmes and such like; see Brock 2002). Space prohibits a full discussion of the motivations and problems for applying fictionalism in these areas, but it is useful to mention them, so that you can see how fictionalism is deployed as a general technique to try and alleviate certain unwanted ontological commitments.

Further reading: Balaguer (2008); Eklund (2009); Nolan (2008)

FISSION

Fission occurs when we start out with just one thing, *a*, and end up, later on, with two things, *b* and *c*, each of which has a claim to being identical with *a*. This proves problematic because **identity** is a **one-to-one** relation: at most one of *b* and *c* can be identical with *a*. Fission cases (such as the Ship of Theseus) crop up in discussions of **identity over time** generally, but here we will mainly be concerned with a standard fission case (sometimes known as the 'split-brain case') that appears in the debate about **personal identity**.

We seem to be able to conceive scenarios we would intuitively describe as 'one person splitting into two'. Philosophers refer to these scenarios as cases of 'fission'.

It is possible for a human being to continue to live with only one hemisphere of their brain intact. It also seems possible in principle to remove the brain of one human being *a* and insert it in the head of some other human being *b*, such that the result is a person that has the body of *b* but is psychologically continuous with *a*. These two possibilities in conjunction make for some very interesting **thought experiments**.

Suppose that both hemispheres of the brain of the Queen of England are removed, and one is inserted into Barack Obama's body, whereas the other is inserted into the body of David Cameron (the brains of both of these men are scooped up and disposed of). Suppose further that this is done in some kind of way such that the result is two persons – one with Obama's body and one with Cameron's body – both of whom are psychologically continuous with the Queen (see **psychological continuity**). Philosophers describe this kind of situation, in which in some sense (to say more than 'in some sense' would involve us in philosophical controversy) 'one person becomes two' as 'fission'.

Besides being lots of fun to think about, this scenario presents a serious challenge to psychological continuity theories of **personal identity**. The bare bones of such a theory are: person *x* at some time is identical to person *y* at some other time if and only if *x* is psychologically continuous with *y*. However, in the situation described above *two* people are psychologically continuous with Her Majesty: the post-operative person with Obama's body and the post-operative person with Cameron's body. If we stuck to the bare bones of the theory, we would have to say that *both* of the post-operative persons are identical to Her Majesty. However, because **identity** is a **transitive relation** – if *a* = *b* and *b* = *c* then *a* = *c* – this implies that both the post-operative persons are identical to each other. This seems implausible. The person with Obama's body and the person with Cameron's body could go off and live totally different lives; if the post-operative person with Obama's body committed a crime it would surely not be fair to punish the post-operative person with Cameron's body for it. However, what is the alternative? Supposing that both the royal hemisphere recipients are equally psychologically continuous with Her Majesty pre-operative, it seems arbitrary to single out one of them as identical with Her Majesty.

One of the ways psychological continuity theorists respond to these worries is by adding a 'no-branching clause' to their analysis of personal identity, so that the analysis becomes something like: person x at a certain time is identical to person y at some other time if and only if (i) x and y are psychologically continuous, (ii) fission does not take place in the chains of psychological continuity between x and y (call (ii) the 'no-branching clause'). On this view, a person ceases to exist at the moment of their fission. A similar but more nuanced adjustment is to add a *best-candidate clause*, rather than a no-branching clause, to the analysis. A best-candidate clause specifies that where there is fission, the post-fission person most psychologically continuous with the pre-fission person is identical to the pre-fission person (if both post-fission people are equally psychologically continuous, the pre-fission person ceases to exist).

The main objection to both the no-branching and the best-candidate versions of psychological continuity theories is that they infringe what is sometimes called the 'only x and y principle', a principle many philosophers find intuitive. This is the principle that whether x is identical to y is wholly grounded in facts about x and y and relations between them; it cannot depend on matters external to x and y. Suppose that I am kidnapped by evil terrorists and told that tomorrow my left hemisphere is to be transplanted into another body to form a person we can call 'Dave', and my right hemisphere will either be (i) transplanted into a different body to form a person called Alan (such that both Alan and Dave will be equally psychologically continuous with me) or (ii) be destroyed. Will I be identical to Dave tomorrow? In both situations, the **intrinsic** nature of me today and Dave tomorrow and the relations between us are exactly the same; the two situations differ only in matters extrinsic to me (now) and Dave (tomorrow) – namely, in what happens to the right hemisphere of my brain after it has been removed, and yet, according to the no-branching/best-candidate versions of the psychological continuity theories, it is only in the second of those possible situations that I am identical with Dave. This is the sense in which these theories are in tension with the intuitive 'only x or y principle'.

Lewis defends an alternative response on behalf of the psychological continuity theorist to fission cases: the Multiple Occupancy Thesis. On this view, given any human body with fission in its future/past, there are two persons located in that body, both persons thinking the same thoughts and feeling the same feelings. At the point of fission, these persons separate out, coming to occupy distinct bodies. The Multiple Occupancy Thesis makes most sense against the background of **perdurantism**. For the perdurantist, the multiple occupancy of two or more persons is a matter of those persons sharing some of their **temporal parts**.

We have so far presented cases of fission as a challenge to psychological continuity theories of personal identity. However, many philosophers think that there are analogous difficulties for any theory of personal identity that is reductive (see **reductionism**) in the sense of accounting for facts about the **diachronic identity** of persons in terms of more fundamental facts. We can imagine situations that we would describe as one human body or human animal splitting into two, and such situations will present the **animalist** and **bodily continuity theorist** with challenges analogous to those faced by the psychological continuity theorist. It seems that any relation R, be it psychological, physical or biological, which is offered in some **reductionist** account as sufficient for personal identity, might branch (unless a 'no branching' stipulation – which might be seen as an *ad hoc* addition to the theory – is included in the definition of the relation). One neat way of avoiding the difficulties associated with branching is to simply reject reductionist accounts of personal identity by advocating the **simple view of personal identity**.

It is, at least in part, reflection on cases of fission that motivate Parfit's well-known and startling thesis that 'identity is not what matters in **survival**': according to Parfit, it is neither psychological continuity that is the problem, nor the attempt to provide a reductive analysis of personal identity, but the identity relation itself.

Fission cases do not always relate to personal identity. For example, the case of the Ship of Theseus is also a fission case (see **identity over time**).

Further reading: Noonan (1989, Chapter 7); Parfit (1971, § 1)

FLOW OF TIME

Space does not flow. Objects from across the universe are not all dragged inexorably in one particular direction, say eastwards. That would be a bit weird. Instead, we are free to move around space much as we like (albeit that gravity sometimes makes it harder – but not impossible – to go in some directions than others). Time does not seem to be like that. Regardless of where in time you want to go, you find yourself continually advancing through time, second after second, day after day and year after year. There is nothing you can do about it. In other words, time *flows* whereas space does not (that is, if we ignore the possibility of **backwards causation**, and the possibility of such a thing may well bear on the question about time flowing). (Note that to say that time flows is different to saying that time has a direction; see **direction of time**. The current of a river has a direction, but you can swim upstream. Backwards causation aside, you cannot move backwards through time.)

That, at least, is the intuitive view. That it is intuitive is sometimes taken to be good reason to think that we should believe that time is tensed, or that only the present exists (see **tensed and tenseless theories of time** and **presentism**). Those who do not endorse such theories (the **eternalist**, the tenseless theorist and the static theorist) take themselves to have to explain the apparent flow of time. For instance, they might say that the apparent flow of time is just a result of how our memory works. Although the world might, say, be tenseless and static, it just so happens that at one point in time I have a certain set of memories whereas at another, later, time I have *more* memories. This accumulation of memories, they say, gives me the impression that time flows. (This has also been wheeled out as an explanation of the **direction of time**.)

Conversely, some think that if there was an objective flow of time we would, in fact, have a problem. If time flows, they say, it could flow at a different rate, that is, just like a river can go faster or slower, time itself – if it flowed – could flow faster or slower. However, that does not seem to make any sense. It seems bizarre to say that time could flow at, say, the rate of one second per year. It is not even clear what that would mean. Moreover, even an answer like 'one second per second' looks bizarre for just the same reason – is there any sense to be had, we might ask, in saying that time flows *at all?* As various theories of time involve a commitment to the flow of time, this philosophical problem can be quite vexing.

Further reading: Markosian (1993); Le Poidevin (2009)

FORM AND MATTER

The distinction between 'form' and 'matter' is central to **Aristotle's** metaphysics. What exactly Aristotle means by these terms is a matter of considerable scholarly debate, but the basic idea is quite intuitive. The 'matter' of an object is what it is made up of, the 'form' of an object is the principle of organisation that makes it the kind of thing it is. My toaster is made of metal: the metal is the 'matter' of which the toaster it made. What makes it a toaster, as opposed to, say, a can opener, is that that metal has been arranged to fulfil the function of toasting bread; its being so constitutes its 'form' (see also **platonism**).

FOUR-DIMENSIONALISM

The term 'four-dimensionalism' is ambiguous. There are three theories it can refer to. First, it might refer to **perdurantism**: objects are extended in time and are thus four-dimensional, having different **temporal parts** at different times. Second, it might refer to **eternalism**: every moment (past, present and future) exists, along with everything at those moments, so the Universe (and everything in it that lasts for longer than an instant) is, in a sense, four-dimensional. Third, it is sometimes used to refer to a package deal consisting of perdurantism, eternalism and the **tenseless view of time**. Hence, when you come across the term in the literature, you must take care over what the author is referring to.

FRANKFURT'S NEFARIOUS NEUROSURGEON

Incompatibilists hold that acting freely – and therefore **moral responsibility** – requires the ability to do otherwise. This requirement is often known as the **Principle of Alternate Possibilities** or 'PAP' for short.

In his classic 1969 article, Frankfurt presents a famous **thought experiment**, often referred to as the 'nefarious neurosurgeon' case, which purports to show that PAP is false. The case runs more or less as follows (in fact, Frankfurt presents a lot of different cases, but this is the one that has caught philosophers' imaginations. Cases that are similar to this case are often known generically as 'Frankfurt-style cases'). Black, our nefarious neurosurgeon (sometimes known as the 'counterfactual intervener'), wants Jones to do something (kill Smith, let us say), so he implants a device in Jones's brain that he can activate by remote control. If activated, the device will make Jones decide to kill Smith. However, Black does not want to be implicated in Smith's murder if he can help it, so he waits until Jones is about to make his decision and will only activate the device if it becomes clear that Jones is about to decide *not* to kill Smith. (Black is a very good predictor of Jones's behaviour. Perhaps, Black knows that Jones always twitches when he is about to decide to do the morally right thing – in this case, refrain from killing Smith – so Black can activate the device if he sees the twitch, or perhaps, Black can directly monitor Jones's thoughts through monitoring his brain activity by the device, so again he can tell what Jones is about to decide.) In fact, Jones decides on his own to kill Smith; Black, having predicted that this is what Smith was going to do, does not activate the device.

Frankfurt contends that although Jones could not have decided other-wise – he was bound to decide to kill Smith, either on his own or through Black activating the device – he is clearly morally responsible for murdering Smith. After all, Black played no role whatsoever in Jones's decision-making process; the process ran exactly as it would have done had Black never implanted the device in the first place. And so the thought experiment is a counter-example to PAP: moral responsibility does not require the exis-tence of alternate possibilities – that is, alternative decisions or actions that the agent could have made or performed – because there is at least one possible case of moral responsibility without alternate possibilities.

This is good news for **compatibilism**, because it looks as though if Jones was morally responsible, then he also acted freely – despite the fact that he could not have done otherwise – which would mean that one of the premises in the **Consequence Argument** for incompatibilism (and against compatibilism), namely PAP, is false.

An incompatibilist response

A standard incompatibilist response to the nefarious neurosurgeon case is to pose a dilemma. Is the decision-making process that actually leads to Jones's decision (i.e. without the activation of the device) supposed to be deterministic or indeterministic? If deterministic (see **determinism**), then the incompatibilist will hold that Jones would not be morally responsible even if there were no nefarious neurosurgeon on the scene, because Jones would not, even then, be able to do otherwise, so, trivially, he is not morally responsible in the case where we add the nefarious neurosurgeon either. In other words, in the deterministic version of the case, the falsity of PAP is simply presupposed by the thought experiment, and the incompatibilist will reject that presupposition.

On the other hand, if the decision-making process is supposed to be indeterministic (see **indeterminism**), then Black cannot predict with certainty what Jones will decide to do, contrary to what Frankfurt assumes: even if Black knows all the relevant facts about the past and all the **laws of nature**, he still could not know for sure, right up until Jones actually makes his decision, what that decision will be. Given that Black has to decide not to activate the device *before* Jones makes his decision, and given that it will not be determined at that time what decision Jones will make, it is perfectly possible that Black's prediction will be wrong, that is, that he decides not to activate the device, but Jones then decides not to kill Smith. Hence, Jones could, in fact, have decided differently – he could have decided not to kill Smith – so the fact that he is morally responsible for killing Smith does not undermine PAP. Either way, then, the case is not a counter-example to PAP. Whether this dilemma really is fatal to Frankfurt's attempt to refute PAP remains a hotly contested question; the literature on Frankfurt-style cases is huge.

Further reading: Frankfurt (1969); Fischer (1995, Chapter 7); Fischer (1999, §§ II and III)

FRANKFURT-STYLE CASES

See **Frankfurt's nefarious neurosurgeon**.

FREE WILL

Traditionally, what is often known as 'the problem of free will' is the problem of reconciling freedom of the will with **determinism**, the thesis that everything that happens – including all your decisions and actions – is determined by facts about the past together with the **laws of nature**. The expression 'freedom of the will' dates back several centuries, to a time when philosophers thought of the mind as having several distinct 'faculties', one of which (alongside the intellect, the imagination and the senses) was the will. The will was taken to be responsible for determining what a person chooses or decides, on the basis of what they want or desire (or 'will' – as in the expression 'God willing'). The central issue was, thus, whether the will – conceived as a mental faculty – is free. These days, many philosophers avoid the expression 'freedom of the will', preferring to talk about freedom of *action* (including the freedom of mental actions such as choosing, forming intentions, and deciding), although some still make a distinction between freedom of action and freedom of the will (see **compatibilism**).

'The' problem of free will has evolved into several distinct problems, and there are many different solutions on offer. The basic, and original, problem is that of reconciling free will with determinism. **Incompatibilists** argue that free will and determinism cannot be reconciled (one such argument is the **Consequence Argument**). Hence, either determinism must be false (in other words, **indeterminism** must be true) or else, contrary to what we normally think, we never act freely.

This incompatibilist conclusion answers the original question (are free action and determinism compatible? No), but raises a host of new questions. Some incompatibilists subscribe to **libertarianism**, according to which at least some of our decisions really are undetermined by the past and the laws. However, on what grounds do libertarians reject determinism, rather than the claim that we (at least sometimes) act freely? It would seem to be the business of science, not philosophy, to figure out whether or not determinism is true, and no conclusive answer has so far been reached, but that seems to leave us in the uncomfortable position of not knowing whether we have free will. And this is no mere philosophical discomfort, it is very widely thought that only freely performed acts can be ones for which we have **moral responsibility**, and so not knowing whether or not we ever act freely entails not knowing whether or not we are ever morally responsible for anything we do. (Many philosophers now accept that we do not have any particular reason to think that determinism is true. For this reason, the traditional philosophical positions of **hard determinism** and **soft determinism** – which amount to a combination of determinism on the one hand and, respectively, incompatibilism and compatibilism on the other – are not especially popular any more.)

There are also further problems, aside from the possibility that determinism is true, looming for the view that we sometimes act freely and therefore responsibly. One is the **problem of luck**. Suppose that our decisions are not determined by the past plus the laws, so that the traditional problem of free will does not apply. In that case, it looks like we lack *control* over our decisions: what we decide to do is a matter of luck, being no different, in effect, to deciding what to do on the basis of the toss of a coin. Some philosophers hold that the only way to be a truly free and morally responsible agent is to 'agent-cause' one's decisions. However, – even supposing we can make sense of the idea of **agent causation** – what grounds, if any, do we have for thinking that we really do, in fact, agent-cause our decisions? Some philosophers have concluded that free will is in fact an illusion (see **illusion of free will**); free will is incompatible both with determinism and with any version of indeterminism that is at all likely to be true. There have also, recently, been arguments from neuroscience and psychology to the conclusion that free will is an illusion (see **neuroscience and free will**).

However, some philosophers – those who subscribe to **compatibilism** – think that there is no tension between free will and determinism in the first place. The alleged problem arises because determinism seems to rule out the possibility that we can ever do otherwise than what we actually do (because what we do is determined by things completely outside our control, namely facts about the past and the laws). However, some compatibilists argue that the ability to do otherwise is not required for acting freely (see **Frankfurt's nefarious neurosurgeon**), and others argue that there is a relevant sense of 'being able to do otherwise' that is entirely consistent with determinism (see **Principle of Alternate Possibilities**).

It can get a bit confusing to distinguish all the various positions in the free will debate. Table 1 may help; a 'Y' means that the position is committed to the relevant thesis's truth (e.g. a soft determinist is committed to the truth of determinism), an 'N' means the opposite (e.g. a libertarian is committed to the falsity of determinism), and a question-mark means that the position is neutral with respect to the thesis (e.g. a compatibilist may or may not believe that actual agents sometimes act freely – although in practice virtually all of them *do* believe this).

Table 1

Position	Determinism	Determinism compatible with free will	Actual agents sometimes act freely
Compatibilism	?	Y	?
Incompatibilism	?	N	?
Libertarianism	N	N	Y
Soft determinism	Y	Y	Y
Hard determinism	Y	N	N
Illusionism	?	N	N
Agent causalism	?	?	?

Further reading: O'Connor (2008); Blackburn (1999, Chapter 3); Beebee and Dodd (2006, Chapter 2)

FUSION, MEREOLOGICAL

'Fusion' is a term in **mereology**, and in this context does not have anything to do with two objects getting welded together and becoming a single object (though 'fusion' in this sense is sometimes discussed in the debate about **personal identity**, being the opposite of **fission**; see Parfit 1971: § IV).

In mereology, 'fusion' has two usages. One says that x is the fusion of the ys if and only if the ys compose x. Hence, saying 'a fusion' is just a way of saying 'a composite object'. Similarly to say that the x fuses the ys is just to say that x is composed of the ys (and if you suspect that philosophers just use the word 'fusion' and its cognates rather than talking about composition, solely in an effort to sound that bit funkier – well, we could not possibly comment). Hence, you are composed of all your various body parts: your body is a fusion of all those parts, or 'fuses' them.

The second usage is rarer. Here a fusion (or 'sum') is defined as a particular type of composite object, where its modal and temporal properties are such that it can never have different parts. That is, if the fusion has the ys as parts then it essentially has the ys as parts. If the parts changed, or ceased to be, the fusion would cease to exist. For instance, with this usage, imagine a house made entirely of some bricks. We might say that the house is the fusion (or mereological sum), in this sense, of all the bricks. This would then commit us to saying that the sum of the bricks cannot change its parts (for they are, by definition, had essentially). This is obviously a far cry from the first usage, according to which the house is a fusion simply in virtue of being a composite object. 'Mereological essentialists' think that *all* mereological fusions in the first sense defined above are also fusions in the second sense; *everything* necessarily has the parts it actually has.

Exactly which meaning is intended you will have to figure out from the context, although usually it is the first meaning.

GEDANKENEXPERIMENT

German for **thought experiment**

GENERAL CAUSAL SENTENCES

General causal sentences/statements are just those that express **type-level causation** (such as 'smoking causes cancer').

GLOBAL REALISM

See **realism and anti–realism (global)**.

GOD'S EYE VIEW

It is sometimes argued by global anti realists (see **realism and anti–realism (global)**) that realism presupposes the intelligibility of a 'God's eye view' of reality, and that this presupposition is false. Putnam, for example, in his discussion of the sceptical hypothesis that we are all **brains in vats**, claims that the intelligibility of this hypothesis

> ... assumes a God's Eye point of view from the start ... [f]or *from whose point of view is the story being told?* Evidently *not* from the point of view of any of the sentient creatures *in* the world. Nor from the point of view of any observer in another world who interacts with this world; for a 'world' by definition includes everything that interacts in any way with the things it contains ... So the supposition that there could be a world in which *all* sentient beings are Brains in a Vat presupposes from the outset a God's Eye view of truth, or, more accurately, a No Eye view of truth – truth as independent of observers all together.

> Putnam (1981: 50)

Note that the claim that (global) realism – and therewith **scepticism** – presupposes the intelligibility of a God's eye (or 'no eye') view, just by itself, is not really an *objection* to realism; after all, the realist can simply retort that, yes, truth is indeed independent of observers. The use of the 'God's eye view' claim is really only a way of making vivid the (alleged) commitments of realism. To generate a genuine objection to realism, one would have to argue that the notion of a God's eye view is really unintelligible.

Putnam himself (see **brains in a vat**) mounts such an argument by focussing on what a brain in vat could possibly *mean* when they consider whether the claim 'I am a brain in a vat' is true. Dummett (1991: 345) claims that the realist has to form, 'by analogy with our own faculties, the conception of a being with superhuman powers': a being, that is, that could somehow survey the whole of reality and see it as it really is, as opposed to actual human beings, who can only observe small portions of reality, and so can only gather *evidence* for the truth of claims about the parts that lie outwith that small portion. And of course one might argue that we cannot *really* form a conception of a being that can survey the whole of reality in this way.

Kirk (1999: 139–41), however, argues that the global realist is not really committed to the idea of a God's eye view at all. After all, it is the global anti-realist, and not the realist, who holds that truth must be truth *from some perspective*. And, arguably, it is that thought that generates the idea that, if truth is independent of *our* theorising or our available evidence or our **conceptual scheme**, then there must be *some* perspective from which our theories or conceptual scheme can be seen to be in error, or perhaps incomplete. However, of course, the realist just denies all of this: the realist is, or should be, happy to hold that there may be facts about the nature of reality that cannot be grasped from *any* perspective that we can even begin to imagine.

Further reading: Kirk (1999, Chapter 9)

GRANDFATHER PARADOX

See **time travel**.

GROWING BLOCK THEORY

Whereas **presentism** is the thesis that only the present moment exists, and **eternalism** is the thesis that past, present and future moments exist, growing block theorists hold that present and past times exist, but future times do not. In this fashion, the universe 'grows', for as time passes the 'block' of times that exist becomes ever greater (as more and more moments are added to the past), whereas the present moment forever remains at the edge of this growing block. Of the theories concerning the ontology of time, growing block theory is the least popular, although it does have its supporters and the pedigree of having been defended by C. D. Broad.

Motivations

Contemporary motivations for growing block theory all revolve around some alleged need for a serious metaphysical difference between the past and future (and metaphysical differences do not get more serious than the difference between existence and non-existence). Tooley notes that causation is asymmetric, in that an effect depends upon its cause in a way that the cause does not depend upon its effect. Believing that the only way to account for this asymmetry is by holding that, at the time the cause kicks into action, the cause exists whereas the effect does not, Tooley concludes that the past and present exist whereas the future does not. He finds similar asymmetries when analysing **counterfactual conditionals** (Tooley 1997: Chapter 4). More recently, Diekemper has focused on the asymmetry of fixity. We intuitively think that facts about the past are 'fixed' and will never change in truth value, for example it is true, and has been for many years, that dinosaurs once roamed the earth, and it will be true from now until the end of time. The future, however, is (intuitively) 'open', in the sense that propositions about the future may change in truth value. For example, it is not true *right now* that I will die in AD 2030, but if I have an unfortunate accident that year, then it will *become* true. This asymmetry between past and future propositions can only be accounted for, argues Diekemper (2005), if you endorse the growing block theory.

Objections

The most popular objection to the growing block theory is the *dead past* objection (Bourne 2002; Merricks 2006). Given the growing block theory, in AD 1220 Ghenghis Khan thought that it was the present moment. The present moment has moved on by several hundred years, but Ghenghis Khan still exists and (tenselessly) thinks what he once thought. Hence, Ghenghis Khan is sat in AD 1220 *incorrectly* thinking that the time he exists at is 'present'.

The dead past objection argues that there is no way for you to know you are not in the same position as Ghenghis Khan, ergo there is a good chance that you are wrong about what time is the present moment. Finding this to be absurd, we should ditch growing block theory and endorse either presentism or eternalism. Presentists avoid the problem since past people do not exist and so cannot think incorrect things. Eternalism (when combined with a tenseless theory of time – see **tensed and tenseless theories of time**) solves the problem because, for the eternalist, 'now' is an indexical term. Hence, although Ghenghis Khan does exist in AD 1220 thinking his time is present, that belief is true, because (given a tenseless theory of time) 'now' is whatever time you happen to be at (which, for Ghenghis, is AD 1220).

There have been rejoinders to the dead past objection. Forrest (2004) argues that only beings in the present moment are conscious, and when they pass into the past they are relegated to an unconscious zombie state, unable to entertain beliefs at all. Button (2006) has a different response, arguing that the problem goes away when we disambiguate whether the 'is' in 'is this moment present?' is tenseless or tensed.

GUIDANCE CONTROL VS REGULATIVE CONTROL

A distinction, due to Fischer, made in the **free will** debate. Guidance control is normally claimed to be compatible with **determinism**: you control (in the guidance control sense) when you get up by deciding when to set your alarm clock, setting it, and then getting up when it goes off; the truth of determinism does not undermine this. Regulative control requires alternative possibilities (see **Principle of Alternate Possibilities**) and so may not be compatible with determinism (**see compatibilism**).

GUNK

'Gunk' (or 'atomless gunk') is a term from **mereology**. Something is made of atomless gunk when every **part** of it has a **proper part** – that is, no part of it is such that it does not itself have any proper parts (i.e. is not a **simple**). Hence, it might turn out that you and I are made of gunk if, say, physics one day discovers that we have no simples as proper parts.

Do beware: being gunky is different from being infinitely divisible. First, an object might be made of gunk but not be *divisible* at all – it might have an infinite number of parts, all of which are so tightly connected that it is impossible to split them. Second, an object can be infinitely divisible without being made of gunk. If an object was made up of an infinite number of point particles (i.e. particles with no spatial extension) then it could be infinitely divided but would, nonetheless, have proper parts that themselves had no proper parts (namely the point particles). Hence, although gunk might be infinitely divisible, refrain from asserting that they amount to the same thing.

Further reading: Hudson (2007)

HAECCEITISM

Haecceitism is the view that the identity of an object across **possible worlds** is brute, in the sense that it does not **supervene** on the qualities or relations instantiated by that object. This becomes clearer with an example. Imagine a world, call it '*w*', that is just like ours in every respect, except that in *w* Elvis Presley has all the (qualitative) **properties** that Napoleon has in the actual world, and Napoleon has all the (qualitative) properties that Elvis has in the actual world. Hence, in *w*, Napoleon was born in 1935 in Mississippi and grew up to become the world's best known rock and roll singer in the 1950s and 1960s, whereas Elvis was born in 1769 in Corsica and grew up to become Emperor of the first French Empire. In other words, for the haecceitist, there are worlds that, despite instantiating *all the same qualities and relations*, are nonetheless different; this difference being a matter of the **identity** of the objects existing in those worlds.

One potentially confusing thing to bear in mind is that belief in haecceit*ism* is not the same as belief in haecceit*ies*. Haecceities − if there are such things − are 'non-qualitative' properties that ground the identity of a thing (a property is 'non-qualitative' if an object's having that property is not a matter of its instantiating any qualities or relations). For the believer in haecceities, some object has the non-qualitative property of *being Elvis*, and it is in virtue of having that property that the object is Elvis. Hence, what distinguishes the actual Elvis from our imagined Napoleon-at-*w* (who is exactly like the actual Elvis with respect to all *qualitative* properties) is that the two differ with respect to their haecceities: actual Elvis has the property of *being Elvis*, whereas Napoleon-at-*w* has the different property of *being Napoleon* (a property he shares, incidentally, with the actual Napoleon).

Believing in haecceities is *one way* of believing in haecceitism. However − and you may have had this thought yourself while reading the preceding paragraph − haecceities are generally seen as a very weird kind of entity, and not many people believe in them. Many philosophers who believe in haecceitism take the identity of objects to be brute, not grounded in the possession of haecceities. For such philosophers it is just a brute fact that the person who is actually called 'Elvis' is identical with the person in *w* who is called 'Napoleon', and that the person who is actually called 'Napoleon' is identical to the person in *w* who is called 'Elvis'.

Many philosophers take haecceitism to be a view of objects which is to be understood analogously to **quidditism** about properties.

Further reading: Adams (1979); Lewis (1986a, § 4.4); Mackie (2006)

HARD DETERMINISM

Hard determinism is the view that (a) **free will** is incompatible with **determinism** (hence, it is an **incompatibilist** position) and (b) determinism is actually true (compare **soft determinism**). Hard determinism's popularity has waned considerably in recent times, as philosophers have come to accept that **indeterminism** might well be true.

An obvious consequence of hard determinism is that nobody is ever, in fact, morally responsible for anything they do. Some philosophers have argued that this consequence is a good reason to think that hard determinism is false. In particular, Strawson (1962) argues that if hard determinism were true, our practices of blame, praise and punishment, and what he calls our 'reactive' attitudes such as resentment, gratitude and forgiveness, would all be unjustified. However, it is psychologically impossible for us to give up these attitudes, Strawson argues; in effect, it would amount to giving up on the very possibility of interpersonal relationships. Thus, the truth of hard determinism – once its implications are grasped – is simply not something that we, being the kind of creature that we are, could possibly seriously endorse. Other philosophers, however, have argued that belief in hard determinism need not amount to giving up on the possibility of interpersonal relationships (see for instance Pereboom 1995: § 7).

HOLES

Within the study of **ontology** we might wonder whether or not holes exist. For instance, if my jeans had a hole in them, then we would (**nihilism** aside) endorse the existence of my jeans, but would we go further and endorse the existence of the *hole*? At first sight, it looks as though we should; after all, I have just said that *there is a hole* in my jeans. Hence, am I not asserting that a hole (in my jeans) exists?

Anti-realism about holes

We might decide not to include holes in our ontology, on the grounds that they are an **ontological commitment** we can do without (see **theoretical virtues**). To do this we might try and offer a **paraphrase** of sentences about holes. For instance, we might paraphrase the sentence about my jeans as 'my jeans are singly perforated'. In this new sentence we are quantifying over only one thing – the pair of jeans – and saying that some predicate applies to them ('__ is singly perforated'). The commitment to holes is avoided. However, this strategy has problems with harder sentences, such as 'the hole in the tooth was smaller than the dentist's finest probe' (Geach 1968) and 'there were as many bullet holes in his corpse as there were dirty cops on the force'. We leave attempts to find paraphrases for such sentences to the interested reader. However, even if paraphrases can be found, the worry is that no *general method* to work out what the paraphrases are could be formulated, and that this lack of a general theory may be reason enough to think the paraphrasing strategy fails.

Realism about holes

Realists just endorse the existence of holes. Hence, there exists something, a hole, that is part of my jeans; there exists something, a hole in a tooth, and it is smaller than the tip of a particular probe; there exist some things, some of which are holes in a body and some of which are dirty cops, and there are as many of the latter as there are of the former.

Among the realists, metaphysicians are divided over what a hole might be. Some endorse the 'Ludovician' theory that a hole is the *hole lining* (Lewis and Lewis 1970). That is, the object that is the edge of the hole turns out to be identical to the hole. However, if we had a hole in an object like the one depicted on the left below (Figure 1), and then made that hole bigger, as depicted on the right hand side, we would have made the hole *lining* smaller. So, the fear is that the hole and the hole lining cannot be identical, as then the hole would have gotten both bigger *and* smaller, which is absurd (see Casati and Varzi 1994: Chapter 3 for more).

Some instead say that holes are actually certain regions of space – namely those regions surrounded by the hole lining. One problem with this is that

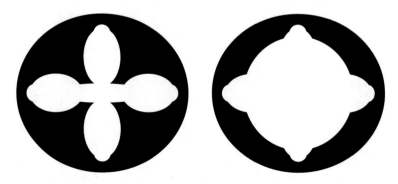

Figure 1

regions of space cannot move (objects move in space, but space itself stays where it is). However, if I move my jeans surely the hole moves with it. It is not as if it is a different hole every time the jeans change location.

Finally, some think that holes are *sui generis* entities – that is, they are entities in a category of their own, which cannot be identified with a type of entity from any other ontological category. Obviously the worry here is one of 'ontological profligacy' – it is desirable to keep the different types of entities in your ontology to the lowest number possible (see **theoretical virtues**).

Further reading: Casati and Varzi (2009)

HUME, DAVID

David Hume (1711–76) was a Scottish philosopher and historian. His most famous philosophical works are *A Treatise on Human Nature* (1739–40), *An Enquiry concerning Human Understanding* (1748), *An Enquiry concerning the Principles of Morals* (1751), and *Dialogues concerning Natural Religion* (1779). However, during his lifetime he was better known as a historian, and his six-volume *History of England* (1754–62) was a bestseller.

Hume was the last of the three great British Empiricists, after **John Locke** and **George Berkeley**. All three held that all of our 'ideas' must come from experience, and hence that we cannot have any innate knowledge about the world, for we come into the world without any ideas at all (ideas being the building-blocks of thought; we can roughly think of them as **concepts**). Hume's **empiricism**, however, was more hard-hitting than Locke's and Berkeley's. Locke, for example, held that we can know about the external world (thereby avoiding **scepticism**) because we have good reason to think that our 'impressions' (roughly, sensory experiences) are caused by objects that resemble those impressions. Hume denied that we could have any grounds for such a belief. After all, it is not as though we can step outside our own experiences and verify that any of them have been caused by objects that resemble them; and any causal hypothesis must, if it is to have any credibility at all, be backed up by evidence. *Contra* Berkeley, Hume argued on empiricist grounds that we have no reason to believe in God, or at least in a being with the qualities (such as omniscience, omnipotence and benevolence) attributed to God by the Christian Church.

Hume is a huge figure, both in the development of atheism (which got him into trouble: he failed to be appointed to a Chair at the University of Edinburgh because of his views on religion) and in the history of metaphysics. In continental Europe, Hume's influence on **Immanuel Kant** was explicitly recognised by Kant himself, who, in the introduction to his *Prolegomena to any Future Metaphysics* (1783), credited Hume's discussion of **causation** with interrupting his 'dogmatic slumber' and prompting him to write the mighty *Critique of Pure Reason* (1781).

In the Anglophone world, where empiricism continues to be the dominant philosophical tradition, Hume's philosophy has helped to shape nearly three centuries of philosophical thought; and, particularly in the areas of **causation** and **laws of nature**, philosophical positions are often broadly divided into 'Humean' and 'anti-Humean' positions. **David Lewis** even named a principle – **Humean supervenience** – after him. (In these areas, 'Humeanism' is often understood as the view that there is no **natural necessity**.)

Further reading: Hume's major philosophical works are all freely available online from various sources. 'Translations' into contemporary English of some of Hume's works (including the *Enquiries*, the *Dialogues* and the first three books of the *Treatise*) can be found on Jonathan Bennett's Early Modern Texts website (www.earlymoderntexts.com/f_hume.html)

HUMEANISM

'Humeanism' is so-called because it bears at least some relation to the views of **David Hume**. The epithet 'Humean' normally denotes a theory that either eschews **natural necessity** or, more generally, abides by the thesis of **Humean supervenience**. Thus, the **regularity theory of causation** is a Humean theory, because it holds that causal facts do not depend for their truth on facts about natural necessity. The **counterfactual theory of causation** is arguably Humean for the same reason, as is the **Ramsey–Lewis view** of **laws of nature**.

HUMEAN SUPERVENIENCE

'Humean supervenience' is a metaphysical thesis advanced by **David Lewis** that has been widely discussed in metaphysics in recent years. (NB, you may need to read the section on **supervenience** before proceeding.) Some class of facts or entities *A supervenes* on another, *B*, if, roughly, you do not get any difference in the *A*-facts without any difference in *B*-facts. For example, facts about the mental (beliefs, desires, and so on) supervene on facts about the physical (facts about subatomic particles, say) just if there can be no difference in mental facts without a difference in physical facts. For example, if John and Jack are identical twins, and indeed are identical right down to the states of their brains at a particular time t, it cannot be the case that one of them is happy and the other is sad at t. Supervenience claims are alleged by some philosophers to allow us to be **realists** about something (the A-facts) while holding that those facts are really 'nothing over and above' the B-facts. For example, we can (some philosophers think) accept that it is perfectly true that John is happy, or is thinking about dinner, while still upholding the view that mental states are really 'nothing over and above' physical states (see **supervenience** for more on this).

The thesis of Humean supervenience is a thesis about what the 'supervenience base' is (the B-facts in the above formulation) for all the facts there are to be had (the A-facts) about the actual world (and indeed worlds reasonably similar to it, see **possible worlds**). And the thesis is this (to quote Lewis himself): 'all there is to the world is a vast mosaic of local matters of particular fact, just one little thing and then another . . . For short, we have an arrangement of qualities. And that is all . . . All else supervenes on that' (Lewis 1986b: ix–x).

The general idea is this. We first need the concept of a point-sized thing – a thing that is as small as can be. Lewis never claimed to know what these things were, thinking physics would settle the matter, but candidates would be tiny sub-atomic particles, or points of spacetime. These point-sized things have certain intrinsic **properties**, and stand in certain spatiotemporal relations to one another (say, being a certain distance from one another, and separated by a certain interval of time). Given Humean supervenience, once you have fixed what point-sized things there are, what properties they have and what spatiotemporal relations they stand in (what Lewis calls the 'local matters of particular fact'), this fixes *everything* else about the world. This includes all the facts about macroscopic objects, like tables and donkeys, but also all the facts about **causation**, **laws of nature**, **personal identity**, and so on. In other words, *everything* else supervenes on the nature and distribution of the point-sized things.

The thesis is named after **David Hume**, who Lewis (1986b: ix) describes as 'the greater denier of necessary connections', reflecting the fact that what Humean supervenience primarily rules out is the existence of necessary connections between 'distinct existences', or what is sometimes known as **natural necessity**. Thus, Lewis's accounts of, for example, **laws of nature** and **causation** (allegedly) respect the principle by providing truth conditions for claims of the form 'L is a law of nature' and 'c caused e' that do not appeal to natural necessity. These accounts do, however, appeal to other possible worlds. However, the existence of other possible worlds is supposed to be consistent with Humean supervenience; indeed, the main point of Lewis's theory of **modality** (i.e. of **necessity and possibility**) is that necessity, on that theory, is a matter of relations *between* possible worlds and not an **intrinsic** feature of any particular possible world (modality is an 'inter-world' and not an 'intra-world' matter). Hence, there are plenty of facts about what is necessary and what is possible, but none of these facts depend on the existence of natural necessity.

For example, for Lewis, it is true that the laws of physics are 'physically necessary'. However, that does not amount to saying that there is some kind of necessity that is a feature of the actual world and which distinguishes the laws from merely accidentally true generalizations ('all the pens in my pocket are blue', say). Rather – given his account of laws – what makes them physically necessary is the mere definitional fact that something is physically necessary if and only if it is entailed by the laws of nature. Any given law of physics is trivially entailed by the laws of nature (because it is one of those laws), whereas 'all the pens in my pocket are blue' is not entailed by the laws and so is not physically necessary.

Lewis also (perhaps controversially) takes Humean supervenience to rule out, for example, Cartesian dualism (immaterial minds would violate the requirement that all there is a 'vast mosaic of local matters of particular fact', not least because, lacking spatio-temporal location, they are not in any sense 'local') and **endurantism** (see **perdurantism**). However, he takes Humean supervenience to be only contingently true (indeed he accepts that it *might* not be true at all). For example, while he thinks an account of the *actual* nature of mental states can be given that obeys Humean supervenience, this is consistent with the view that Cartesian souls exist at other possible worlds.

Further reading: Lewis (1986b, Introduction); Weatherson (2010, § 5)

IDEALISM

See **phenomenalism and idealism**.

IDENTITY

Let us start by explaining an important distinction that can often confuse people: the distinction between 'qualitative identity' and 'numerical identity'.

Imagine you and your friend have the misfortune to show up at the same party wearing the same dress. Done it? Right. Now, what did you imagine just then? Chances are you did not imagine you and your friend somehow squeezing into the very same dress – perhaps taking one sleeve each and leaving the zip undone so that you would both fit in. (Of course, you *might* have imagined that, if you are a particularly contrary person. However, most people would not have done.) Probably, what you imagined is that you were both wearing *very similar*, or perhaps (if you are the same size) *exactly similar* dresses, that is, what is sometimes described as 'qualitative identity', and it contrasts with numerical identity, which is what we would have if you really were, literally, wearing the very same dress.

Failing to distinguish between qualitative and numerical identity (and difference) can get you into trouble. For example, in the debate about **personal identity**, we are interested in what it is that makes a person *A* at time 1 (you this morning, say) the *same person* as person *B* at time 2. This is a question about numerical identity. If you confuse it with qualitative identity, you will be liable to say things like 'when I got a haircut, I became a different person'. You did not – you just started out with longer hair and ended up with shorter hair. There is a qualitative difference between the earlier you and the later you, but – at least in the absence of a good argument to the contrary – that is no reason to think that the later 'you' is literally (i.e. numerically) a different person.

Philosophers, being aware of the dangers of failing to be precise, will very rarely use 'the same *X*' to mean 'an exactly similar *X*'; indeed they tend to avoid talk of 'qualitative identity' all together. Hence, when they talk about identity, you can be pretty sure they mean 'numerical identity'. Things can get a little less clean-cut, however, when we think about **properties**. Imagine that you and your friend are wearing dresses that are the same colour. Is this qualitative or numerical identity? Those philosophers who believe in **universals** – features of objects that can literally be present in two different places at once (e.g. in two different dresses) – will think that the dresses are qualitatively identical (at least with respect to their colour) *because* of the *numerical* identity of the colour of your dress and the colour of your friend's dress: it is literally the same universal that is instantiated in both dresses. (Actually most believers in universals deny that there are colour-universals, but let us leave that point aside.) Those who disbelieve in universals will say that the qualitative identity of the two dresses is *not* to be explained by any numerical identity; they may say instead that the dresses each contain a colour **trope** such that the two (distinct) colour tropes maximally resemble each other, or they may say that the dresses are the 'same colour' only in the sense that each one satisfies the predicate 'is red' (or whatever) (see **nominalism**).

A second important distinction is that between 'synchronic' and 'diachronic' identity. Synchronic identity is a matter of some thing, x, being (numerically) identical to some thing, y, at the same time. Diachronic identity is a matter of x at one time being identical to y at a *different* time. Both synchronic and diachronic identity are rich sources of metaphysical debate. In the case of synchronic identity, one issue is whether all true identity claims (i.e. claims of the form $a = b$) are **necessary**, or true in all **possible worlds**. In his famous work on the **necessary *a posteriori*, Saul Kripke** claims that all identities are indeed necessary. However, some philosophers have disputed this. Here is a classic example, due to Gibbard (1975). Imagine that you fashion a lump of clay (call the lump 'Lumpl') into a statue of Goliath (call the statue 'Goliath'). Is Lumpl identical with Goliath, that is, are they one and the same object? If you think the answer is 'yes', then you appear to be committed to a contingent identity claim, because we can imagine Lumpl existing without Goliath. (You might not have fashioned the clay into a statue of David, say, in which case Goliath would never have existed.) Hence, 'Lumpl = Goliath' *might* have been false. If you think the answer is 'no' – perhaps on the grounds that all identities are necessary – then you seem to be committed to the rather curious claim that there are actually *two* objects here – Lumpl and Goliath – which are nonetheless constituted by exactly the same matter, arranged in exactly the same way (there is just the one lump of clay, after all, which happens to be fashioned into the shape of a biblical character). For some issues concerning diachronic identity, see **personal identity** and **identity over time**.

Further reading: Noonan (2009)

IDENTITY OF INDISCERNIBLES

See **Leibniz's Law**.

IDENTITY OVER TIME

Identity over time, sometimes called *diachronic* identity, concerns when some thing, x, at one time is numerically identical to some thing, y, that exists at another time (this is in contrast to x being identical to y at the same time, which is *synchronic* **identity**). For instance, you might look at an old photograph of an eight-year-old child and say, plausibly enough, 'look, that's me!'. In other words, the eight-year-old in the picture is *numerically identical* to the person reading this entry right now. (We will drop the 'numerically' from now on; see **identity** if you are not sure what it means.)

However, you clearly *are not* identical to Ghenghis Khan, a young Mel Gibson or a table that existed in the 1600s. Hence, you are diachronically identical to some things but not to others. (The observant will have noticed a problem with phrasing in that previous sentence – for of course you are not identical to some thing*s* (plural), but only some *thing* (singular), namely you and *only ever* you. However, we can charitably ignore such grammatical inconveniences.)

In metaphysics, identity across time crops up in three inter-related areas. One area is addressing what the conditions are for some *x* being identical to some *y*. Most commonly, this question is asked with reference to a specific **sortal**, for instance 'person'. In that case, you would be investigating what it is for one person to be identical to another person at a different time – which is just the question of **personal identity**. More rarely you will see discussions of what it is for *any* kind of *x* to be identical to some given *y* at a different time (with one commonly proposed answer being that *x* and *y* are spatiotemporally continuous with one another).

The next area that identity across time appears is in dealing with certain puzzles. One example is the Ship of Theseus (a **fission** case, where one object appears to become two objects). At some time t_1 Theseus owns a ship, which is made of planks; call it Ship$_{original}$. Slowly, over time, each plank is replaced by a new plank until, at some later time t_2, every plank has been replaced. We end up with a ship, call it Ship$_{replace}$. The intuition is meant to be that a ship can survive such a replacement (i.e. Ship$_{original}$ at t_1 is identical to Ship$_{replace}$ at t_2). However, imagine also that the planks that were taken away were stored somewhere else and then, again at t_2, reassembled to make a new ship: call it Ship$_{reassemble}$. Ship$_{reassemble}$ has exactly the same parts, in exactly the same arrangement, as Ship$_{original}$ had at time t_1. The intuition is meant to be that Ship$_{reassemble}$, at t_2, made of the original planks, is identical to Ship$_{original}$ at t_1 (for, after all, ships are like tents and can survive being disassembled and reassembled – indeed, sometimes exactly that was done to ships to take them across stretches of land).

However, if Ship$_{original}$ is identical to both Ship$_{replace}$ *and* Ship$_{reassemble}$, then, because identity is **transitive**, Ship$_{reassemble}$ is identical to Ship$_{replace}$. However, that, so the problem goes, is not right, as they are clearly two *distinct* ships at t_2. Unsurprisingly, issues over the conditions under which one thing is (diachronically) identical to another thing bear on the debate about how to resolve this puzzle. Issues of identity over time also figure in problems like that of the statue and the lump of clay (see **perdurantism, endurantism** and **identity**).

Finally, some metaphysicians are worried about *how* objects can be identical across time. They think either that such a fact demands a metaphysical explanation, or that there is a problem with how things can be identical across time given that they change from one moment to the next (this is similar to the problem of temporary intrinsics; see **perdurantism**). In either case, metaphysicians who think there is a problem here generally think that endorsing endurantism or perdurantism will be a solution, that is, that an object's perduring will explain how objects can be identical across time (alternatively, that an object's enduring will yield such an explanation).

Further reading: Gallois (2009)

ILLUSION OF FREE WILL

Pretty much all philosophers agree that most people ordinarily *think* they have **free will** and hence are **morally responsible** for their actions. However, some philosophers hold that this view is mistaken; hence, according to them, free will is an illusion.

Actually, we need to be careful when describing something as an 'illusion'; not just any old false belief counts as an illusion. Many people think Sydney is the capital of Australia. They are not suffering from an illusion; they merely have a false belief. To call a belief an 'illusion' suggests that the belief in question is somehow based on perceptual (or perhaps inner) experience. Hence, for example, we might say that people who think the sun moves round the earth are suffering from an illusion: they believe that the sun moves round the earth because that is how it *looks*.

Some philosophers think that free will really is an illusion in something like this sense. It *seems* to us that when we make decisions, we could have done otherwise (see **Principle of Alternate Possibilities**), or because it seems to us that we are uncaused causes of our decisions (see **agent causation**). However, in fact, things are different to how they appear to be: perhaps because **determinism** is true, so it is not true that we could have done otherwise (see **hard determinism**); or perhaps because we – as opposed to our mental states – do not cause our decisions, or because we are caused to make those decisions by prior states of our brains. Other philosophers think that free will is an illusion, but in a different sense. Sigmund Freud took an illusion to be a belief that is motivated by wish-fulfillment (thus, for Freud, belief in God is an illusion, not because it perceptually seems to people that God exists but because their belief in

God is motivated by their desire for God to exist). Smilansky (2000: 145–50) holds that free will is an illusion in this sense.

Those who think that free will is an illusion are typically **incompatibilists** (i.e. they hold that free will is incompatible with determinism), although some of them also think that free will is incompatible with **indeterminism** too, or at least with the kind of indeterminism that is suggested by our current best science, that is, quantum mechanics. Such philosophers thus think that it does not much matter whether it turns out that the Universe is deterministic or indeterminstic: free will is an illusion either way. (Pereboom (2001) calls this position 'hard incompatibilism'.) It has also recently been claimed that findings in neuroscience and psychology reveal free will to be an illusion; see **neuroscience and free will**.

Further reading: Pereboom (2001, Chapter 5)

IMMANENT REALISM ABOUT UNIVERSALS

Immanent realism about **universals** is the view that a universal is wholly present in each object which instantiates it. It stands in opposition to the **platonist** view that universals exist outside space and time. One consequence of immanent realism (as opposed to platonism) is that there are no uninstantiated universals: if there were never any spherical objects, say, then the universal *being spherical* would not exist.

Immanent realism originated in the writings of Aristotle. Perhaps its most famous contemporary defender is **David Armstrong** (see **universals** for more on this view).

IMPROPER PART

See **part**.

INCOMPATIBILISM

Incompatibilism is the view that acting freely is incompatible with **determinism** (the thesis that everything that happens – including all our actions – is determined by the past plus the **laws of nature**). Incompatibilism contrasts with **compatibilism**, according to which **free will** *is* compatible with determinism.

One motivation for incompatibilism is the thought that acting freely requires the ability to do otherwise. Imagine some action you performed at nine o'clock this morning (made a cup of tea, say), and call this action *A*. You probably assume that you did *A* freely, or 'of your own free will'. What exactly doing something freely requires is of course a controversial question, but it is widely thought that one requirement is that you *could* have done something else instead. You might well assume that your doing *A* meets this requirement. After all, when you were deciding whether to have tea or coffee, say, you presumably thought that you *could* do either of those things – otherwise why would you have been deliberating about it? And your meeting this requirement does seem to be connected to the idea that you did *A* freely. After all, if someone had forced you to make tea, or if some evil neuroscientist had rigged up a remote-control device to your brain and by pressing a button, had *made* you decide to make the tea – even if making the tea was what you wanted to do anyway – then it looks as though you did not make the tea freely because you *could not have done otherwise* than what you did.

Assuming that acting freely does indeed require the ability to do otherwise (see **Principle of Alternate Possibilities**), a problem looms, because, according to the **Consequence Argument** for incompatibilism, this ability is incompatible with **determinism**. Hence, if you were determined to make the tea – even if what determined you to do it was not the intervention of an evil neuroscientist but just your own, perfectly ordinary situation plus the laws of nature (you wanted tea more than you wanted coffee, you knew how to make it, there were teabags in the cupboard, the kettle was working, and so on) – then you did not, in fact, make it freely.

A second popular argument for incompatibilism, sometimes called the 'causal chain argument', locates the problem that determinism poses for free will not in the fact that it closes off alternative possibilities, but rather in the fact that on a deterministic worldview, all the *sources* of our actions lie, ultimately, outside ourselves. Because what we do is fully determined by the laws of nature together with facts about the distant past – and we can go as far back as we like, for example to a time before our grandparents were born – *we* are not the ultimate sources of our actions. Determinism thus appears to rob us of what is sometimes called 'ultimate responsibility' for our actions. The buck does not stop with us; we are mere conduits through which causal processes pass. Incompatibilists who are persuaded by this argument typically require that agents must directly cause their own actions (or at least some of them – their decisions, say) in order for them to act freely (see **agent causation**).

Nothing follows from incompatibilism just by itself about whether we do, in fact, have free will. After all, incompatibilism is just a thesis to the effect that two claims – determinism, and the claim that agents sometimes act freely – cannot *both* be true. Accordingly, different incompatibilists take different views about which claim we should give up. In particular, **hard determinists** hold that determinism is true, and thus – because free will is incompatible with determinism – that we never act freely. A more popular variety of incompatibilism, however, is **libertarianism**. Libertarians hold that we do, at least sometimes, act freely and thus that **indeterminism** rather than determinism is true: at least sometimes, what we do, or what we decide to do, is not fully determined by facts about the past plus the laws of nature.

Hard determinists and libertarians differ over which thesis – determinism or the claim that we sometimes act freely – is true. Some incompatibilists, however, reject *both* theses. For example, Pereboom (2001) holds that free will is incompatible with determinism, but also with the kind of indeterminism that is arguably delivered by our best science, that is, quantum mechanics. Hence, although he thinks that *in principle* indeterministic agents could act freely, he thinks it unlikely that they actually ever do (see also **illusion of free will**).

Further reading: Clarke (2008); Vihvelin (2008)

INDETERMINISM

Indeterminism is, as you might expect, the denial of **determinism**, that is, the thesis of indeterminism says that it is *not* the case that $(P_t \& L)$ logically entails a statement that describes the exact state of the Universe at any other time, where P_t is a statement that describes the exact state of the whole Universe at a particular time t, and L is a statement that describes all the **laws of nature**.

A common view among philosophers is that quantum mechanics – which is a phenomenally successful theory of how the sub-atomic realm works – shows determinism to be false. For example, radioactive atoms have a 'half-life': the time period within which there is a probability of ½ that a particular atom will decay. (Radioactive decay is very dangerous to human beings and other animals, and some radioactive atoms have a very long half-life, which is why nuclear waste is such a problem. For example, strontium-90 was spread over large areas of Europe after the Chernobyl nuclear accident in 1986. Because strontium-90 has a half-life of 28 years, probably less than half of it has decayed so far.)

You might think that probabilistic laws like the one concerning the half-life of strontium-90 (i.e. the law that there is a 50 per cent probability that a strontium-90 atom will decay within 28 years) are merely an expression of our ignorance about hidden causes: if we knew everything there was to know about this particular strontium-90 atom, and all the laws relevant to radioactive decay, we would know either that it will decay within 28 years (so this has probability 1) or that it will not (probability 0). After all, many of the probabilities we think about in our daily lives fall into this category. For example, a good poker player will assess the probability that the next card to be dealt will be an ace. However, it is already determined what the card will be – it is right there at the top of the pack – so her assessment of the probability of an ace only reflects her less-than-complete information about what the card is (e.g. there are 20 cards left and only one of them is an ace, so the probability that the next card is an ace is 1/20).

However, many scientists – and so also many philosophers – think that (for example) the probability of ½ that a given strontium-90 atom will decay within 28 years is a 'rock-bottom' probability or **chance** (note that this is a technical sense of 'chance' that does not have much to do with how we ordinarily use the word). There are no further facts about the atom such that, if we knew them, we would know exactly when it will decay (unlike in the poker case, where there is such a further fact, namely which card is at the top of the pack: the 'rock-bottom' probability – the chance – that the next card is an ace is therefore either 1 or 0). So, even if we knew all the past facts about the Universe and all the laws of nature, we would not be able to infer when a given strontium-90 atom will decay. Hence (if the scientists and philosophers are right) determinism is false.

Whether quantum mechanics really shows determinism to be false is debatable, however. In particular, the claim that quantum mechanics delivers only probabilities of events (e.g. the probability of ½ that a strontium-90 atom will decay within 28 years) depends upon a particular interpretation of quantum mechanics. In particular, it depends on solving what is known as the 'quantum measurement problem' by postulating a 'collapse of the wave function'. (We do not have the space to go into that here, but see Penrose (1989: Chapter 6) for a reasonably accessible introduction to quantum mechanics.)

All things considered, the jury is out on whether indeterminism is true. However, note that even if it *is* true, it does not follow that *nothing* that happens can be predicted with certainty from complete information about the laws and the past. First, it is perfectly consistent with the truth of indeterminism that, say, the motion of a snooker ball when you hit it is a deterministic process, even if not *every* event is determined to happen by the past and the laws.

Second, as we have already seen with the poker example, the fact that we can sensibly assign probabilities to events is perfectly compatible with those events being fully determined by the past plus the laws. Think of a horse race: the odds offered by bookmakers reflect how likely they think it is that the different horses will win. Of course, the bookmakers have *some* information about the horses, on the basis of which they set the odds, but not *all* relevant information. Hence, the genuine *chance* (in the technical sense) that a given horse will win is unlikely to be the same as the bookies' estimate. When the race starts, is it already determined which horse will win? It is safe to say that nobody really knows the answer to that question or, indeed, the answer to any such question about events outside the quantum realm. Are the outcomes of coin tosses determined? Is it determined, now, whether it will rain in Birmingham in the next three hours, or whether Roger Federer will win the next point, or whether I will have a sandwich for my lunch? Again, it is safe to say that nobody really knows.

This point is particularly important when we consider the position of **libertarianism** in the **free will** debate, because libertarians claim explicitly that at least some of our *decisions* (for example, my decision about what to have for lunch) are not determined by the prior facts plus the laws.

Further reading: Penrose (1989, Chapter 6); see also the *Further reading* for **determinism**

INDEXICAL

An indexical is a referring expression that refers to different things depending upon the context in which it is uttered (or written). For instance, 'I' and 'here' are both indexical expressions. When uttered, the word 'I' refers to different things – when I utter the word it refers to me; when you utter 'I' it refers to you. Similarly for 'here'. When Angela Merkel utters 'I am here' when standing in Berlin, the 'I' refers to Angela Merkel and the 'here' refers to Berlin. When Barack Obama utters 'I am here' when in the White House, the 'I' refers to Barack Obama and the 'here' to the White House.

Indexicals, and how they are used, are relevant in numerous areas of metaphysics. For example, **David Lewis** is a genuine **modal realist** who thinks that some things exist – namely **possible worlds** – without *actually* existing. It makes sense for these things to exist without actually existing, says Lewis, because 'actual' is an indexical term, referring to the world at which the person uttering the words 'actual world' is located (so actual existence is not a special *kind* of **existence** any more than existing *here* is a special kind of existence). In the same way that something can fail to be 'here' without failing to exist (for instance, in Birmingham the Eiffel Tower is not 'here' whereas in Paris it is) the inhabitants of other possible worlds can exist without being actual. For instance, Gandalf does not *actually* exist, for Gandalf is not located at the actual world (i.e. the world we inhabit). In a possible world where Gandalf does exist, all utterances asserting that he actually exists turn out to be true, because for the inhabitants of any given Gandalf-world, 'the actual world' refers to *that* world.

Similarly, tenseless theorists (see **tensed and tenseless theories of times**) take 'now' to be an indexical, that is, things that presently exist (i.e. that exist *now*) are not metaphysically special in any way; they are just the things that happen to be temporally local to you (in the same way that things which are 'here' are not special in any way; they are just the things which are *spatially* local to you).

Further reading: Braun (2008)

INDISCERNIBILITY OF IDENTICALS

See **Leibniz's Law**.

INFINITY

Infinity gets deployed a lot in metaphysics, especially in the philosophy of time and in other areas of ontology. Two features are of particular metaphysical interest.

Classical themes

It is **Aristotle** who provides one of the more pervasive classical theories of the infinite. Aristotle holds that infinity cannot be a number, because any number can be counted to and nobody can possibly count to infinity. Hence, because for any things there must be a number of those things, there cannot be an infinite number of things. For instance, time cannot go on for eternity because that would involve an infinite number of seconds, and objects cannot be infinitely divisible as then they would have an infinite number of parts.

Aristotle's view is, however, at odds with various scenarios you might think are intuitively possible: what if time never comes to an end, or what if there just is not any stage where we get down to a part of an object that is too small to be divided? In those cases it is surely correct to say that time is infinite in duration or that objects are infinitely divisible.

Aristotle resolved the tension by saying there are two brands of infinity: potential infinity and actual infinity. Some things are actually infinite in number if an infinite number of such things exist. Something is potentially infinite if the process that gives rise to the increasing number of things is never-ending – so those things might not exist, but *potentially* could exist. Hence, for example, an object may well be infinitely divisible in the sense of potential infinity: if we started dividing it into **parts**, we would never get to a point where we could not divide it any more. However, at every stage in this process we would have made only a finite number of divisions, and so only a finite number of objects (parts of our original object) would exist. For instance, if we divide one object into two, then the two parts into four, then the four parts into eight, etc. it could go on forever, but at every stage there would be a finite number of parts we had divided the object into. That was fine, said Aristotle. However, we could never have an *actual* infinite number of things – we could never *complete* the process of dividing the infinitely divisible object (so Aristotle would not have believed one could carry out **supertasks**). The parts that we get from the process of division only potentially exist before the division; they do not exist all along waiting to be divided up. Hence, at no stage is it true that there is an infinite number of parts that the object has. Whether these different types of infinity are cogent, for instance whether deploying them will solve the problems Aristotle wanted to solve (such as **Zeno**'s paradoxes), is up for debate.

Cantor

Aristotle's disdain for infinity did not cut it with Cantor (1845–1918). His work on set theory (see **class**) allowed him to say more informative things about the notion of infinity. For instance, Cantor established that infinity was more like a number than Aristotle thought. Indeed, Cantor established that there are different *sizes* of infinity. This fact sometimes gets deployed in metaphysics, so it is worth explaining briefly here. Cantor endorsed a principle (originating with **Hume**) that two collections of things are the same in number if and only if they can be placed in one-to-one correspondence with one another (so if I have got two things, *a* and *b*, and two more things, *c* and *d*, there are as many of the former as the latter because *a* can be paired with *c*, and *b* with *d*). Hence, if we take all the positive integers (1, 2, 3, . . .), there is an infinite number of them, and there are exactly as many of them as there are negative integers (-1, -2. -3, . . .) because they can be paired one-to one with one another (1 with -1; 2 with -2; 3 with -3, etc.).

Bizarrely, however, there are also as many positive integers as there are integers (i.e. the positive and the negative integers combined). We can order the integers like so: 1, -1, 2, -2, . . . Furthermore, we can pair up the positive integers with that list: 1 pairs with 1, 2 with -1, 3 with 2, 4 with -2, and so on. At no stage will you 'run out' of positive integers: for any integer (positive or negative), however large (say, -1,265,482,501), there will be some positive integer paired with it. (We will leave it to you to figure out which positive integer this would be, given the method just described.) Perhaps even more surprisingly, the same is true of the integers vs the *rational* numbers (such as 1.344 or 4.2874 – rational numbers are those that can be expressed as ratios, so 1.344 is 1,344/1,000, etc.; the rationals include the integers, because, trivially, 1 is 1/1, 2 is 2/1, etc.). Hence, the rationals are *countable*: you can pair them up with the integers.

Some infinites, however, cannot be so paired with the integers (or, equivalently, with the rational numbers), and so are *uncountable*. Take the *real* numbers – that is, not just the rational numbers but also the irrational numbers (those that cannot be expressed as ratios, such as π or 0.2222222 recurring). The reals *cannot* be paired one-to-one with the rationals. The proof ('Cantor's Diagonal Argument') is too lengthy to detail here, but does demonstrate that the set of reals is bigger than (has a greater 'cardinality') the set of rational numbers – that is, they are both *infinite*, but one infinity is bigger than another.

These different sizes of infinity (or, to be more mathematically precise, the different cardinalities of the different infinite sets) even get names. The smallest infinity is 'aleph-zero' ($\aleph_0$) – this is the cardinality of the set of integers (and also the set of positive integers, the set of rationals, the set of positive integers, . . .). The next largest is 'aleph-one' ($\aleph_1$) – the cardinality of the set of reals.

Further reading: Moore (2001)

INSTANTIATION

'Instantiation' and 'exemplification' are equivalent names for the relation-ship which holds between an object and its **properties** (or 'features' – such as redness and roundness). Some philosophers who are both realists about **universals** and substance-attribute theorists (see **bundle theory vs substance-attribute theory**) hold a non-**reductionist** view of this relation; such a view is thought to face the problem of **Bradley's regress**. As a way of avoiding this problem, others deny that instantiation is really a *relation* at all (**David Armstrong** describes it as a 'non-relational tie'; see **Bradley's regress** and **states of affairs** for more on Armstrong's position).

Other accounts of properties give a reductionist account of the instan-tiation relation. For example, if properties are identical with classes of objects, so that redness is just the class of red things (see **class nominal-ism**), then for an object *o* to instantiate property *P* is just for *o* to be a member of *P*.

INTRINSIC VS EXTRINSIC PROPERTIES

The crude definition of *intrinsic* properties is that they are the **properties** that concern how the object is 'in itself'. The extrinsic properties are the non-intrinsic properties – in other words, those properties that an object only has because of the way the rest of the world is. To illustrate, consider properties of mass and weight. An object has a certain mass, which remains constant as long as the object itself remains unchanged. Mass, then, is intrinsic. However, the weight of the object can vary even though the object itself remains unchanged. For instance, on Earth an object has one weight; in the depths of space it has no weight; when near Jupiter it has a radically increased weight. The object's weight is dependent upon how close it is to other things – the object can remain the same ('in itself'), even though its weight changes. Hence, its weight is extrinsic.

Other common examples of intrinsic properties include being a certain height, being **concrete**, being **abstract**, having hair, having a hand and being a liquid. Other common examples of extrinsic properties include being an uncle (because that depends on there being other people – a brother or sister with a child); being hated by small children (as that depends on small children hating you); and being married (as that depends on the existence of someone else, and whether or not they engaged in certain rituals with you). Hence, again, those latter properties can change whilst you remain the same in and of yourself. The event of a child's birth that took place on the other side of the world would not bring about any *intrinsic* change in you, but it would (in making you an uncle) bring about an *extrinsic* change. Note that in ordinary language 'intrinsic' can have a stronger meaning than it does in philosophical contexts: in ordinary language an intrinsic feature is part of an object's **essence** or 'essential nature'. In philosophical contexts, having hair, say, is an intrinsic property, but it is unlikely to be a part of anything's essence.

One philosophical puzzle is how to give an **analysis** of what it is to be intrinsic/extrinsic (usually one analyses what 'intrinsic' is and then simply defines 'extrinsic' as not being an intrinsic property). For instance, Jaegwon Kim and Roderick Chisholm analyse 'intrinsic property' as:

G is an intrinsic property $=_{df}$ it is possible that an object could have G even though no other objects existed.

You could not be an uncle, or be hated by small children if nothing else existed, ergo they are not intrinsic properties (and so are extrinsic). An immediate problem with this analysis is that the property of being such that nothing else exists (what is usually called 'being lonely' in the literature) turns out to be an intrinsic property, for you could (indeed would) have *that* property if nothing else existed. However being lonely should be an extrinsic property, as it depends on what other things exist (for if other things *did* exist, then you would not be lonely any more).

An alternative analysis, due to **David Lewis**, is given in terms of 'qualitative duplication'. Roughly, a qualitative duplicate of an object is the thing that would appear if the object was placed into a magical cloning machine that duplicated everything perfectly. For instance, if you stepped into such a machine, then your clone would be the same height and mass as you, they would have hair if you have hair, etc., but they would not be an uncle (they would only just come into existence, so do not have any siblings, never mind nieces and nephews); nor would we think that they were hated by small children (for they had never even met *anyone*, never mind any small children). With that in mind we might say that a property is intrinsic to an object if and only if all possible duplicates of that object have that property. The point of talking about *possible* duplicates is that it does not matter that objects do not (usually) have any actual duplicates, for we are looking at the duplicates of that object at other **possible worlds**. Hence, because in every possible world anything that is my duplicate is exactly the same height as me, then my height turns out to be an intrinsic property.

When it comes to counter-examples, this analysis takes care of loneliness (because some duplicates are not lonely, existing at other possible worlds alongside other things). However, it does mean that some intuitively extrinsic properties might turn out to be intrinsic. For instance, if **numbers** exist necessarily then they exist at every possible world. That means they exist at every possible world where anything has a duplicate. Therefore, the property *being such that the number 7 exists* turns out to be an intrinsic property when it should not be – intuitively that property somehow involves the existence of another object (albeit an object that exists necessarily). These two examples should give you some taste of the debate that is had in this area.

We can extend the notion of intrinsic and extrinsic to relations as well. One way to do this is to take the analogue of an intrinsic property to be an 'internal relation'. A relation is internal if and only if it would hold if its **relata** remained the same in themselves (i.e. if it **supervenes** on the intrinsic properties of the relata). Otherwise a relation is 'external' (the analogue of being extrinsic). For instance, if Jack and Jim are both the same mass then they stand in the *same mass as* relation. Given that Jack has the intrinsic properties that he does, and given that Jim has the intrinsic properties he does, that relation *has* to hold, and hence is an internal relation. Whereas Jack and Jim can remain exactly as they are in themselves while changing the distance between them – so the relation *being 20 metres away from* is an external relation.

A more permissive sense of 'intrinsic relation' is sometimes used, however, particularly in the debate about **causation**, to mean something more like 'local'. Suppose I flip a switch and thereby cause the light to go on. Arguably the causal relation here is not *internal* – the switch-flipping and the light's going on could have happened just as they did, without one being a cause of the other (e.g. someone might have flipped another switch at just the same time, which both cut the electricity supply from my switch and itself caused the light to go on – this is a case of **pre-emption**). However, we can argue about whether the obtaining of the causal relation was 'intrinsic' in a different sense; does the fact that the flipping and the lighting are causally related depend just on the nature of those two events plus 'local' facts, for example, facts about the flow of electrons from the switch to the lightbulb? 'Anti-Humean' views of causation typically take causation to be an intrinsic relation in this sense, whereas Humean views do not (because such a relation would violate **Humean supervenience**). Humean theories of causation appeal to extrinsic facts, such as the obtaining of regularities (see **regularity theory of causation**) or the truth of certain counterfactuals (see **counterfactual theory of causation**). Some philosophers (e.g. Menzies 1996) take it to be a 'platitude' – part of the 'folk theory' of causation – that causation is an intrinsic relation (see **Canberra Plan**).

Further reading: Cameron (2009); Weatherson (2008)

INUS CONDITIONS

Imagine I place a bomb on a bridge in just the right place so that, when detonated, the bridge collapses. When the timer reaches zero, the bomb explodes destroying the bridge. The timer reaching zero seems to be a cause of the bridge collapsing. Also, my placing the bomb seems to have been a cause of the bridge collapsing. Neither cause, however, is *sufficient* for the effect to take place. If I had placed the bomb correctly but there was no timer to set it off, the bridge would have remained intact. If the timer had reached zero but I had not bothered to place it on the bridge, instead staying at home in bed, then the bridge would have remained intact (and if I would stored the bomb at home, I would have had a rude awakening). Nor are these causes *necessary* – the bridge could have collapsed without either cause taking place, for instance if it had become rusted, or someone had loaded heavy weights on it until it collapsed, or someone else had bombed it.

However, the condition of my *both* placing the bomb (b) *and* the timer reaching zero (z) *is* sufficient for the bridge to be destroyed (in fact other events will be needed too, such as the timer being connected to the explosives, but for purpose of example ignore such complications and pretend that only these two events were needed). That, broader, sufficient condition – (b & z) – is, again, not necessary for the bomb's destruction (for the rust in the bridge might destroy it, etc.). Hence, (b & z) is an *unnecessary* but *sufficient* condition for the bridge collapsing. Meanwhile, each of b and z by itself is (obviously) *insufficient* for that broader condition (b & z) to obtain, but is *necessary* for (b & z) to obtain (you need both b and z to get, well, b & z). Hence, the two things we picked out as causes, the placing of the bomb and the timer reaching zero – that is, b and z – may not, individually, be sufficient conditions of the bridge collapsing, but each is an 'INUS' conditions of it – that is, each is an **i**nsufficient but **n**ecessary part of a condition that is itself **u**nnecessary but **s**ufficient to destroy the bridge.

According to Mackie's (1965) analysis of causation (a variant on the **regularity theory of causation**), c is a cause of e if and only if c is (at least) an INUS condition of e. Unfortunately, the INUS account came in for quite a lot of criticism (e.g. Kim 1971) and has fallen into disrepute, though interestingly the 'NESS test' for causation in legal contexts (a causes is a '**n**ecessary **e**lement of a **s**et of conditions jointly **s**ufficient' for the effect), on which the INUS account was closely based is still going strong.

Further reading: Mackie (1965); Kim (1971)

KANT, IMMANUEL

Immanuel Kant (1724–1804) spent his whole life in the German city of Königsberg – now the Russian city of Kaliningrad. He worked at the university, which was recently renamed the Immanuel Kant State University of Russia in his honour. He has had, and continues to have, a huge influence on philosophy, in both the analytic and the continental traditions. As far as metaphysics is concerned, Kant's two major works are the hefty *Critique of Pure Reason* (1781) – which Kant (1783: 8) himself describes as 'dry, obscure, opposed to all ordinary notions, and moreover long-winded' – and the rather lighter-weight *Prolegomena to Any Future Metaphysics* (1783).

Kant's bête noire was **David Hume**, whom Kant, not unreasonably, credited with having launched a terrible attack on metaphysics. Hume 'threw no light on this species of knowledge', he says in the *Prolegomena* (again not unreasonably, because Hume thought that metaphysical knowledge was impossible), but 'he certainly struck a spark from which light might have been obtained, had it caught some inflammable substance and had its smouldering fire been carefully nursed and developed' (1783: 3–4) – perhaps an unfortunate metaphor given Hume's recommendation that all speculative metaphysics should be consigned to the flames. Kant's (1781: 7) aim was to rekindle that fire (his fire, that is, not Hume's bonfire), and thereby to re-establish metaphysics as (as he puts it in the *Critique*) 'the Queen of all the sciences'.

Kant's basic idea goes something like this. Hume – being an **empiricist** – thought that all our **concepts** (or 'ideas') derive from experience. For example, the idea of 'necessary connection' or **causation** derives from repeated experience of one kind of event (*A*) being followed by another kind of event (*B*), whence we form the habit of inferring, on encountering an *A*, that a *B* will also occur. By contrast, Kant thinks that we need to have the concept of causation in order to be capable of having any experience at all. Thus, that concept cannot itself be the product of experience, but must have its source in the 'pure understanding'. Similarly for other concepts that are the bread and butter of metaphysics: unity (or **identity**), **substance, possibility, existence**, and so on. This being so, we can (*pace* Hume) come to know principles of metaphysics *a priori*.

The downside, however, is that these principles that we can know *a priori* – and indeed any claim we can meaningfully make about the world at all – will apply only to (as Kant sometimes puts it) 'objects of experience' (or 'phenomena') and not to 'things in themselves' (noumena). Hence, Kant is what is sometimes known as a 'transcendental idealist' (note that this is a different sense of 'idealism' to that found in **phenomenalism and idealism**). We can have no knowledge of – and indeed (at least on some interpretations of Kant) cannot even formulate meaningful claims about – things in themselves, because our concepts can only apply to objects of experience, and not to whatever it is that lies behind those experiences. For example, we cannot even say that our experiences are *caused* by things in themselves. Causation is one of the *a priori* concepts or 'categories' that determine how we experience and conceptualise the world, we therefore cannot meaningfully apply it to unconceptualised, noumenal reality.

Kant is thus very close to being a 'global anti-realist', according to our definition of the term (see **realism and anti-realism (global)**). Kant holds that virtually all of our talk and thought about the world refers only to the world-as-conceptualised-by-us: it refers to the phenomenal world of cats, chairs and planets. Unlike full-blown anti-realists, however, he does appear to think that there is one (and perhaps only one) concept that really does apply to the world as it is in itself, namely the concept of the world as it is in itself (or 'noumenon'). Kant holds that noumenal reality exists, but (arguably) that nothing meaningful can be said about it *apart* from that it exists. This is a claim that full-blown anti-realists (on our definition) deny, on the grounds that you cannot meaningfully assert that something exists when there is literally nothing else you can meaningfully say about it (see Nagel 1986: 93–4 and 99–103).

Further reading: Scruton (2001)

KRIPKE, SAUL

Saul Kripke (born in 1940) is a philosopher and logician whose work has had a huge effect on metaphysics in the last 40 years or so, for two main reasons. First, he laid the foundations for 'possible worlds semantics' for modal logic, according to which a proposition is necessarily true if it is true 'in all possible worlds', and possibly true if it is true in at least one possible world. Thanks to the work of Kripke and **David Lewis**, it is now quite hard to find any work in metaphysics that does not make use of the terminology of **possible worlds**. (Incidentally, Kripke started publishing on modal logic while still a teenager.) Second, he wrote *Naming and Necessity* (1980), based on three lectures he presented at Princeton in the early 1970s, which quickly became a classic text in both metaphysics and the philosophy of language. A far as metaphysics is concerned, two of the influential theses contained in *Naming and Necessity* are the **necessity of origin thesis**, and the claim that there is a category of truths that are metaphysically necessary but knowable only *a posteriori* (see **necessary *a posteriori* truths**).

Further reading: Ahmed (2007)

LAW OF NATURE

A law of nature is a general fact that does not merely happen to be true. That $e = mc^2$ (assuming it is true) is not a mere 'accidental regularity': it does not just happen to be the case that the energy of any object is equal to its mass times the speed of light squared. By contrast, the fact that all lumps of solid gold are smaller than ten metres in diameter *is* an accidental regularity: if someone were rich enough and odd enough, they could amass that much gold and fashion it into a giant sphere. See **causation and laws**, **Ramsey–Lewis view of laws**, and **Dretske-Tooley-Armstrong view of laws**. Laws of nature also crop up in the **Consequence Argument** for **incompatibilism**.

LEIBNIZ'S LAW

Leibniz had two famous principles: the *indiscernability of identicals* (if x and y are identical, then everything that is true of x is true of y – they are indiscernible); and the *identity of indiscernibles* (if everything that is true of x is true of y and *vice versa* – if x and y are indiscernible – then x is identical to y).

The former is usually taken to be uncontroversially true: if Barack Obama is 1.87 m tall, and Obama is identical to the President of the United States, then *of course* the President has to be 1.87 m tall. Similarly for every other attribute of Obama and the President: *of course* the properties have to be the same, for being identical means there is just one person, and someone cannot have some properties while simultaneously *not* having those properties. Hence, few people dissent from the truth of the indiscernability of identicals. The latter, on the other hand, is much less popular, for it seems *prima facie* possible that there could be two indistinguishable objects that are nonetheless distinct (see Forrest 2009 for more discussion). For instance, there could be a universe with nothing but two electrons: they would (allegedly) be qualitatively alike in every way, but would not be identical.

It is a grave misfortune that some philosophers use the term 'Leibniz's Law' to apply to one of those principles, whereas other philosophers use the term to apply to the other. Usually, however, they will be explicit as to which principle they mean, so if you pay close attention you won't get caught out. If in doubt, then if the philosopher in question is taking their 'Leibniz's Law' to be obviously true, they probably mean the indiscernability of identicals. If they take their 'Leibniz's Law' to be doubtful, or requiring some argument, they probably mean the identity of indiscernibles.

Further reading: Forrest (2009)

LEWIS, DAVID

Born in 1941, in Oberlin, Ohio, David Kellogg Lewis became one of the most influential analytic philosophers of the twentieth century. He initially studied chemistry, but while visiting Oxford he attended lectures by Gilbert Ryle on the philosophy of mind. Upon his return to America, he immediately switched to studying philosophy. After completing his degree, he went to Harvard and took his PhD under the supervision of **W. V. Quine**. Although he spent most of his academic career lecturing at Princeton, he often visited Australia for extended spells. Indeed, he held great affection for Australia, including its football and bush songs (which he was often found singing at conferences).

Lewis wrote widely on numerous areas of analytic philosophy; an exhaustive list of the topics he contributed to would be too extensive to list here. Within metaphysics he is most famous for his work on **possible worlds** and his own brand of **modal realism**, but he also invented the **counterfactual theory of causation** and was partially responsible for the **Ramsey–Lewis view of laws**. He also made important contributions to debates over **perdurantism, time travel, compatibilism**, the existence of **universals, nominalism, truthmakers**, the philosophy of **classes** and **personal identity**. In covering so many areas of philosophy, as well as taking every opportunity to help and encourage his fellow philosophers, Lewis was massively influential. He continued to write until his death in 2001.

Lewis's work in metaphysics was, in the main, driven towards demonstrating that a particular thesis, which he dubbed **Humean Supervenience**, is true (or, at least, is tenable). Thus he provided theories of causation, laws of nature, mental states, and so on, which were (or so he hoped) compatible with Humean Supervenience.

Further reading: Hall (2010); Nolan (2005)

LIBERTARIANISM

Libertarianism, in the context of discussions of **free will** (not to be confused with the position in political philosophy also known as 'libertarianism'), is the view that (a) agents actually act freely, at least sometimes, but (b) acting freely requires **indeterminism** to be true: we can only act freely if our acts are not determined to happen by facts about the past plus the **laws of nature**. Given (b), libertarianism is an **incompatibilist** position.

Motivations for the incompatibilist component of libertarianism (i.e. (b) above) come from two main sources: the **Consequence Argument** and the 'causal chain argument' (see **incompatibilism**). According to the Consequence Argument, free action requires the ability to do otherwise. Libertarians who are convinced by this argument (sometimes known as 'leeway libertarians' because indeterminism is claimed to provide the 'leeway' required for an agent to have a genuine free choice between more than one possible alternative) thus typically uphold the **Principle of Alternate Possibilities**: in order for an action A to be free, it must be the case that the agent could have done otherwise than A.

According to the causal chain argument, by contrast, **determinism** blocks free will by locating the ultimate source of our actions outside ourselves, because our actions are determined by facts that were in place long before we were born (together with the laws of nature). Correspondingly, libertarians who are convinced by this argument (sometimes known as 'source libertarians' or 'causal history libertarians') tend to think of freedom of a given action as depending not so much on whether the action itself is undetermined by the past plus the laws, but on whether the agent is the ultimate causal source of the action. Source libertarians therefore sometimes take a rather more relaxed attitude towards the Principle of Alternate Possibilities: what is important, in determining whether a given action was freely performed, is whether the ultimate source of that action lies within or outside the agent. As long as the ultimate source lies within the agent, source libertarians are open to the possibility that the action is determined *at the time the agent performs it.*

For example (to use the same example as in the section on the **Principle of Alternate Possibilities**), suppose Sam is the kind of person who never resorts to violence – say, hitting an annoying person in the face of fairly mild provocation. For the source libertarian, what is important for Sam's freely refraining from hitting the person is not whether, at the time of provocation, she could have done otherwise. Rather, what is important is how it is that Sam came to be the kind of person that she is – the kind of person who does not resort to violence. If Sam 'made' herself into that kind of person – if she is the ultimate source of her own character traits – then we can say that she freely refrained from hitting out, even if, now being the kind of person she has made herself be, she could not have done otherwise.

Although source libertarians are sometimes more relaxed than leeway libertarians when it comes to the Principle of Alternate Possibilities, they sometimes also carry an additional commitment, namely a commitment to **agent causation** as a requirement on free action: to the claim that free actions must trace back to a choice or decision that was not only undetermined by facts about the past plus the laws, but was also 'agent-caused': caused directly by the agent herself, and not merely by her beliefs, desires, and so on.

Is there any evidence for libertarianism?

As we saw, libertarians are not just committed to views about what is *required* for acting freely; they are also committed to holding that these requirements are, at least sometimes, actually satisfied. Hence, libertarians (of whatever variety) are committed to the truth of indeterminism. Indeed, they are committed to the stronger claim that the processes *that lead to some of our actions* are indeterministic. Hence, for example, in the above case, the source libertarian who holds that Sam freely refrained from hitting out is committed to holding that at *some* point in the past, Sam made a decision or choice that affected the kind of person she would become, such that that decision or choice was not determined by facts about the past plus the laws of nature. And the leeway libertarian will (typically) be committed to the claim that Sam's decision or choice *not to hit out* was itself not determined by the past plus the laws.

One question to ask the libertarian is how they can claim to know, or at least reasonably believe, that the required indeterminism really does obtain. It is an empirical question whether or not indeterminism is true; and even if we think our best current science gives us good reason to believe that indeterminism really is true, our best science does *not* appear to provide any good reasons to think that the relevant causal processes that lead up to agents' decisions or choices are typically, or ever, indeterministic (see **indeterminism**). Libertarians sometimes suggest that we can just tell by introspection that we have alternative choices or decisions available to us: it *seems* to me, when I am deciding between tea and coffee, that I *could* make either decision, and so I have good reason to think that I really could, in fact, make either decision. (After all, when it seems to you that it is raining, that is normally a very good reason to think that it is, in fact, raining.) However, once we appreciate that what the libertarian means by 'I could make either decision' is 'it is not determined by the past plus the laws which decision I make', it is rather unclear why we should think that the 'phenomenology' of our decision-making – how it seems to us when we are deliberating about what to do – is a reliable guide to which possibilities are genuinely left open by the past plus the laws.

That said, if we are convinced that **compatibilism** is false, then libertarianism does look like a rather more attractive option than its main rivals (**hard determinism** and 'illusionism' – see **illusion of free will**). Hence, the libertarian might claim that even if we do not have any concrete empirical evidence that some of our decisions are undetermined, at least her view has intuitive plausibility, in that it has the consequence that agents do at least sometimes act freely.

Further reading: Clarke (2008)

LINGUISTIC FRAMEWORK

See **metametaphysics**.

LINGUISTIC TURN

'The linguistic turn' refers to a general tendency in the mid-twentieth century of philosophers to turn their attention away from thinking about the nature of reality (often on **empiricist grounds**) and onto thinking about the nature and purpose of our language (see **metametaphysics**).

LOCKE, JOHN

John Locke (1632–1704) was the first of the three great British Empiricists (followed by **George Berkeley** and **David Hume**). As far as metaphysics is concerned, Locke's (1690) important work is *An Essay concerning Human Understanding*, the primary aim of which is to uncover the sources and extent of human knowledge. Despite this epistemological aim, the book is also a rich source of metaphysical theses and arguments, and Locke's work has been very influential in shaping debates concerning **personal identity**, **essence**, **primary** and **secondary qualities** and **universals**.

Locke's influence, however, is not restricted to metaphysics and epistemology. Locke was a friend and correspondent of both Newton (1642–1727) and his fellow scientist Boyle (1627–91). All three were early members of the Royal Society, and Locke played a part in the spread of what we now know as science (then called 'natural philosophy' or '**experimental philosophy**'), which itself was such a major part of the Enlightenment.

Locke's (also 1690) work in political philosophy, especially his *Two Treatises of Government*, has also been hugely influential. In particular, parts of the US Declaration of Independence of 1776 are closely modelled on Locke's ideas, and Thomas Jefferson, its principal author, describe Locke as 'one of the three greatest men who have ever lived' (the other two being Newton and Francis Bacon).

Further reading: Locke's major philosophical works are all freely available online from various sources. A 'translation' into contemporary English of Locke's *Essay* can be found on Jonathan Bennett's Early Modern Texts website (www.earlymoderntexts.com/f_locke.html)

LOGICAL TRUTH

See **conceptual vs logical truths**.

MCTAGGART, J. M. E.

John McTaggart Ellis McTaggart (1866–1925) was given his forenames after his great-uncle (John McTaggart). As part of receiving his great-uncle's inheritance, it was further stipulated he should take his surname as well – hence the two 'McTaggart's' that appear in his name. He spent most of his life as a lecturer at Trinity College, Cambridge. McTaggart was famous for putting on breakfasts (although no food was provided at them) to which he would invite people to discuss philosophy. Attenders included both G. E. Moore and Bertrand Russell (notably, though, things soured somewhat when McTaggart later played a role in having Russell dismissed from Trinity College for his anti-war activities).

McTaggart was an idealist (though in fact more of a phenomenalist given the way we have defined these terms – see **phenomenalism and idealism**) and was heavily influenced by Hegel. Although he was a committed atheist, he believed that all that really existed were immortal, reincarnating souls bound to one another by love. His philosophical output was aimed at proving this mystical thesis to be the case. His most famous philosophical position was that time does not exist, and it is his argument for this that (see **unreality of time**) has most influenced analytic philosophy. For instance, it was responses to that argument which were the main cause for the contemporary debate over **tensed and tenseless theories of time**.

Further reading: Geach (1979)

MEINONGIANISM

Meinongians believe that there are some things that do not exist (indeed, that some things do not **subsist** either) (see **non-existent objects**).

MEMORY THEORY

The memory theory of personal identity, rooted in the work of **John Locke**, attempts to account for **personal identity** in terms of facts about memory. The rough idea is that a certain person x at an earlier time is identical to a certain person y at a later time if and only if y remembers the experiences of x (see **psychological continuity** for more information on this view).

MEREOLOGICAL FUSION

See **fusion, mereological**.

MEREOLOGY

Mereology is the study of parts and wholes (from 'mereos', which is Greek for 'part'). It became a formalised field of study during the early twentieth century after the efforts of the Polish logician Stanisław Leśniewski, and was brought to the attention of non-Polish audiences by Henry S. Leonard and Nelson Goodman during the 1940s.

There are various different mereological systems, which differ over exactly what the features of parthood are. For instance, there is a division over the logical properties of the parthood relation: the vast majority of metaphysicians think it is **transitive** – others demur. There is a division over whether everything has **proper parts** (and therefore everything is made of **gunk**) or whether some things have no proper parts (and are so **simple**). There is a division concerning the circumstances under which objects come to compose a further object; for instance, whether or not some atoms arranged in the formation of a table compose a table (which we would naturally think is the case) and whether or not several atoms scattered haphazardly across the galaxy compose a bizarre, scattered object (which we would naturally think is not the case; see **Special Composition Question** for more). And there is a dispute over whether or not if two objects have exactly the same parts they are identical.

Classical mereology

Classical mereology (confusingly sometimes just called 'mereology') is the system of axioms and theorems that have traditionally been endorsed; notable supporters include **David Armstrong, David Lewis** and **W. V. Quine**). Classical mereologists say that parthood is a **transitive**, nonsymmetric (*x* can be a part of *y* without *y* being a part of *x*) and reflexive (everything is a part of itself) relation. Note that although parthood is nonsymmetric and reflexive, *proper* parthood is such that it is transitive, *asymmetric* and *irreflexive* (see **part** for more information). Also, according to classical mereology everything *always* composes a further object (this is called **universalism**), and if two things have the same parts, they are identical (a principle sometimes called 'mereological extensionality' or 'uniqueness').

Classical mereology was once widely accepted but has come under a lot of recent scrutiny – particularly when it comes to the latter two claims. There are, then, other alternatives on offer, disagreeing over the conditions under which parthood holds, its relation to the identity relation, and so on.

Nomenclature

Usually, mereological relations are represented using the following notation:

$x < y =_{df} x$ is a **part** of y

$x \ll y =_{df} x$ is a **proper part** of y

$x \leq y =_{df} x$ is an **improper part** of y

$x \circ y =_{df} x$ overlaps y (i.e. x and y have a part in common, for instance in the case of terraced houses they might have a wall in common – hence they would overlap).

$x \int y =_{df} x$ is disjoint from y (i.e. x and y do not have any parts in common, for instance as I am not a conjoined twin I do not have any parts in common with anyone else, so am disjoint from every other person).

Further reading: Varzi (2009)

METAMETAPHYSICS

Metametaphysics is philosophical enquiry into the nature of metaphysics. When we are doing metametaphysics, we ask questions like: what is metaphysics? How, if at all, is metaphysics possible? What is its method? What are the limits of metaphysical enquiry?

Often metametaphysical debates are debates between those philosophers we might call 'metaphiles', who hold a traditional conception of metaphysics as an *a priori* enquiry capable of yielding substantive truths about the nature of mind-independent reality, and those we could call 'metaphobes', who have a less grand conception of the discipline or are positively hostile to it. Metaphobia comes in a variety of strengths: there is the view that metaphysical questions are meaningless, the view that metaphysical questions are meaningful but unanswerable, or the view that metaphysical questions are meaningful and answerable but concern only the nature of our experience or **conceptual scheme** rather than the nature of mind-independent reality.

We find in **David Hume** an early form of metaphobia. Hume distinguishes between 'relations of ideas', knowable *a priori*, and 'matters of fact', knowable through experience. Any alleged knowledge that does not fall into either category is 'sophistry and illusion' and should be consigned to the flames of (as it is sometimes called) Hume's bonfire. In effect, Hume was dismissing much of traditional metaphysics. **Immanuel Kant**, very much influenced by Hume's thought, wrestled with the following challenge to metaphysics: how is it possible for there to be *synthetic a priori truths*? (Roughly, analytic truths are those which are solely true in virtue of what the individual words mean, for example, 'all bachelors are unmarried men'; synthetic truths are those which are not analytic; see **analytic vs synthetic truths**.) Kant's answer to this challenge is that metaphysics is enquiry into the *necessary structure of experience*, rather than the nature of reality as it is in and of itself. Although Kant had a much more positive view of metaphysics than Hume, his view might still be classed as a form of metaphobia in that he denies that metaphysical enquiry yields truths about the nature of mind-independent reality. (There is thus a connection of sorts between metaphilia and global realism, in that metaphiles take metaphysics to aim at a true description of mind-independent reality; see **realism and anti-realism (global)**.)

For a large part of the twentieth century, from the 1930s to the 1970s, analytic philosophy was dominated by metaphobia. It is likely that this was partly caused by unfavourable comparisons between science and metaphysics. Although empirical science over the past few hundred years had continued to develop an impressive body of knowledge, metaphysics, in its 3,000 years history, had failed to achieve consensus on anything. The logical positivists of the first half of the twentieth century – influenced by Hume – dismissed metaphysical statements as unverifiable (a statement is unverifiable if sensory experience cannot settle whether it is true or false) and hence meaningless. A more nuanced rejection of metaphysics is to be found in Ludwig Wittgenstein (1889–1951), who tried to show that the urge to ask metaphysical questions was grounded in confusion about the nature of language.

Not all analytic philosophers in this period were as extreme as Wittgenstein and the positivists in rejecting metaphysics as nonsense, but most followed what has become known as the '**linguistic turn**', the trend in philosophy for thinking that philosophical puzzles were to be solved by linguistic analysis. For example, we find Strawson (1959) advocating 'descriptive metaphysics' – the attempt to map general features of our conceptual scheme – as opposed to 'revisionary metaphysics', the attempt to alter our conceptual scheme to make it fit better with the nature of reality. However, from the 1970s onwards, there began a gradual re-emergence of traditional metaphysics, with the result that metaphysics is now once again, rightly or wrongly, an active and valued area of philosophy.

The great comeback of traditional metaphysics may in part be due to the work of **W. V. Quine** a couple of decades earlier (although ironically Quine's own austere, naturalistic approach to metaphysics is a far cry from the high-flown metaphysics found in some philosophy departments these days). Quine's contribution to metametaphysics is perhaps best seen as a reaction to the particular brand of metaphobia advocated by the German logical positivist Rudolph Carnap. Carnap distinguished between 'internal questions' and 'external questions' concerning a linguistic framework (roughly a 'framework' is a class of terms together with rules governing their use, e.g., the framework of numbers or the framework of physical objects). Internal questions are those which arise from within a framework, such that the method for answering them is determined by the rules of the framework. Carnap thought of the work of mathematicians and scientists, the employment of straightforward empirical or mathematical methods, as the answering of internal questions. External questions in contrast are questions posed from outside any framework at all. Carnap sees external questions either as completely meaningless or as purely pragmatic questions about which framework it is most useful to adopt. Metaphysical questions, for Carnap, are non-pragmatic external questions and hence are meaningless. (Carnap thus arguably counts as a global anti-realist by our lights; see **realism and anti-realism (global)**.)

Hence, for example, the answer to the question, 'do **numbers** exist?' *qua* internal question is a clear 'yes': from within the framework of mathematics (and also physics), it is straightforwardly true that there are numbers (and indeed other more abstruse mathematical entities) – it follow from, for example, the fact that there are infinitely many prime numbers, which any maths student should be able to prove. *Qua* external question, either the answer is 'yes' again (if conceived as a pragmatic question about whether the framework of mathematics and physics is a useful one to adopt) or else the question is meaningless. Thus, there simply is no distinctively metaphysical question to be answered about the nature and existence of numbers.

Quine's most influential response to Carnap, and to logical positivism as a whole, was his famous rejection of the distinction between analytic truths and synthetic truths. If there is no clear distinction between the analytic and synthetic, then there is no clear distinction between mathematics and logic on the one hand (which the logical positivists took to analytic) and metaphysics on the other (which the logical positivists, like Kant, categorised as synthetic – or rather metaphysical truths *would* be synthetic if there were any, which, *contra* Kant, there are not). If there is no clear distinction between maths/logic and metaphysics, then there is no way of embracing the former while rejecting the latter.

Also, in his manifesto 'On what there is', Quine (1948) laid out a rigorous metametaphysical theory, which became the dominant way of approaching metaphysics thereafter. For Quine, the job of the metaphysician is to tell us what things exist. She does this by taking our best, scientifically informed, theory of reality and translating it into quantificational logic. The things that exist according to this theory are the things that the quantifiers of this formalised theory range over. This is Quine's criterion of **ontological commitment**: belief in the theory *ontological commits* us to the existence of those things the formalised theory quantifiers over. Hence, for example, on Quine's view, numbers exist, because mathematics 'quantifies over' numbers (e.g. 'there are prime numbers greater than 57'). **Properties,** on the other hand, do not, because (according to Quine) nothing in our best scientifically-informed theory of the world requires us to quantify over properties (see **nominalism** and **austere nominalism** for more on these issues).

Carnap, as we have seen, held that asking questions that precede the adoption of a framework (unless they are purely pragmatic questions about which framework it is useful to adopt) are meaningless. Quine supposed that the question, 'what things exist?', or, 'what things do our completely unrestricted quantifiers range over?' can be asked without adopting any framework. In this way, he offers the hope that the findings of metaphysics can be 'objective', in the sense of not being relativised to some framework or other. (If you want something a bit more difficult, there is an interesting contemporary debate on whether Quine was right about this. The 'neo-Carnapian' Eli Hirsch defends 'quantifier variance', the view that there are a number of equally good meanings of the logical quantifiers; choosing one of these frameworks is to be understood analogously to choosing a Carnapian framework. Theodore Sider opposes this by defending the 'neo-Quinean' view that only one of these meanings 'carves nature at the logical joints'. See **carving nature at its joints** for brief discussion on this and references to their work – Sider and Hirsch also have papers on this subject in Chalmers *et al.* (2009)).

The comeback of metaphysics against twentieth-century metaphobia is impressive, but the discipline has not returned unchanged. For one thing, many metaphysicians do not think of metaphysics as a purely *a priori* investigation into the nature of reality: **conceptual analysis** plays a much larger role than it did prior to the 'linguistic turn', and consistency with our best scientific theories is generally seen as a constraint on a good metaphysical theory. Relatedly, contemporary metaphysicians tend to show a greater humility than metaphysicians of old with respect to what it is possible for metaphysics to achieve. René Descartes (1596–1650) and Kant hoped that one day their metaphysical systems would be universally adopted; contemporary metaphysicians tend not to view the achieving of such consensus as a realistic aim. It is usually accepted that there are few knock down arguments for or against a given metaphysical view, with which such consensus could be achieved. Rather, arguing for a metaphysical view tends to take the forms of building a case, appealing to the relative advantages of the view across a wide range of criteria, such as economy, explanatory power, fit with other metaphysical views and with **common sense** (see **theoretical virtues**). To use an analogy of **David Lewis** – perhaps the most influential metaphysician of modern times – the metaphysician sets up her stall as best she can, but has no way of guaranteeing that other metaphysicians will be interesting in buying her wares.

Further reading: Chalmers *et al.* (2009); Quine (1948, 1951)

METAPHYSICAL REALISM

The position, implicitly endorsed by many metaphysicians, that most things in the world (definitely sheep, potatoes and stars, but perhaps not colours or smells or moral values) exist independently of our minds, beliefs, language or experience (see **realism and anti-realism (global)**).

MODALITY

Modality is the field of metaphysics concerned with the nature of possibility and its many facets. For instance, take **propositions** (or sentences). Not only do they have a truth value (true or false), they also have a *modal* status. They might be true *necessarily* (so they *must* be true, e.g. mathematical statements like '2 + 2 = 4'); or true *contingently* (so they are true but *might have been* false, for example, 'Barack Obama is President of the United States' is actually true but *might have been* false, e.g. if he had lost the 2008 election); or *possibly* true ('John McCain is President of the United States' is false but *might have been* true – he might have won the election; 'Obama is President of the United States' is also, trivially, possibly true because it is *actually* true); or *impossible* (*could not* have been true, e.g. '2 + 2 = 6'). Modal status as it applies to propositions is called *de dicto* modality. It is often represented in 'boxes' and 'diamonds', so that 'necessarily, *P*' is represented as $\Box P$, and 'possibly, *P*' as $\Diamond P$.

There is also *de re* modality (or arguably so; **W. V. Quine** famously argued that the notion of *de re* modality is incoherent) – the issues here concern whether or not predicates apply to their subjects accidentally or essentially (see **essence**). Hence, we might say I am *essentially* human (if we thought I could not possibly have been anything other than a human). Conversely, it seems natural to say that my being a philosopher is only an *accidental* feature of me (for instead of going to university and becoming a philosopher I might have instead decided to become a professional fisherman). These issues of *de re* and *de dicto* modality are not the only modal matters, however. For instance, the topic of modality also concerns itself with **counterfactual conditionals** – statements concerning what *would* or *might* be the case, if something else were the case ('if I fell off the Empire State Building I would die' or 'if I had not gone to university, I might have become a fisherman').

It is commonplace nowadays, though not universally accepted, to use **possible worlds** to help investigate such modal concepts (this, in turn, raises questions about whether such 'possible worlds' exist – see **modal realism**).

MODAL REALISM

A modal realist believes that **possible worlds** exist, and that possible world talk is literally true, not just some useful way of speaking. Possible world talk is deployed pervasively in metaphysics these days, primarily (but not exclusively) as a way of understanding **modality**. For example, to say that something is *necessarily* true is to say (according to 'possible worlds semantics') that it is true in all possible worlds, and to say that something is *possibly* true is to say that it is true in *at least one* possible world (see **possible worlds** for more on this).

Not surprisingly, if we endorse a given modal claim (that it is possibly true that cats are an extinct species) and buy into possible worlds semantics, it looks like we also ought to endorse the corresponding claim about possible worlds (e.g. that 'cats are an extinct species' is true in at least one possible world), and so it looks like we are **ontologically committed** to the existence of possible worlds – which would make us modal realists. (Plenty of philosophers engage happily in possible-world talk without being card-carrying modal realists, however; see **possible worlds** for other options.)

Although modal realists agree that possible worlds *exist*, they disagree concerning what they *are*. There are two main schools of thought: genuine modal realism and *ersatz* modal realism.

Genuine modal realism (GMR)

Sometimes called '**concrete** modal realism' and sometimes (just to be terminologically annoying) simply 'modal realism', GMR maintains that possible worlds are just like the actual world, but are not spatiotemporally connected to our actual world. Hence, possible worlds exist and, just like our world, are universes containing physical, concrete objects. For example, it is possible that everyone in the world spontaneously decides to don clown outfits and sing Ricky Martin's *Livin' la Vida Loca*. Strange as it would be, it *could* happen. Hence, in possible world talk, there is a possible world at which this all takes place. Given GMR, that means that there exists a universe containing people just like you and me, who all apply face paint and start singing Latin pop. That world is, like ours, made up of physical objects but – according to GMR – is not spatiotemporally connected to our universe. Similarly for *every* possibility, no matter how strange or weird.

That there is an infinite number of such disconnected universes where every possibility plays out, and that we can discover this merely by doing metaphysics, is initially repugnant to most people. Nonetheless, GMR has proved to be an important theory in metaphysics. Its main advocate is **David Lewis**, who argues that odd as the theory may sound, it is superior to the alternative treatments of possible worlds.

The first alleged benefit is that, given GMR, we can reduce modal facts down to facts about what things exist (see the entry on **reductionism** for more on reducing facts). For instance, the fact that we all *could* be clowns singing Ricky Martin songs is true because there exists a world at which people a lot like us *are* clowns singing Ricky Martin songs. That latter fact, that there is a universe containing singing clowns, is not a modal fact. Hence, the modal fact is true in virtue of a non-modal fact, and we have reduced the modal facts down to the non-modal. (This is particularly important for Lewis and other **Humeans**, who want to uphold the thesis of **Humean supervenience** and, in particular, the thesis that there is no **natural necessity** in the world.)

More alleged benefits of including concrete possible worlds include getting a parsimonious **ontology**. **Propositions**, for instance, need not be extra entities in addition to the worlds and their contents. Lewis believes that, given GMR, we can identify propositions with the set of worlds where certain things are true. Hence, the proposition <John Lennon was assassinated> is identified with the **set** of all worlds in which John Lennon existed and went on to be assassinated. **Properties** get a similar treatment, as GMR allows a workable theory of **class nominalism**, where we identify properties with the set of everything that has that property. Hence, the property *redness* is identified with the set of every red thing from every possible world.

The GMRist will also tend to play down the alleged weirdness of her theory. For instance, although the GMRist must admit that Santa Claus exists (because there are possible worlds at which he exists), it is not as if they have to say that Santa Claus *actually* exists. He does not *actually* exist at all – for what actually exists, says Lewis, is what exists as part of the actual world (i.e. the world we are in). 'Actuality', then, is an **indexical** term. Hence, even though we have to say Santa exists (which sounds weird) we still get to affirm that he does not *actually* exist (and Lewis thinks that is good enough to meet the demands of your intuitions). In addition, Lewis rejects the complaint that there is something repugnant about GMR as not really an objection at all. He calls it the 'incredulous stare': not an objection as such – more of a funny look. So, the argument goes, on balance of the costs and benefits, we should endorse GMR.

Ersatz modal realism

The alternative position is ersatz modal realism. Where GMR says that possible worlds represent what is possible by *being* that way (so a concrete world represents the possibility that everyone sings *Livin' la Vida Loca* by being such that everyone sings it) ersatz modal realism says that, worlds exist but that they represent possibilities without being the way that the possibilities say they are. Here is an analogy: a picture might *represent* two people arguing even though the picture is just a sheet of canvas – it is not *itself* two people arguing. Similarly, a 'world' may represent *that everyone sings*, even though the world itself is just an **abstract** entity of some sort.

Exactly which entities do the representing (and *how* they do it) is a matter for dispute. **Universals**, sets (or **classes**) of propositions, sets of sentences and sets of **states of affairs** are just some of the things that have been proposed as being candidates for such ersatz possible worlds. Hence, although in each case the ersatzer denies GMR, and all ersatzers are agreed that possible worlds *are not* concrete spacetimes, there is a lot of dispute concerning exactly what ersatz worlds should be identified with.

Let us take sets of propositions as an example identification. It is *possible* that everyone is dressed like a clown and singing *Livin' la Vida Loca*. Hence, we need a possible world that represents that possibility, and the suggestion is that that possible world is a set of propositions. How would that go? Well, the set would include propositions that are true at the actual world, such as <the Earth exists> and <the United States is a representative democracry> but also propositions that are false at the actual world, such as

<Barack Obama is dressed like a clown and singing *Livin' la Vida Loca*>, <Mel Gibson is dressed like a clown and singing *Livin' la Vida Loca*>, and so on, for everyone who actually exists. What is true at that possible world is just whatever propositions are members of that set. Because propositions are abstract, sets of them will be abstract too. Hence, clearly, possible worlds would not be concrete entities as they are in GMR.

However, there are downsides. This theory cannot reduce modal facts to non-modal facts like GMR, as some sets of propositions have to be disqualified from counting as possible worlds. For instance, only sets which are *consistent* (i.e. all the propositions could be true at the same time) can be possible world. Inconsistent sets of propositions cannot be possible worlds for obvious reasons: if a set of propositions included inconsistent propositions (such as <Obama is President of the United States in 2010> and <Obama is not President of the United States in 2010>) then, if that set counted as a possible world, it would be *possible* for Obama to both be, and not be, President of the United States at the same time. However, clearly that is impossible. Hence, only consistent sets of propositions can be possible worlds. But consistency is a *modal* notion (because two propositions are consistent if and only if they *could* both be true at the same time), so, if we accept ersatzism, we would not be able to reduce modal facts to non-modal facts about possible worlds, as we need a modal notion to figure out what the possible worlds are in the first place.

Further benefits of GMR are denied to the ersatzist. Clearly, if possible worlds are sets of propositions, we cannot reduce propositions to sets of possible worlds (as GMR can) without that reduction being circular. It also looks difficult to make the identification of **properties** that GMR permits. Although ersatzists have an ontology containing possible worlds, they *do not* have the *contents* of those worlds – what are called '*possibilia*'. For example, according to GMR there are possible talking donkeys – they are real, flesh-and-blood inhabitants of other possible worlds. Although the ersatzist can agree with the GMRist that <there are talking donkeys> is possible, on the ersatzist account this amounts merely to there being at least one consistent set of propositions that includes the proposition <there are talking donkeys>. Possible worlds, on the ersatzist account, do not really have 'inhabitants' at all – there are no *possibilia* and in particular no talking donkeys. (To put it another way: a possible talking donkey would surely have to be a concrete object. However, (for the ersatzist) a set of propositions is an abstract object, as are all of its members.)

Why does this matter? Well, we might – as Lewis does – combine GMR with **class nominalism**, and so identify the property *redness* with the red *things* from all the possible worlds, that is, all the red *possibilia*. Lacking such *possibilia*, the ersatzist cannot do the same. Indeed, *possibilia* crop up nearly as often as possible worlds in metaphysics (often under the thinly-veiled disguise of being 'inhabitants' of other possible worlds), so to have the latter without the former seems a bit odd (see Melia 2003 for more information).

The GMRist position is that no matter what ersatzist theory we invent, be it identifying worlds with sets of propositions or universals or states of affairs or whatever, similar problems emerge. Ersatzists, on the other hand, either argue that they were never seeking such benefits – or that the alleged benefits are not benefits at all (although the question then arises of what benefits they think they *do* get from being modal realists) – or they try and offer a more complicated ersatzism that *can* get the benefits that GMR offers. In either case, the ersatzist takes it that the main plus point of their theory is that we are getting an ontology of possible worlds *without* endorsing GMR, and hence without taking possible worlds to be concrete entities.

Further reading: Divers (2009); Melia (2003, Chapters 5–7)

MOOREAN FACTS

When Bob the Philosopher says that a certain proposition *p* expresses a 'Moorean fact', he means that (i) *p* is a proposition of **common sense**, and (ii) our pre-philosophical justification for believing *p* is so great that we should not take seriously any philosophical argument to the conclusion that *p* is false. The phrase is named after G. E. Moore, who argued against **scepticism** about the external world (the philosophical view that we have no reason to believe that there is an external world) by raising his hands and declaring, 'Here is one hand . . . and here is another'. In effect, Moore was arguing that the pre-philosophical certainty we have that, say, we have hands and therefore that an external world exists (your hands, if they exist, are part of the external world; therefore if your hands exist so does the external world), is so great that we should have no time for any philosophical argument to the contrary, even if we cannot see what is wrong with the argument. As **David Armstrong** (1980: 441) puts it, to account for the Moorean facts is to answer the 'compulsory questions in the philosophical examination paper'.

Among the propositions most commonly claimed to express Moorean facts are that there is an external world, and that other human beings have minds. Armstrong (1980) frames debates between **nominalists** and realists about **universals** as opposing attempts to account for the Moorean 'fact of sameness of type'.

Further reading: Moore (1925, 1939)

MORAL RESPONSIBILITY

In metaphysics, moral responsibility is important in the context of the **free will** debate. Performing an action freely is generally taken to be necessary for moral responsibility: someone who does not act freely is not morally responsible for what they do. Those philosophers who subscribe to **incompatibilism** hold that acting freely, and so morally responsibly, is incompatible with **determinism**, whereas the **compatibilists** hold that there is no tension between freedom and moral responsibility on the one hand, and determinism on the other.

However, what *is* moral responsibility? Different answers to this question can affect how we think about the issue of the compatibility of moral responsibility and determinism. One dimension of disagreement concerns whether the concept of moral responsibility is, as one might put it, a 'metaphysically shallow' or a 'metaphysically deep' notion. According to a deep conception, in order to be truly accountable for one's actions, one must, in a metaphysically distinctive sense, be the originating cause of it (see **agent causation**) or perhaps one must be able to do otherwise in the incompatibilist sense (see **incompatibilism** and **libertarianism**). On the other hand, one might think of moral responsibility in metaphysically shallow terms. For example, one might think that the purpose of the notion of moral responsibility is something like social cohesion: the point of praising and blaming people (i.e. holding them morally responsible) is in a sense similar to the point of rewarding and punishing a dog: it is a tool for modifying behaviour to make living with each other easier. Such a view is metaphysically shallow because it appears to place few metaphysical constraints on moral responsibility. In particular, the truth of determinism would not in the least undermine the claim that the practices of praise and blame are conducive to social harmony.

One concept of moral responsibility or two?

Are these two kinds of account of responsibility in competition to be *the* concept of moral responsibility? Traditionally, compatibilists have tended to argue that 'moral responsibility' is a metaphysically shallow notion and incompatibilists have argued that it is a deep notion. However, recently some philosophers have argued that there are simply two distinct concepts of moral responsibility in play, so that if determinism is true we are morally responsible in the shallow sense, but if libertarianism is true (and perhaps if we are agent causes of our actions) we are morally responsible in the deep sense.

Some philosophers hold that the ordinary notion of moral responsibility is incompatibilist, but that this notion is simply confused and we would be much better off adopting a shallow, compatibilist concept of responsibility (see Smart 1961: 303–6). There has also been interesting work done recently in **experimental philosophy** that aims to test whether the ordinary notion of moral responsibility is in fact compatibilist or incompatibilist (see for example Nichols and Knobe 2007).

Moral responsibility and reactive attitudes

A somewhat different approach to moral responsibility is famously taken by Strawson (1962). On Strawson's view, we should not ask what conditions an agent must satisfy in order for what he calls our 'reactive' attitudes – such as gratitude and resentment – to be justified. The legitimacy of those attitudes cannot seriously be called into question (as they are by, for example, **hard determinists**), Strawson thinks, because even if we were capable of abandoning those attitudes (which, he thinks, we are not), doing so would result in catastrophe; indeed, the very possibility of interpersonal relationships would be ruled out (see **hard determinism** for more on this). Strawson thus rejects both the deep and the shallow approaches described above: the reactive attitudes are, in an important sense, constitutive of who we are and cannot be shown to be unjustified (as is threatened by the deep conception of moral responsibility) nor are they merely practical devices for promoting social cohesion.

Further reading: Fischer (1999); Eschleman (2009)

MOVING SPOTLIGHT THEORY OF TIME

The moving spotlight theory of time comprises two parts: **eternalism** and the tensed theory of time (see **tensed and tenseless theories of time**). Hence, every time exists but the present moment is still metaphysically privileged. It is, like the name says, as if the different times are houses down a street and the present moment is a moving spotlight that is shined upon them one by one. The moving spotlight theory appears to be what **J. M. E. McTaggart** had in mind when he attacked the existence of time.

MULTIPLE OCCUPANCY THESIS

This is a thesis in the **personal identity** debate that aims to solve the problem of 'fission': one person 'becoming' two people, for example, by having their brain hemispheres separated and rehoused in two separate bodies that have previously had their brains removed. According to the Multiple Occupancy Thesis, there were two people housed in the original body all along (see **fission**).

NATURAL KINDS

A natural kind is a grouping of objects that **carves nature at its joints**. Hence, for example, there is a class of things that are all ravens-or-writing-desks but it does not constitute a natural kind, whereas the class of electrons or the class of samples of water or (perhaps) the class of tigers *does* constitute a natural kind.

How to account for this difference between non-natural and natural kinds is (of course) a matter for much dispute. Some philosophers, such as Ellis (2001), have a fundamental **ontological commitment** to natural kinds: there are natural-kind **universals** (*being an electron, being water* and so on), whereas there is no universal *being a raven-or-a-writing-desk*. Others (in fact, this class of philosophers overlaps with the first class) take the natural kinds to be just those kinds that are susceptible to **necessary *a posteriori*** 'theoretical identifications', such as 'water = H_2O' and 'gold is the element with atomic number 79', where what comes after the identity sign ('the element with atomic number 79', etc.) is the **essence** of the kind (where 'essence' is supposed to mean something more than just the criteria by which something gets to be a member of the kind in question).

Others are much more relaxed about natural kinds. Dupré (1993), for example, argues for a 'pluralist' position, according to which the natural kinds are just whatever categories best serve the purposes of explaining and predicting natural phenomena. What makes this kind of view pluralist is the thought that there is no one correct, mind-independent way to carve nature. For example, take psychological categories, such as *belief, desire, decision,* and so on. From the point of view of physics (and assuming physicalism), these are not 'natural' categories; they do not map onto divisions in nature that physicists are at all interested in. However, they are, nonetheless, hugely useful categories; indeed, they are central to our ability to predict and explain human behaviour. On a pluralist view, this is (arguably) sufficient for them to count as natural kinds, notwithstanding the fact that, from the point of view of physics, they look like utterly arbitrary and disunified categories. (By contrast, it is unlikely that the category *raven-or-writing-desk* will ever come to have any explanatory or predictive utility, so we can all safely agree that it is not a natural kind.)

Further reading: Bird and Tobin (2008)

NATURAL LAW

Another way of saying 'law of nature'.

NATURAL NECESSITY

'Natural necessity' is sometimes used to denote any kind of 'intra-world' necessity. According to **David Lewis**, and indeed all Humeans (**see Humean supervenience**), all necessity is 'inter-world': all claims about necessity (and possibility) are to be analysed as claims about what is true in all **possible worlds**, so that necessity is not an **intrinsic feature** of any particular possible world (including the actual world) (see **modality**). To assert that there is natural necessity is to deny this claim: to hold that the intrinsic nature of the (actual) world does indeed include facts about necessity.

The three main places where non-Humeans tend to claim that natural necessity is to be found are in fundamental dispositional properties (see **categorical vs dispositional properties**), **causation and laws**. Here, briefly, is why. First, fundamental dispositional properties. If it is a 'rock-bottom', irreducible fact about an object *o* that it is disposed to do *x* in circumstances *C* (e.g. an electron will repel another electron if sufficiently close to it), then an electron with that dispositional property (call it *D*) *must* repel another electron (i.e. it *necessitates* the repulsion) in the relevant circumstances. And this necessitation is guaranteed just by facts about the actual world, namely the fact that the electron has property *D* (along with facts about the background circumstances); so, it is intra-world, rather than inter-world, necessity.

Second, causation. Humeans claim that 'cause' can be analysed in such a way that the truth of '*c* caused *e*' does not depend on any **intrinsic** (and so intra-worldly) tie or bond between c and e. Non-Humeans deny that any such analysis is possible and hold that there *is* such a tie or bond – which is to say, a relation of natural necessity. (It is necessity because causes *make*, or *guarantee that*, their effects happen. Though if **indeterminism** is true, 'necessity' is not really the right word. Maybe 'natural probibilification' or 'tendency' would be better; see also **chance**.)

Third and finally, laws of nature. In fact, 'natural necessity' is sometimes used in a narrower sense to refer explicitly to the relation of 'contingent necessitation' postulated by **David Armstrong** in his account of laws: for Armstrong, it is a law that all Fs are Gs if and only if the **universals** F and G stand in the relation N, where N is the relation of contingent necessitation (see **Dretske-Tooley-Armstrong view of laws**). Again, N is a real, intrinsic relation between F and G – it is a universal and so an inhabitant of the actual world. Again, N is *necessitation* because things *have* to obey the laws. It does not just *happen* to be the case that all Fs are Gs; if something is an F, it *must* be a G, if it is a law that all Fs are Gs.

NATURAL PHILOSOPHY

See **experimental philosophy**.

NATURAL PROPERTY

Some philosophers think that a certain subclass of properties, commonly called the 'natural properties', **carve nature at its joints**.

NECESSARY *A POSTERIORI* TRUTHS

In *Naming and Necessity*, **Saul Kripke** (1980) famously claims that truths such as 'Hesperus is Phosphorus', 'water is H_2O' and 'gold is the element with atomic number 79' are necessarily true and yet knowable only *a posteriori* (i.e. can only be known on the basis of empirical investigation). This is (or was at the time) a radical claim. Traditionally, it had been thought that **necessity** and knowability *a priori* automatically go together: if something is a necessary truth, we can know *a priori* that it is true, and *vice versa*, or, to put it another way, all necessary truths are true in virtue of the meanings of words. Hence, once you understand the meaning of, say, 'all bachelors are unmarried', you will thereby know that this statement is necessarily true, because 'bachelor' just *means* 'unmarried man' (see also **conceptual vs logical truths** and **analytic vs synthetic truths**). Although Kripke does not deny that this is often the case (say with 'all bachelors are unmarried'), he does deny that it holds universally: there are *some* necessary truths such that you can know all there is to know about the meanings of the constituent terms (such as 'Hesperus is Phosphorus') without being able to tell whether or not the claim is true.

The basic idea is that when we give an object a proper name ('Hesperus', 'Plato', 'Cleopatra's Needle'), we automatically designate or refer to the same object across all **possible worlds**, and that this conflicts with traditional, 'descriptivist' theories of the meaning of proper names. On a descriptivist view, the meaning or 'sense' of a proper name is some description that the object referred to uniquely satisfies; hence the meaning of 'Plato' might be 'the teacher of Aristotle', say. Kripke claims, however, that whatever description we attempt to cast as the meaning of a proper name, it is always possible that the object referred to fails to satisfy the description. Hence, 'Plato' would still have referred to Plato – to that particular person – even if Aristotle had never been born or had had a different teacher. Imagine Plato's mum saying, while looking at her new son, 'I'm going to call *you* "Plato"'. That act, just by itself, fixes the reference of the name 'Plato'. Plato's mum *is not* saying, 'I define "Plato" as the name of my first-born son'; if she were, it would be necessarily true that Plato had no older brothers, which obviously it is not.

Names thus *directly* refer to their referents; they do not do so via some description (such as 'the teacher of Aristotle'). Moreover, they refer to or designate *the same object* in every possible world: they are 'rigid designators'.

How does this get us to necessary *a posteriori* truths? Well, consider the truth 'Hesperus is Phosphorus'. 'Hesperus' was the name given by ancient astronomers to a heavenly body visible in the evening sky, and 'Phosphorus' was the name of a heavenly body visible in the morning sky (these heavenly bodies were also known as 'the Evening Star' and 'the Morning Star'). It was then *discovered* that Hesperus and Phosphorus are, in fact, the very same heavenly body, namely the planet Venus. However, what was thereby discovered was a metaphysically necessary truth, because (or so Kripke claims) all **identity** claims are necessary: if it is true that *a* is the very same object as *b*, it could not have been false that *a* = *b*. After all, it does not merely *happen* to be true that Venus is identical with Venus. Of course,

'Venus = Venus' has the form '*a* = *a*', and not '*a* = *b*' (as 'Hesperus is Phosphorus' does). However, given Kripke's view that names are rigid designators, this difference is not a genuine difference in *meaning*: 'Venus', 'Hesperus' and 'Phosphorus' all mean the same thing, in the sense that (a) they all designate the same object and (b) which object a proper name designates exhausts its meaning (it has no additional descriptive meaning or 'sense'). Hence, 'Hesperus is Phosphorus' is necessarily true but not knowable *a priori*: it took scientific investigation to reveal its truth.

Similarly, Kripke claims, we can name a kind of substance or some other **natural kind** of thing (using names such as 'water' or 'gold') even if we do not know its **'essence'** – we do not know what it *is* that makes something water or gold or a horse or whatever, or, to put it another way, we can perfectly successfully use the term 'water' without associating some description – such as 'the stuff that flows in the rivers and lakes' – with the name (analogous to 'the teacher of Aristotle') such that a sample of the kind in question must satisfy that description in order to count as *water*. After all, people quite happily – and successfully – went around talking about water before chemistry came along and discovered that water is, in fact, H_2O. And, Kripke thinks, chemists did not merely discover that water is *in fact* H_2O; they discovered that it is of water's *essence* that it is H_2O.

According to Kripke (and also Hilary Putnam, who hit on roughly the same idea at around the same time), this latter claim about water's essence is established by what has come to be known as a 'Twin Earth' **thought experiment**. Imagine a possible world that is just like the actual world, except that what flows in the rivers and lakes (and is colourless and drinkable) is some substance that does not exist here on Earth: it is not H_2O but XYZ. (This particular example is due to Putnam, although Putnam actually asked us to imagine that Twin Earth is a distant planet and not a different possible world.) Question: is that substance on Twin Earth *water*? According to both Kripke and Putnam, the answer is no: were we to travel to Twin Earth and discover the nature of the stuff flowing in the rivers and lakes there, we would say that we have discovered a new kind of substance and not that we had discovered that water also exists on Twin Earth. The upshot is that 'water is H_2O' is a necessary truth: it is of the **essence** of water that it is composed of H_2O molecules. Nonetheless, it is a truth that cannot be known *a priori*: we cannot discern that water is H_2O without doing some scientific investigation, and in particular we cannot discern it merely by reflecting on the meaning of the word 'water'. In other words, 'water is H_2O' belongs in a category previously thought not to exist: the category of necessary *a posteriori* truths.

One reason why Kripke's thesis is interesting is that it makes vivid the possibility that there are some necessary truths – known as 'metaphysically necessary truths' – that are neither **conceptual truths** nor logical truths. For example, the sentence 'Hesperus is Phosphorus' is not a logical truth (because it has the form '$a = b$' and not '$a = a$'). Nor, on Kripke's view, is it a conceptual truth: the ancient astronomers had the concepts 'Hesperus' and 'Phosphorus' but no amount of reflection on the meanings of those terms could reveal that Hesperus *is* Phosphorus.

Further reading: Ahmed (2007, Chapters 2 and 3)

NECESSITY

Necessity is a *modal* notion: to say that something is necessary is to say something not just about how things *in fact* happen to be, but how they *must* be (see **modality**). Necessity (and its close relative, possibility) often gets cashed out in **terms of possible worlds**, so that to say that P is necessarily true (often represented at $\Box P$, where $\Box$ is the 'necessity operator') is to say that P is true *in all possible worlds*. Metaphysicians also often distinguish between different 'kinds' of necessity, such as epistemic necessity, physical necessity and metaphysical necessity; see **possible worlds** for the standard way to distinguish between them. It is sometimes claimed (by anti-**Humeans**) that at least one kind of necessity, namely **natural necessity**, cannot be cashed out in terms of possible worlds (see also **essence**).

NECESSITY OF ORIGIN THESIS

The '**necessity of origin**' thesis is defended by **Saul Kripke** (1980) in his famous *Naming and Necessity*. The basic idea is that it is an essential feature (see **essence**) of a particular object that it has the 'origin' or source that it actually has. For example, assuming that Stella McCartney is the biological offspring of John and Linda McCartney (i.e. they provided the sperm and egg respectively that eventually resulted in Stella), it is an essential feature of her that Paul and Linda are her biological parents: she *could not* have had different biological parents. To put it in terms of **possible worlds**, no inhabitant of any other possible world, no matter how similar they are to Stella, will *be* Stella if they have different biological parents. For example, there is a possible world w where John Lennon and Yoko Ono produce a daughter, whom they call 'Stella', who looks like the actual

Stella, goes on to design Madonna's wedding dress, and so on, while Paul and Linda remain childless. According to the necessity of origin thesis, *w* is not a possible world where Stella is the daughter of John and Yoko; rather, it is a possible world in which Stella does not exist at all. Similarly, the desk you are currently sitting at *could not have been made* from anything other than what it is actually made of. Assuming the desk is made of pine, it could not have been made from plastic or fibreboard or oak. Indeed, it could not even have been made of pine from a different tree. In other words, it is essential to that desk that it was made from the very hunk of pine that it was in fact made of. (Of course, you could have been sitting at an oak desk. However, the desk you would then have been sitting at would not be the *same* desk as the desk you are *actually* sitting at.)

Even if we grant the intuitive plausibility of these examples, however, the necessity of origin thesis starts to look a bit less plausible when we consider some other intuitions. Take your desk. Imagine that one of its legs breaks and you get that leg replaced by a very similar one. According to the necessity of origin, it looks like the resulting desk is literally a different desk to the one you had before: it is not 'numerically identical with' the original desk (see **identity**), no matter how qualitatively similar it may be to the original desk. For it (taken in its entirety) does not have the same origin as the original desk; most of it does, but the new leg has a different origin. However, ordinarily it seems that we would describe the situation as one in which your desk has a new leg and not one in which the old desk no longer exists. Similarly, we ordinarily take it for granted that you can replace the chain on your bike or your car can get a new engine, and so on – and we don't think that these replacements result in your coming to own a different bike or car. (see also **identity over time**.)

Further reading: Ahmed (2007, § 3.1)

NEGATIVE FACTS

Negatives facts are a type of **fact** that, unsurprisingly, concern negative aspects of the world, for example, the fact that there are no unicorns; the fact that there is no air in deep space; and the fact that I am not on fire. In a trivial sense of 'fact', where 'it is a fact that *p*' just means '*p* is true', it is indeed a fact that there are no unicorns. However, if we think of facts as genuine constituents of reality, it is less clear that we should believe in them (see **facts** and **states of affairs**).

Negative facts, if there were such things, would be useful in a few areas of philosophy. For instance, they could be the **truthmakers** for negative existential **propositions** such as <There are no unicorns> and <There is no air in deep space>, or they could be **causal relata**. For instance, if I was ejected from the airlock of a spaceship I would suffocate. We might then want to say the fact that there is no air in deep space caused me to die – that one fact, a negative fact, caused the fact that I died (see also **causation by absence**).

However, although some famous names have believed in negative facts (such as Bertrand Russell), they come in for a hard time. One concern is that they are weird entities to begin with (and that everything that exists should be somehow 'positive'). Another is a concern from ontological parsimony: that for there to be no unicorns we just need a lack of something, not the inclusion of some entity such as a negative fact (see also **theoretical virtues**).

NEURON DIAGRAM

Neuron diagrams (Figure 2) were introduced by **David Lewis** to depict putative counter-examples to the **counterfactual theory of causation**. They are representations of neurons (the cells inside your brain). They are represented with circles. Neurons can fire and stimulate other neurons – this is represented by arrows. However, neuron diagrams are generally taken to represent, much more generally, cases of **events** causing (or not causing) other events. The circles now represent the events and the arrows represent one event causing another. So, if two bricks are thrown at a window, smashing it simultaneously, that gets represented by the same diagram that represents two neurons firing and both activating a third neuron:

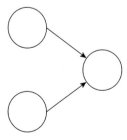

Figure 2

Other situations can be represented as well. For instance, to represent a neuron firing, whereby that firing *stops* another neuron from activating, a line with a reverse arrowhead is used (Figure 3). The neuron, as it does not fire, is represented by dotted lines, as are the firing patterns it *would have had* were it to have fired. Hence, you end up with something like this:

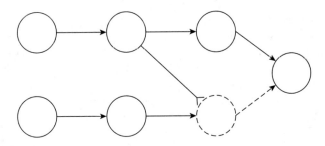

Figure 3

However, this diagram can also be taken to represent an alleged counter-example to the counterfactual theory, namely **pre-emption**. The circles again represent events; the reverse arrowhead represents one event causing another event *not* to take place (that is to say, *preventing* it; and the dotted circles represent events that *would have taken place* had they not been prevented. Hence, the above diagram also represents the case of two bombers going to blow up a bridge. The second event of the top row might be the first bomber planting and setting his bomb. As a result, the other bomber, who sees this, does not bother to set his bomb (the first bomber's action prevents the second bomber from doing what he would otherwise have done). The event of the second bomber setting his bomb never takes place and is represented by the dotted circle. The reverse arrowhead represents the event of the first bomber placing his bomb caus-ing the dotted-circle event to *not* take place. We might then take the circle on the far right to be the event of the bridge being destroyed. It is caused by the first bomber's actions, whereas the dotted line from the dotted circle represents the fact that *had* the event of the second bomber placing his bomb taken place, it *would have* caused the bridge to collapse. (Pre-emption is a problem for the very simple version of the counterfactual theory of causation, because although the first bomber's act clearly caused the bridge to collapse, the latter does not *counterfactually depend* on the former: had the first bomber not acted, the second one would have done, and so the bridge would have collapsed anyway.)

Sometimes alternative notation is used. For instance, sometimes shaded in circles represent neurons firing/events that take place, whereas non-filled circles represent neurons not firing/events that did not occur. Furthermore, the reverse arrowhead is sometimes replaced by a line and a dot (Figure 4). Hence, an alternative representation of the case of pre-emption from above would be:

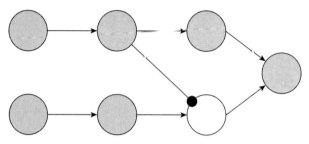

Figure 4

Neuron diagrams are used both because it is easier to draw a diagram rather than laboriously explain an appropriate scenario (so used by some to save on time giving extensive expositions), and because some of the scenarios are so complex a diagrammatic representation of it is of tremendous help.

NEUROSCIENCE AND FREE WILL

In recent years, there has been some debate about whether there is neuro-scientific evidence that **free will** is, in fact, an illusion (see **illusion of free will**). In a 1999 article provocatively titled 'Is free will an illusion?', neuro-scientist Benjamin Libet provides experimental data which, he claims, shows that the role for what he calls 'the conscious will' is extremely limited.

Libet's basic experiment works roughly as follows. Experimental subjects had their scalps wired up to a monitoring device, which tracked electrical changes in the brain. (Note, this is an actual experiment and not a **thought experiment**! The similarity to **Frankfurt's nefarious neurosurgeon** ends here.) They were asked to say when they experienced an 'urge' to flex their wrist, by looking at a clock with a fast-moving hand and saying where the hand was when they experienced the urge. These timings were then compared with 'spikes' in electrical activity (called 'readiness potentials' or RPs) in the brain.

Libet found that in general the RPs occurred about 350 milliseconds – that is around a third of a second – *before* the subjects felt the urge to flex and he concluded that the initiation of voluntary acts occurs unconsciously in the brain; hence, what we would like to think is the 'conscious will' turns out to be no more than the awareness of a 'choice' that one's brain has already made. (Actually things are more complicated than this, because Libet allows that the conscious will may still have a 'veto' function: we may be able to consciously suppress intentions that have already been formed by our brains. However, we will ignore that complication.)

Objections to Libet

Libet's work has received a lot of attention – much of it critical – from philosophers (see e.g. Mele 2008: §§ 1–6). Libet appears to assume that because a causal precursor to the flexing of the wrist has already (unconsciously) happened at the point where the subject is (as he puts it) 'aware of the urge' to flex, what he calls the 'awareness of the urge' itself plays no causal role in the flexing. However, there are (at least) two worries here. One is that what Libet calls the 'awareness of the urge' might, consistent with the experimental data, really be the formation of an intention, namely the intention to *flex now*; and the formation of that intention might well itself be a cause of the flexing. Hence, there are no grounds for saying that the mental activity that the subjects report plays no causal role in the flexing.

The other related worry is that Libet appears to presuppose that genuinely free action would require that genuine exercise of the 'conscious will' must have no physical causal ancestry at all: the conscious mental activity that subjects report cannot be the exercise of the conscious will and so cannot render the flexing free, because it is itself caused by prior activity in the brain. However, although such a view has its place in the philosophical literature – it amounts to something like an **agent–causal** view of free will – there are many other options available. From a **compatibilist** perspective, for example, it should come as no great surprise – and it should certainly not cast any doubt on the claim that our conscious decisions or intentions are freely made or formed – if it turns out that those decisions or intentions are caused by prior events in the brain. After all, our mental activity is itself a part of the causal order and not a mysterious uncaused or non-physical intervention, from the outside, on that causal order. **Libertarians** similarly do not require that our conscious decisions and intentions are completely uncaused; they just require that they are not *determined* by facts about the past. Libet's results do not show that they are so determined, because he does not claim to know what the relevant laws are; he merely shows that there is a correlation between RPs and the 'awareness' of the urge to flex. Even if this correlation were 100 per cent reliable, this would not show that the correlation is underpinned by deterministic laws; from a libertarian perspective, the fact that I have never murdered anyone despite countless opportunities to do so does not show that on each occasion the laws plus the past guaranteed that I would refrain from murder.

Neuroscience is only one area of science that has recently been argued to reveal that we do not really have free will; the psychologist Wegner (2002) cites psychological evidence for the same conclusion. It has been argued, however, that Wegner, like Libet, has a very demanding conception of what it would be to have free will (see Mele 2008: §§ 7–9).

Further reading: Mele (2004, 2008)

NIHILISM

In metaphysics, this normally has one of two meanings. The most common is *mereological nihilism* – that no things ever compose further objects. The other, less commonly used, meaning is *ontological nihilism* – that nothing *whatsoever* exists. Ontological nihilism is a rare position indeed, and although a few people have toyed with the theory, it remains a niche position.

Further reading: See the entry on the **Special Composition Question** for more information on nihilism and composition. Information on ontological nihilism is limited and almost without exception very challenging to read. One such contemporary source is O'Leary-Hawthorne and Cortens (1995).

NOMINALISM

The word 'nominalism' is used in two different ways in metaphysics. Sometimes we use the word 'nominalism' to refer to the view that there are no abstract objects, in other words the view that **platonism** is false (thus, for example, Field (1980) describes his **fictionalism** about mathematical entities as 'nominalist'). Sometimes – and perhaps more commonly – we use the word 'nominalism' to refer to view that there are no **universals**, where universals are properties – things like redness, beauty and sphericity – construed as constituents of objects which are *repeatable*, in the sense that one and the same universal can be had by (or be 'wholly present in') two distinct objects. **David Armstrong** is a 'nominalist' in the former sense but not the latter. **W. V. Quine** (in his later work) was a 'nominalist' in the latter sense but not the former. This section will examine 'nominalism' understood as the view that there are no universals.

Some nominalists worry about the intelligibility of the notion of a universal, particularly when universals are taken to be entities located in space and time. If the colour red is wholly present in the lamp on my desk but also wholly present in the curtains next to my desk, it follows that the colour red is a metre away from itself. It is not obvious that we can make sense of something being a certain distance from itself. Other nominalists doubt the coherence of universals on the grounds that we lack clear, non-circular criteria for distinguishing the situation where we have two universals that are **numerically identical** (i.e. to say, *one* universal), from the situation where we have *two* universals that are numerically distinct. (This worry is most closely associated with Quine, who coined the slogan 'no entity without identity' to express the general need for such a criterion with respect to any entity to which we have an **ontological commitment**.) For example, we cannot provide such a criterion for a given universal in terms of the objects that exemplify that universal – so that universals F and G are distinct if there are some objects that instantiate one but not the other – because two distinct universals might be instantiated by all and only the same objects, for example, *having a heart* and *having kidneys* are instantiated by exactly the same objects. In other cases, nominalism is defended on the grounds that a commitment to universals falls foul of **Bradley's regress**.

All these arguments present challenges to the coherence and attractiveness of **realism** about universals, and in doing so lend support to the nominalist position. However, these concerns do not get to the heart of the motivation for nominalism. As a general rule, most nominalists embrace nominalism out of a yearning for parsimony (see **theoretical virtues** for more on the importance of parsimony) – a 'taste for desert landscapes', as Quine famously put it. Realists about universals believe in two categories of entity: universals and **particulars**; nominalists believe in only one: particulars. Realists believe in universals on the grounds that they can explain similarity and property possession (see **universals** for how this is done). However, if a nominalist theory can satisfactorily explain those phenomena without committing to universals, then it looks like nominalism, as the more parsimonious view, is the theory to be preferred.

All nominalists claim that we do not need universals to explain similarity and property possession. However, a minority of nominalists claim that this is because we do not need to explain similarity and property possession at all, at least not in more metaphysically fundamental terms than: the predicate 'red' truly applies to the lamp *because the lamp is red*, the lamp and the curtains are similar in that *they are both red*. This kind of nominalism is called **austere nominalism** (sometimes rather uncharitably known as 'ostrich nominalism').

However, most nominalists share with realists about universals a belief that similarity and property possession need to be explained; they just think that they can be satisfactorily explained without a commitment to universals. Suppose my lamp and curtains resemble each other in that they are both red. The realist about universals explains this fact in terms of the fact that my lamp and my curtains instantiate a common universal, namely *redness*. Below are some of the main forms of rival nominalist explanation:

- *Predicate nominalism:* The lamp and the curtains are both red in virtue of the fact that a single predicate, 'is red', applies to both of them.
- *Concept nominalism:* The lamp and the curtains are both red in virtue of the fact that a single concept, that is the concept of *redness*, applies to both of them.
- *Class nominalism:* The lamp and the curtains are both red in virtue of the fact that they are both members of the class of red things (see **class nominalism**).
- *Resemblance nominalism:* The lamp and the curtains are both red in virtue of their resemblance to other red things (see **resemblance nominalism**).
- *Trope theory:* The lamp and the curtains are both red in virtue of the fact that they both have a red trope (see **trope theory**).

We can see, then, that the kind of nominalism we have been examining in this section is a broad church. It encompasses a wide range of metaphysical views from austere nominalism to trope theory, united only by their refusal, driven on the whole by a desire for parsimony, to ontologically commit to repeatable entities.

Further reading: Armstrong (1989); Loux (2006, Chapter 2); Oliver (1996)

NON-EXISTENT OBJECTS

Unsurprisingly, a non-existent object is an object that does not exist. There are two contexts in which this may come up. One is that some objects might be said to 'subsist' rather than exist. Bertrand Russell (1872–1970) had this view: **abstract** things, such as **universals** or **numbers**, do not exist *per se*, but do have some sort of **being**. In this context the word 'exist' is reserved solely for **concrete** things.

The second context is related. It was common until the twentieth century to think that some things do not exist in *any* sense, that is, do not have any sort of being. Examples would be things like fictional objects (Santa Claus, Sherlock Holmes, etc.); merely intentional objects (if my nephew is scared of the monster under his bed, the monster is the object of his fear but it does not exist); as well as impossible objects like round squares ('impossibilia'). The theory that some things are like this is often called 'Meinongianism', after Meinong who believed that there are things such that it was not true of them that they existed. (Not everyone says this, for instance Priest (2005) believes that (a) everything that there is exists, but (b) it is true of some things that there are not such thing; so Priest believes some things are non-existent but unlike Meinong – who denies (a) – Priest denies that *there are* such things).

During the twentieth century, it stopped being so common to believe that some things do not exist. Russell, initially a Meinongian, baulked at the idea that there were contradictory objects such as round squares. He instead detailed how to avoid believing in non-existent objects by using definite descriptions. Here is a quick summary of how that is supposed to work. Take the sentence, 'the King of France does not exist' – a sentence that is, apparently, true. 'The King of France' is a referring expression (in grammatical terms, it is a 'noun phrase') – and so the sentence would appear to say *of* that object, the King of France, that it does not exist. Hence, the sentence appears to entail that there is a non-existent object.

In 'On denoting', Russell (1905) argues that the sentence 'the King of France does not exist' should be understood instead simply as saying that there does not exist any object satisfying the description 'the King of France' (where satisfying that description is a matter of being *a* king of France, and there not being any *other* kings of France). So, reference to allegedly non-existing objects is neatly avoided.

The next blow against Meinongianism came from **W. V. Quine** (1948) in 'On what there is'. There, Quine lays out his theory of **ontological commitment**: 'what there is' is just what our best theories quantify over using the existential quantifier. Specifically with Meinong in mind (the article uses the pseudonym 'Wyman' to represent Meinong), Quine concludes that whatever there is will also be such that it exists, and so it cannot be the case that there are any things that do not exist. From then on, most of contemporary metaphysics has (rightly or wrongly) ignored non-existent objects.

Further reading: Priest (2009); Reicher (2008)

NUMBERS

Numbers (and indeed other far more esoteric mathematical entities) have proved to be a rich source of puzzlement for metaphysicians. Take the claim that there are at least five prime number bigger than 2. (Actually there are infinitely many of them.) This claim is clearly true, and, what is more, it would seem that we can know it *a priori*: we do not have to check any empirical facts about the world in order to satisfy ourselves that it is true. (This contrasts with, say, 'there are at least five cities bigger than Birmingham'.) However, our claim, 'there are at least five prime numbers bigger than 2', asserts that *there are* (prime) numbers: in other words, *that numbers exist* (see **existence**). Hence, what kinds of things could numbers *be*, such that we can know *a priori* that they exist?

One answer to this question – more popular among mathematicians than philosophers – is **platonism**: roughly, the view that numbers and other mathematical objects are a special kind of object, unlike chairs and molecules in that they are eternal (they do not come into existence or go out of existence), do not causally interact with **concrete** objects like chairs and molecules, and are **necessary** existents: they (unlike chairs) exist in all **possible worlds**. (This explains why mathematical truths are necessary – they cannot be false.)

There are several reasons to be sceptical about platonism, however. One is that it is unclear how if numbers are platonic objects, we could come to know about them. It has been claimed (for example by the mathematician Kurt Gödel, 1906–78) that we have – or at least, trained mathematicians have – a special faculty of mathematical intuition: we can just 'see' that the axioms of arithmetic, say, are true. However, that does not seem entirely plausible. Moreover, there is the question of how facts about this mysterious platonic realm of objects are supposed to impinge upon the world of chairs and molecules. Mathematical truths apply to the world of concrete objects – you cannot distribute thirteen whole oranges equally between six people, say. How can this be? If the fact that 6 does not divide 13 is a fact about eternal, platonic objects that are completely disconnected from the realm of oranges and people?

Some philosophers have adopted a 'formalist' position, according to which mathematical truth is a matter of being derivable from a set of axioms. The axioms themselves – and so the truths they imply – are not taken to be 'about' anything at all; they are not taken to represent any feature of reality. On this view, the question of the nature of numbers is one that does not arise: the truth of 'there are at least five prime numbers greater than 2' is due solely to the fact that this statement can be derived from the axioms of arithmetic.

A different approach that has been the focus of much recent attention is **fictionalism** about numbers. On this view, mathematical statements really are claims about the existence of numbers, but we should treat mathematical discourse as a 'fiction'. Hence, saying that there are at least five prime numbers greater than 2 is a bit like saying that Sherlock Holmes lived at 221b Baker Street: just as the latter is true within the fiction of the Sherlock Holmes stories, so 'there are at least five prime numbers greater than 2' is true within the 'fiction' of mathematics.

Further reading: Horsten (2008)

OCKHAM'S RAZOR

Also known as 'Occam's razor', and named after William of Ockham (1288–1348), this is the principle that our theories should be as parsimonious as possible as far as **ontological commitment** is concerned. It might be summarised as: 'do not believe in something unless there is a really, really good reason to'. Ontological parsimony is generally (but not universally) held to be a **theoretical virtue** in metaphysics.

ONE-TO-ONE RELATION

A relation R is a one-to-one relation if and only if, necessarily, there is at most one thing on either side of the relation. *Being married* is an example of a one-to-one relation (in British law, at any rate); marriage is a relation that holds between one person and one person. *Being on the left of* is not a one-to-one relation; John might be on the left of a plurality of things: George and Paul and Ringo and the Eiffel tower.

Most philosophers believe that identity is a one-to-one relation: it cannot be the case that one thing is identical to *more* than one thing. That might seem obvious – John can only be identical with himself, and not with George and Paul and Ringo and the Eiffel tower – but it is less obvious when we think about **identity over time** (diachronic identity): when an amoeba divides, you might – if you do not think about it very hard – say that the original amoeba *is* now two amoebae.

This is important in the metaphysics of **personal identity**, as some of the relations philosophers use to account for personal identity, for example

psychological continuity, seems not to be one-to-one relations (cases of **fission** and **fusion** are *prima facie* cases where one thing is psychologically continuous with two or more things). It is difficult to account for a relation that is one-to-one – such as personal identity – in terms of a relation that is not one-to-one – such as psychological continuity (one option is to add a *no-branching clause* to the analysis of personal identity: the relation of *being psychologically continuous in a non-branching way* is one-to-one; see **fission**).

ONLY *X* AND *Y* PRINCIPLE

See **fission**.

ONTOLOGICAL COMMITMENT

A sentence that is ontologically committed to certain things is such that if it were true, those things would exist. For instance, 'Jack went to the cinema' seems to be ontologically committed to the **existence** of both Jack and of at least one cinema; 'the explosion was caused by too much uranium' seems to be committed to uranium, but might also be committed to an **event**, namely 'the explosion', whereas 'a leprechaun mugged me last night' seems to be committed to leprechauns. One can also talk about how a theory (rather than just a sentence) has ontological commitments. Hence, a theory of quantum physics might be committed to the existence of certain sub-atomic particles; Johann Joachim Becher's theory of phlogiston is committed to phlogiston; and a detective's theory that the murderer did it with the candlestick in the library would be committed to the existence of candlesticks and libraries.

Note that just because there is a theory or sentence with certain commitments does not mean that those things exist. They only exist if the theory or sentence has the commitments *and is true*. Becher was wrong about phlogiston: his theory is committed to phlogiston but the theory is false and so there is not any such stuff. As I was not mugged by an Irish fairy, although the sentence 'a leprechaun mugged me last night' is committed to leprechauns, there are not any such things.

Note also that the commitments of a sentence or theory are not uncontentious. It is not obvious that believing that the average family has 2.7

children commits us to the existence of such a thing as the average family, let alone such a thing as 0.7 of a child. Whether or not sentences/theories that mention events commit us to **events** (or, as it is sometimes put, to having events in our **ontology**), or whether sentences/theories that talk about objects *being a certain way* (red, for instance) commits us to **universals**, or even whether sentences/theories that talk about people and objects commit us to people and objects (because one might be a **nihilist**) is all up for debate (see also **paraphrase** and **holes**).

There are competing theories of ontological commitment. The most common is **W. V. Quine**'s. He said that we should translate a theory into first-order logic and whatever that theory quantifies over (i.e. whatever ends up being a variable attached to the existential quantifier) exists, according to the theory. This was summed up in the slogan 'to be is to be the value of a bound variable' (you do not need to worry about the 'bound' bit because, in the classical first-order logic you are probably acquainted with, every variable is bound); this is often known as 'Quine's criterion of ontological commitment'. Quine went on to say that what we *should* say exists is what our best scientific theory is committed to in this sense. So, we take our best scientific theory, translate it into classical first-order logic, and the commitments are whatever we are quantifying over.

However, there are alternatives. For instance, P. F. Strawson thought that we are committed to whatever features as a subject in our sentences. Others, such as **David Armstrong**, think we are only committed to the **truthmakers** of our sentences.

Further reading: Macdonald (2005, Chapter 1); Quine (1948)

ONTOLOGY

'Ontology' is used in two senses in metaphysics. First, when someone talks about 'my ontology' or 'Armstrong's ontology', or whatever, she just means whatever entities she, or Armstrong, is committed to. Hence, if someone says, 'ghosts are no part of my ontology', she just means that she is not ontologically committed to ghosts – that is, that, according to her theory, there are no such things as ghosts (see **ontological commitment**).

Ontology in the second, more interesting (and related) sense is the name of a sub-discipline of metaphysics. Note that in other fields of study such as computer science, 'ontology' may refer to something entirely different, so do be careful. Ontology as a field of study within metaphysics is concerned with what things **exist**. This is not to say that ontologists simply catalogue what things we commonly think exist, spending hours making lists such as 'my spectacles, my left hand, the Eiffel Tower, Jupiter, . . . ', and so on. Instead, ontologists are interested more generally in what *kinds* of things exist, and when they say 'kinds' they do not mean 'cars' or 'pandas', they mean categories far broader than that. For instance, all of those things (cars, pandas, my spectacles, the Eiffel Tower) will fall within the category of '**concrete** object'. Hence, that is one category of entity. There are also interesting ontological questions about what sort of concrete entities there are (such as whether there are **temporal parts** or **holes**).

Ontology is also interested in other, broader categories: are there **events** or **states of affairs** or **possible worlds**? Are there such **abstract** things as **numbers**, platonic **universals** and **classes**? For instance, ontologists may agree that there are pandas but wonder whether the property *being a panda* exists; or agree that it is true to say that there is a prime number between 5 and 11 but wonder whether this entails that the number 7 exists. (see **ontological commitment** and **metametaphysics** for theories concerning how to resolve such matters.) They may also wonder about what populates a given category; so they might agree that universals exist but disagree over whether there is a universal *redness*, or they might agree that facts exist but disagree about whether **negative facts** exist. Hence, ontological questions are far broader, more abstract, and more esoteric than simply making a roll call of the things that exist.

However, do not presuppose that every ontologist believes these questions are all open questions, or even sensibles questions, For instance, some ontologists think it is *obvious* and *trivial* that all of the kinds of entity listed above exist, and do not see why metaphysicians are wasting their time asking such silly questions (Thomasson 2008). Whether or not the questions ontology deals with are open questions that cannot be settled easily is the current focus of the **metametaphysics** debate. Further, some of those involved in that debate have come to believe that ontology is not so much about saying what things *exist*, but is rather about saying which things are *fundamentals* and which things are such that everything else ontologically depends on them (Schaffer 2009). Thus, for example, one might or might not hold that states of affairs are more fundamental than particulars and universals (see **Bradley's regress**), or that categorical properties are more fundamental than dispositional properties (see **categorical vs dispositional properties**), and so on.

Further reading: Obviously a large number of entries in this book are relevant to ontology. For more on how ontologists categorise the things that exist, see Thomasson (2009)

OSTRICH NOMINALISM

A perjorative term for **austere nominalism**.

OVERDETERMINATION

Imagine you and I both throw a brick at a window, where both bricks pass through it simultaneously. Each brick throwing is a distinct event, but both appear to be causes of the window shattering – it is not that one caused it and the other did not, for they both have as much right as the other to count as a cause. However, each is a **redundant** cause of the window shattering. If the first brick had not thrown, the second brick would have shattered the window, and vice versa. This is a case of **over-determination** (sometimes called 'symmetric overdetermination'): *each* of the two causes has an equal claim to being a cause of the effect. (It contrasts with **pre-emption**, another form of redundant causation, where only one of the potential causes has a claim to being a cause of the effect, as when the washing dries because you hung it out, but if you had not hung it out someone else would have done – so it would still have got dry.)

Cases of overdetermination have been suggested as counter-examples to the **counterfactual theory of causation**. If the event of throwing the first brick had not occurred then the window would still have shattered, so the window shattering does not counterfactually depend in the appro-priate manner upon the first brick being thrown – therefore, according to the naïve version of the counterfactual theory, it does not *cause* it either. Nor does it do so according to the more sophisticated version described in **pre-emption**: there is no 'chain' of causal dependence running from either of our putative causes to the effect, so, again we get the wrong answer that neither of them are causes. Hence, nobody shattered the win-dow! Hence, at least, goes the problem.

One response, due originally to Bunzl (1979), is to deny that overdeter-mination is really possible. Consider the exact manner in which the win-dow broke. It would not have broken *in just that manner*, had you thrown your brick just as you did but I had desisted, or if I had thrown and you had desisted. In other words, we can think of the shattering of the window – and indeed events generally – as what Bunzl calls 'maximally modally frag-ile'. That is, for any event *e*, any difference whatsoever to the time or manner of *e*'s occurrence would amount to the occurrence of a *different* event. In this case, the window would still have shattered, but it would not have been the *same* shattering – the same event – as the one that actually occurred (see **events** for a little more on fragility).

Bunzl's response has not proved terribly popular, and one reason why is that it gets us a whole lot of 'spurious causation': causal claims that are intuitively false will turn out to be true, given maximal modal fragility. Someone says 'hello' to you causing you to say 'hello' back. At the same time, an apple you ate earlier is working its way through your digestive system. Was your eating the apple a cause of your saying 'hello'? Intuitively not. However, if you had not eaten the apple, it would not now be inside you and so – on Bunzl's account – the event that actually occurred – your saying-hello-with-an-apple-working-its-way-through-your-digestive-system – would not have occurred. Instead, a similar but distinct event – your saying-hello-with-no-apple-inside – would have occurred.

David Lewis's response to the problem of overdetermination is, in effect, to tough it out. In such cases, he says, it 'may be unclear whether to say that each is a cause or whether to say that neither is a cause (in which case we can still say that the combination of the two is a cause) ... Because it is unclear what we want to say, these symmetrical cases are not effective test cases for proposed analyses of causation. Set them aside' (2000: 182). One may or may not find this response convincing, of course.

Further reading: Schaffer (2003)

OVERLAP

One thing overlaps another if and only if they have a part in common (see **mereology**).

PARAPHRASE

Take a sentence that seems to explicitly attribute some property to some entity, for example, '7 is a prime number', 'blue is my favourite colour' or 'the average family has 2.7 children'. You might think that taking such sentences to be true would commit you to the existence of certain things (see **ontological commitment**), for example, **numbers**, **universals** or the average family (plus two children and, more gruesomely, 70 per cent of a child). If you were an **anti-realist** about any such things, you would want to avoid such commitment. With that aim in mind, a 'paraphrase' is sometimes offered of those sentences. A paraphrase is, very roughly, a sentence that is 'just as good as' the original sentence but *does not* quantify over the worrisome entity. So to avoid committing to the existence of numbers one might endorse some sort of **fictionalist** paraphrase (e.g. 'according to the fiction of platonism about numbers, 7 is a prime number'). To avoid commitment to universals, one might be an **austere nominalist** and rely on the paraphrases they offer. To avoid believing in an average family and its partially dismembered children, one might paraphrase the above sentence as 'the number of children divided by the number of families is equal to 2.7' (although, note, this paraphrase would still commit you to numbers; so a nominalist about numbers would need to take a different tack).

Exactly how a paraphrase is meant to help is not entirely clear. For instance, is it that the paraphrase is intended to *mean* the same as the paraphrased sentence? If you can offer a paraphrase, is the original sentence nevertheless true (as van Inwagen (1990: 10–11) says) or is it false but somehow still worth asserting (as Merricks (2001, Chapter 7) says)? However, although different metaphysicians will have a different take on exactly what work a paraphrase is meant to do, the general idea is that if a paraphrase is offered that avoids quantifying over the type of entity in question, then ontological commitment to that type of entity is avoided (see also **conceptual analysis**).

PART

In **mereology** – roughly, the study of the relations between parts and wholes – the phrase 'proper part' corresponds to what we generally mean by 'part' in English. So, one proper part of a table is one of its legs (another would be one of its atoms, another would be the tabletop, etc.). The phrase 'improper part' is a technical term that is defined such that *everything* is an improper part of itself. So the *improper* part of the table would be the table itself. Finally, in mereology, the word 'part' takes on a special meaning such that anything that is either a proper or improper part of an object is a part of it. So the table has, as parts, its legs, its various atoms, the table top (both of which are amongst its proper parts) and itself (which is the table's improper part). So, in the papers and books you are reading, the word 'part' might be being used in this special technical sense.

PARTICIPATION

See **instantiation relation**.

PARTICULARS

A particular is a **concrete** entity that occupies a single spatial location at any time at which it exists (ignoring cases of **time travel**). Tables, chairs, trees, persons, animals, stars and planets are all examples of particulars. Particulars are contrasted with **universals**, which can (if they exist, which is by no means universally agreed on) be instantiated by multiple objects in different spatial locations at the same time. **Trope theorists** take **properties** to be particulars: the wisdom of Socrates is a distinct 'trope' from the wisdom of Plato.

PARTICULARS AND UNIVERSALS

Metaphysicians are interested in finding out what *objects* there are in the world: are there souls as well as bodies? Does God exist? But they are also interesting in finding out *what it is in general to be an object*. Take any old object, say, the chair you are sitting on. **Bundle theorists** think that chair is wholly constituted by its **properties** – its size, its shape, its colour etc. – standing in some kind of relation (such as 'compresence') to each other. Substance-attribute theorists (see **bundle theory versus substance-attribute theory**), in contrast, believe that, as well its properties, there is some constituent of the chair, its 'substratum', which *bears* the properties of the chair. Metaphysicians also have different theories about the properties themselves. Realists about **universals** take properties to be genuine constituents of objects which are *repeatable*: the hardness of your chair might be one and the same thing as the hardness of my chair. Such philosophers are divided between those who follow **Aristotle** in believing that a given universal is wholly located in each object that instantiates it and **Platonists** (following Plato, obviously), who believe that universals exist outside space and time.

The view that there are no universals is known as '**nominalism**', and there are many different forms. Some nominalists believe in properties but just deny that they are universals. **Trope theorists**, for example, take properties to be unrepeatable **particulars**: the hardness of your chair may resemble the hardness of my chair, but strictly speaking what we have are two distinct 'hardnesses'. **Class nominalists** identify the hardness of your chair with the class of hard things. Other philosophers, known as **austere nominalists**, do not believe in properties at all: although the chair is hard there is no such thing as the hardness of the chair.

PERDURANTISM

Objects have spatial parts, for example, my hand is a (spatial) part of me, and a wheel is a (spatial) part of a car. Perdurantism is the thesis that objects also have **temporal parts**. It contrasts with **endurantism**, according to which an object is wholly present at every moment at which it exists; hence objects do not have temporal parts.

The perdurantist's temporal parts are material objects that are parts of the larger whole, just as your hand is a material object that is part of the larger whole, namely you. For example, Napoleon (1769–1821) has a temporal part that exists from 1769 to 1770, another temporal part that exists from 1770 to 1771, another that exists from 1771 to 1772, etc. Indeed, he does not just have year-long temporal parts but decade-long temporal parts, day-long temporal parts, and so on (just as your left index finger is a part of your hand, which in turn is part of you). So, for the perdurantist, just as a table is an object composed of a table top and four legs, Napoleon is composed of these temporal parts (indeed, for the perdurantist, each and every **particular** is composed of such temporal parts). For more detail on how temporal parts are supposed to work, see **temporal parts**; in this section we shall concentrate on general arguments for and against perdurantism.

Motivations

There are numerous motivations for perdurantism, but we will concentrate on three.

The argument from temporary intrinsics

Hulk Hogan was once, as a child, 2′ tall but is now 6′7″ tall. These properties are apparently incompatible – no object can be *both* 2′ and 6′7″ tall – so we have a contradiction. The obvious move to avoid the contradiction is to say that, because Hogan has **persisted**, these properties are had *at different times*. However, not every metaphysician is satisfied with that – they want to know what it is about an object's persisting that means the contradiction is avoided. In other words, why does the object having the properties at different times *explain* the lack of a contradiction? The perdurantist explanation is that at the earlier time Hogan has a temporal part that is 2′ tall, whilst at the later time he has a temporal part that is 6′7″ tall. Just as it is no contradiction for one part of me to have one property (say, for my hand to have fingers) and for another *not* to have that property (say, for my head to have no fingers), contradiction is avoided as the allegedly incompatible properties are had by different (temporal) parts. So, for the perdurantist, it is those temporal parts, and the properties they have, that explain why Hogan manages to change his intrinsic properties over time.

Alternative, non-perdurantist, attempts to avoid the contradiction include saying that intrinsic properties are *relational*. So a property like *being 2′ tall* is actually a relation to a time (just like *being the child of* is a relation between yourself and your parents). To return to the example, Hulk bears the *being 2′ tall* relation to the earlier time, but the *being 6′7″ tall* relation to the later time.

Contradiction is now avoided, for recall the original problem: that Hogan changes from being 2′ tall to *not* being 2′ tall. On the relationist view, Hogan is *always* '2′-tall-related' to that earlier time, and *that* never changes, even if Hogan bears other height properties to other times. Nor is it a problem that he bears one relation (*being 2′ tall* or *being 6′7″ tall*) to one time and not another, in the same way that it is not a problem for me to bear the relation *is a child of* to some people (my parents) and not to others (everyone who is not my mother or father).

Other non-perdurantist solutions include endorsing **presentism** (the view that only the present – and not the past and the future – exists), whereby Hogan only ever has the properties he *presently* has, so it is not true that he is 2′ tall at all, because that is not a property he presently possesses. Again, the contradiction is avoided.

The argument from coincidence

Imagine that a lump of clay is shaped into a statue. As the lump of clay has existed for longer than the statue, their properties are different. From **Leibniz's Law**, because their properties are different, the objects must be distinct. However, that means there are *two* objects (the statue and the lump) in the same place at the same time. Perdurantists often find this conclusion to be objectionable and believe perdurantism can avoid it.

Consider yourself and your hand. You occupy the same hand-sized region of space that your hand does, so in a sense there are two things in the same place at the same time, but this is not a problem as your hand is a *part* of you. Similarly, given perdurantism the statue is a temporal part of the lump and so it is okay for them to both be in the same place at the same time. Some respondents try to allay the problem without relying on perdurantism (see **endurantism** for more details), whereas others have argued that the perdurantist response does not, in fact, avoid the problem (Wasserman 2002).

The third argument is *the argument from* **Humean Supervenience** (Lewis 1983b: 73–7). The controversial commitment of perdurantism is that not only do I exist, but there are a bunch of other objects each existing for but an instant (namely my instantaneous temporal parts). However, it is uncontroversial that there *could have been* such things, for example, a person who popped into existence for but an instant before vanishing again. **David Lewis** imagines a world similar to our own, but which only contains such instantaneous objects. For instance, although in fact Napolean persisted for 51 years, Lewis imagines a world where, at *every* instant *t* at which Napolean existed (for example, on the stroke of midnight on 24 April, 1805), there is a person who pops into existence at *t*, who has exactly the same intrinsic properties that Napoleon has at *t* in the actual world, and in the next instant pops out of existence again to be replaced by another instantaneous person. Similarly for *everything* in the universe. So, at any given instant, Lewis's imaginary world is intrinsically identical in every way to the corresponding instant at the actual world. Lewis then endorses a version of Humean supervenience, whereby everything about a world **supervenes** on how the world is at the individual instants. As Lewis's imagined world and the actual world are the same when it comes to the individual instants, they must therefore be the same in *every* way. Thus, because Lewis's world contains all of these instantaneous objects, so too must the actual world; ergo perdurantism is true. (For a response, see Noonan 2003.)

This does not exhaust the motivations for perdurantism. There are also motivations from vagueness (Sider 2001: 120–39), and considerations to do with the nature of space-time (Sider 2001: 110–19), **relativity** and **time travel**.

Objections

Objections to perdurantism are less common than motivations. Traditionally, opponents have assumed that perdurantism is a revisionary position, populating our ontology with all kinds of strange instantaneous objects that we do not intuitively believe in. And so they think it is sufficient to undermine motivations for perdurantism, rather than having to specifically offer objections to the position itself.

However, there are exceptions. Thomson (1983) argues that perdurantism entails a ridiculous commitment to there being a constant stream of objects (namely the temporal parts of persisting objects), which appear from nowhere before promptly vanishing again for no apparent reason. Other objections revolve around the modal properties of perduring objects (van Inwagen 1981) or the alleged difficulties of combining perdurantism with certain, popular, versions of **supervenience** (Sider 2001: 224–36)

Further reading: Sider (2001, Chapters 3–5)

PERSISTENCE

An object persists if and only if it exists at one time, and also exists at another, distinct, time. So, if David Cameron existed in 1980 and exists in 2010, then he persists. There are serious metaphysical questions about persistence; see **perdurantism** and **endurantism**.

PERSONAL IDENTITY

Most metaphysicians working on **personal identity** occupy themselves with trying to give an account of the *diachronic* **identity** of persons, that is, the identity of persons over time. The central question here is: what is it for a certain person existing at one time to be one and the same person as a certain person existing at another time? To take a specific case: what is it for grey-haired Old Jack in 2010 to be one and the same person as Wee Johnny who ran in the 1952 Olympics in Helsinki? Perhaps the most popular way of answering this question is to ground personal identity in facts about **psychological continuity**. Rival views include the identification of persons with human animals (see **animalism**) or the identification of persons with their bodies or brains (see **bodily continuity**). Proponents of **the simple view of personal identity** reject any kind of **reductionist** account of personal identity: the fact that Old Jack is identical to Wee Johnny cannot be explained in more fundamental terms.

Some of the most interesting issues in this area arise from reflection on cases of **fission**, which include cases in which a person's brain is split in half and each half put in a distinct body. Derek Parfit has an argument, starting from consideration of such cases, for the startling conclusion that we have no non-derivative reason to try to ensure our future existence: we only have reason to do so *because* we have reason to ensure our future *survival* and to survive is *in fact* (in the absence of fission) – but only as a matter of contingent fact – to continue to exist (see **survival**).

PHASE SORTAL

A phase sortal is a **sortal** (which for brevity we can think of as a 'count noun', such as 'cat' – you can count cats, but you cannot count, say, water or wisdom) that applies to an object only for part of its existence. So 'kitten' is a phase sortal – it applies to a cat for only part of its existence – as are 'child' and 'pensioner'. According to **animalism** – a theory of **personal identity** – 'person' is a phase sortal. A person is identical with a human animal, but not for the animal's entire existence (e.g. not when it is a foetus).

PHENOMENALISM AND IDEALISM

Phenomenalism and idealism are closely related philosophical positions and basically amount to the view that the external world (and the familiar objects that populate it – trees, cars, bananas, and so on) is really no more than a collection of sensations or experiences or 'sense data'. As **George Berkeley** put it, 'esse est percipi' or 'to be is to be perceived'. Phenomenalism and idealism are thus both versions of anti-realism (see **realism and anti-realism (global)**), because on both views the existence and nature of the external world are mind-dependent (indeed the external world just *is* mental, it is just a collection of sensations).

Roughly, the idea is this. Intuitively, you might think that there is a sharp distinction between the banana you see and feel and taste, and those experiences themselves. The banana is a real object, existing independently of your mind, and your experiences give you information *about* this object; how it looks and tastes, for example. According to the phenomenalist (and idealist), however, there is no such distinction. All there really is to the banana is its visual appearance, smell, taste and tactile qualities; and these 'qualities' of the banana are really just a collection of *your* experiences. The banana just *is* that collection of experiences or sense data.

Now so far we have rather a crude and obviously problematic philosophical position. In particular, surely the banana still exists when you put it in the cupboard – that is, even when you are not observing it. The phenomenalist or idealist who denied this would have a view according to which a huge amount of what we believe about the world ('the milk is in the fridge', 'my feet still exist while I'm asleep' etc.) is straightforwardly false; and violating **common sense** to this extent is generally thought to be bad form.

Phenomenalists and idealists do not want to deny obvious facts such as the fact that my feet still exist when I am asleep, and the difference between them comes to exactly how they account for those facts. *Idealism* – the position advocated by Berkeley – appeals to the existence of God: *you* might not experience your feet when you are asleep, but God is all-seeing, and *he* perceives your feet, thus ensuring their continued existence. This position is nicely summarised in a well-known pair of limericks (whose author is lost in the mists of time):

> There was a young man who said, 'God
> Must find it exceedingly odd
> To think that the tree
> Should continue to be
> When there's no one about in the quad'.

> 'Dear Sir:
> Your astonishment's odd;
> I am always about in the quad.
> And that's why the tree
> Will continue to be
> Since observed by,
> Yours faithfully,
> God.'

Phenomenalism makes no such appeal to God. On the phenomenalist view, an object is (as J. S. Mill put it) a 'permanent possibility of sensation'. The basic idea is that claims about the world are really disguised *subjunctive* claims (roughly, **counterfactual conditionals**). For example, to say that there is a tree in front of me (when my eyes are closed) is really to say something like 'if I were to open my eyes, I would have a visual tree-experience', 'were I to have a walking-ten-yards-experience and a reaching-out-my-hand experience, I would have a tactile bark-experience', and so on.

Why would anyone want to adopt phenomenalism or idealism? Well, Berkeley (1710: §§1–70) does have an argument for idealism. The basic starting-point is a rejection of **John Locke**'s distinction between **primary**

and secondary qualities. Grant that Locke establishes that qualities such as heat, cold, taste and colour (the secondary qualities) exist only in the mind (though it is unclear whether Locke really thinks this). Why, then, should we think, as Locke does, that the alleged *primary* qualities (extension, solidity, motion, and so on) do not? Indeed, Berkeley argues that it does not even make sense to suppose that these alleged primary qualities exist outside the mind. One might initialy, naively suppose, he says, that our *idea* of, say, solidity 'resembles' some mind-independent feature of an object (i.e. its solidity). However, upon reflection we realise that it is impossible for some mind-independent feature of reality to resemble an *idea*. So when we talk about solidity, we must really be talking just about the *idea* of solidity, rather than some feature of extra-mental reality. Phenomenalists and idealists have generally taken their view to be a consequence of **empiricism**, the view that all our knowledge of the world comes from experience. (These days, most philosophers would hold that a suitably sophisticated version of empiricism does not entail phenomenalism or idealism.) If all we have to go on are our ideas, and all our ideas come from sensory experience, how could we possibly acquire even an idea – let alone knowledge – of something that exists outside our experience? Fortunately, this argument is generally agreed to be fatally flawed (see Nagel 1986, Chapter 6).

One advantage of phenomenalism (and idealism), however, is that it provides a response to **scepticism**. The phenomenalist denies that there is any distinction between the way the world is and the way our experience represents it as being. Hence there is simply no possibility of being deceived by Descartes' evil demon, or of being a **brain in a vat**: if to be is to be perceived, then the evil demon hypothesis (or the brain-in-a-vat hypothesis) is really unintelligible, because trees and elephants are every bit as real in the alleged sceptical scenario (the demon hypothesis) as they are in fact. Elephant-experiences beget elephants, and the question of what it is, outside the realm of ideas, that causes those experiences is one that we cannot so much as intelligibly ask, because to try to answer it would be to assume that we can form an idea of something that is not itself an idea.

A standard contemporary argument against phenomenalism is a '**truthmaker**' argument. Take the claim that the sentence 'there is a tree in front of me' really means something like 'if I were to open my eyes, I would have a visual tree-experience'. What makes this sentence true? The phenomenalist appears to have no answer to this question: it is just a brute fact that if I were to open my eyes, I would have a visual tree-experience (so – to put things rather anachronistically – the phenomenalist rejects the standard **possible worlds** semantics for counterfactuals, according to which facts about other possible worlds make counterfactuals true). However, (it has been argued) this is not good enough; this is not the kind of fact that can serve as a truthmaker. The realist, by contrast, has a perfectly good truth-maker available, namely the tree itself, which, were I to open my eyes would cause me to have a tree-experience. (Note that idealism does not seem to be susceptible to the truthmaker argument, because according to the idealist there *is* a truthmaker for the relevant claim, namely the fact that God is 'always about in the quad'.)

Note that some care is needed with the expressions 'phenomenalism' and 'idealism', because not everyone defines the positions in the way we have just done. Thus some philosophers will talk about 'Berkeleian phenomenal ism' (rather than idealism), and some philosophers take idealism to be a much broader philosophical thesis, sometimes amounting to what we are calling 'global anti-realism' (see **realism and anti-realism (global)**).

Further reading: Dancy (1985, Chapter 10)

PLATONIC HEAVEN

Plato believed that when you are dead, you would pass through a realm of Forms (what were, effectively, **universals**, but the **platonic** version thereof) and by seeing such Forms would – upon being reincarnated – be able to recognise those things that exemplified them. This realm was 'Platonic Heaven' – a supernal place where the Forms and other such things were to be found. However, the phrase is no longer used in this literal manner. Instead, when someone says that something is in Platonic Heaven, they mean that it is an **abstract** thing that exists but is not located in space and time. So, sentences such as '**numbers** are in Platonic Heaven' or '**classes** (or sets) are up there in Platonic Heaven' should be taken metaphorically – they are not 'in' any place; talk about them being 'up there' is just a heuristic device, not a commitment to a literal otherworldly place where these things are to be found.

PLATONISM

'Platonism' in contemporary metaphysics is generally taken to denote the view that there are *abstract objects*: roughly, entities that have no spatio-temporal location and are not capable of causal interaction (see **abstract vs concrete**).

'Platonism' gets its name, of course, from Plato, and in particular, from his Theory of Forms. The basic idea behind the Theory of Forms is a fairly intuitive distinction (though one that is not much used in contemporary metaphysics) between 'matter' and 'form'. Roughly, any object – a dog or a chair or a planet – is a hunk of matter. However, it is not just any old hunk of matter; in order to *be* a dog, as opposed to a chair, the matter has to have a certain 'form'; it has to be organised in such a way as to make up a dog and not a chair. However, what is it for matter to be 'organised' in the right way? Plato's answer is that there is a 'Form', *dog*, in which dogs 'participate' (and indeed for any **property** *F*, such as being a chair or being round or being red, an object gets to have that property in virtue of its participating in the relevant Form). Plato's Forms fall into the category of what contemporary metaphysicians call abstract objects: they do not have spatio-temporal location and they are eternal and changeless (although Plato did not take them to lack causal efficacy). Plato sometimes talks of the Forms as though they exist in some special realm (and philosophers continue to talk about the 'realm' of Platonic Forms, or **Platonic Heaven**), but, of course, we have to take this with a pinch of salt: the Forms being non-spatio-temporal, it is not as though they exist somewhere *else*; they are not a part of the material world, but they are not literally located in some *other* place. The same goes for abstract objects generally.

In contemporary metaphysics, to be a platonist about some entity (sometimes spelled with a small 'p' in recognition that the view is only loosely associated with Plato's own view) is to hold that the entity in question is an abstract object. Most philosophers disagree with Plato about the Forms, seeing no reason to think that **properties** are abstract (see **immanent realism about universals**). However, many philosophers hold that there are other abstract objects: **numbers**, say, or **classes** (sets). Sometimes the debate is about whether a given entity is abstract or concrete; for example, **David Lewis** holds that **possible worlds** are concrete objects, whereas some of his opponents hold that possible worlds exist but are abstract objects (see **modal realism**).

If you are feeling a little wary of embracing platonism about *any* kind of object – perhaps on the grounds that it is just very odd to think that there are objects that have no spatio-temporal location – you are certainly not alone. 'Abstract' objects derive their name from **John Locke**'s theory of *abstraction*. For Locke, we get the **concept** or 'idea' of redness, say, simply by observing a lot of red things and 'abstracting away' from the differences between them (size, shape, and so on). What we are left with at the end of this psychological process is the idea of *redness*. However, on Locke's **nominalist** view, there is no need to think that we have discovered and given a name to some *entity*, redness. The 'abstract idea' of redness is merely an idea or concept, formed by a certain kind of psychological process; it does not correspond to any abstract *object.* Similarly, one might try to argue for, say, numbers: 'two' is just the abstract idea that we get when we abstract away from the differences between a pair of twins, a pair of oranges and a pair of lamps.

Further reading: Balaguer (2009)

POINT PARTICLE

See **simple**.

POSSIBILIA

Possibilia are (if there are any such things) merely possible entities: not just wizards, hobbits and leprechauns, but also the tree that would have been in your garden if you had not pulled out the sapling several years ago, the birthday party that would have happened if only you had bothered to orga- nise it, time-travelling DeLoreans (arguably), talking donkeys, and so on.

Do possibilia exist? **Quine** (1948) famously mocked the idea: is the pos- sible man in the doorway fat or thin? Is the possible fat man in the doorway identical with the possible bald man in the doorway, or are there two pos- sible men in the doorway? Some philosophers have held that there are **non- existent objects** and have counted possibilia among their number. Others – believers in 'genuine **modal realism**' – hold that possibilia exist but do not *actually* exist: they are inhabitants of real, **concrete** but non-actual **possible worlds** (so there is a possible world where there is a fat man in the doorway, and another where there is a bald man in the doorway, and another where there is a fat, bald man in the doorway, and so on – but none of these possible men are hanging around the *actual* doorway).

POSSIBLE WORLDS

Talk about possible worlds is intimately connected with **modality**. Such talk is commonplace throughout metaphysics and, indeed, other areas of philosophy, so you would be well advised to grasp the basics.

Consider the following sentences:

It *could* be the case that the Queen of England plays the banjo.
Necessarily 2 + 2 = 4.
It is *impossible* for me to fly.

In each case the italicised word is a modal term. Possible world talk drops such explicit modal terms in favour of talking about possible worlds and what is true at those worlds, where a possible world is a total way that our world could be (where 'world' here means the entirety of existence, not just the planet Earth – more like the whole Universe, but more, even than that, if you think, for example, that there are **abstract** objects that exist outside space and time, or God, or whatever). In possible world talk, something is possible if and only if it *is the case* at some possible world. So the first sentence becomes:

There is a possible world at which the Queen of England plays the banjo.

See how the modal term '*could*' has been dropped in favour of talking about possible worlds instead. Similarly, something is necessarily the case if and only if it is the case at *all* the worlds. So the second sentence becomes:

At all possible worlds, it is the case that 2 + 2 = 4.

Finally, something is impossible if and only if it is not the case at *any* of the worlds. So the third sentence becomes:

At no possible world do I fly.

Different types of modality

The last case above is instructive, as you might well want to say that 'it is impossible for me to fly' is true or false depending upon the context you are in. For instance, if I tried to leap from a rooftop, confident that I would fly like an eagle and land safely on the ground, you would (I hope!) try and dissuade me on the grounds that I cannot fly – that it is *impossible* for me to do so. However, in other contexts the sentence does not seem to be true. For instance, we might engage in a theological debate over what an omnipotent being could, or could not, bring about. There we might agree that such a being could endow me with the ability to fly. In that context, then, the sentence seems to be false – I *could* fly under those circumstances: it is not impossible at all.

One of the joys of possible world talk is that it makes it easy to understand how sentences such as 'it is impossible for me to fly' can be true or false in different contexts. Imagine all the ways the world could be, no matter how odd or strange, as long as they do not involve a contradiction. These are the *logically possible worlds*. So there are logically possible worlds where John Lennon was not assassinated, worlds where mankind never evolved, and even worlds where the laws of physics are very different (say, where magic is real and the events of Harry Potter play out). None of these worlds involve a *contradiction*, so they are logically possible worlds.

One of those worlds is special, namely, the world that represents what is *actually* the case. So one of the worlds will be a world where humans did evolve, John Lennon was assassinated, magic does not exist, etc. – down to the last, tiniest detail. That is the *actual world*. With this in place, we can start demarcating the logically possible worlds into smaller sets. For instance, take all the logically possible worlds with the same laws of physics as the actual world. These are the *physically possible worlds* (alternatively, the *nomologically possible worlds*, which are the worlds with the same **laws of nature** – which is usually taken to be the same thing as having the same physical laws). These will include worlds where humans did not evolve and where John Lennon was not assassinated, because they will have different 'initial conditions' from the actual world, but will not include worlds where the events of Harry Potter play out, because many of those events are contrary to the actual laws of nature. Thus to say that *P* is physically possible is to say that there is at least one physically possible world where *P* is true, and to say that *P* is physically necessary is to say that *P* is true in all physically possible worlds. (And so – by definition – all the actual laws of nature are physically necessary.)

Now we can see what is going on in that last sentence. When we say it is impossible for me to fly, we translate that into the sentence:

At no possible world do I fly.

This sentence is true in the first context, when I am trying to leap off a rooftop, because when we say there are no possible worlds where I fly we mean there are no *physically* possible worlds where I do so. When we are discussing what an omnipotent being can do, we mean there are *logically* possible worlds where I fly. So, the possible world talk makes it clear how these two sentences can both be true in their own respective contexts.

These groupings, of logically and physically possible worlds, are not the only demarcations we can make amongst the worlds. For instance take:

For all I know, it could be the case that the Chairperson of the Federation Council of Russia is an atheist.

We can capture this sentence by talking about those worlds such that everything that I know to be true at the actual world is true of those other worlds. They are the *epistemically possible worlds*. To illustrate: if I know that the Queen of England does not play the banjo, then at no epistemically possible world does she play the banjo (and it is epistemically necessary – relative to what I know – that the Queen does not play the banjo, i.e. true in all epistemically possible worlds); if I know the boiling point of water is 100 °C at sea level, then in all epistemically possible worlds that is what the boiling point of water is; if I *do not* know that the boiling point of water is 100 °C at sea level then there will be possible worlds where water boils at all kinds of temperatures that are epistemically possible worlds (epistemically possible for *me*, i.e. they might not be epistemically possible worlds for *you*). We can then translate the sentence into:

> At some epistemically possible world, the Chairperson of the Federation Council of Russia is an atheist.

There are all kinds of restrictions we can make on what possible worlds we are talking about, and all kinds of ways to translate sentences into possible worlds talk. It is this versatility that has made possible world talk so common in philosophical literature (see Melia 2003, Chapter 2 for more examples of how possible worlds can make complicated modal statements easier to comprehend).

Some questions about possible worlds

So far we have talked about possible worlds but not explained (i) whether they exist, (ii) what they *are* if they do exist, (iii) how **propositions** (like <the Queen plays the banjo>) are true at them, or indeed (iv) exactly what the relationship is supposed to be between possible-world talk on the one hand and modal claims on the other.

Let us start with (iv) Some philosophers (for example **David Lewis**) are believers in 'possible world semantics'; that is, they take each of the above 'translations' to be a full **conceptual analysis** of the relevant modal claim (similarly for **counterfactual conditionals**). This is particularly important for **Humeans**, who eschew **natural necessity** and so like the idea that modal facts are reducible (see **reductionism**) to facts about possible worlds. Such philosophers thus appear (insofar as they take the original modal claims to be true) to be committed to the existence of possible worlds, because, for example, the truth of 'the Queen might have played the banjo' entails that *there is* a possible world where the Queen plays the banjo. 'Genuine **modal realists**' happily embrace this consequence and hold that there really is a possible world – a concrete entity, just like the actual world – that is inhabited by a real, flesh-and-blood, banjo-playing Queen of England.

'Ersatz **modal realists**' also sign up to the existence of possible worlds, but take possible worlds to be **abstract** objects of some sort, sets of propositions being a popular choice. Some ersatz modal realists subscribe to possible worlds semantics; however, it is standardly thought that they are not really entitled to do this, because ersatzers are left with the unanalysed **primitive** notion of 'consistency', which is itself a modal notion (See **modal realism** for an explanation of this, and for further information on ersatz modal realism.)

Finally, some modal **fictionalists** (see e.g. Rosen 1990) sign up to possible worlds semantics (or something very close to it), holding that 'it is possible that *P*' is to be analysed as 'according to the *fiction* of genuine modal realism, there is a possible world where *P*'. So some fictionalists endorse possible worlds semantics but are not committed to the existence of possible worlds.

Other philosophers who deploy possible world talk do not sign up to full-blown possible worlds semantics: they do not think that modality is really to be *analysed* in terms of possible worlds. Instead, they regard possible world talk as merely a convenient heuristic device: a useful substitute for modal talk, on occasion, but not something that gives the *meaning* of modal claims. Some 'ersatz **modal realists**' – having granted that they cannot fully *analyse* modality in terms of possible world talk (see above) – fall into this camp, as do some fictionalists.

As will by now be clear, opinion is also divided over questions (i) and (ii). On (i) – whether possible worlds exist – the fictionalist says 'no', whereas the ersatzer and genuine modal realist both say 'yes'. On (ii), the ersatzer and genuine modal realist disagree. Finally, on (iii), again see **modal realism**.

The take-home message is that, although possible world talk is pervasive in metaphysics, different philosophers have different views about what exactly they are doing when they deploy it; and you cannot assume, just from the fact that someone deploys possible worlds talk, that they are a modal realist.

Further reading: Divers (2002, Chapters 1–2); Melia (2003, Chapter 2)

POSSIBILITY

Possibility is a *modal* notion: to say that something is *possible* is to say something not about how things *are*, but how they *might be* or *might have been* (see **modality**). Possibility (and its close relative, necessity) often gets cashed out in terms of **possible worlds**, so that to say that P is possible or possibly true (often represented at $\Diamond P$, where $\Diamond$ is the 'possibly operator') is to say that P is true *in at least one possible world*. Metaphysicians also often distinguish between different 'kinds' of possibilities, such as epistemic possibility, physical possibility and metaphysical possibility; see **possible worlds** for the standard way to distinguish between them.

POSTMODERNISM

Postmodernism – at least the aspect of it that is relevant to a book about metaphysics – is an intellectual movement that rose in popularity in the second half of the twentieth century. Authors who might be described as 'postmodernist' include Michel Foucault, Jacques Derrida, Jean Baudrillard and Richard Rorty. The literary theorist Eagleton (1996: vii) describes postmodernism as 'a style of thought which is suspicious of classical notions of truth, reason, identity and objectivity, of the idea of universal progress or emancipation, of single frameworks, grand narratives or ultimate grounds of explanation'.

Although postmodernist thinking can be (and has been) applied to virtually any facet of contemporary culture from physics to pop music – indeed its roots lie not in philosophy but in art, architecture and politics – as the passage from Eagleton suggests, it has at its heart some distinctly metaphysical claims about the nature of reality. And these claims are broadly anti-realist (see **realism and anti-realism (global)**): postmodernists reject the idea that there is in principle one true theory of the way the world really is (as seen, perhaps, from the **God's eye view**) and replace it with a much more **relativist** view.

Further reading: Rorty (1989, Chapter 1); Kirk (1999, Chapter 9)

PRAGMATISM

Pragmatism is a variety of global anti-realism (see **realism and anti-realism (global)**) and has its roots in the work of the American philosophers C. S. Pierce (1839–1914), William James (1842–1910, brother of the novelist Henry James) and John Dewey (1859–1952). (Actually many pragmatists would describe themselves as realists; however, we are working with a definition of anti-realism according to which the anti-realist holds that reality is not mind-independent, and pragmatists subscribe, implicitly at least, to that thesis.) The basic tenet of pragmatism is that what is true is tied to the *practical* difference that is made by asserting or believing a given claim or theoretical framework. Different pragmatists have had different views about how the notion of a 'practical' difference should be spelled out and these have resulted in different kinds of theory, some more radically anti-realist than others.

One way to get into the pragmatist way of thinking is to think about the purpose of theories – in science, or history, or religion, or whatever. What is the point of having a theory of something? One answer is to say, 'well, so that we can find out the *truth*!' If we never theorised about anything, our understanding of the world would be vastly impoverished because we would never have made discoveries about evolution or the cosmos or the causes of AIDS or whatever. If pressed, we might go on to say that the truth of a theory is a matter of some sort of 'fit' or 'correspondence' between the way the theory says things are and the way they really are; and we might claim that testing the predictions of the theory is a good method for finding out whether or not the theory is true in that sense (see **truth**).

But we can think of theories in another way. Consider, say, Freudian psychoanalysis and let us suppose for the sake of the argument that psychoanalysis has proved to be hugely effective: it has helped vast numbers of people to deal effectively with serious psychological problems. Freudian psychoanalysis is based on a theory about the mind. For example, Freud distinguishes between the ego, the superego and the id. These three aspects or parts of the mind are used to explain various psychological problems and psychoanalytic therapy depends on understanding the mind in these terms. Now, from a realist perspective, it seems that we can separate out the (assumed) fact that psychoanalysis is hugely effective and beneficial from the question of whether the theory is *true*: are there *really* these three aspects of the mind – the ego, the superego and the id? Or are these just inventions of Freud's, which, luckily enough, underpin successful therapy? However, from a different perspective, we might ask whether this second question (whether the theory is true) is at all important, when considered as a question that is distinct from the first one. Why does it matter whether or not the psychoanalytic categories really map onto features of reality? Is not it enough that the theoretical framework *works*? After all, on the whole we are better off adopting that framework than we would be without it. And, if we agree that the fact that it works – that it is practically *useful* – is a good reason to endorse it, we might then broaden our view and ask the same question about theories in general. Is it not enough that a theory works: that it yields successful predictions, allows us to build bridges and cure diseases, or perhaps (in the case of religion) comforts us or makes us more likely to behave well? What more could we want of a theory, after all? Why should it matter, in addition, that the theory 'corresponds to the way the world really is'?

This is a broadly pragmatist way of thinking. Indeed, pragmatists go further. It is not so much that it is unimportant whether our theories are *true*; rather, the very notion of truth as correspondence to 'the way the world really is' is to be replaced with a notion of truth according to which truth just *is*, as James (1975: 42) puts it, 'whatever proves itself to be good in the way of belief, and good, too, for definite assignable reasons'.

Pragmatism is a variety of anti-realism (in our sense) because the pragmatist conception of truth is thereby also a conception of reality: you cannot have the former without the latter. For example, if you think that the truth of psychoanalytic theory is determined by its usefulness, you cannot also hold that there is still a fact of the matter about whether the ego, superego and id 'really' exist that is independent of the usefulness of the theory. That is because to say that the ego, superego and id 'really' exist is to say no more than that it is *true* that the ego, superego and id (really) exist; and that question just *does*, for the pragmatist, depend on the usefulness of the theory. Questions about what the world is really like, independent of the usefulness of our theories or beliefs, are not questions that make any sense from a pragmatist perspective. So the nature of reality really does depend on the usefulness of our theories or beliefs.

Further reading: Hookway (2010)

PRE-EMPTION

Pre-emption scenarios are usually introduced as (alleged) counter-examples to the **counterfactual theory of causation**. In general they all involve coming up with a situation where one **event** (or **fact**, depending on what you think the **causal relata** are), *c*, intuitively causes another event, *e*, but there is no counterfactual dependence of *e* on *c* (i.e. if *c* had not occurred *e* would still have occurred). This is a problem for the more naïve version of the counterfactual analysis, which says that for one event to cause another the effect must counterfactually depend on the cause.

Here is a concrete example. Imagine I decide that by midday a bridge I have taken a dislike to must be destroyed. I arrive at 10 am, bomb in hand, to discover that you are already there planting your own bomb. Quite surprised, but not wanting to waste good explosives, I go home and back to bed. At midday your bomb explodes destroying the bridge. Clearly you are causally responsible for the destruction of the bridge. However, if you *had not* have set your bomb then, when I arrived at 10 am, I would not have turned around and gone home: I would have continued to set up my own bomb, which would then have destroyed the bridge at midday. Even though you are causally responsible for its destruction, if you had not blown the bridge up I would have. So the **counterfactual conditional** 'if you had not planted the bomb the bridge would not have been destroyed' is false and, given the naïve counterfactual analysis of causation, you *did not* cause the bridge to blow up. As that is false – clearly, you did cause it – we have a counter-example to the naïve counterfactual analysis.

This very simple pre-emption scenario gives some idea of how the counter-examples work. The counterfactual theorists do have remedies. For instance, Lewis's original counterfactual analysis of causation is not, in fact, the naïve version just described; instead, it says that:

> *c* causes *e* if and only if *e* stands in the **ancestral relation** of counter-factual dependence to *c* (see Lewis 1973a).

That is, *c* causes *e* if (and only if) there is a *chain* of events, one after another, and each event in that chain counterfactually depends on the event before. (So, like all ancestral relations, the causal relation is **transitive**). Usually the final event will counterfactually depend on the first event (so, if the first event had not taken place the final event would not have either). Here is the rub: the pre-emption cases are not your usual cases. They are scenarios where the final event (the bridge blowing up) happens *not* to depend on the first event (you planting the bomb). However, *each event in the chain* counterfactually depends on some earlier event in a way that links the first event to the last. So, the bridge blowing up counterfactually depends on the blasting cap firing, which in turn counterfactually depends on the blasting cap being placed correctly by you, which in turn counterfactually depends on you being there (at 10 am) to place it. So the event of the bridge blowing up does not counterfactually depend on you being there planting it at 10 am, but it *does* stand at the end of a chain of such dependent events. Given Lewis's more sophisticated analysis, you planting the bomb *does* cause the bridge to blow up.

The above shows how we get pre-emption style counter-examples (often represented by **neuron diagrams**) and how the counterfactual theorists fix their theory. There are more complicated scenarios which are counter-examples to those fixes (and in turn more complicated tweaks to the theory). However, many of these counter-examples are very similar in spirit and are all collectively called 'pre-emption cases'.

Two kinds of pre-emption that are harder to deal with are 'late pre-emption' and 'trumping pre-emption'. The case described above is a case of 'early pre-emption': there is some event in the chain between c and e that 'cuts off' the alternative process that would have led to e (in this case, you planting the bomb – which I saw, causing me to go back to bed). Late pre-emption happens when it is the effect *itself* that prevents the 'back-up cause' (i.e. the event that *would* have caused the effect, had the actual cause not done so) from doing its work. Imagine Billy and Suzy (they crop up quite a lot in this literature) throwing rocks at a window at the same time. Suzy's throw (c) is slightly quicker than Billy's (d), so her rock gets there first; Billy's follows close behind but, of course, by the time his rock arrives, the window is already broken (call the window's breaking 'e'). The thing that stops d from causing e is e itself, not any prior event in the causal chain from c to e. (If Suzy's rock had somehow intercepted Billy's and knocked it off course, and *that* had been what stopped d from causing e, that would have been a different matter – and would have been early pre-emption. However, that is not the case we are imagining.) Lewis's analysis, described above, cannot – as it stands – deal with late pre-emption, for this reason: take any event in the chain from c to e, excluding e itself. (Call that event f.) We will get a nice chain of counterfactual dependence running from c to f, but – no matter which event we choose – e will not counterfactually depend on f. It will always be the case that had f not occurred, the window would still have been broken. So c is not, on Lewis's analysis, a cause of e – which is obviously the wrong answer.

'Trumping' pre-emption cases are easiest to see using magic examples (though many people – Lewis included – think that there are perfectly good non-magic examples). Grizelda the Witch casts a spell at midnight (c) to turn the prince into a frog the following midday (e). Gandalf the Wizard casts the same spell at 2 am (d). Let us stipulate that, in the **possible world** we are imagining, there is a **law of nature** that says that the first spell cast 'neutralises' all further spells: if you cast a spell that has already been cast by someone else, it just does not do anything. Also, magic – being magic – works by 'action at a temporal distance'. There is no chain of events linking spells to their effects; the spell is cast and then, later on, the prince turns into a frog with nothing in between. Here, again, c preempts d, the back-up cause: even though d has no effect on the prince, if c had not happened, d *would* have caused e, so e would have happened anyway. However – as with late pre-emption, but for a different reason – we cannot fix the problem by appealing to a chain of counterfactual dependence running from c to e. This is because there simply is (by stipulation) no chain of events at all that links c to e.

Lewis (1973a, 1973b) himself was worried enough about late and trumping pre-emption to abandon his earlier counterfactual analysis and propose a very different (though still counterfactual) analysis; see Lewis 2000. However, plenty of counter-examples have been proposed to his new analysis too (e.g. Schaffer 2001). And so it goes on.

Further reading: Schaffer (2000); Lewis (2000)

PRESENTISM

Presentists believe that the only concrete things that exist are those that presently exist. For example, the concrete things that exist (at the time of me writing this) include George Bush and dolphins, but do not include George Washington or the dinosaurs. This may sound trivial, but various theories say otherwise, such as **eternalism** (that concrete things from all times exist) and **growing block theory** (that all concrete things from the past and present, but not the future, exist).

Presentism concerns only concrete things, so can allow that abstract objects (see **abstract versus concrete**) exist even though, being outside space-time, they do not *presently* exist. This extends even to times. Although many presentists believe that only one time exists (the present moment, obviously) some presentists believe that all times exist, but that those times are abstract. They are *ersatz* times (just as *ersatzists* about possible worlds think possible worlds are abstract rather than concrete (see **modal realism**)).

Motivations

Generally, presentists argue that it is *intuitive* that the only concrete objects that exist are presently existing ones. Given this intuition, they take their view to be the incumbent – it is to be believed unless there is good reason *not* to believe it.

There are other motivations beyond this alleged intuitive appeal. Presentists have argued that only their theory provides a good response to **McTaggart**'s argument for **the unreality of time**. Secondly, some presentists have argued that only their theory is consistent with other, allegedly appealing metaphysical theories (such as **endurantism**; see Crisp 2003) or solves certain problems other metaphysical theories face (for instance, it offers a solution to the problem of temporary intrinsics; see **perdurantism**). Finally, motivations for presentism are often parasitic on those for tensed theories of time in general (see **tensed and tenseless theories of time**). If one has good reason for thinking that the only plausible tensed theory is a presentist theory (repudiating views like the growing block theory or **moving spotlight theory**) then any motivation to be a tensed theorist will double as a motivation for presentism.

Objections

The first objection is metaphysical: that presentism has difficulties with **truthmaking**. Given presentism, it is difficult to see what makes **propositions** about the past and future true. Whereas eternalists rely upon past and future objects (and past and future states of affairs), the presentist cannot. For example, the proposition <there were dinosaurs> is, for the eternalist, made true by dinosaurs being located in the past. For the presentist dinosaurs do not exist, so they cannot say this.

Here, presentists break into two camps. One camp denies that truthmaking is a worthwhile project and offers objections to the truthmaking enterprise as a whole (see Merricks 2007, especially Chapter 6). The other camp accepts the truthmaking challenge, introducing extra abstract objects (such as properties, facts or **haecceities**) to play the appropriate truthmaking role (see Keller 2004; Zimmerman 2008). Of course, their opponents think that these extra entities are too great a cost, and that the truthmakers eternalism offers are to be preferred.

The second objection to presentism is logical. In classical logic, propositions containing singular terms entail that entities named by those terms exist. For example, <Ghenghis Khan was a Mongolian> is true and we might represent that proposition as 'Fa', where a is the singular term and F is the predicate '__ was a Mongolian'. In classical logic, Fa implies $\exists x$ ($x = a$), that is, that the thing named by the singular term ('Ghenghis Khan') exists. Or another example: we might represent <Tony Blair admires Winston Churchill> as aRb, where a is a singular term standing for Tony and b for Winston. In classical logic aRb entails $\exists x$ ($x = b$), that is, that Winston exists. In both these cases, classical logic seems to entail that non-present things (Winston and Ghenghis) exist and therefore that presentism is false.

One response is to reject classical logic and deny that the fact that singular terms appear in true propositions entails that the things they name exist. Alternatively, presentists may deny that the example propositions really have a logical form containing the problematic singular terms. For instance, the presentist may introduce new logical operators to deal with past and future truths: the WAS and WILL operator. Rather than thinking <Ghenghis Khan was a Mongolian> is best represented by 'Fa' (where F is the predicate '__was a Mongolian') we deploy operators to give a different representation. Let

G stand for the predicate '__is a Mongolian' (rather than *was* a Mongolian). We then deploy a WAS operator to get 'WAS *Ga*', which (in English) is 'it *was* the case that Ghenghis Khan *is* a Mongolian'. From that we cannot conclude '$\exists x \ (x = a)$', whereby Ghenghis Khan exists even though he is not present, but only conclude 'WAS $\exists x \ (x = a)$' (in English: 'it was the case that there exists something identical to Ghenghis Khan'). The presentist will accept *that*, for that only asserts that it *was* the case that Ghenghis Khan *existed* and not that he *exists*. So the WAS and WILL operators end up being like the possibility operator: the proposition $<\Diamond \exists \ x \ (x = \text{Santa Claus})>$ (in English: 'Santa Claus could have existed') is true, let us suppose; but it does not follow that Santa Claus *does* exist, only that it *could* have been the case that he exists. Similarly, the presentist does not move from it being the case that there *did* exist a man named Ghenghis Khan, to concluding that there *is* a man named Ghenghis Khan (see Markosian 2004 for discussion).

The final objection is that presentism flounders in the face of contemporary science. Given Einstein's Theory of **Relativity**, the relation of simultaneity is relative to inertial frames. That is, if two objects are in motion relative to one another, then events that are simultaneous for one object may not be simultaneous for the other. However, it is natural to think that everything that presently co-exists with an object is simultaneous with it (and *vice versa*). The problem then is that, as simultaneity is relative, so what counts as *present* is relative to inertial frames. Because, for the presentist, what exists is what is present, then *what exists* is relative to inertial frames. So, if I am travelling at a different velocity to you, what exists for me is different from what exists for you! That what exists may depend upon how fast one moves seems deeply counterintuitive to most philosophers, and thus they generally repudiate presentism.

At this juncture, some presentists bite the bullet saying that existence *is* relative to inertial frames. Others argue instead that it is consistent with our best science to believe a theory that replaces Einstein's theory, where the replacement theory *does not* relativise simultaneity (Bourne 2006, Chapters 6–8; Tooley 1997, Chapter 11).

Further reading: Bourne (2006, especially Chapters 2 and 3); Crisp (2003); Zimmerman (2008)

PRIMARY AND SECONDARY QUALITIES

The debate about the distinction between primary and secondary qualities goes back several centuries (the distinction is present in the work of both

Galileo and Descartes), the most well-known protagonists being **John Locke** and **George Berkeley**.

Locke (1690, Book II, Chapter 8) famously distinguishes between primary and secondary qualities. Primary qualities, roughly, are qualities (or **properties**) whose existence in no way depends upon our perception; moreover, our sensory impression of the quality resembles the quality itself. Locke includes extension (roughly, the fact that an object takes up or is 'extended in' space), shape and solidity. Secondary qualities, by contrast, are supposed to be those whose existence depends in some way on our perception. Standard (alleged) secondary qualities are colours and smells: to say that an object is red, or has a particular smell is not, Locke thinks, to say something about how the object is 'in itself'. Rather, it is to say something about how the object *affects us* – and in particular, how it affects our *senses*. Secondary qualities, on Locke's view, are powers to produce certain kinds of sensation *in us*: they are, to use a contemporary term, **response dependent**. So, although our visual impression of roundness really does resemble some feature of the object – roundness is a primary quality – our visual impression of red, say, does not resemble any feature that the object has independently of us.

Moreover, objects have those powers to produce sensations in virtue of their primary qualities, and in particular in virtue of the primary qualities of the 'corpuscles' which (according to the 'corpuscularian hypothesis' that was popular at the time Locke was writing) constitute the object. Locke's distinction between primary and secondary qualities thus has some affinity with the distinction between **categorical and dispositional properties**, with the primary qualities acting as the 'categorical basis' of the secondary qualities, which are powers or dispositions to affect our senses in certain ways.

Some of Locke's arguments for the distinction between primary and secondary qualities are, unfortunately, rather dubious. For example, he justifies the claim that secondary qualities such as heat are not really 'in the object' by pointing to the fact that the same water can seem hot to one hand and cold to the other (if, for example, you have been out in cold weather wearing only one glove); yet clearly the same object cannot possess two contradictory properties at the same time. This and other arguments are pounced on by Berkeley (1710: §§1–15), who points out that the same thing is true of alleged primary qualities: the same coin can appear round to one observer and elliptical to another, depending on the angle from which they view the coin. Berkeley notoriously concludes that primary qualities are not really 'in' material objects either; indeed, he goes further and concludes that the very notion of 'matter', conceived as mind-independent, makes no sense (see **phenomenalism and idealism**).

The popularity of the distinction between primary and secondary qualities has, however, endured (unlike the popularity of phenomenalism and idealism). One reason for this is that it promises to effect at least a partial reconciliation between what are sometimes called the 'manifest image' and the 'scientific image': the common-sense, ordinary conception of the world that we deploy in our everyday lives, and the rather different conception of the world delivered by contemporary science. Indeed, this may well have been part of Locke's point: according to the corpuscularian hypothesis, objects are composed of tiny corpuscles, the size, shape and motion of which are responsible for the object's properties and behaviour. How, then, do we account for the fact that objects have colours and smells – how can an object be red, when all the object is really composed of are corpuscles, with particular sizes and shapes, in motion? Answer: colours and smells are mere powers of the object to produce sensations *in us*; and those powers exist because of the size, shape and motion of its constituent corpuscles. Thus we can hold that material objects are merely collections of corpuscles (with their primary qualities of shape, size and motion) – this is the 'scientific image', or at least it was in Locke's day – and also hold that material objects have colours and smells (the manifest image): there is, it turns out, no incompatibility between these two conceptions of the nature of reality. (Of course, the corpuscularian hypothesis was eventually discredited. However, the same sort of move can arguably be made with respect to the contemporary scientific worldview.)

Further reading: Blackburn (1999, Chapter 7)

PRIMITIVE

A primitive of a theory is a predicate (or sometimes a **concept**) that has no **conceptual analysis** according to that theory. For instance, the predicate '__ is a brother of__' could be analysed in terms of '__ is male' and '__ is a sibling of__' (i.e. x is a brother of y if and only if x is male and x is the sibling of y). So, a theory that endorsed such an analysis would not take '__ is a brother of __' as primitive. Or consider the predicate: '__ is located in space'. Many (although not all) theories will say that no analysis can be given of that predicate – that there is nothing more to be said about what it is for something to be located in space. So, in that case, '__ is located in space' would be a primitive. Note that a predicate's being a primitive is always relative to a theory: what one theory says is a primitive, another theory may say is not.

It is standard to believe that it is a **theoretical virtue** for a theory to have as few primitives as possible. If you can do the same work with fewer primitives – that is, fewer concepts left unexplained – this is a good thing. This is not to say that a theory should not have *any* primitives – virtually everyone thinks this is impossible, and that every theory must take *some* predicates as its stock of primitives. Moreover, and this is important, there might be other theoretical virtues that outweigh the cost of including primitives. For instance, one theory might have fewer primitives but have a bloated ontology or fail to have as much explanatory power as another theory. In such cases, the cost of including the primitives may be balanced by the gains made in avoiding such problems. However, there are no clear, fixed rules with which to decide such choices, and you will often find metaphysicians disagreeing about where the addition of primitives is justified.

One good examples of such a debate is that between the 'realist' about **universals** which are abundant (who analyse predication in terms of objects instantiating universals, although they might take some things – like **instantiation** – as primitive; so they lower the number of primitives at the cost of including more things, the universals, in their ontology) and the **austere nominalist** (who thinks we should eliminate as many *things* as possible, such as universals, but then has to take hordes of predicates as primitive – **paraphrasing** away all apparent reference to **properties** tends to result in a proliferation of predicates). Another example is that between the genuine **modal realist** (who wants to eliminate *all* modal primitives by introducing lots of **concrete possible worlds** into their ontology) and those who disagree such as *ersatz* modal realists or modal **fictionalists** (who take *some* modal concepts as primitive, but repudiate the existence of concrete possible worlds).

PRINCIPLE OF ALTERNATE POSSIBILITIES (PAP)

The Principle of Alternate Possibilities, or 'PAP' for short, is the principle that an agent S is **morally responsible** for performing an action A only if they could have done otherwise than A. PAP is relevant to the debate between **compatibilism** and **incompatibilism** about **free will** – a debate about whether or not acting freely is compatible with **determinism** (the thesis that everything that happens, including our acts, is determined by the past plus the **laws of nature**). PAP (which is a thesis about moral responsibility) is relevant to this debate because acting freely is generally taken to be a precondition for being morally responsible. So if PAP is false (as **Frankfurt's nefarious neurosurgeon case** is alleged to show), it must also be false that S performs A *freely* only if they could have done otherwise. (If S is morally responsible for doing A, and moral responsibility for doing A requires that S does A freely, then S does A freely. So if S is morally responsible for doing A despite lacking the ability to do otherwise, it must also be that S does A freely despite lacking that ability.) One reason why PAP is important for the free will debate, then, is because it is related to the principle that acting *freely* requires the ability to do otherwise; and this is a premise in the **Consequence Argument** for incompatibilism.

Weakening PAP

In fact, most incompatibilists subscribe only to a weaker principle than PAP. Imagine that Sam gets very drunk but decides to drive home anyway. She drives far too fast and kills a pedestrian. Intuitively, Sam is morally responsible for killing the pedestrian; but it might be that, given the speed at which she was driving, she could not have avoided doing so. Many incompabilists will say that PAP is restricted to those actions for which we are *directly* morally responsible, and that in this case Sam is only *indirectly* morally responsible for killing the pedestrian: she is morally responsible for it because there was some *previous* act A, for which she was directly morally responsible, but which was such that she *could* have done otherwise than A. Perhaps she could have driven more slowly. Or, if she was too drunk to have been able to do that, perhaps she could have decided not to drive home. Or perhaps, if she was too drunk to have been in a position to make *that* decision, she could at least have refrained from getting drunk in the first place. So, Sam was directly morally responsible for putting herself in a position where she was going to drive dangerously, and – in line with a version of PAP restricted to 'direct' moral responsibility – she was, at that time, able to refrain from putting herself in that position. And so she is indirectly moral responsible for later killing the pedestrian, even though, at the time she did *that*, she was unable to do otherwise.

Compatibilism and PAP

Compatibilists fall into two broad categories when it comes to PAP. Some hold that there is a perfectly good sense of 'could have done otherwise' that is (contra the Consequence Argument) compatible with **determinism**. So, determinism is no bar to being able to do otherwise and hence no bar to acting freely and morally responsibly. Many such compatibilists subscribe to what is known as the 'conditional analysis' of the ability to do otherwise. The basic idea is that 'S was able to do otherwise than A' (and so had 'alternative possibilities' available to her) should be understood to mean that S *would* have done otherwise, if she had *chosen* to do otherwise. Even if determinism is true, I could have done otherwise than make a cup of tea because, if I had chosen to make coffee instead, I would have made coffee and not tea.

The standard incompatibilist objection to the conditional analysis is that it just delays the problem: what makes it the case that I could have *chosen* to make coffee instead, given that I was determined to choose tea? It looks like the defender of the conditional analysis must say that there is some further possible choice or action A_1, such that had I chosen or done *that*, I would have chosen to make coffee rather than tea. However, it is hard to see what that choice or action might be; and in any case, even if we managed to find a suitable candidate for A_1, the question would simply reappear: in order for it to be true that I could have done A_1, there must be some further choice or action A_2, such that if I had chosen or done A_2, I would have done A_1. And so on, *ad infinitum*.

The second kind of compatibilist view about PAP is that it is simply false (see, e.g., Dennett 1984, Chapter 6 and **Frankfurt's nefarious neurosurgeon**). Suppose that Sam is the kind of person who is literally psychologically incapable of hitting someone who is being particularly annoying, in normal circumstances (e.g. the annoying person is not threatening to kill Sam's family if she does not hit them! Perhaps in those circumstances Sam could hit them; but those are not the circumstances we are imagining). It is just part of Sam's character that she is not the kind of person who resorts to violence in the face of mild provocation. Does it really follow that Sam is not morally responsible – in particular, that she is not praiseworthy – for refusing to resort to violence? Many compatibilists think that the answer to this question is clearly 'no': the fact that hitting the annoying person was not a possibility that was open to Sam in no way nullifies the intuitive praiseworthiness of her behaviour.

Of course, the incompatibilist might respond that this is just another case of indirect moral responsibility: Sam's praiseworthiness depends upon there having been some previous time at which, say, she could have chosen *not* to become the kind of person who does not resort to violence. So her indirect praiseworthiness for not hitting the annoying person derives from her direct praiseworthiness for some previous choice. The compatibilist, in turn, will simply dispute the relevance of the existence of such a prior choice. It simply does not matter whether there was some prior choice Sam made – a choice that she could have refrained from making – when it comes to her praiseworthiness for not hitting the annoying person. That simply is not an issue we consider when we praise someone for not resorting to violence. In other words, it simply is not part of our ordinary notion of moral responsibility that we take it to depend upon whether the agent could have done otherwise, either now or at some point in the past.

Further reading: Dennett (1984, Chapter 6); see also the *Further reading* for **Frankfurt's nefarious neurosurgeon**

PROBABILISTIC THEORIES OF CAUSATION

Until around the 1960s, philosophers tended to assume that **causation** must be deterministic, so that a cause is not only 'necessary for' its effect (the cause is required in order for the effect to occur) but also 'sufficient for' – that is, guarantees – its effect. The sufficiency requirement connects with the thesis of **determinism**, according to which a complete specification of the facts about the Universe at a given time, together with the **laws of nature**, entails a complete specification of the facts at any later time. So the general idea is that, given the background conditions (the electricity is on, there is water in the kettle, and so on), if the cause occurs (flipping the switch on the kettle, say), the effect (the water boiling) *must* occur: given the laws of nature, the background conditions and the cause, there is just no possibility of the effect failing to occur. The 'necessary for' requirement also connects with determinism. If we extract the alleged cause (putting the kettle on) from all the other relevant features of the situation (water in the kettle, etc.), then it is guaranteed (given the laws) that the effect *would not* occur: the water cannot boil unless you switch on the kettle (well, this is in the normal run of things, excluding cases of **pre-emption** and **over-determination**).

Since around the 1960s, however, philosophers have taken seriously the possibility that **indeterminism**, and not determinism, might be true. Many of them have correspondingly taken seriously the idea that causes need be neither necessary nor sufficient for their effects after all.

Consider the following (doubtless rather unrealistic) **thought experiment**. Eva, who is a malicious but rather capricious bomb-maker, is going to flip a coin that is rigged up to a machine. (We are assuming here that it is a genuinely indeterministic matter whether the coin lands heads or tails – that is, that the probabilities below are genuine **chances** in the technical sense.) If the coin lands heads, the machine will in turn detonate a bomb; if it lands tails, it will not. Now, suppose that Eva plans to toss a particular coin, and there is a 50 per cent chance that this particular coin will lands heads. However, Eric happens to have in his possession a special, weighted coin, and there is a 90 per cent chance that *that* coin will land heads if tossed. Eric is even more malicious than Eva and he also wants the bomb to go off. And he knows he can switch the coins without Eva knowing. So he switches the coins (call this event c), thus increasing the chance of the bomb going off from 50 per cent to 90 per cent. (i.e. if Eric had not switched the coins, there would have been a 50 per cent chance of the bomb going off. However, with the coins switched, the chance is 90 per cent.) In fact, when Eva tosses Eric's coin, it does land heads and the bomb goes off (event e).

Was event c – Eric's switching the coins – a cause of the explosion? According to most philosophers, the answer is 'yes'. Why? Well, one reason to think so is that Eric is surely at least partly morally responsible for the explosion (as is Eva – it was her bomb, after all, and she flipped the coin knowing full well that it might lead to an explosion). He deliberately switched the coins with the intention of making the explosion more likely to happen, and it did happen, just as he hoped it would. However, why would he be morally responsible, if what he did was not a cause of the explosion?

Note, however, that c – the switch – was neither necessary nor sufficient for e, the explosion. c was not sufficient for e because the chance of e occurring once the switch had been made was only 90 per cent: there was still a chance that the coin would land tails and the bomb would not go off. And c was not necessary for e either, because even if Eric had not made the switch, there would still have been some chance (a 50 per cent chance, in fact) that the bomb would go off anyway. Hence, assuming indeterminism – that is, assuming that there are 'rock-bottom' chances other than 0 per cent and 100 per cent – an event c can cause event e even though c is neither necessary nor sufficient for e.

Without going into the thorny details, a standard way of analysing causation that accommodates this claim is to say that a cause *raises the probability* of its effect. (In fact, some philosophers think that it is only a *change* in probability that is required and not an *increase*; see, for example, Beebee 1998.) How we are to understand 'raising the probability' is a contentious question, but one straightforward account, due to **David Lewis**, is a version of his original **counterfactual theory of causation**. According to this account, c caused e if and only if had c not occurred, the chance of e would have been lower than it actually was. (This account gets the Eva/Eric case right, because if Eric had not switched the coins, the chance of the explosion would have been lower. However, plenty of counter-examples and amendments to the analysis have been proposed since Lewis first introduced it.)

The term 'probabilistic theory of causation' is sometimes applied to any theory of causation according to which causation should be analysed in terms of **probability** or **chance**, as in the analysis just described. However, sometimes the term is reserved for what are sometimes called 'statistical' or 'statistical relevance' analyses of causation; see **probabilistic theories of causation (type-level)**.

Further reading: Beebee (1998)

PROBABILISTIC THEORIES OF CAUSATION (TYPE-LEVEL)

Probabilistic theories of type-level **causation** (sometimes just referred to as 'probabilistic theories of causation') deal with so-called 'type-level causation' (as in 'smoking causes cancer') rather than **token–level causation** (as in 'Eric's switch was a cause of the explosion', or 'John's smoking caused him to get cancer'). 'Type-level causation' goes by a variety of alternative names, including 'population causation', 'property-level causation' and 'generic causation'. Also, probabilistic theories are sometimes called 'statistical' or 'statistical relevance' theories.

The basic idea behind such theories, as with token-level **probabilistic theories of causation**, is the idea that causation is a matter of increase (or perhaps just change) in **probability**. However, here the probabilities in question are not the individual **chances** of individual events happening (e.g. the bomb going off); instead, they are statistical claims about *frequencies* within populations. (Correspondingly, the probabilities deployed in these theories need not all be 0 or 1 if **determinism** is true – but that depends on the details of the theory in question that we shall ignore here.) So, for example, we might, as a first pass, hold that some 'causal factor' (such as smoking) causes another (cancer) in a particular population (the UK population, say) if and only if the probability of cancer (*C*) *given* smoking (*S*) is higher than the probability of cancer given not-smoking – that is, if and only if $P(C/S) > P(C/{\sim}S)$.

Intuitively – but not entirely accurately – we can think of $P(C/S)$, for example, as being a matter of the *proportion* of smokers who get cancer. So – again, not entirely accurately – $P(C/S) > P(C/{\sim}S)$ just if proportionally more smokers than non-smokers get cancer. The 'population' is just whatever collection of people, objects or events we are interested in: it might be the UK population, or the cat population of Macclesfield, or all the tea in China, or all fourth-division football games held in Lancashire during the 1970s. Or it could be a much more open-ended population, such as all cats, including those that will exist in the distant future.

Unfortunately, this crude analysis will not work, and here is a counter-example. The probability of rain (R) given that a barometer points to 'rain' (B) is higher than the probability of R given not-B (barometers would not be any good for predicting rain if this were not so), but barometer-readings do not *cause* rain. Rather, low atmospheric pressure (A) is a 'common cause' of both B and R. So the simple analysis described above is no good. However, we can get the troublesome statistical correlation between B and R to disappear if we 'hold fixed' A. In other words, if we compare $P(R/B \& A)$ with $P(R/\sim B \& A)$, we will find that the two probabilities are the same: in cases of low atmospheric pressure, whether or not the barometer is pointing to 'rain' (which is to say, whether or not the barometer is actually working) makes no difference to the likelihood of rain. So, according to a more plausible (and more complex) probabilistic theory of type-level causation, 'smoking causes cancer' is true in a given population only if (i) smoking increases the probability of cancer, and (ii) that increase in probability is not 'screened off' by any other factor. (In the barometer case, the correlation between B and R is screened off by atmospheric pressure – which is to say, if you hold A fixed, the correlation between B and R disappears.)

Needless to say, there are problems with this analysis too, and so we embark, as we often do when it comes to analysing causation, on a long cycle of counter-examples, revisions to the analysis, more counter-examples, more revisions, and so on. Lest we lose sight of the wood for the trees, though, it is important to note that a long-standing metaphysical issue is at stake here. The underlying question is simply 'what *is* type-level causation?' Some proponents of probabilistic theories are motivated by the desire to uphold a '**Humean**' theory of causation, according to which (type-level) causation is a matter of regularity – as with the original **regularity theory of causation**. It is just that now the regularity is a matter of *frequent* conjunction (i.e. statistical correlation) rather than *constant* conjunction. Others are motivated by the thought that our metaphysics of type-level causation ought to tie up in a fairly straightforward way with its *epistemology*: how it is that we actually and legitimately go about gaining *evidence* for the truth of, say, 'smoking causes cancer'. After all, a whole branch of medical science, namely epidemiology, is concerned with finding out the causes within the population of various ailments. It is hard to deny that a metaphysical account of type-level causation ought to cohere with our best methods for finding out about it.

Further reading: Hitchcock (2008)

PROBABILITY

Probability is a topic in metaphysics in its own right – the central question here being, 'what *are* probabilities?' This is sometimes cast as a question about what the right 'interpretation' of probability is. Mathematically, a 'probability' is just anything that satisfies the axioms of the probability calculus (see later). However, that does not tell us how we should 'interpret' that calculus: what in the world makes a claim that involves appeal to probability true? Probability also crops up elsewhere in metaphysics, in particular in discussions about **causation**, where **indeterminism** appears to require us to adopt a **probabilistic theory of causation**.

Metaphysical issues

There are several views about the metaphysical underpinnings (or 'interpretation') of probability. The *classical* picture is that the probability of some sentence P being true is the number of possibilities where P is true divided by the number of total possibilities. For instance, the probability of a die coming up 6 when you roll it is 1 in 6 (i.e. about 0.17) as there are six different possible outcomes, only one of which is a '6'.

The standard problem for the classical view is that the possibilities have to be *equal* possibilities. For instance, when it comes to me spontaneously combusting right this very instant there are only two possibilities – either I do or I do not. In one of those possibilities I do spontaneously combust, so (given the version of the classical view laid out here) the chance of me spontaneously combusting right now is 1 in 2. Since the chance of me so combusting is *not* fifty-fifty, something is terribly wrong. The proposed solution is that we only consider cases which are 'equally possible' like they are in the die-rolling scenario. However, this appears to be circular, for what can 'equally possible' mean other than 'equally *probable*' – and figuring out the probability of things (hence, what things are *equally* probable) is what the classical theory is meant to do in the first place.

There are alternatives. For instance, *frequentists* say that the probability of something occurring is just the frequency with which it occurs. So to say that the probability that a particular coin will land heads on a particular occasion is 0.5 is just to say that half of all coins that are ever tossed (including in the future) land heads-up. Frequentism about probabilities, like the **regularity theory of causation**, has problems with accidental regularities, however. For instance, it seems perfectly possible that the probability of heads could be 0.5, and yet, by coincidence, 55 per cent of all the coins ever tossed land heads. However, the frequency theory rules

189

out this possibility. A standard move at this point is to say that the frequency includes not just all *actual* coin tosses, but also merely *possible* coin tosses, so that (say) the probability of a particular coin landing heads is the same as what the frequency of heads *would* tend towards, if we carried on tossing coins indefinitely.

Another popular theory is the *propensity view*. This view says that there is a dispositional property – a propensity – that things have to produce certain results (see also **categorical versus dispositional properties**), and that this disposition has a certain quantitative value (e.g. 0.5). The probability of that result occurring is not the *frequency* of it occurring, but the *propensity* for it to do so. So our coin has (say) a propensity 0.5 to land heads, and this is consistent with the possibility that 55 per cent of all coins land heads when tossed (just as it is perfectly possible for something to be soluble and never actually dissolve).

One problem with the propensity account is that it seems only to assign probabilities to events that are genuinely undetermined by the past plus the laws (see **indeterminism**); in other words, the propensity account at best gives us an account of one *kind* of probability, namely 'rock-bottom' probability or **chance** (in a special, technical sense of 'chance' that is by no means universally used, so beware!). By analogy, you might assume that a particular pane of glass is *fragile* – it is disposed to break when struck by, say, a brick. If you then hurled a brick at it and it did not break, you would revise your opinion and say it was not fragile after all (maybe it is special, reinforced glass). The fragility of the glass does not depend on what you do or do not happen to *know* or *believe* about it; either it is fragile or it is not.

If probabilities are dispositions, then they are a bit like fragility. However, most probability-talk does not work like that. A poker player, for example, might judge that the probability that the next card to be dealt will be an ace is 1/7, since she knows that there are 21 cards left and 3 of them are aces. However, nothing has the *propensity* of 1/7 to be an ace; either the card at the top of the deck is an ace or it is not, which is to say that its 'propensity' to be an ace is either 1 or 0. So our poker player would just be *wrong* about the probability of an ace. Similarly, even if **determinism** is true, it would still seem to make perfectly good sense to say that the probability of this coin landing heads is 0.5, even though, again, its *propensity* to land heads (or its chance of landing heads) is either 1 or 0.

Nomenclature

There is some common nomenclature used in the literature, often without any explanation of what it means. This short introduction should help. The probability of a proposition coming about is often represented as '$P(A) = x$', where '$P(A)$' represents the probability of A being true, and x is a number between 0 and 1. (Probabilities are sometimes denoted by 'Pr' rather than 'P'.) So, if A was the proposition <the fair coin came up heads> we would express that as '$P(A) = 0.5$'. If A was the proposition <the ball landed on zero on the roulette wheel>, it would be '$P(A) = 0.027027...$'.

Other nomenclature that is commonly used includes:

$P(A \& B)$ represents 'the probability of both A and B being true'.

For instance, if A is <coin A came up heads when tossed at time t> and B is <coin B came up heads when tossed at time t>, then the probability of them *both* coming up heads is ¼; in other words, $P(A \& B) = 0.25$.

$P(A \mid B)$ represents 'the probability of A being true given that B is true'.

For instance, if A were the proposition <next week, I will have to constantly go to the toilet in front of other people>, you might think that $P(A)$ would be quite low. However, if B were the proposition <next week, I will be in jail> then, even though the chance of me being in jail this time next week is itself miniscule, the chance of me regularly having to go to the toilet in front of other people *given I will be in jail*, represented by $P(A \mid B)$, is exceedingly high.

Indeed, given $P(A)$ and $P(B)$, one can calculate both $P(A \& B)$ and $P(A \mid B)$ quite easily (see Mellor 2005: 14–5). However, such mathematical detail probably will not prove necessary, as to understand the metaphysics of probability you almost certainly will not need much more than this basic introduction to the nomenclature.

Further reading: Mellor (2005); Hájek (2010)

PROBLEM OF LUCK

The **Consequence Argument** purports to show that **free will** – and so **moral responsibility** – is incompatible with **determinism**: if our decisions and actions are determined by facts about the distant past together with the **laws of nature**, then we cannot do otherwise, and so our actions are not free and we are not morally responsible for them. The problem of luck, by contrast, is a problem about the compatibility of moral responsibility and **indeterminism**.

Why might moral responsibility be thought to be incompatible with indeterminism? Well, imagine that tossing a coin is an indeterministic process, so that the initial conditions plus the laws deliver a 50 per cent **chance** that the coin will land heads. (Coin tossing may not really be indeterministic; perhaps if you constructed a coin-tossing machine that tossed the coin in exactly the same way every time, and if you used exactly similar coins and activated the machine in exactly the same circumstances, the coin would land heads up every time. However, let us imagine that it is in fact impossible to build such a machine, given the laws of nature.) If tossing a coin really is indeterministic, is it possible to *control* the outcome of a toss? It seems not: whether the coin lands heads or tails is just a matter of luck. After all, imagine that the coin lands heads. There is another **possible world** that has exactly the same laws of nature as the actual world, and is exactly like the actual world right up until the point where the coin is tossed, except that in that world the coin lands tails. (Note that it does not matter what the relevant probabilities are here, so long as they are between 0 and 1. It would still be a matter of luck if you tossed a biased coin that had a 90 per cent chance of landing heads, since you would still have no control over whether it landed heads or tails.)

If our decisions are similarly not determined by the initial conditions plus the laws – that is, if, right up until you actually decide what you are going to do, more than one decision is left open by the past plus the laws – then it looks as though the decision you actually make is no less a matter of luck than is the outcome of a coin toss, and so you are no more responsible for the former than you are for the latter. To put the point more vividly, imagine that Jane is on her way to a very important business meeting (this example is taken from Kane 1999). On her way, she comes across someone being assaulted in an alley. She has to decide whether to help the victim or attend the meeting. Eventually she decides to help the victim, and intuitively her behaviour is morally praiseworthy. However, let us assume that it really is not determined, right up until Jane makes her decision, what she will decide to do, so that the condition that **incompatibilists** require for free will and moral responsibility – namely the ability to do otherwise – is met. In that case, there is another possible world that has exactly the same laws of nature as the actual world, and is exactly like the actual world right up until the point where Jane decides, except that in that world Jane decides to go to the meeting instead. So it looks as though Jane is not really morally praiseworthy for her decision to help the victim, given that nothing in her decision-making process determined her to make the decision she actually made; she was not really in control of her decision, any more than she would have been if she would decided what to do on the basis of the toss of a coin.

The problem of luck reveals a worrying tension in our thinking about free will and moral responsibility. On the one hand, there seems to be a tension between acting freely and determinism: determinism seems to rob us of a genuine *choice* between alternative actions. On the other hand, *in*determinism seems to rob us of genuine *control* over which of the alternative actions we perform. However, of course, if free will is incompatible *both* with determinism *and* with indeterminism, then the unavoidable conclusion is that free will is impossible, since one out of determinism and indeterminism must be true (see **illusion of free will**).

A solution to the problem of luck?

Kane (1999) has argued that the problem of luck can be overcome. Roughly, his claim is that in cases such as Jane's, where there is a sort of internal conflict about what to do, the agent is *trying* to make two incompatible choices (in Jane's case, trying to choose to help the victim and simultaneously trying to choose to attend the meeting). However, we *can* be responsible for doing what we try to do, even when the link between our trying and our eventual success is indeterministic. (Imagine shooting someone using a gun that had some chance of jamming. You tried to shoot them and you succeeded; so even though the trying did not fully *determine* that you would succeed – the gun might have jammed – it seems that you were still morally responsible for shooting them because you did what you were trying to do.) So in Jane's case, whichever decision she makes, she succeeds in making a decision that she was trying to make and so she is morally responsible for it.

Further reading: Kane (1999); Mele (2006, Chapter 1)

PROCESS THEORIES OF CAUSATION

One way to think about the debate between supporters of the **regularity theory of causation** – and, indeed, any theory inspired by the thesis of **Humean supervenience** (for example, the **counterfactual theory**) – and their rivals is to think about what kinds of entity we want cropping up in our fundamental **ontology**. Humeans think we should adopt a theory of causation that eschews **natural necessity**; and they tend, traditionally, to assume that *any* kind of fundamental, irreducible or **intrinsic** relation between causes and effects will either just *be* natural necessity (perhaps by another name), or will be equally dubious.

Those who adopt a 'process theory' of causation typically reject this assumption. The basic idea is that we can think of causation as a fundamental, intrinsic and yet entirely non-mysterious relation, that most certainly is not simply natural necessity by another name; and this relation is (according to one proposal) *energy transfer*. So, for example, when one billiard ball hits another and causes it to move, the causal relation is not constituted either by any regularity (e.g. billiard ball movements of the first kind being 'constantly conjoined' with movements of the second kind) or by the existence of a relation of natural necessity; rather, it is constituted by the transfer of energy from the first ball to the second. Other obvious cases would include flipping a switch and a light going on, or turning on the heating and the room warming up. However, process theorists claim that this generalises to all genuine cases of causation.

Different process theorists disagree about what, exactly, is transferred; some hold that it is energy or energy-momentum, and others (for example, Dowe 2000) claim that the transfer of any 'conserved quantity' recognised by physics will do.

One advantage of the process theory is, as we have already seen, the thought that it renders causation non-mysterious, but avoids the problems associated with the regularity and counterfactual theories of causation. Causation is non-mysterious because energy, momentum and conserved quantities generally are things we need to believe in anyway if we are to endorse our best physical theory about how the world works. So – as with the regularity theory (and, arguably, the counterfactual theory) – no addition to our **ontology** is needed in order to account for causation. However, the regularity and counterfactual theories face well-known problems, particularly in accounting for phenomena such as **pre-emption**. By contrast, pre-emption would seem to be easily dealt with by the process theory. For example, if Suzy throws her rock at the window just before Billy throws his, so that Suzy's gets there first, the process theory obviously delivers the right result that Suzy's throw caused the window to break and not Billy's, because energy is transferred from Suzy's rock to the window but not from Billy's: Billy's just sails straight through the hole created by Suzy's rock.

On the 'costs' side, however, one alleged problem with the process theory is that it rules out **causation by absence**. If you fail to water your neighbour's plant while she is on holiday and it dies, many philosophers claim that it is intuitively obvious that your omission causes the plant's death. However, clearly no energy is transferred from you to the plant. Another objection is that the process theory does not aim to provide a **conceptual analysis** of causation and so cannot tell the whole story: there are **possible worlds** with different **laws of nature**, where there is no energy or momentum or any conserved quantity, but where there is, arguably, plenty of causing going on. (For example, some such worlds might work by the direct intervention of a deity, or by the casting of spells by witches and wizards – see the 'trumping pre-emption' case in **pre-emption**.) Process theorists generally do not want to commit to claiming that such worlds are devoid of causation – a wizard who turns a prince into a frog surely causes the prince's unfortunate fate even though no energy is transferred – but that means that they are unable to explain what it is in virtue of which the wizard *does* the prince to turn into a frog. (see **Canberra Plan** for a possible way to deal with this problem.)

Further reading: Dowe (2000, Chapter 1); Dowe (2008)

PROPERTIES

Properties are *characteristics* of things: redness, solidity, squareness, beauty are all examples of properties. **Austere nominalists** are **anti-realists** about properties: although they grant that claims like 'the cricket ball is red' are often true, they deny that there is any such thing as *redness*. There are many different kinds of **realism** about **properties**, each of which gives a different account of their nature: realists about **universals, trope theorists, class nominalists** and **resemblance nominalists**.

Some care is needed with the term 'property'. First, even austere nominalists are normally quite happy to indulge in property-talk; if the pillar box and the Coke can are both red, for example, the austere nominalist may happily say that they share a property. However, she understands their 'sharing a property' to amount merely to the fact that the pillar box is red and so is the Coke can (see **paraphrase**). Second, some philosophers take '*a* has property *F*' (as opposed to merely '*a* is *F*') to mean that *a* has some distinctive metaphysical intrinsic *nature*. On that construal of 'property', only believers in universals and tropes count as realists about properties. Class nominalists, for example, think that to be *F* is merely to be a member of the class of red things, so there is no item of **ontology**, present in *a* itself, that constitutes its *F*-ness. Hence on this restrictive reading of 'property', '*a* has property *F*' is false as far as the class nominalist is concerned (though '*a* is *F*' may still be true).

PROPER CLASS

See **set**.

PROPER PART

See **part**.

PROPOSITION

One way of thinking about propositions is as the things that are true or false (what are called '**truthbearers**').You might think it is only sentences which are true or false, but this can land you into trouble. For instance, it is eminently plausible to think that even if mankind had never existed, it would still be true that the world was round. However, if mankind does not exist then nobody ever says anything, and if nobody ever says anything then there are no sentences. So, the argument goes, if sentences are the truthbearers, then if none existed, nothing would be true or false. Allegedly, then, we need something mind-independent to be the truthbearers – and in step propositions. (Note that in this book we sometimes talk about sentences and sometimes propositions; usually there is no deep reason for this, and when there is, it should be obvious from the context.)

To use a metaphorical image, propositions are like sentences written down in God's Big Book of Reality, wherein God has written down every possible statement and scribbled 'true' or 'false' next to it accordingly. Whether or not mankind existed, the proposition <the Earth is round> (that sentence in God's Big Book that reads 'The Earth is round') would be true. Note that the symbols < and > around the sentence indicate that it is a proposition (as opposed to a sentence, which we surround with ' and ').

Propositions are usually thought of as **necessarily** existing **abstract** objects.This is a good way of ensuring (in the absence of God and his Big Book) that there enough of them hanging about the place to do the job. For example, if there were no **concrete** objects, <there are no concrete objects> would surely be true. However, if propositions were themselves concrete objects, there would then *be* no proposition to *be* true. What if there were no *abstract* objects? Would not we then lack the proposition <there are no abstract objects>? Well, no worries because propositions (like, it is normally thought, abstract objects generally) are *necessary* existents: so it is guaranteed that the proposition <there are no abstract objects> exists, and what is more that proposition is guaranteed to be false.

Propositions are not merely useful for acting as truthbearers, however, and they are sometimes pressed into service to perform other roles. For instance, propositions are sometimes thought to be the object of intentional states. If I fear there is a monster under my bed, then given this view of propositions, I stand in the *fearing* relation to the proposition <there is a monster under my bed>. If I really want the Monster Raving Loony Party to win the next election, then I stand in the *really wanting to come true* relation to <the Monster Raving Loony Party win the next election>. Propositions are also sometimes said to be the meanings of sentences – that is, sentences *express* propositions. If two scientists are discussing the shape of the Earth and they both say that it is round, then there would be two different utterances, both of which meant the same thing. So those two sentences would both express the proposition <the Earth is round>. Similarly, if I say 'snow is white' and Jacques says 'la neige est blanche', although the sentences sound different they mean the same thing – they both express <snow is white>. This might look a bit circular. Is not the proposition (as opposed to the sentence) <snow is white> still, well, *in English*? True enough. We can only *refer* to propositions by stating them in a language – there is no other way to do it. However, the thought is that *what* we are referring to is not, itself, a bit of the English language (or any other language, for that matter).

There are serious metaphysical questions about propositions and whether they should be included in our **ontology** or not. Some people hold that propositions exist as abstract objects in a category of their own; others (like **David Lewis**) give a **reductionist** analysis, holding that propositions are to be identified with certain **classes** of **possible worlds** (namely those possible worlds at which the proposition is the case); although still others will deny the existence of propositions altogether, trying to offer **paraphrases** for proposition talk.

Further reading: Loux (2006, Chapter 4); McGrath (2007)

PSYCHOLOGICAL CONTINUITY

Perhaps the most popular approach to the metaphysics of **personal identity** – that is, the **identity over time** of persons – is to try to ground personal identity in *psychological continuity*. For grey-haired Old Jack in 2010 to be identical to Wee Johnny who ran in the Olympics in Helsinki in 1952 is for Old Jack and Wee Johnny to be psychologically continuous; in general for person x at t_1 to be identical to person y at t_2 is for x to be psychologically continuous with y.

This tradition has its roots in **John Locke**'s 'memory theory' of person identity, according to which Old Jack is identical to Wee Johnny in virtue of the fact that *Old Jack remembers the experiences* of Wee Johnny, for example, Old Jack remembers winning the 100 metres in 1952. There are two well-known difficulties with Locke's memory theory, originally articulated by Locke's contemporaries Joseph Butler (1736) and Thomas Reid. Firstly, the fact that identity is a *transitive* **relation**, although *remembering the experiences of* is an *intransitive* relation, makes problems for Locke's account.

To illustrate, suppose that during the 1970s Old Jack was captain of a ship and was known to his crew as 'Captain McFaddon'. Let us suppose further that (i) Old Jack in 2010 remembers sailing the seven seas as Captain McFaddon, but no longer remembers being a young man (we can imagine that senility is setting in such that the only thing Jack can recall is his proud sailing career), and (ii) Captain McFaddon in 1974 remembers being Wee Johnny winning the 100 metres in 1952. By Locke's analysis we ought to conclude that (A) Old Jack is identical to Captain McFaddon (since he remembers the experiences of Captain McFaddon), (B) Captain McFaddon is identical to Wee Johnny (since he remembers the experiences of Wee Johnny), but (C) Old Jack is not identical to Wee Johnny (since he does not remember the experiences of Wee Johnny). However, if (A) is true and (B) is true, it follows by the transitivity of identity that Old Jack is identical to Wee Johnny contrary to (C). We thus derive a contradiction: Locke's theory implies that Old Jack both is and is not identical to Wee Johnny.

The second difficulty is that analysing personal identity in terms of memory seems to be circular, as the concept of memory is partially analysed in terms of the concept of personal identity. Part of what it is for Captain McPhaddon to *genuinely remember* winning the 100 metres in the 1952 Helsinki Olympics, as opposed to *merely thinking he remembers* winning the 100 metres in the 1952 Helsinki Olympics, is for it to be the case that Captain McPhaddon is identical to the person who won the 100 metres in the 1952 Helsinki Olympics. It is part of the concept of memory that you cannot remember someone else's experiences. Because of this, ascriptions of memory *presuppose*, and so cannot *explain*, facts about personal identity.

We can solve the first problem by distinguishing between memory connections and memory *continuity*. There are memory *connections* between x and y if and only if y remembers (some of) the experiences of x (or vice versa): Old Jack has direct memory connections with Captain McPhaddon in virtue of remembering the captain's experiences. There is memory *continuity* between x and y if and only if there are chains of overlapping memory connections between x and y: Old Jack has memory continuity with Wee Johnny in virtue of the fact that there are memory connections between Old Jack and Captain McPhaddon, and memory connections between Captain McPhaddon and Wee Johnny. The relation of memory continuity, like identity, is **transitive** and so by defining personal identity in terms of memory continuity rather than memory connections, we avoid the first difficulty. (This works because memory continuity is the **ancestral relation** of memory connection, and ancestral relations are always transitive.) A standard contemporary solution for the second difficulty is to use *quasi-memory* (or '*q*-memory' for short), rather than memory, in the analysis of personal identity

Later, philosophers attracted to the spirit of Locke's view have found it natural to involve other psychological connections in addition to memory in the analysis of personal identity. The fact that the intentions of Wee Johnny result in the actions of Captain McPhaddon, the fact that the beliefs, desires and character traits of Wee Johnny bring about the beliefs, desires and character traits of Captain McPhadden, all of these psychological causal connections seem as relevant to our concept of a single person as do connections in memory. We can say then that x at time t_1 and y at time t_2 are 'psychologically connected' if and only if the mental states of y are directly caused by the mental states of x (many theories of psychological continuity will qualify this with some kind of restriction on the kind of causal connection required), and that x at t_1 and y at t_2 are 'psychologically continuous' if and only if there are overlapping chains of psychological connectedness between x and y.

Again, psychological continuity is the 'ancestral' of psychological connectedness, so is transitive – which is what we need, given that identity is transitive. Again there are worries about circularity analogous to the worry in the memory case, for example, it seems that the concept of *intending* is partly analysed in terms of personal identity, in the sense that I can only intend that *I* do something. As with the simpler memory theory, most proponents of psychological continuity theories of personal identity try to avoid this worry by using quasi-states in their analyses – see *quasi-memory/quasi-state*).

One advantage of defining personal identity in terms of psychological continuity, of giving a 'psychological criterion of personal identity', as it is sometimes put, is that it allows us to make sense of the conceptual coherence of body swapping. Suppose Barack Obama's brain is put into David Cameron's body and David Cameron's brain put into Barack Obama's body, such that the person with Cameron's body post-op is psychologically continuous with Obama pre-op and the person with Obama's body post-op is psychologically continuous with Cameron pre-op. Many philosophers find it extremely natural to describe this situation as one in which the two men have swapped bodies: post-op Cameron has Obama's body and vice versa (see **thought experiment** for some discussion of a similar case). This is exactly the result a psychological criterion of personal identity gives us. In contrast, theories which account for the persistence of a person in terms of the persistence of their whole body struggle to account for the intuition that two people could in principle swap bodies. Those who identify the person with the brain, as opposed to the whole body, can make sense of body swapping in the above case, but it is not obvious that such a view is a stable middle way between psychological continuity theories and those views that identify the person with the whole body; see **bodily continuity**. See **animalism** for a related attempt to solve the problem.

The deepest challenges for psychological continuity theories of personal identity are raised by consideration of cases of **fission**. Having said that, some of the most interesting aspects of metaphysics of personal identity have resulted from proponents of a psychological continuity theories reflecting on these cases, and trying to work out what they ought to say about them, for example, **David Lewis**'s Multiple Occupancy Thesis (see **fission**), and Derek Parfit's claim that 'identity is not what matters in survival' (see **survival**).

Further reading: Chapters 2 and 3 of Noonan (1989) discuss Locke's memory theory and objections to it; Chapters 7–10 deal in depth with issues closely related to the psychological continuity theory of personal identity. See also Williams (1970) and Olson (2008)

PSYCHOLOGISM

See **concept**.

QUASI-MEMORY/QUASI-STATES

There is a well-known problem, originally posed by **John Locke**'s contemporary Butler (1736), for metaphysical theories that try to account for **personal identity** either in terms of memory or in terms of **psychological continuity**. The problem is that the concept of memory and the concepts of other aspects of psychological continuity are partially analysed in terms of the concept of personal identity. Part of what it is for Captain McPhaddon to *genuinely remember* winning the 100 metres in the 1952

Helsinki Olympics, as opposed to *merely thinking he remembers* winning the 100 metres in the 1952 Helsinki Olympics, is for it to be the case that Captain McPhaddon is identical to (i.e. is the same person as) the person who won the 100 metres in the 1952 Helsinki Olympics. It is part of the concept of memory that you cannot remember someone else's experiences. Because of this, ascriptions of memory *presuppose*, and so cannot *explain*, facts about personal identity.

Similarly, the concept of *intending* is partially analysed in terms of personal identity: it is a conceptual truth that a person can only intend that *she herself* perform a certain action. I cannot intend that *you* study hard for your exams (although I can obviously *desire* that you study hard for your exams). Again, there is the threat that any theory of personal identity which involves intending in the analysis will be circular.

The most popular response to this dilemma by memory and psychological continuity theorists of personal identity is to appeal to *quasi-memory* ('*q*-memory' for short) and *quasi-intending* (*q*-intending), and *quasi* mental states in general (*q*-states), in the analysis (see, for example, Shoemaker 1970 and Parfit 1971). As explained above, the problem with the concepts of memory and intending is that the concept of personal identity is one of the components involved in their analysis. The concepts of *q*-memory and *q*-intending are just like the concepts memory and intending, except that an analysis of them can be given without involving this troubling component. So *q*-memory is just like memory except you can *q*-remember someone else's experiences; *q*-intending is just like intending except you can *q*-intend to do someone else's actions. We can define *q*-memory in the following way:

> *X q*-remembers an experience *E* if and only if (i) *X* has an apparent memory of *E*, (ii) someone did have *E*, (iii) *E* caused *X* (in something like the way a memory is caused by the experience of which it is a memory).

Imagine that person *A*'s memories could somehow be 'fed' into person *B*'s mind. *A* genuinely remembers going on holiday to the Caribbean, let us say. *B* cannot *remember* the holiday, of course, since she did not go. However, she can (thanks to the memory-feed) *q*-remember it. 'Remember that sunset dinner I had on the beach?', *A* may ask *B*. 'No, obviously not', says *B*, 'but I *q*-remember it well. The wine was excellent, was not it? You really enjoyed yourself that night'.

Assuming that the notion of a *q*-memory is coherent, memories are a subclass of *q*-memories: memories are *q*-memories of experiences such that the person who originally had the experience and the person who is *q*-remembering the experience are one and the same person. (Of course, *in fact* there is no such thing as a memory-feed. So *in fact*, all our *q*-memories are memories. However, they would not be, if we *did* have memory-feeds.)

We can extend the notion of a *q*-memory to cover any mental state that involves the concept of personal identity in its analysis, so that we have the notion of *q*-intending, and so on. Removing the concept of personal identity from the analysis gives the analysis of the '*q*' version of that mental state. An account of personal identity in terms of *q*-memory and/or other *q*-states will not be subject to the circularity objection, for *q*-states do not involve the concept of personal identity in their definition.

There is some debate concerning whether we can make coherent sense of the phenomenology of a *q*-memory (which is not a memory). I automatically assume that my apparent memories, at least if they are veridical, are memories of experiences I myself had. Each of us makes this assumption automatically (and indeed quite rightly). Derek Parfit argues that this assumption is grounded in the contingent fact that people only *q*-remember their own experiences. If we lived in a world where people regularly had the *q*-memories of others implanted into them – just like in the film 'Total Recall' – then we would not automatically make this assumption; people would naturally think, 'I know I *q-remember* seeing the award ceremony. . . but I am not sure if I *remember* it'.

However, Schechtman (1990) has argued that the phenomenology of memory is more bound up with personal identity than can be accommodated by the notion of a *q*-memory. We experience the world a certain way because of who we are. French sounds very different to someone who understands French than it does to someone who does not. Places and people look different when they are familiar to when they are unfamiliar. Sausages smell different to an insatiable carnivore than they do to a meat-hating vegan. Suppose, Jacques is a Parisian who loves sausages, and Jack is monoglot English meat-hating vegan who has never been to Paris. Imagine that Jacques' *q*-memory of tucking into a plate of sausages in a Paris café with which he is very familiar, surrounded by French chatter, is implanted into Jack's head. There are two possibilities:

1   Jack's *q*-memory is qualitatively very different to Jacque's *q*-memory: the sausages would smell and look disgusting instead of inviting, the café unfamiliar instead of familiar and the chatter incomprehensible instead of meaningful. If so, it looks like there is no experience *E* such that Jacques remembers *E* and Jack *q*-remembers *E*. After all, Jacques did not feel disgusted by the smell of the sausages, he understood the conversation, and so on. So condition (ii) of the above analysis is violated.

2   Jack's q-memory is qualitatively identical to Jacques': the sausages smell delicious, and so on. In this case the q-memory seems be a *delusional*: it would seem to Jack, when 'reliving' the experience that *he* liked sausages, knew Paris very well and knew French, when in fact, of course, he does not. This shows, according to Schechtman, that the phenomenology of an apparent memory of an experience cannot be so easily separated from the identity of the person who originally had the experience: it is the fact that Jack is a very different kind of person to Jacques that leads to the q-memory being delusional.

For these reasons, Schechtman does not believe it is possible, contrary to what the proponents of q-memory assume, to take the concept of memory and distil from it a concept untainted by involvement with the concept of personal identity, which is what is required to get round the circularity objection. The notion of 'q-memory', for Schechtman, is an incoherent philosophical fiction.

Further reading: Noonan (1989, Chapter 8); Parfit (1971, Section III); Olson (2008); Schechtman (1990)

QUIDDITISM

Not to be confused with the rather dangerous sport enjoyed by Harry Potter and his chums at Hogwarts, 'quidditism' is the belief that the identity of a property is brute, in the sense that the identity of a property is independent of how objects with that property behave (including how they appear to us or are detected by measuring devices).

Scientists characterise mass and charge in terms of the **dispositions** that things with those properties manifest: things with mass fall to the ground, and things with negative charges are disposed to repel other things with negative charge (of course, the relevant dispositions are much more complex than this, but let us keep the example simple). For the quidditist, although we pick out mass and negative charge in the actual world with reference to these dispositions, there is no necessary connection between mass/negative charge and the dispositions they happen to endow objects with in the actual world. There is a **possible world**, according to the quidditist, where objects with mass behave just like objects with charge (for example, they repel other things with mass), and things with negative charge behave just like things with mass (for example, they fall to the ground).

The anti-quidditist is most likely to believe that properties just *are* dispositions: if the property of negative charge just is the disposition to repel other negatively charged objects, then of course there are no possible worlds where objects have negative charge and yet are do not have a disposition to repel other negatively charged things. Quidditists, in contrast, take properties to be 'quiddities': properties, which are only contingently connected to the dispositions of their bearers.

Quidditism is thus sometimes claimed to be an inevitable consequence of **Humean supervenience**, according to which (among other things) all the fundamental properties of things are *categorical* (see **categorical and dispositional properties**): to accept that an object is **intrinsically** disposed to behave in certain ways is tantamount to believing in **natural necessity**, which **Humeans** eschew. Anti-quidditists take this to be a good reason to abandon the view that the fundamental properties are categorical (Bird 2007, Chapter 4). Some of their opponents, however – notably **David Lewis** (2008) – simply bite the bullet and embrace quidditism.

Many philosophers take quidditism to be a view of properties that is to be understood analogously to **haecceitism** about objects.

QUINE, W. V.

Willard van Orman Quine (1908–2000) grew up in Akron, Ohio. Interested in mathematics, he was divided over what to study at university. After a suggestion from a fellow poker player to look at Bertrand Russell's philosophy of mathematics, he settled on studying philosophy, completing his PhD at Harvard on Whitehead and Russell's epic *Principia Mathematica*. During World War II, he served for three years in the Navy (attaining the rank of Lieutenant Commander) before returning to Harvard and becoming a full professor in the Department of Philosophy. He never limited himself to the United States, however, and travelled far and wide, visiting a total of 118 countries. Nor was travel his only passion – in his spare time he enjoyed Dixieland jazz and even played a banjo in various jazz groups.

Philosophically, Quine concentrated on the philosophy of language, logic and, of course, metaphysics. Quine is renowned for playing a key role in kick-starting contemporary **ontology**. His work on that area is best summed up in his famous 1948 article 'On what there is', where he lays out his theory of **ontological commitment**. He argued that the entities we are committed to are those that the sentences we hold true quantify over. As a die-hard naturalist (believing that philosophy is continuous with science), Quine believed that we only need to look at our best scientific theory and see what that quantifies over to figure out what the correct ontology is. Up until his death on Christmas Day 2000, he continued to write on metaphysics, notably arguing for **austere nominalism**, although he later changed his mind and settled on a form of **class nominalism**. Quine is also famous for arguing that there is no distinction between **analytic and synthetic truths**, and for being very sceptical about *de re* **modality**, which he took to be pretty much equivalent to – and so just as bad as – essentialism (see **essence**) (see also **metametaphysics**).

Further reading: Orenstein (2002)

RAMSEY–LEWIS VIEW OF LAWS

The Ramsey–Lewis view of laws (RLV) dates back to Ramsey (1928); in fact, an earlier version is to be found in John Stuart Mill (1806–73) – so it is sometimes called the Mill–Ramsey–Lewis view – but the flesh was put on the bones by **David Lewis** (1973b: 72–7). RLV aims to give a **conceptual analysis** of what it is for a proposition to be a law of nature, with an eye to avoiding a commitment to **natural necessity**. The simplest version of the theory is that:

> L is a law of nature $=_{df} L$ features as an axiom or theorem in the best deductive theory of the world.

In other words, we look to science to find out what system of axioms best fits with what goes on in the world, and whatever propositions feature as part of that system are the laws of nature.

RLV is thus sometimes known as a 'sophisticated' **regularity theory of laws**: a regularity theory because the best system just contains generalisations about what happens in the Universe (or that is the hope, anyway), and 'sophisticated' because it is a lot fancier, and better, than the 'naïve' regularity theory, according to which L is a law of nature if and only if L is a true universal generalisation. For example, accidental regularities such as 'all lumps of gold are smaller than one mile in diameter' do not come out as laws of nature according to RLV, since 'all lumps of gold. . .' is certainly not going to be one of the axioms of our best theory of the Universe – it is hardly up there with $e = mc^2$.

What is the best theory?

What RLV *does not* mean is that laws are the axioms of the theory we *currently* think is best. Ptolemaic science might have held that the Earth was at the centre of the universe and (we might imagine) was the best science of the day. However, that does not mean that, back in the time of ancient Greece, it was a law of nature that the Earth was the centre of everything! Instead, what is intended is that we look to the best theory *even if we do not know it yet*. So, it is the theory that scientists would come up with if they were given enough time and resources to make a theory that was better than any other theory that could be.

Even then, some issues remain concerning what counts as best. Lewis takes the best theory to be the theory that has the best balance between simplicity and strength. Both are straightforward notions. A *simple* theory is one that has only a small number of axioms. Let theory A consist of only a single axiom ('all dogs are mammals'); theory B be a theory like that offered by contemporary physics (which would be a rather large and complicated list of axioms); and theory C just be a list of every true proposition (which would be an even larger, indeed infinitely large, list of axioms). In that case, theory A would be the simplest, B not as simple and C very complicated indeed. A *strong* theory is one that entails many true propositions. So theory A entails only that dogs are mammals. There is not much more to it – it is a very weak system. Theory B is relatively strong – as strong as contemporary science can be in entailing what goes on around us (which is not everything, after all contemporary science still fails to entail certain things). Theory C is the strongest – in simply being a list of every true proposition it clearly entails every true proposition, and so it is as strong as a theory could be. Hence, although A is simple, it is weak; although C is very strong, it is insanely complex; so of our three theories, B would be the best theory with regards to the best *balance* of strength and simplicity. Of course, the best theory would not be any of A, B or C – it will be some other theory we are yet to discover. However, the above discussion should give you some idea of the criteria used for determining which is best.

Problems for the Ramsey–Lewis view

Here are two sample problems.

Problem one: There are difficulties concerning simplicity. What is simple to one person might be complicated to another. Imagine a weird universe that contains large cubes and spheres, medium cubes and spheres and small cubes and spheres. The large cubes and spheres are all black, the medium and small ones are either blue, yellow or pink. We observe that the medium and small cubes and spheres are accompanied by a certain sound when they pass by us, but the large are accompanied by no sound. In this weird universe we come up with the following competing scientific theories (which have but one axiom each):

- *Theory 1*: All objects smaller than a certain size cause a certain sound.
- *Theory 2*: All blue, yellow or pink cubes or blue, yellow or pink spheres cause a certain sound.

Both theories are as strong as one another, for – given what goes on around us – they both entail the observations we make about the objects and the sounds they produce. However, the first theory seems *prima facie* simpler, so according to RLV is the best theory.

But now imagine a different culture. They have no phrase for 'smaller than'. They are also less interested in colour: they have no distinction between blue, yellow or pink, calling such things 'blellink'. However, they are very interested in shape, and have an enormous range of words for shapes of different sizes. Large spheres are 'leres', large cubes are 'lubes', medium spheres are 'meres', medium cubes are 'mubes', small spheres are 'smeres' and small cubes are 'subes'. They come up with the following competing theories:

- *Theory 1**: All meres, mubes, smeres and subes cause a certain sound.
- *Theory 2**: All blellink things cause a certain sound.

For this culture, Theory 2* appears to be simpler. However, Theory 2* is just a translation of Theory 2 into their language – so if Theory 2 is not the best theory, Theory 2* cannot be either. The problem is that the best theory determines the laws of nature, so if the best theory depends upon what language you are speaking so too do the laws. However, that seems ridiculous – that the speed of light is ~300,000 km/s is an *objective* law of nature, and a law for *everyone*, not just, say, the French.

Problem two: RLV rejects intuitively possible situations. For instance, at our world it is a law of nature (let us suppose) that salt dissolves in water. Imagine another **possible world** with different contents – where there is only a single particle moving in a straight line. The problem is that, intuitively, what the contents of the world are will have no bearing on what the laws of nature are at those worlds, so it seems possible that in the latter world it is still a *law* that salt dissolves in water, even though there is no salt. However, given RLV that is not possible. In the second world, the best system will always exclude the law that salt dissolves in water, for it would be an extra law (hence, added complexity) that never added any predictive power to the theory (for there is no salt to predict will dissolve in water). So it would always add complexity for no benefit in strength – hence the best system will always be the system *without* the law that salt dissolves in water. Therefore the second world is *impossible*, when it should not be.

Further reading: Beebee (2000); Psillos (2002, Chapter 5)

RATIONALISM

According to its website, the Rationalist Association 'promotes reason and evidence in the understanding of life'. This is not what philosophers mean by 'rationalism'; you would be hard-pressed to find a respectable contemporary philosopher who shuns reason and evidence. Rationalism is instead the name given to a philosophical trend exemplified by some of the early modern philosophers, in particular René Descartes (1596–1650), Baruch Spinoza (1632–77) and Gottfried Leibniz (1646–1716) and contrasts with **empiricism**. Roughly speaking, the rationalists signed up to the view that we can know some things about the nature of reality by *a priori* reasoning alone, for example that every event has a cause or that God exists. (They also claimed that we can have innate knowledge – knowledge that everyone is born with.)

Although rationalism is an epistemological doctrine, concerned with the origin and justification of knowledge, it is relevant to metaphysics because on the one hand metaphysics concerns (or is often claimed to concern) the nature of reality, on the other hand it apparently involves no empirical or experimental investigation (see the Introduction to this volume). The arch-empiricist **David Hume** claimed that no such trick can be turned, and the very last sentence of his first *Enquiry* provides an incendiary recommendation for any philosophical work purporting to manage it: 'Commit it then to the flames: for it can contain nothing but sophistry and illusion' (Hume 1748/51: 165).

This passage still has the power to make contemporary metaphysicians shift nervously in their seats. Although **Immanuel Kant**'s *Critique of Pure Reason* was a direct response to Hume aiming to reclaim metaphysics as the 'Queen of the sciences', it did so at the cost of admitting that our access to reality is limited to the 'phenomenal world', the world of possible experience – a road down which few contemporary metaphysicians want to tread, for it is likely to lead us into global anti-realism (see **realism and**

anti-realism (global)). For part of the twentieth century, the standard response to Hume (the '**linguistic turn**') was to admit that he was right, so that all that we metaphysicians can hope to achieve is **conceptual analysis**. Many contemporary metaphysicians have abandoned the linguistic turn and would therefore appear to implicitly endorse a form of rationalism (although most are unlikely to admit to this if you ask them). The recent study of **metametaphysics** can be seen, at least in part, as a new attempt to get to grips with the old question raised by Hume: does attempting to figure out the nature of reality using philosophical methods alone constitute a form of rationalism, and if so, does it belong on Hume's bonfire?

REACTIVE ATTITUDES

See **moral responsibility**.

REALISM AND ANTI-REALISM

'Realism' and 'anti-realism' are terms that are hard to define because different philosophers mean different things by them. Broadly speaking, though, debates between realists and anti-realists are debates about the existence or nature of some disputed entity or kind of entity. Often, 'realism' is taken to denote the view that the entity in question not only exists, but also has some distinctive ontological status: the realist holds that the entity is not 'reducible' to something else (see **reductionism**) or that the existence of the entity is a wholly mind-independent matter. So, for example, someone who thinks that causation is not a fundamental feature of the world but is just a matter of regularity (see **regularity theory of causation**) would count as an anti-realist about causation in this sense. So would someone who holds a **response dependence** view of colours, according to which to be red (say) is to be disposed to produce certain kinds of visual sensation in human beings, rather than being a matter of instantiating some **intrinsic** property that is wholly independent of our perception.

However – and this is the meaning we shall use – 'realism' about some entity X can also be taken simply to denote the view *that X exists*, and 'anti-realism' to denote the view that X does not exist. On this way of defining realism, the reductionist about causation is a realist *about causation* – they hold that there are plenty of truths of the form 'c caused e' – but an anti-realist about irreducible or fundamental causal relations. Similarly, someone who holds that colours are response dependent is a realist about colours (they agree that London buses are red), but an anti-realist about *intrinsic* or *mind-independent* colours: they deny that there are any such things.

A note of caution: use of the terms 'realism' and 'anti-realism' does not always follow either of the above usages. In particular, some philosophers define 'realism' so that it includes both a metaphysical and an epistemological component, so that to be a realist is not only to believe that some entity X exists, but also that we can come to know, or find out about, the nature of X (see Wright 1992, 1–3).

Some arguments for anti-realism

So much for the terminology. A more interesting question is: what reasons might someone have to adopt either realism or anti-realism about a given entity or kind of entity? One kind of argument for anti-realism is epistemological (i.e. it concerns consideration of what we can come to know or have good reasons to believe). Someone who believes that God does not exist, for example, might argue for this on the basis that we have no evidence that God exists – God is not something one can directly observe. (Eye-witness accounts of miracles can always be disputed. **David Hume** (1748/51: §10.) famously argued that there will always be more reason to think that the eyewitness is mistaken than reason to think that a miracle really has occurred; see his *Enquiry Concerning Human Understanding*.) Similarly, someone who believes that there are no irreducible causal relations might argue for this on the basis that we have no evidence of such relations, since we cannot directly observe causation (Hume – again – claims that all we ever observe is one thing *following* another, and not one thing *causing* another). Of course, such epistemological claims can be disputed. One could take issue with Hume's claim about miracles; similarly, some philosophers hold, *contra* Hume, that causation *can* be directly observed. Moreover, one can dispute the assumption that evidence requires direct observation; see below.

A second argument for anti-realism – one that was very popular in the first half of the twentieth century, but less so now – appeals to claims about *meaning*, often in the context of **empiricism**. Hume (again) held – along with other traditional empiricists – that all our 'ideas' (roughly: **concepts**, for example, the idea or concept of a tree or the self) must come from our experience. Trees are unproblematic – we certainly have experience of *them* – but other entities are more controversial. Take causation again. Assuming Hume is right that we do not see any **intrinsic** causal relation between causes and effects, the traditional empiricist line (and, arguably,

Hume's own view) is not simply that we cannot therefore have any *evidence* that such a relation exists. It is rather that we do not even so much as have an 'idea' or concept of such a thing, since such an idea would violate the requirement that ideas must come from experience. On this view, talk of intrinsic causal relations between objects or events is not false, or lacking in justification, but meaningless: we do not really mean anything at all if we make claims about such things. (That goes for the claim that intrinsic causal relations do *not* exist as much as it does for the claim that they do. Both claims could only make sense if the expression 'intrinsic causal relation' had a meaning, which, on the current proposal, it does not.) This kind of empiricism is sometimes known as 'meaning empiricism' and it has fallen out of favour in recent decades.

Some arguments for realism

On the other side of the debate, realism is sometimes motivated by *inference to the best explanation*. We can sometimes have very good reasons to think that something exists, even if we cannot observe it. For example, if I see mouse droppings in my kitchen, and the bread I left on the table overnight shows signs of having been nibbled, it is perfectly reasonable of me to conclude that a mouse has taken up residence in my house. The fact that I never actually *see* the mouse means that, in principle, something else *could* explain these phenomena – perhaps someone snuck in overnight, nibbled the bread and planted the droppings. However, the *best* explanation is the existence of a mouse. Similarly, some philosophers argue, for entities that are more philosophically controversial than mice. Some people hold that the best explanation for the existence of intelligent life (namely, us) is that we were designed by a benevolent, omnipotent creator, namely God. This claim is widely thought to have been undermined by the fact that evolution is a much *better* explanation of the existence of intelligent life. And if it *is* a better explanation, then inference to the best explanation of the existence of intelligent life does not provide justification for belief in God.

A second kind of argument for realism comes from the theoretical advantages that the positing of an entity brings with it. **David Lewis**, for example, argues that positing **possible worlds** brings enormous theoretical advantages: once we hold that they exist (or 'allow them into our **ontology**', as it is sometimes put), we can provide philosophical accounts of all kinds of other things: **modality, propositions, causation and laws of nature** and **supervenience**, for example.

The above discussion focuses on realism and anti-realism about particular entities (causation, the mind, God, **universals, natural necessity, time,** and so on). However, there is also a long-standing philosophical debate about what might be called 'global' realism vs anti-realism: that is, realism vs anti-realism about *the nature of the reality (or the world) itself* – not just specific entities, but all of them: chairs, bananas, galaxies, the whole lot. Here, realists are those philosophers who think that the world exists *independently of us*: that is, independently of what we happen to experience, of what our concepts happen to be, and so on. Anti-realists, by contrast, hold that the world's existence *does* depend in some way on us; in other words (to maintain consistency with the definition of realism given above), they disagree that there is such a thing as *mind-independent reality* (see **realism and anti-realism (global)**).

Further reading: Miller (2008, §§ 1–5)

REALISM AND ANTI-REALISM (GLOBAL)

Many disputes in metaphysics can be characterised as disputes between realists and anti-realists, who disagree about whether an entity or kind of entity exists (see **realism and anti-realism**). One long-standing dispute, however, concerns what we are calling 'global' realism and anti-realism. The central question here is whether there is such a thing as – and indeed whether it even makes sense to suppose that there *might* be such a thing as – *mind-independent reality*. It might seem just obvious that things like trees, cats, clouds and planets are mind-independent, that is, that their existence in no way depends on us. (This is the position generally known as 'metaphysical realism'.) After all, we did not create them, they are not figments of our imagination, and surely they would still exist even if human beings were to die out, and indeed, even if we had never existed. Why, then, would a philosopher want to question the mind-independent status of such things?

One way into the anti-realist's way of thinking is to consider the fact that our experience of the world is not a completely untainted representation of how things really, mind-independently, are: the way in which our minds are causally affected by our environment, via our senses, depends to a great extent on facts about our perceptual and cognitive apparatus. Colours, for example, arguably appear as though they are real, mind-independent properties of objects; but the fact that something looks red (and so, arguably, the fact that it *is* red) is partly due to the way our eyes and brains work (see **primary and secondary qualities** and **response dependence**). Moreover, there is no objective, mind-independent reason why we divide the colour spectrum up in the way we do into red, orange, yellow, and so on. Beings with very different sensory apparatus might not experience colour at all or they might have utterly different colour concepts to ours.

Some global anti-realists will maintain that what goes for the mind-dependence of colours applies across the board: *all* of our concepts, linguistic expressions and theories – including scientific theories –are *our* attempts to organise and explain *our* sensory experience. What *we* find to be a simple or satisfying explanation or a predictively adequate theory (given the limitations on what we can experience, and so on what predictions we can confirm, as well as the fact that experiences that confirm predictions are, again, infected by our own cognitive and sensory mechanisms) may be very different to what some other kind of being with very different cognitive and sensory apparatus finds simple or satisfying or predictively adequate.

The (global) anti-realist concludes that the reality we experience and describe, in our scientific theorising as much as in everyday life, is not really mind-independent: it is the world-as-conceptualised-by-us and not (as it is sometimes put, following **Immanuel Kant**) 'the world as it is in itself'. Indeed, most global anti-realists proper will deny that it even makes sense to suppose that there is such a thing as 'the world as it is in itself'. After all, by hypothesis this is a world that we could never experience or attempt to describe, since any such experience or description would automatically be an experience or a description of the world as conceptualised (or experienced) by us and not the world as it is in itself at all. So, we cannot so much as formulate any coherent thoughts about such an alleged mind-independent reality – including the thought that it *exists* (see **Kant** for a little more on this). To put it another way, our conception of reality is constrained by our **conceptual scheme**.

The anti-realist thus holds that reality is mind-dependent, but not – or at least, not necessarily – in the sense that we literally create it, or that it is a mere figment of our imagination, or that it would not exist if we did not exist. That planets are not created by human beings, that lions are not mere figments of our imagination, and that dinosaurs would still have existed even if human beings had never evolved are all obvious facts about the world according to our best theory or our conceptual scheme. However, these facts are in turn mind-dependent in the sense that they are facts about the world-as-conceptualised-by-us and not about the world as it is in itself.

Anti-realism of this kind is considered and rejected by Nagel (1986, Chapter 6). On Nagel's view, although it is true that much of our experience and theorising about the world is infected by our undeniably limited perspective, we can – and science does – attempt to achieve a less limited perspective. We can make progress towards what he calls 'the view from nowhere': a conception of the world that is not a conception of the world as viewed from a particular perspective, but is rather a conception of the world as it is in itself. For example, although conceiving of the world as containing red and blue objects (and other secondary qualities) is a function of the cognitive and sensory peculiarities of human beings, it might well be that primary qualities such as shape and extension really are features of 'things in themselves' (see **primary and secondary qualities**).

Varieties of anti-realism include **pragmatism, phenomenalism** and **postmodernism**. Pragmatism emphasises the thought that language is a kind of *tool* for living: it is fundamentally a practical device, like a hammer or a spear. Armed with a spear, you can go and hunt for your dinner. Armed, in addition, with language, you can organise a hunting party, tell someone that there is a boar hiding just over to the left, or warn them that they are in danger of treading on a poisonous snake. Language, in this case, primarily helps you get what you want, viz, to find some dinner and remain alive long enough to eat it. **Truth**, on this view, is not a matter of a sentence or theory corresponding to some portion of mind-independent reality; it is rather a matter of that theory's serving a practical purpose.

One potential consequence of anti-realism (one that is wholeheartedly embraced by postmodernists) is **relativism**: the view that it is not an absolute matter what is true. Rather, truth is always relative: relative to a particular kind of being (human beings, say), or, more radically to particular cultures or even to individual people. So, for example, a cultural relativist might say that the ancient Greeks' belief in the gods of Mount Olympus was not *false*. Rather, it was true-for-them: it served a purpose, given the circumstances in which the ancient Greeks lived, and there was no better theory in the offing that served those purposes any better.

An apparent advantage of anti-realism is that it provides a response to the thorny philosophical problem of **scepticism**. How can we know that the external world is really the way we think it is when our sensory experience would be exactly the same if we were **brains in a vat**, cleverly manipulated by non-envatted neuroscientists? One anti-realist answer is that this alleged possibility really makes no sense: in setting up the **thought experiment** we are presupposing that there is something like a '**God's eye view**' of the world, or 'view from nowhere', from the perspective of which all our beliefs about the world can be seen to be mistaken. However, there is no such perspective genuinely available to us: our very understanding of the nature of reality is constrained by the theories we hold true, and the world, according to those theories, is a world of trees and cats and planets, and not a world of brains, vats and manipulative neuroscientists. (see **phenomenalism and idealism** for a different anti-realist response to scepticism.)

Further reading: Blackburn (1999, Chapter 7); Kirk (1999); Miller (2008); Nagel (1986, Chapter 6); Beebee and Dodd (2006, Chapter 3), this includes an abridged version of Nagel (1986, Chapter 6)

REDUCTIONISM

The word 'reduction' is often used in metaphysics and in philosophy generally, but you have to be careful as it is not always used in the same sense. Broadly speaking, a reductionist (or reductive) account of a certain kind of entity K is a theory which claims that (i) Ks exist but (ii) the existence of Ks can be wholly accounted for in terms of some description of reality which does not make reference to Ks. Physicalist theories of mind are reductionist in this sense: (i) minds exist, (ii) the existence of minds can be wholly accounted for in terms of a physical description of reality which makes no reference to minds. Having said that, the word 'reduction' generally means something slightly different in philosophy of mind. In philosophy of mind, it is common to distinguish between 'reductionist' physicalist theories, which claim that each mental type is identical to some physical type, from 'non-reductionist' theories, which deny this but nonetheless hold that the mental **supervenes** on the physical.

On our definition of 'reductionist', the definition more common in metaphysics, both of the above views count as reductionist. For example, **bundle theories of the self or person** are reductionist: (i) persons exist, (ii) the existence of persons can be wholly accounted for in terms of a description of mental events standing in certain relations to each other. The **regularity** and **counterfactual theories** of **causation**, and the **Ramsey–Lewis view of laws of nature** are also reductionist theories.

Reductionism typically goes hand-in-hand with **conceptual analysis**. If you can analyse the *concept* 'K', that is, provide an analysis that says 'something is a K if and only if P' (such as 'c causes e if and only if e counterfactually depends on c'), and 'P' does not make any reference to Ks, then, in effect, you are saying that all there is to being a K is its being the case that P (so you satisfy condition (ii) above). And, so long as you are pretty confident that P is sometimes true, you will then be in an excellent position to hold that condition (i) is satisfied too.

215

Reductionist theories of *K*'s are a middle way between **anti-realist** theories, which deny the existence of *K*'s, and strong **realist** theories of *K*'s, which take *K*'s to be fundamental constituents of reality. In contrast to these extremes, reductionist theories believe in the existence of *K*'s, but take them to be 'nothing over and above' the existence of certain other entities. Some contemporary metaphysicians, a prominent example being Merricks (1999, section IV), claim not to be able to make sense of such a middle way. For these metaphysicians, we must either think that minds (or persons or whatever) exist and hence are an extra item in our **ontology**, or we must think that minds (or persons or whatever) do not exist; there is no middle way. This increasingly common attitude may be the result of adopting the Quinean approach to metaphysics (see **metametaphysics**), which roughly construes the job of the metaphysician as answering existence questions. If the job of the metaphysician is just to say, 'Yes, *x*'s exist', or 'No, *x*'s do not exist', then there is no room for the more nuanced answer: 'Well, '*x*'s exist, but they are nothing over and above *y*'s'.

Schaffer (2009) has recently argued that we should replace this Quinean approach to metaphysics with what he calls a 'neo-Aristotelian' approach, in which reduction plays a central role. The neo-Aristotelian approach makes a distinction between *fundamental* entities and *grounded* entities, the latter being nothing over and above the former. Although we are **ontologically committed** to the grounded entities, they come at no ontological cost in the sense when judging the economy of a hypothesis (see **theoretical virtues**) we should only take into consideration the fundamental entities. Once we have the fundamental entities, the grounded entities come for free.

Whether or not one is comfortable with reduction makes profound differences to how one approaches metaphysics. Merricks (2001) spends a great deal of time considering the issue of whether or not inanimate composite objects exist: whether there are tables and chairs or just atoms arranged in table-like ways and chair-like ways. Because he does not allow for the possibility of a reductionist theory of tables and chairs, he has only two options to choose from: *realism*, the view that tables and chairs exist and *anti-realism*, the view that tables and chairs do not exist (Merricks sides with anti-realism). For Schaffer, in contrast, there are three options to choose from: *strong realism*, the view that tables and chairs are fundamental entities, *mild realism*, the view that tables and chairs are grounded entities (perhaps grounded in atoms and their arrangements), and *anti-realism*, the view that tables and chairs do not exist. In other words, the metaphysician who is open to reductionism has more options.

Further reading: Schaffer (2009)

REDUNDANT CAUSATION

'Redundant causation' is usually used to mean '**pre-emption** or **over-determination**'. What unites these phenomena is that in each case the cause is 'redundant', in that, had it not occurred, the effect would have happened anyway. You hang the washing out – but if you had not, your flatmate would have done it. So the washing getting dry did not *depend* on your hanging it out – it would have got dry anyway. That is pre-emption. Or: two members of the firing squad both shoot the victim and either of their shots would, on its own, have killed him. So the victim's death does not depend on either shot – without it, the victim would still have died, killed by the other one. However – intuitively (or at least arguably) – each of the shots was still causally responsible for the victim's death. That is overdetermination.

REGULARITY THEORY OF CAUSATION

Regularity theories may be concerned with *causation*, or with what are sometimes called *causal laws* (what we are calling 'type-level causation'; see **probabilistic theories of causation (type-level)**) or with laws of nature (see **regularity theory of laws**). In each case, the intention is to give an account which avoids embracing **natural necessity**. Unsurprisingly, then, all versions of the regularity theory find themselves rooted in the works of natural necessity's arch-nemesis **David Hume**. We shall just discuss the regularity theory of causation here.

The regularity theory reduces causation to the regular occurrence of certain events. The canonical formulation, where c and e are events, is:

> c causes e if and only if (i) c is spatiotemporally contiguous with e (or there is a chain of contiguous causes and effects between c and e); (ii) c precedes e in time; (iii) all events of the type that c is are followed by events of the type that e is.

This is a close paraphrase of Hume's (1739–40: 172) famous 'first definition' of causation, but beware: it is unclear whether he was really intending to *define* causation at all. It is best to avoid interpretative controversy and think of the regularity theory as a '**Humean**' theory, rather than *Hume's* theory.

217

Each conjunct proves problematic. The first proves problematic because some think unmediated causation – action at a spatial and/or temporal distance – is possible. These are cases where the cause and effect are separated in space or time, with no chain of causes and effects linking them. For instance, we might believe it is logically possible for, say, Gandalf to sit at home and cast a magic spell that strikes dead the evil Balrog that lives many miles away, and that this just happens with no mediating chain of causes and effects. Allegedly, although a fantastic tale, it is surely not *impossible*. More pressingly, some people believe that the best interpretations of quantum mechanics involve this type of causation at a distance. So, the scenarios that demonstrate conjunct (i) is not necessary are not fantastical at all, but part of the everyday occurrences of the sub-atomic world.

The second conjunct proves difficult if you endorse the possibility of **backwards causation** whereby events in the future (Marty getting into the time travelling DeLorean in 1985) have effects in the past (Marty arriving back in 1955 by using his time machine). Clearly such possibilities are ruled out by the second conjunct. Finally, the third conjunct has problems with 'accidental regularities'. Imagine that, by chance or design, we arrange the world such that every time a clock with a wood casing 'ticks', a second clock with a metal casing 'tocks'. Now it would be the case that the tickings of the wooden clock are always followed by the tockings of metal clock – but we would not think that the former *causes* the latter. The regularity is not a result of causation but of accident. (Even though there is an explanation for why the tocks follow the ticks – both clocks tell the time, after all, and are designed to keep ticking and tocking at the same speed – it is still not the case that the ticks of one clock cause the tocks of the other.)

The regularity theory of causation (and, similarly, the regularity view of laws) does not have many admirers these days because it is, frankly, hopelessly inadequate. However, the spirit of the theory can be seen – at least if you squint hard enough – in the **counterfactual theory of causation** (in the case of laws, in the **Ramsey–Lewis view of laws**). These more sophisticated views try to capture the heart of the Humean enterprise, in particular the denial of natural necessity, and do so by taking whether or not one thing causes another, or whether or not something is a law, to be a matter, in the end, of the obtaining of regularities. You have to squint in the case of the counterfactual theory of causation because counterfactual dependence does not obviously have anything to do with regularities. However, because Lewis analyses counterfactual dependence in terms of similarity of **possible worlds**, and the major criterion for similarity is sameness of the laws of nature, *and* he has a sophisticated regularity theory of laws, in the end causation – at least for Lewis – boils down to the obtaining of regularities.

Further reading: Armstrong (1983, Part I); Psillos (2002, Chapter 1)

REGULARITY THEORY OF LAWS OF NATURE

The regularity theory of laws – very similar to the **regularity theory of causation** – says that it is a **law of nature** that all *F*s are (or are followed by) *G*s if and only if all *F*s are (or are followed by) *G*s. One might try to add some bells and whistles to this theory to avoid the most obvious counter-examples ('all the carpets in my house are beige', 'all unicorns are made of cheese'), but it is generally agreed that it is a lost cause. Still, the **Humean** spirit of the regularity theory is preserved in the rather more sophisticated **Ramsey–Lewis view of laws**.

Further reading: Armstrong (1983, Chapters 2–4)

REGULATIVE CONTROL

See **guidance control vs regulative control**.

RELATA

The relata of a given relation are the things that are related by that relation (and 'relatum' is the singular form). If Jack and Jim are twenty metres from one another, then Jack and Jim stand in the *20 metres away from* relation. So, Jack and Jim are the relata of that relation (Jack is a relatum and so is Jim). If Jack hates Jill, then Jack stands in the *hating* relation to Jill. So Jack and Jill are the relata of that relation. If Jack, Jim and Jill are in a love triangle together, then they are all the relata of the *in a love triangle with* relation.

It is even easier to see when represented in first-order logic (which just goes to show that logic courses are useful for you to study). For the

propositions:

> *Rab*
> *Rac*
> *Rabc*

a and *b* are the relata of the first relation; *a* and *c* are the relata of the second relation; and *a*, *b* and *c* are the relata of the third relation.

People also talk more generally of the types of relata that relations may have. So, objects are the type of thing that are the relata of the *20 metres away from* relation. Since only people can hate, but they can hate anything including inanimate objects (and maybe even **abstract** objects if they tried), the relata of the *hating* relation are always such that one is a person and the other can be anything; whereas the relata of the *in a love triangle with* relation are always all people. Rather more philosophically interesting is the debate about what the relata of **causation** are (e.g. **facts** or **events** or **states of affairs** or even agents – see **agent causation**).

RELATIVISM

Relativism is generally conceived as a philosophical thesis about **truth** (although, as we shall see, one can also think of relativism as a thesis about *meaning*). However, as we say in the section on truth, it is important to remember that one's theory of truth is not independent of one's theory of the way the world is. For any proposition or sentence *p*, '*p*' is true if and only if *p* (so, for example, 'God exists' is true if and only if God exists). So, if you are a relativist about truth (and so about the truth of 'God exists'), you are also going to be a relativist about *the existence of God* or, equivalently, about *the fact that God exists*.

So, what is relativism? Well, obviously, it is the view that truth is relative – to something. Different relativists have different views about what the 'something' is; but they tend to agree that the 'something' has something to do with human beings (and other actual or possible beings that have language). We survey some options below. Anyone who thinks that truth is relative to some feature of human or other beings is an anti-realist in the sense of 'anti-realism' used in this book; that is, they are an anti-realist about mind-independent reality (see **realism and anti-realism (global)**). (If you think that the truth of 'God exists' is relative to, say, the religious beliefs of a particular society, you must also think that the existence of God is also relative to the religious beliefs of a particular society, and hence that the existence of God is a mind-dependent matter.)

Varieties of relativism

There are stronger and weaker forms of relativism, and there also broader and narrower forms of relativism. By 'broader' and 'narrower', we mean that someone might be a relativist about one particular domain of discourse but a non-relativist about some other domain. For example, someone might be a relativist about moral or aesthetic truth, but a card-carrying realist about, say, scientific truth. To think that the truth of moral claims – that euthanasia is wrong, say, or that bigamy is morally acceptable – is relative to, say, a particular culture, does not require you to also think that, for example, the truth of claims about the speed of light or the circumference of the Earth is also relative to a particular culture. (Though whether it is really a good idea to talk about relativism about *truth* in this context, rather than relativism about meaning, is a question we return to below.)

Along the stronger/weaker axis, there are different things one might relativise truth to. On one end of the spectrum, you might think that truth is thoroughly subjective: what is true is just what is true *for me*. So if I say that God exists and you say that God does not exist, we are not (contrary to appearances) really disagreeing with each other; what I say is true-for-me and what you say is true-for-you. Unfortunately, although this radically subjectivist view is a good way of preventing heated arguments (after all, you do not really disagree with anyone!), it is wildly implausible. It entails, for example, that none of your beliefs are false. It also entails that rational disagreement is impossible, since there are no facts of the matter, independent of your beliefs, for you to disagree with anyone else about. It would also make communication rather difficult. ('Watch out! There is a car coming!' 'Yeah, well, that may be true for *you* . . .') Of course, there are *some* domains within which this kind of view makes some sense ('Do not eat that, it has got olives on it, and olives taste horrible!' 'Yeah well, that may be true for you, but I *like* olives!'), but not many.

More plausible versions of relativism relativise to something rather bigger than the individual: perhaps a particular society or culture, or a particular theoretical framework (quantum physics, say, or evolutionary biology), or perhaps a language (German or Swahili). This establishes a realm of facts that are independent of what any *particular* person happens to think *within* the culture or framework or language, so that genuine disagreement is possible; but it makes disagreement *across* cultures or frameworks or languages impossible. So, given relativism about theoretical frameworks, two evolutionary biologists can have a perfectly sensible dispute such that in fact one of them is right and one of them is wrong, but an evolutionary biologist and a proponent of Intelligent Design cannot; it is true relative-to-evolutionary-biology that we descended from apes but false relative-to-Intelligent-Design. Nothing to argue about!

Relativism, truth and meaning

Should we really think of relativism as a doctrine about *truth*, however? Suppose you are inclined towards relativism in, say, the case of the taste of food ('olives are horrible!') but not elsewhere. In making sense of this view, there is really no need to say that there are two *kinds* of truth: one for claims about the taste of food and another everywhere else. Instead, one can just say that when someone makes a claim such as 'olives are horrible!', what they *mean* is that olives taste horrible *to them* – just as, if Sam in Birmingham is on the phone to Jo in Sydney, it is true for Sam that it is 10 pm and true for Jo that it is 9 am; but that is because, uncontroversially, 'it is 10 am' (given some assumptions about context) just *means* 'it is 10 am in my current geographical location'.

Relativism that locates the source of relativism in meaning, as opposed to truth, is closely associated with the work of Kuhn (1962) and the thesis of *incommensurability*. Kuhn holds that the language of a new scientific theory or 'paradigm' (such as the theory of relativity in physics – note that this is a completely different sense of 'relativity'!) that replaces an old theory (such as Newtonian physics) cannot be translated into the vocabulary of the old theory. Even if many of the words used by the two theories are the same (such as 'mass' or 'planet'), those words have different and incommensurable – that is, to say, not-mutually-translatable – meanings. Proponents of the old and new paradigms cannot rationally debate which theory is closer to the truth or a better description of how things are, since there is no common language within which such a discussion might take place; so the new theory cannot be seen as a more accurate representation of some theory-independent reality. (see also **conceptual scheme**.)

Arguments for relativism

One kind of argument for relativism focuses on the question of what a genuine fact of the matter in the domain under discussion might look like. It is easy to imagine a race of aliens, say, who just find human beings hideously ugly. It is not clear why we should think that they are making a *mistake* when they say that all human beings, without exception, are ugly, because it is unclear what kind of facts of the matter we could appeal to in order to settle the dispute: it would be odd to say that there is something defective about their visual or cognitive apparatus (after all, from their point of view, it is us who have a peculiar view and not them). So, perhaps, beauty is not exactly in the eye of the beholder, but is relative to features of human beings in general or, perhaps, features of particular cultures. Philosophers who take a 'global' relativist position – who are relativists not just about beauty or the taste of food or ethics but also the existence of planets and chairs and elephants – claim that something similar is true across the board· in the case of radically different worldviews or **conceptual schemes**, we cannot imagine a vantage point or **God's eye view** from the perspective of which it would be clear which one represented reality more accurately. Hence it really does not make sense to suppose that there *is* a unique 'reality' that is represented differently by the two conceptual schemes.

Further reading: Kirk (1999, Chapter 3)

RELATIVITY

In 1887, Albert Michelson and Edward Morley conducted experiments that showed the speed of light in a vacuum (which is roughly 299,792,458 metres per second or m/s, and denoted by the letter c) was the same for everything no matter how fast it is moving relative to anything else. This was an extraordinarily weird result. Imagine you are stationary (relative to the Earth) and there are two people running away from you. The first, Bill, is moving at 3 m/s, whereas the second, Bob, is moving at 4 m/s. From Bill's perspective, Bob is only moving at 1 m/s (i.e. Bob's velocity from your perspective minus Bill's velocity from your perspective i.e. $4 - 3 = 1$ m/s). However, the Michelson-Morley experiment demonstrated that no matter what your perspective the speed of light (unlike the speed of Bob) is the same. So, light is travelling at c from your perspective, but rather than travelling at $c - 3$ m/s from Bill's perspective, and $c - 4$ m/s from Bob's perspective, as would seem natural, it *still* goes at c from their perspectives. If that doesn't strike you as weird, imagine someone who is trying to chase a photon (a particle of light), and who is, from your perspective, travelling at 299,792,457 m/s. From your perspective, the photon is going at c m/s, and the person is travelling just 1 m/s slower than it. However, from *their* perspective the photon is not travelling at a measly 1 m/s, for it is *still* zooming along at nearly three million metres per second!

Scientists proposed an explanation. When things move at fast velocities relative to you, they undergo *time dilation*, as if time is 'slowed down' for them. They also undergo *length contraction*, appearing to be thinner than they would be if they were at rest. This explains why the two different perspectives diverge. From your viewpoint, someone moving at $c - 1$ m/s, who tried to measure the distance a photon travels during a period of one second, would get it wrong. Their clocks would be ticking slower, so what they *thought* was a second would (from your perspective) be a much longer period of time, during which that extra metre per second the photon has on the fast traveller would have led to it getting a huge distance away from him. Further, when that traveller tries to measure that huge distance, he seemingly gets that wrong too as his metre rules are all shorter, so he thinks that the distance the photon travelled is greater than it is from your perspective. The combination of these two factors means that he would report that during what was (from his perspective) a single second, the light travelled (from his perspective) nearly 300 million metres. (Even weirder, because *you* would be travelling very fast from *his* perspective, he thinks *you are* undergoing time dilation and length contraction and getting *your* results wrong in the same way you think he is!).

Einstein's Special Theory of Relativity (STR) accounts for these bizarre phenomena of length contraction and time dilation. Intuitively, we think that simultaneity is *absolute*; that is, if one event is simultaneous with another event, this fact is true no matter who you are or what perspective you have on the world. STR does away with that intuition. Instead, simultaneity is relative to how fast you are going. So for those of us on Earth (who are all, more or less, stationary with regards to one another) your reading this entry is simultaneous with some event on the other side of the planet, say, an Australian drinking a beer. However, for someone travelling *very* fast, at a speed close to the speed of light, these two events will be temporally separated such that the beer drinking occurs long before your reading of this entry. Once we make simultaneity relative in this fashion, and accept STR, the time dilations and length contractions that explain the weird problems described above are predicted. Although counterintuitive, relativity has become part of mainstream physics and the predictions it makes have been confirmed many times.

It is this relativisation of simultaneity that makes relativity such an interesting theory when it comes to the philosophy of time. It bears directly on **presentism** (dealt with in that entry) and there are arguments from relativity for **perdurantism** (see Balashov 1999; Gibson and Pooley 2006; and Gilmore 2006).

Further reading: A good introduction to special relativity is Sklar (1992, Chapter 2). For more on the metaphysics see Hawley (2009)

RESEMBLANCE NOMINALISM

Resemblance nominalism is a variety of **nominalism** according to which everything is a particular. there are no **universals**. So we cannot explain why, say, the Coke can and the telephone box are the *same colour* by appealing to some entity – a universal – that is present in each of them.

Resemblance nominalism takes resemblance between particular objects as a **primitive** and tries to explain facts about **properties** in terms of facts about resemblance. An object is red in virtue of its resemblance to all the other red things. The resemblance nominalist may be an **anti-realist** about **properties** – offering **paraphrases** of sentences containing terms that appear to refer to properties, such as 'red is a colour' – or she may identify properties with classes of resembling objects.

We can see resemblance nominalism as a view that is slightly less parsimonious, but slightly more intuitively satisfying, than **class nominalism** (see **theoretical virtues** for an explanation of 'parsimony', but roughly a theory is more parsimonious if it has fewer **ontological commitments**). The class nominalist takes it as basic that particular objects are members of a given class, and tries to explain facts about resemblance in terms of this primitive fact. By making an investment in a **primitive** resemblance relation, the resemblance nominalist has a deeper explanation of what binds the members of, say, the class of red things together, namely their resemblance to each other. By explaining class membership in terms of resemblance rather than vice versa, the resemblance nominalist gives a slightly more intuitive order of explanation.

However, resemblance nominalism faces many of the same difficulties as class nominalism. Just as in the case of class nominalism, it is difficult to see how the resemblance nominalist can account for co-extensive properties. We might say that a given thing with a heart resembles all the other things with a heart, and attempt to explain that things having a heart in terms of its resembling all the other things with a heart. However, each thing with a heart also resembles all the things with kidneys (since everything that has a heart has kidneys). If at a fundamental level we just have a single class of things, those things that have a heart and kidneys, and a single resemblance relation between them, how can we distinguish between the having of a heart and the having of kidneys? It is tempting to distinguish between *resemblance in virtue of having a heart* and *resemblance in virtue of having kidneys*, but, of course, this would be to reintroduce *having-a-heart* and *having-kidneys* into the account, the very thing we started off trying to analyse, and so the account becomes circular.

Furthermore, resemblance nominalism is counterintuitive in many of the respects in which class nominalism is counterintuitive. An object seems to have no nature in and of itself; it is only in virtue of its relationship (of resemblance) to other round things that the ball is round. And although resemblance nominalism gives a more intuitive order of explanation with respect to resemblance and class membership, it gives a counterintuitive order of explanation with respect to predication and resemblance. It is surely more natural to think that red objects resemble each other in virtue of being red, rather than vice versa. However, the resemblance nominalist, by the definition of the view, reverses the order of this explanation.

Bertrand Russell objected to resemblance nominalism as a way of elim- inating universals on the grounds that the view needs to believe in, at least, one universal, namely the universal of resemblance. However, it is not clear why the resemblance nominalist cannot just avoid this difficulty by deny- ing the existence of the universal of resemblance, while taking it as prim- itive that objects resemble each other (compare: the **trope theorist** takes it as primitive that tropes resemble each other).

Further reading: Armstrong (1989, Chapter 3); Lowe (2002, 355–60); Loux (2006)

RESPONSE-DEPENDENCE

Many philosophers claim that some of our **concepts** are 'response-dependent'. In particular, secondary quality concepts ('red', 'smooth', 'tasty') are often thought to be response-dependent (see **primary and secondary quali- ties**). To say that a concept ('red', say) is response-dependent is to say, roughly, that something's *being* red – the concept's correctly applying to an object – is at least partly determined by some feature of our *response* to that object. In this case, the response in question is a visual experience: red things look a certain way to us and it is (partly) constitutive of something is being red that it looks that way to us.

Response-dependence is an important notion in debates about **realism and anti-realism**. The way we are defining realism, if you think that a certain entity or property (red, say) is picked out by a response-dependent concept, you are a realist about it, in the sense that you think that red things exist. However, you are an anti-realist about **intrinsic** or mind- independent colours, since on this view the existence of redness is not fully mind-independent: there are no mind-independent colours. (The existence of redness depends on the fact that there are human beings, or beings with similar perceptual mechanisms, to whom certain objects look a certain way.)

One immediate apparent problem with a response-dependent account of, say, redness is that clearly an object does not get to *be* red just because it happens to look red to a particular person on a particular occasion: a red apple is still red when you turn the lights out, and it is still red even when observed by a colour-blind person; and a white wall is still white even if you put on a pair of red-tinted spectacles so that it *looks* red. The response-dependence account deals with this kind of worry by saying that something is red if it looks red *to a normal observer in normal circumstances*. So, for example, someone who is colour-blind is not, in this context, a 'normal' observer; and normal circumstances include there being sufficient light and not wearing red-tinted spectacles.

Response-dependence is a useful notion because it allows us to make a distinction between facts about the world that are (in one particular way) mind-dependent from those that are not. A red cube is equally red and cubic, but (one might claim) its redness is at least partly a mind-dependent feature of it, whereas its being cubic (shape being a primary quality) is not. This can help us to resolve some metaphysical problems; in the colour case, for example, it helps us to resolve the tension between the rather obvious fact that there are red things, and the equally obvious fact that in some sense redness is not really 'in' objects at all: put a red apple under a sufficiently powerful microscope and it no longer looks red (see **primary and secondary qualities** for a bit more on this).

Philosophers disagree among themselves over exactly which concepts are response-dependent. For example, some philosophers think that shapes are response-dependent too: something's being triangular just *consists* in the fact that if you counted the corners, you would get the answer '3', plus the fact that triangular objects visually appear a certain way, and so on. Response-dependence is also a big issue in meta-ethics (roughly, the study of what grounds the truth of moral claims). Some philosophers hold that moral concepts (like 'good' and 'vicious') are response-dependent: someone's behaving viciously is in part *constituted* by the fact that (normal) people have certain kinds of emotional reactions (distaste, horror, or whatever) to whatever it is the person is doing. Again, this kind of view can be thought of as attempting to resolve a philosophical puzzle: we want to be able to correctly say that some actions (a murder, say) are vicious, but we might also have metaphysical scruples about thinking that viciousness is an objective or **intrinsic** feature of the action. (The person squeezes the trigger, the bullet is released, it embeds itself in the victim's body; where, exactly, is the viciousness located in that sequence of events?)

Further reading: Joyce (2009, § 5)

SCEPTICISM

In ordinary language, to be 'sceptical' about something is normally to doubt its truth (so, you might be sceptical about whether Labour will win the election, meaning that you are in some doubt about whether they will win). In contemporary philosophy, however, 'scepticism' is not normally taken to describe a psychological state – that of doubting that something is true. Instead, scepticism is a philosophical position: the position that some particular claim or class of claims (e.g. the claim that the future will resemble the past, or any claim about the external world) cannot be known or, more strongly, that there is no reason whatsoever to believe it.

The term 'scepticism' is normally (but not always) reserved for scepticism *about the existence or nature of the external world*. That is, to say, the sceptic holds that we cannot know – or indeed that we have no reason to believe – that the external world is more or less the way we ordinarily take it to be, or perhaps even that it exists at all. For example, the sceptic will claim that we cannot know that familiar objects such as chairs and trees and elephants exist. There are also more restricted varieties of scepticism, for example inductive scepticism (we have no reason to believe that the unobserved resembles the observed, e.g. that the sun will rise tomorrow) and scepticism about other minds (we have no reason to believe that other people have minds, as opposed to simply manifesting behaviour that is not caused by mental states at all). Here we shall be concerned solely with scepticism about the external world, or 'global' scepticism, as we shall call it (though note that 'global scepticism' is sometimes defined as 'scepticism about absolutely everything').

Scepticism is a worrying position: if scepticism is true, then it is no more rational to believe in trees and chairs than it is to believe in fairies and little green men. So, are there any good arguments for scepticism? Unfortunately, it appears that there are.

René Descartes (1596–1650) asks you to consider the possibility that you are really a disembodied mind, being fed all of your sensory experiences by an evil demon whose (successful) aim is to ensure that all your beliefs about the external world are false (Descartes 1641, Meditation 1). For example, you believe that there are chairs and elephants and planets, but really all that exists, according to this 'sceptical scenario', is your (immaterial) mind, including your sensory experience, and the demon. This is sometimes called the 'evil demon hypothesis'. (A contemporary version of the evil demon hypothesis is the **brains in a vat** hypothesis.)

Now the question is: do we have any reason at all to think that the evil demon hypothesis is false? It would appear not. Our evidence for the existence of chairs, elephants, and so on, comes entirely from our senses: from what we see or what we read in books and newspapers and what other people tell us. However, if the evil demon hypothesis were true, our sensory experience would be exactly the same: we would have experiences as of chairs, as of reading books and newspapers and as of people telling us things; but all those experiences would just be the work of the demon. So, according to the sceptic, none of our sensory experience is *really* evidence for the existence of the external world at all, given that that experience would be just the same if there were no external world and just the demon.

Scepticism, it is important to note, does *not* amount to the view that the evil demon hypothesis *is* true; nor is it simply the view that the evil demon hypothesis *might* be true. Rather, the view is that *even if all our beliefs about the world are true* – even if we really do live in a world of chairs and elephants and planets – there are no rational grounds for those beliefs. So the sceptical worry is not merely that we might, consistent with our evidence, be being deceived by the evil demon; it is that even if we are not being deceived, and even if we continue to (truly) *believe* that we are not being deceived, we still have no rational *grounds* for that belief.

Scepticism is, of course, an *epistemological* position: it is a thesis about what we can know (or reasonably believe). What, then, is it doing in a book on metaphysics? The answer is that some responses to scepticism are *metaphysical* responses. Such responses attempt to show that the alleged sceptical scenario – the evil demon hypothesis, say – is incoherent, and they do so (though not always explicitly) by appealing to a version of global *anti-realism* (see **realism and anti-realism (global)**).

How do such responses work? Well, the general idea is this. Scepticism presupposes that we can draw a sharp distinction between the way the world *seems* to be and the way it really is, in itself. Or, to put things in a way that is less reliant on sensory experience, there is a distinction between how our best theories describe the world and – again – how it really is. That is to say, scepticism presupposes a *realist* position about the nature of reality: its nature is independent of our experience of it and/or the theories we use to describe it. And then the sceptical claim is that these two things might, for all we can tell, be radically different. The world *seems* to be a world of trees, chairs, and so on (or: our best theories describe the world as containing trees, chairs, and so on); nonetheless, it might be that it is actually an evil-demon world, and all our sensory experience is (or our best theories are) radically mistaken.

Anti-realists deny that there is such a distinction to be drawn. **George Berkeley**, for example, argues for idealism: as Berkeley puts it, 'to be is to be perceived'. On this view, there is no more to the world than our experience of it. Hence no distinction can be drawn between how the world seems to us and how it really is; and hence the sceptical argument cannot get going (see **phenomenalism and idealism**).

Berkeley's argument for idealism trades on a thesis about *meaning*: roughly, his view is that the notion of a *mind-independent* material world does not make any sense. More recent anti-realists reject idealism (and its secular counterpart, phenomenalism), but argue, like Berkeley, that there are limits to what we can conceive and those limits make it impossible to formulate the sceptical scenarios that underpin scepticism. One core idea here is that realism (and hence scepticism) presupposes the notion of a **God's eye view** – a kind of neutral perspective, from the vantage-point of which one could tell whether our theories of what the world is like correspond to the way it really is like. Anti-realists argue that the notion of a God's-eye view really does not make sense, however; we lack the conceptual resources to be able genuinely to imagine breaking out of our own theoretical perspective or **conceptual scheme** and viewing the world as it really is.

Further reading: Descartes (1641, Meditation I); Blackburn (1999, Chapter 1); Stroud (1984)

SET

A set is a type of **class**. For the most part, you can probably treat the words 'set' and 'class' as synonymous, even though they can come apart. Normally, classes can be **members** of other classes (such that, say, the classes $\{a\}$ and $\{b\}$ are members of $\{\{a\},\{b\}\}$). However, to avoid certain paradoxes (the details of which are interesting, but there is no space to describe them here) some set theories take it that there are classes that are so big that they *cannot* be members of another class. These are called 'proper classes'. The word 'set' is then reserved to refer to all of the remaining classes, which *are* members of other classes.

SHIP OF THESEUS

See **identity over time**.

SIMPLE

'Simple' is a term from **mereology**. Something is a simple if and only if it has no **proper parts** (it is important that we say *proper* parts, for everything has a **part** – namely itself). Generally, those who believe that there are simples identify them with the elementary particles (such as quarks or superstrings). Some people think simples cannot be extended in space, for if they were then they would have, say, a left and a right proper part – and if they had proper parts, they cannot be simples. In that case, simples would be 'point particles' – objects that exist but fail to be extended in any spatial dimension (so called '0-dimensional objects'). Others disagree saying that simples could be extended (so-called 'extended simples'). With that in mind, some people think that extended simples could be quite big sometimes even far bigger than the sub-atomic size. At the extreme, some people follow the cue of the Greek philosopher Parmenides and think the entire universe is a giant simple, and that we are wrong to think that the universe has any parts whatsoever (the position of monism – see **special composition question**).

Not everyone endorses the existence of simples. The alternative is to think that the world is made up of **gunk** (or else that there are not any objects whatsoever; that would make you an ontological **nihilist**).

Further reading: Hudson (2007)

SIMPLE VIEW OF PERSONAL IDENTITY

Most theories of **personal identity** offer a **conceptual analysis** of what it is for a person at one time to be identical to a person at another time (i.e. an account of the **identity over time** of persons). Psychological theories claim that personal identity over time is grounded in **psychological continuity**. **Animalism** and **bodily continuity theories** claim that personal identity over time is grounded in the biological continuity of an animal, or the continuity of a body or a brain. All these theories are **reductionist**: they all try to account for facts about personal identity in terms of more fundamental facts.

Proponents of the simple view of personal identity reject all such reductions. The fact that a given person at a certain time is identical to a person at a distinct time is taken to be a primitive fact, not capable of being reduced to some more fundamental class of facts.

Perhaps the most straightforward way of adopting the simple view is by holding that a person is a fundamental non-physical entity, such as soul or a Cartesian ego. If souls exist and persist through time, then it looks like there is nothing more to be said about what it is for a certain soul existing on Wednesday to be identical to a certain soul existing on Thursday; they are just one and the same soul and that is that (the same might be true of fundamental particles, if there are such things).

However, we must be careful. A mere commitment to dualism, the belief in non-physical souls or Cartesian egos, does not commit us to the simple view of personal identity. **John Locke** was inclined to dualism, but gave a psychological account of personal identity: although the soul is what *produces* the experiences and memories that determine psychological connections across time, it is those connections themselves that determine personal identity, rather than the identity across time of the thing (the soul) that generates them. Also, not everyone who signs up to the simple view is a dualist. Merricks (1998), for example, believes that a person is wholly composed of physical parts, but takes the diachronic ('diachronic' means 'over time') facts about the identity of persons to be primitive.

Support for the simple view can perhaps be found by consideration of cases of **fission** (see final paragraph of **fission**).

Further reading: Merricks (1998); Noonan (1989, Chapters 1 and 5); Olson (2008); Swinburne (1984)

SINGLETON

A singleton is a type of **class** that has only one member. For instance, Brad Pitt's singleton is:

{Brad Pitt}

Singletons can have their own singletons. So Brad Pitt's singleton's singleton would be:

{{Brad Pitt}}

Indeed, any class except a **proper class** can have a singleton.

SINGULAR CAUSAL SENTENCES

Singular causal sentences are just those that express the occurrence of some **token-level causation** such as 'the short circuit caused the fire'.

SINGULARISM

Singularism is a view about the nature of causation (see **causation and laws**). Like many philosophical terms, however, 'singularism' receives various definitions, each very similar but not quite the same. Here are some examples of the many views that 'singularism' might denote:

(a) Causation can take place without falling under a 'covering law' (i.e. some **law of nature**). That is, event *c* might cause *e* even though there is no law of nature saying that events like *c* cause – or are followed by – events like *e*).

(b) The correct **analysis** of causation will not reduce it to anything involving laws of nature (see **reductionism**). For instance, the **counterfactual theory of causation** doesn't qualify as singularist because that reduction involves what goes on at **possible worlds** with very similar laws of nature (see **counterfactual conditionals**). By contrast, a theory that took causation as **primitive** would be a singularist theory, because it would not be offering a reduction of causation that involved appeal to laws of nature.

(c) Causation is not reducible to relations between *types* of event (for example, some authors have argued that we cannot analyse 'smoking causes cancer' without appealing to 'token-level causation', i.e. particular causal relations between particular events (e.g. individual people being caused to get cancer by their smoking).

(d) The **truthmakers** for true causal propositions are local to the **causal relata** (i.e. only facts about the two relata are truthmakers; we do not need facts about what the rest of the universe is like – see **intrinsic vs extrinsic properties**).

Whatever the exact definition, the general gist is clear: singularists are trying to capture the idea that what it takes for one thing to cause another depends only on what goes on between the two relata; it does not matter what is going on in the rest of the universe. So, if you punch me causing me to be in pain, those causal facts depend only on your punch and what goes on in the nerve endings between my skin and my brain. This is unlike, say, the **regularity theory of causation**, according to which c causes e if and only if it is an instance of a universal regularity. In that case, you cannot tell just by looking at two events whether one event caused the other. Far from it: you need to know what is going on in the rest of the universe, to see if this occurrence is an instance of a regularity or not. For it to be the case that your punch caused me to be in pain we need to know more than just what is going on with your punch and my brain – we need to know whether, in general and across the universe, being punched causes pain.

Singularism is fairly popular, having philosophers such as Elizabeth Anscombe, **David Armstrong** and Michael Tooley on its side. One reason to endorse it is, of course, the intuition that causation is a local matter – that we do not need to look at facts across the rest of the universe to discover whether one thing caused another. Note, though, that there are other motivations. For instance, one might be motivated by the failure of the reductive analyses offered – if the theories that reduce causation down to non-local matters (such as the regularity theory or counterfactual theory, etc.) do not work, then one might think we have a good reason to deny that such a reduction can be carried out and hence to embrace singularism. The opposition, of course, will not be so willing to give up on their reductive enterprises, and might worry that endorsing singularism would mean saying that some things occurred by **natural necessity** (which is one of the things their reductive theories are set up to avoid).

Further reading: Anscombe (1971); Moore (2009)

SOFT DETERMINISM

Soft determinism is the view that (a) **free will** is compatible with **determinism** (so it is a **compatibilist** position), and (b) determinism is actually true (compare **hard determinism**). In other words, acting freely is perfectly compatible with our acts being fully determined by what happened in the distant past plus the laws of nature; moreover, our acts are, in fact, so determined.

Soft determinism's popularity has waned considerably in recent times as philosophers have come to accept that **indeterminism** might well be true. These days, most compatibilists are neutral on whether or not determinism is true, and many of them take the truth or falsity of determinism to be simply irrelevant to the issue of free will.

SORTALS

As with so many terms in philosophy, the exact definition of 'sortal' is philosophically contentious. It is uncontroversial that sortals (i) are a kind of linguistic term (or perhaps a kind of **concept**), and (ii) take numerical modifiers, that is, can be associated with numerical adjectives. The word 'cat' is a sortal: it is a linguistic term that takes numerical modifiers, that is, we can say, 'two cats', 'three cats', etc. Outside philosophy, terms which take numerical modifiers are called 'count nouns' and are contrasted with 'mass nouns' such as 'milk', which do not take numerical modifiers – you cannot say 'two milks'. (You can, however, say 'two beers': 'beer' sometimes acts as a mass noun and sometimes as a count noun.)

However, being a count noun is sometimes taken to be necessary, but not sufficient, for being a sortal. Sortals are sometimes understood to be count nouns (or concepts expressed by count nouns) that 'sort' things into kinds in some metaphysically significant sense, perhaps by specifying the **essence** of things of that kind. Sometimes philosophers distinguish sortals which group things into kinds, known as 'pure sortals' or 'substance sortals' – 'cat' or 'electron' – from 'phase sortals', which denote a certain phase of a thing's existence – 'kitten' or 'child' – or from 'restricted sortals', which denote certain kind of substance with a certain kind of property – 'white kitten', 'green car'.

Further reading: Grandy (2008)

SOURCE INCOMPATIBILISM

See **incompatibilism**.

SPARSE PROPERTY

David Lewis uses the term 'sparse property' to refer to the **natural properties**, which he takes to be a relatively small subclass of all the **properties**. He contrasts the 'sparse properties' with the 'abundant properties', the latter being the relatively large subclass of properties which do not **carve nature at the joints**.

SPECIAL COMPOSITION QUESTION

Intuitively, some things *compose* further objects: atoms compose human beings (equivalently, and perhaps more naturally, human beings are composed of atoms). Intuitively, some things do not compose further objects: myself and Brad Pitt's left arm do not compose some monstrosity that has three arms – we are just two different things, a person and an arm, that do not compose anything. van Inwagen (1990) famously demanded to know when this happens: under what circumstances do things go on to compose a further thing? This question is called the Special Composition Question.

Two of the most common answers are, surprisingly, quite extreme. **Nihilists** say that nothing ever composes. Usually this means they believe that all that exists are tiny little atoms or **simples**, and none of the things we normally think of as being composite objects (tables, chairs, mountains, goats, people, etc.) exist. Alternatively, some nihilists (also called *monists*) believe nothing composes because there is only one single entity – for instance, that only the Universe exists and nothing else does (Schaffer 2007). The other extreme answer is **universalism**. Universalists say things *always* compose – so there *is* an object composed out of myself and Brad Pitt's left arm. That object is a scattered object, partially located where I am and partially located where Brad Pitt is, but it is just as much a *bona fide* object as a table or person. And, of course, there are other odd objects – for any collection of things you name there is an object they compose.

Both of those answers sound weird – if they don't, go back and reread what they say. Even the proponents of these positions generally think they are somewhat counterintuitive and thus that there needs to be at least some explanation of why we should believe them. With that in mind, universalists and nihilists are more than ready to bring out arguments to justify their positions. One popular argument starts from a worry about vagueness (Lewis 1986a: 211–3 and Sider 2001: 120–34 argue for universalism, but the argument can easily be modified to argue for nihilism instead).

Another argument in favour of these extreme answers is that there is a distinct lack of competition: less extreme answers, which say that composition sometimes occurs and sometimes does not (what is called *restricted* composition) are, perhaps surprisingly, hard to come by. (You might think it is blindingly obvious that Barack Obama exists and the Eiffel Tower exists, but there is no object composed of Obama and the Eiffel Tower. However, coming up with an answer to the special composition question which entails this is harder than you might think.)

For instance, consider the answer that things that are *fixed* to one another in a certain way compose a further object. According to this answer, my atoms compose me because they are joined to one another with a certain degree of force, whereas myself and Brad Pitt's left arm do not compose anything, because myself and his arm are not connected by any such force and can easily move around independent of one another. That sounds sensible enough, but the answer (allegedly) has some bizarre consequences. For instance, if I stapled myself to you, we would also be fastened to one another, but (so the allegation goes) one would not normally think we thereby composed a further object. Similar worries plague other proposed restricted answers, so although they may guarantee some intuitions, they get others drastically wrong (see also **mereology**.)

Further reading: Effingham (2009); Markosian (2008)

SPLIT BRAIN CASE

See **fission**.

STATES OF AFFAIRS

There is a fundamental divide between philosophers who think that the world is made up of **facts** and philosophers who think that the world is made up of things. The well known Australian philosopher Jack Smart once said that believing in both facts and things is as dangerous as mixing your drinks.

Actually, philosophers use the word 'fact' in two quite different ways. Sometimes philosophers use the word 'fact' just to mean a true **proposition**. However, sometimes philosophers use the word 'fact' to refer to a real, concrete, non-linguistic occupant of reality, but one with a *propositional structure*, that is, a structure that is specified by means of a *that clause*, e.g. *that Socrates is wise, that grass is green*. Such entities are sometimes called 'states of affairs'. When philosophers say the world is made up of facts rather than things, they are using the word 'fact' in the second sense.

David Armstrong defends an **ontology** of states of affairs in which a state of affairs is understood as a fundamental unity of a *substratum bearing immanent universals*, for example, Socrates being wise, grass being green. For Armstrong, metaphorically speaking, when God created the world, he did not bring into existence substrata and universals, and then somehow glue them together. Rather, he created *states of affairs*. Although we can in some sense think of the substratum and the universal in isolation, in reality they exist as inseparable aspects of the unified state of affairs. (see **Bradley's regress** for one reason why this might seem like an attractive option.)

Further reading: Armstrong (1997)

SUBSISTENCE

An object subsists if it has **being** but does not exist. The term 'subsistence' is rarely used nowadays (since most philosophers don't distinguish between 'being' and 'existence'). It was sometimes used by Alexius Meinong and Bertrand Russell in reference to non-**concrete** things like **universals** and **numbers** (see **non-existent objects**).

SUBSTANCE

The word 'substance' is one of those annoying words that has a different meaning in philosophy than it does in ordinary English. In ordinary English 'substance' is a mass noun, which picks out a stuff of some kind, such as copper or magnesium. In philosophy, 'substance' normally means 'irreducible particular thing'; for example, if there are such things as souls, then souls are substances. (So you can have seven souls, but not seven magnesiums: seven *samples* of magnesium would be seven samples of one substance. Seven souls are seven distinct substances.)

The notion of a substance originates in the writings of **Aristotle**, who took the substances – the fundamental constituents of reality – to be organisms. The Aristotelian idea of substance was developed by Aquinas (1225–74), and was a central concept in the scholastic tradition (see **Aristotle** for a brief explanation of what the scholastic tradition is). Descartes (1596–1650) rejected much of the scholastic tradition, but retained the concept of substance, which he defined as something that exists in such a way as to depend on no other thing for its existence. Descartes believing that only God is a substance in the strictest sense of the term, but that minds and physical bodies are substances in the secondary sense that they depend on nothing other than God for their existence. Spinoza (1632–77) went on to argue that there is only one substance in either of these senses, which he called 'God or nature'.

Further reading: Robinson (2009)

SUBSTANCE-ATTRIBUTE THEORY

See **Bundle theory vs substance-attribute theory**.

SUBSTRATUM

The substratum of an object is the constituent of the object, which is not itself a property but which *bears* the object's properties. Substance-attribute theorists believe in substrata (the plural of 'substratum'), see **bundle theory versus substance-attribute theory**.

SUM

'Sum' is a term from **mereology** and usually taken to be synonymous with **fusion**.

SUPERTASK

A supertask is any event in which an infinite number of sub-tasks are completed within a finite amount of time. For instance, if there were an infinite number of grains of sand on a beach, and you counted them within one lifetime, you would have completed a supertask. Obviously, in many cases a supertask is only completed during a **thought experiment** (for, of course, you *could not* count an infinite number of grains of sand within a finite length of time!). It may, however, be the case that supertasks are commonplace (for instance if **Zeno** was correct then every time we move, we complete an infinite series of tasks).

SUPERVENIENCE

Supervenience is a relation of *necessary co-variation*, usually between kinds of property. The basic idea is as follows: *A*-**properties** supervene on *B*-properties if and only if no two things can differ with respect to the A-properties without differing with respect to the B-properties. To take an example, for mental properties to supervene on physical properties is for it to be the case that no two things can differ with respect to their mental properties without differing with respect to their physical properties. So if Jack is thinking about what to have for dinner, and Joe is multiplying 6 by 23 in his head, there must, on the assumption that the mental supervenes on the physical, be some physical difference between Jack and Joe (presumably a difference in the states of their respective brains) that accounts for this mental difference.

This basic notion is tightened up/altered in many different ways in the literature. For example, we can distinguish different kinds of supervenience claim in terms of the kind of **necessity** involved: is the word 'can' in a statement of supervenience such as (S) 'No two things *can* differ with respect to their mental properties without differing with respect to their physical properties', to be read as expressing *metaphysical* necessity or merely *nomological* necessity? If the 'can' in (S) expresses metaphysical possibility, then it is a claim about *all* **possible worlds**. If the 'can' in (S) expresses merely nomological possibility, then it is a claim merely about all possible worlds which have the same **laws of nature** as the actual world.

The kind of supervenience we have talked about thus far concerns *individuals*; this kind of supervenience is known 'local supervenience'. However, supervenience claims are often made in terms of whole possible worlds, rather than in terms of individuals within worlds (such as Jack and Joe). This kind of supervenience is knows as 'global supervenience' and may be defined as follows:

> A-properties globally supervene on B-properties if and only if all possible worlds which *are indiscernible in terms of their B-properties are also indiscernible in terms of their A-properties*.

So, if mental properties *globally* supervene on physical properties, then any two possible worlds which are physically indiscernible are also mentally indiscernible. **Saul Kripke** invokes the metaphor of God creating the Universe to express this idea: for the mental to supervene on the physical is for it to be the case that all God had to do to fix the mental facts (across the whole Universe) was to fix the physical facts.

Global supervenience claims are needed for making sense of *extrinsic* supervenient properties (see **intrinsic and extrinsic properties**). Consider, for example, the value of a pound coin. The value of a coin does not *locally* supervene on physical facts – in a possible world in which coins are not used for currency, a physical duplicate of a pound coin has no value. However, it may be that the value of a coin *globally* supervenes on the physical facts – in any world physically identical to our own a pound coin has the value it has in our world (assuming that if we fix the physical facts, we also fix facts about how people behave, e.g. if you go to the shop and hand over a pound, you are allowed to walk out with a Mars Bar without anyone calling the police; you might even get some change).

The notion of supervenience was introduced into philosophy as a way of characterising the relationship between moral properties and natural properties by R. M. Hare and G. E. Moore (the former, but not the latter, explicitly used the term 'supervenience'). However, supervenience came to the forefront in the work of Davidson, who first used the notion to capture the relationship between the mental and the physical. Since then, it is probably Jaegwon Kim who has been most influential in developing our understanding of supervenience. These days there is a huge literature on the topic, which distinguishes many kinds of supervenience and explores the logical relationships that hold between them.

Some philosophers hope that the notion of supervenience can be used to articulate a sense in which certain properties might be 'nothing over and above' certain other properties (see **reductionism**), for example, that mental properties might be nothing over and above the physical properties. **David Armstrong**, for example, claimed that where there is supervenience there is an 'ontological free lunch'; that is, we are to judge the parsimony (see **theoretical virtues** for an explanation of 'parsimony') of a hypothesis by considering only the entities in the supervenience base (i.e. the entities on which all other properties supervene). Cashing out the *nothing over and above* relation in terms of supervenience would allow us to define physicalism – the view that all properties are nothing over and above physical properties – in terms of supervenience. Supervenience is also (unsurprisingly) used in the definition of **Humean supervenience**.

Further reading: McLaughlin and Bennett (2008); Kim (1993)

SURVIVAL

Many of the most interesting philosophical innovations in the metaphysics of personal identity have come from philosophers trying to work out what on earth to say about cases of **fission** (it is probably best to read the entry on '**fission**' before reading this entry). Of all the things that philosophers have decided to say about such cases, Derek Parfit's conclusions are both the most famous and the most startling.

Suppose that in the year 4000 there is man called Freddy who has a rare disease, such that if his brain stays in his body, or even if his two brain hemispheres stay together, irreparable brain damage will result. The only way of preserving Freddy's brain hemispheres in working order is to remove them from Freddy's cranium and insert each of them into a distinct brand new body. Fortunately, surgeons in the year 4000 have the technology to perform this operation in such a way that it will result in there being two persons psychologically continuous with Freddy, call them New-Freddy 1 (who has Freddy's left brain hemisphere) and New-Freddy 2 (who has Freddy's right brain hemisphere).

Derek Parfit holds a no-branching version of the **psychological continuity theory** (see **fission**) and so takes it that this operation would result in Freddy's ceasing to exist, as neither New-Freddy 1 nor New Freddy 2 (nor the combination of the two) would be identical to Freddy. (This is because **identity**, and so personal identity, is **transitive**: Freddy must be identical either to *both* New-Freddy 1 and New-Freddy 2, or to neither of them. Parfit takes the latter to be the most palatable option.) The only way Freddy could ensure his future existence would be to make sure that the surgeons only put only one of his hemispheres into a new body and destroy the other; in this way he can avoid the branching which would end his existence. If Freddy makes sure that New-Freddy 2 never comes to be (but one hemisphere is hooked up to the body of New-Freddy 1), then Freddy will continue to exist as New-Freddy 1.

However, Parfit takes it to be intuitive that Freddy has nothing to gain from doing this (as opposed to just letting both New-Freddy 1 and New-Freddy 2 come into existence). If the future existence of New-Freddy 1 is something it is rational for Freddy to desire, a result which for Freddy would make the operation a success, why should the fact that New-Freddy 2 also comes to be take away from this?

Thus Parfit draws a very strange conclusion: in this situation Freddy has no reason to ensure his future existence. If Freddy allows fission to take place, then strictly speaking he will cease to be; but the result for Freddy will be just as good as (perhaps even better than) if he had continued into the future. What Freddy has reason to do, thinks Parfit, is to ensure that there exists someone in the future who is psychologically continuous or psychologically connected with him (see **psychological continuity** for an explanation of 'psychological continuity' and 'psychological connectedness'), regardless of whether that person is literally identical to him. Because Parfit thinks fission situations are just as good for the pre-fission individual as continuing to exist in the future, Parfit chooses to describe such situations as 'survival'. We can thus define 'survival', in Parfit's sense, as follows: x at time t_1 survives at time t_2 if and only if there exists at t_2 a person psychologically connected with x at t_1 (there are various slight qualifications Parfit makes to this definition at various stages of his work).

Why is it that in cases of fission an individual loses their reason to secure their future existence? Parfit's explanation is that a person's reason to secure their own existence is not basic, but *derived*; it is derived from a more basic reason to secure one's 'survival' (in the Parfitian sense defined above). As a matter of contingent fact, for each of us, surviving and continuing to exist go together; I will survive tomorrow in virtue of existing tomorrow such that me tomorrow is psychologically continuous with me today. However, it is only because my continuing to exist ensures my survival that I have reason to try to prolong my existence; my prolonging my existence is a means to an end and not an end in itself. This explains why, in cases of fission where survival and continuing to exist come apart, I lose my reason for continuing to exist.

Consider the following analogy which Parfit uses to explain his position. We have an interest in preserving our natural eyes. However, this interest is not basic; it derives from a more basic interest in gaining information about the world and enjoying pleasurable experiences of a certain kind. As a matter of contingent fact, the having of eyes is necessary for a particularly rich way of gaining information about the world, and for the having of certain kinds of experience. If in the future, our eyes could be replaced by artificial mechanisms that allowed us all these things, then we may lose our reason for preserving our natural eyes. In the same way, according to Parfit, should technology allow us to ensure our survival in the future without ensuring our existence in the future (again, because – thanks to fission, say – there will be no person who is *identical* to me), then we may no longer have a reason to ensure our existence in the future.

It is important to note that Parfit's argument above relies on the premise that fission results in a person ceasing to exist, which in turn requires a no-branching version of the psychological continuity theory. This is not uncontroversial and is denied for example by those who follow David Lewis in accepting the Multiple Occupancy Hypothesis (see **fission**). If no person ceases to be in the operation described above, then we have not described a situation where a person's survival comes apart from that person's continued existence, and so have not given reason to think that in such a situation a person ceases to have reason to preserve its own existence.

Having said that, this argument of Parfit's is part of a general strategy of using **thought experiments** to convince the reader that facts about our identity over time are not as 'deep' as we ordinarily take them to be, and that because of this they do not have the kind of significance we ordinarily take them to have. It is well worth reading Parfit directly and judging for yourself how strong his case is for this conclusion.

Further reading: Noonan (1989, Chapter 9); Parfit (1971); Olson (2008)

SYNCHRONIC IDENTITY

The term for identity at a time, as opposed to **identity over time**; see **identity**.

SYNTHETIC TRUTHS

See **analytic vs synthetic truths**.

TEMPORAL PARTS

A temporal part of an entity is 'all of it' throughout a certain period of time. With **events** it is relatively uncontentious that they have temporal parts, and easy to see what they would be. For instance, a football match would be composed of two temporal parts: the first half of the match and the second half of the match (and, indeed, those parts would have further parts, such as the first minute of the match, the second minute of the match, etc.).

However, some people, namely **perdurantists**, think that *objects* have temporal parts as well (and, usually, **endurantists** disagree). If objects have temporal parts then I have a temporal part, which exists throughout, say, only the first year of my life. Such a temporal part is a *bona fide* object, just like my hand or my foot. It starts off the size of a small newly born baby, and then grows to be the size of a one-year old baby. Then that's it – at that point it ceases to exist. Given perdurantism, I also have other temporal parts. If I live for a century I will have one hundred such year-long temporal parts (all of which would then compose me just as the wheels, frame, chain, etc. of a bicycle compose the bicycle). And, just like the football match, those temporal parts themselves have temporal parts (so, if I live for a century, I have 36,425 day-long temporal parts; 874,200 hour-long temporal parts, etc.). Most importantly, perdurantists generally think that I have *instantaneous* temporal parts – that is, temporal parts of me that last for but an instant. Such instantaneous temporal parts are three-dimensional objects, extended in space but not in time, and they are **infinite** in number. It is instantaneous temporal parts of objects that are most often talked about by perdurantists (and crucial to arguments such as the argument from temporary intrinsics; see **perdurantism**).

Over the years there has been a lot of disagreement about how to define exactly what an instantaneous temporal part is meant to be. The definition currently most used in the literature is from Sider (although there is some dissent):

> *x* is an instantaneous temporal part of *y* at time *t* = $_{df}$ (i) *x* is a part of *y*; (ii) *x* exists at, but only at, time *t*; (iii) *x* **overlaps** every part of *y* at time *t*. (Sider 2001: 60)

So, for instance, in fulfilling the first two conjuncts, my current instantaneous temporal part is a part of me at this exact moment, and only exists for a single instant (namely, now). More importantly, in meeting the third conjunct it is also 'as big as me': it is 5'10" (just as I am), it has hands as (spatial) parts at the moment (just like I do), it has feet as parts (just like I do), etc.

Further reading: Sider (2001, Chapter 3)

TEMPORARY INTRINSICS

See **perdurantism**.

TENSED AND TENSELESS THEORIES OF TIME

Some temporal facts are *tensed* – they say that something is past or is present or is future (they are sometimes also called '*A*-facts' following terminology introduced by **J. M. E. McTaggart**). Tensed facts change: what was once future is now present and will later be past and remain forever so. Other temporal facts are *tenseless* – they say merely that one event is earlier than, later than or simultaneous with another (e.g. that the Battle of Hastings is earlier than the American Civil War, or that that American Civil War is later than the American Revolution). The tenseless facts do not change – what was once earlier than another event will always be earlier than it – you will never wake up and find the Battle of Hastings took place after you were born. Tenseless facts are sometimes called *B*-facts, again following McTaggart's lead.

The issue between tensed and tenseless theories revolves around the status of those facts. The debate is expressed in various ways: whether tensed facts can be reduced to tenseless facts, or *vice versa* (see **reductionism**); whether the tensed facts are **intrinsic** to events; whether tensed facts are mind-independent or not; whether tenseless facts are the **truthmakers** for tensed facts; whether tensed facts are more fundamental than tenseless facts; or (moving to talking about **properties** rather than facts) whether tensed properties can be analysed in terms of tenseless properties. (Note that these questions may not amount to the same thing). The tensed theorist (sometimes '*A*-theorist') says that the tensed facts are more fundamental (or intrinsic or mind independent, etc.) whereas the tenseless theorist says the reverse. These theories are traditionally packaged with other theories about time: **presentists** invariably endorse the tensed theory (but not *vice versa*); the same is generally true of **growing block theorists** (although Tooley 1997 is a notable exception); and **eternalism** usually, but not always (see **moving spotlight**), gets coupled with the tenseless theory (and it is that package deal that '*B*-theory' usually refers to).

Tensed theorists often think it is just obvious that there is something metaphysically special about the present, and that tensed facts are privileged in some fashion. The idea that tensed facts are not fundamentally part of the world should, they say, strike us as quite odd. There are a few, subtly different, arguments in this territory. We might argue that the tensed theory is plausible because our perception of time grounds a belief in the tensed theory: we *experience* things as present and have an experience of the present moment. Another move is to say that tensed beliefs are indispensable, and then go from their being indispensable to their being fundamental. For instance, the *A*-facts concerning an event often play a role in motivating your actions in a way that the *B*-facts do not. One such example comes from A. N. Prior's (1959) paper, 'Thank goodness that is over'. His thinking is: while I might know it to be the case that, say, on 18 January 1997 I have a life-threatening operation – a tenseless fact – what really engages my concern are the tensed facts. When the operation is future, I worry. When the operation is present, I am (anaesthetic notwithstanding) suitably perturbed. When the operation is past, I do not worry about that fact at all and indeed might be quite glad of it if the operation cured some serious ailment. This asymmetry in our responses is justified, says Prior, only by thinking that something like the tensed theory is true. Along similar lines, some *A*-theorists believe that tensed sentences ('I am currently cooking dinner' or 'I will be dead in the future') cannot be replaced with a tenseless sentence with an equivalent meaning (we invite the reader to give it a go!). They assume that if our language could never be made tenseless without a loss of meaning, then this indicates that tensed facts are fundamental.

Tenseless theorists then go on both the defensive and offensive. Here is one example of their defensive strategy. When it comes to language, a tenseless theorist might just shrug their shoulders and not give a damn that a language without tensed terms does not have the same expressive power as a tensed language: 'Who cares', they might say 'that language and reality come apart?' But most tenseless theorists do not take this tack, instead trying to offer up a tenseless semantic theory. The *old tenseless theory* (most often associated with Bertrand Russell) relied on the assumption that we can completely translate tensed statements into tenseless statements – that is, that we can find tenseless statements which mean exactly the same as their tensed counterparts. This project is no longer in vogue, and virtually everyone is agreed that the tensed theorist is correct that tensed statements definitely *mean* something different from any tenseless statements.

To replace the old tenseless theory came the *new tenseless theory*, most often associated with Jack Smart (1964) and Hugh Mellor (1998). This says that although we cannot *translate* tensed statements into tenseless statements, we can give the **truth conditions** of those tensed statements in tenseless terms. For instance, suppose in 2010 I utter the sentence 'The Battle of Hastings took place a thousand years ago'; that (tensed) sentence is a **token** of a sentence-**type** (namely the type that all utterances of 'The Battle of Hastings took place a thousand years ago' are tokens of). The tenseless theorist says that that token is true if and only if it is uttered later than the named event, the Battle of Hastings, by 1000 years – so the truth conditions, in relying only on the *later than* relation, are stated in tenseless terms. And the token is (give or take a few decades) later than the Battle of Hastings by a thousand years. So that sentence token is true. Whereas, if I uttered 'The Battle of Hastings took place a thousand years ago', in the year AD 3000, that would be a different sentence token – this time a token that is *two* thousand years later than the Battle of Hastings (give or take). So, as the tenseless truth conditions demand that the sentence token is uttered *one* thousand years later than the Battle of Hastings, it would be false.

Similarly, 'The Battle of Hastings is happening now' would be true if uttered in AD 1066, as that token would be simultaneous with the Battle of Hastings. Whereas, if uttered *now*, that sentence token would be false, as the Battle of Hastings would not be simultaneous with that particular token/

utterance (being, instead, simultaneous with events from the twenty-first century). However, notice that this is not to say that 'The Battle of Hastings is happening now' and 'The Battle of Hastings occurred simultaneous with the utterance of this sentence token' *mean* the same thing – only that the latter sentence states the conditions under which the former sentence is true. Whether this is good enough to calm the fears of the tensed theorist who was concerned that tensed sentences could not be so translated, remains up for debate; whether or not Mellor *et al.* can offer up a theory of tenseless truth conditions for *all* tensed statements is also debatable.

Tenseless theorists also have some offensive strategies. For instance, some argue that the only way to escape **McTaggart**'s argument for the **unreality of time** is to endorse the tenseless theory, or that the tensed theory has problems accounting for the **flow of time**. Others think the tensed theory faces a problem with **relativity**. Just as with **presentism**, the tensed theory says that a particular time is special (indeed, many tensed theorists will say it is special because it is the only time that exists, thus endorsing presentism). However, Einstein's theory of special relativity says that what is simultaneous with what depends upon relative velocity: there will be different facts about simultaneity for two things travelling at different velocities. Given that the present moment is that moment comprised of everything simultaneous with us right now, that means that what counts as present, and *a fortiori* what is metaphysically special, is going to vary depending upon your relative velocity. But then, goes the argument, it seems doubtful that the tensed theorist wants to say that which time is metaphysically special varies according to one's velocity. According to the tenseless theorist, the theory of relativity reveals to us that in the **God's eye view** of the world, there is no objective or metaphysically special 'present moment'. At this point there are a number of responses available to the theorist: she may claim that what is metaphysically special *is* relative to your velocity, or try to replace relativity with a more metaphysically acceptable theory that avoids the metaphysical assumptions of Einstein's theory.

See also **eternalism; presentism; indexical;** *and* **relativity**.

Further reading: Dainton (2001, Chapters 3, 5 and 6); Markosian (2009)

THEORETICAL VIRTUES

Theoretical virtues are 'good making' properties of theories, features such that a theory which has them is in some sense thereby *better off*, perhaps because the fact that a theory has those features gives us some reason to believe that that theory is true. Correspondingly, theoretical vices are 'bad making' properties of theories, features such that a theory which has them is in some sense *worse off*, perhaps because the fact that a theory has those features gives us some reason to believe that that theory is false. Much of metaphysics is taken up with trying to assess and balance the theoretical virtues and vices of various theories; this is one of the main ways in which metaphysicians try to work out what theory they ought to believe in (this process is sometimes known as 'cost–benefit analysis'). In this respect, metaphysical enquiry resembles scientific practice, for scientists also take theoretical virtues into consideration when choosing between theories.

Which features of theories count as theoretical virtues, and which theoretical vices, are – like most things in philosophy – highly contentious. Some commonly accepted examples of theoretical virtues are: being internally unified, having explanatory power, and fit with **common sense** and with other theories. Perhaps the most uncontroversial example of a theoretical virtue is *parsimony*: the property a theory has of *having few **ontological commitments***. The principle that, in our theory choice, we ought to try to keep our theories as parsimonious as possible – sometimes put as the principle that we should not 'multiply entities beyond necessity' – is known as 'Ockham's razor' (or 'Ockham's razor') after the fourteenth-century philosopher William of Ockham (1288–1348).

To give a crude example which captures the general idea, if we have two theories, *A* and *B*, which are equally good in all respects except that *A* but not *B* is ontologically committed to fairies, we ought, if we respect Ockham's razor to go for *A*. To give a real example: it is often argued that Ockham's razor gives us a good reason to prefer a '**Humean**' theory of **causation and laws of nature** (see **regularity theory of causation** and **regularity theory of laws**) over a 'necessitarian' account that invokes **natural necessity**, on the grounds that natural necessity constitutes an ontological commitment that we can do without. Their opponents, however, such as those who endorse the **DTA** of laws, will retort that their theory has better *explanatory power* – another theoretical virtue – since their theory can explain *why* the Universe contains regularities in the first place (the regularities exist because they are necessitated by the laws), whereas for the Humean there is no such explanation: that there are any regularities at all is a brute, inexplicable fact.

Another important (alleged) theoretical virtue is consistency with our 'intuitions' or 'common sense' beliefs about the world, or, as it is sometimes put, our 'folk theory' of a given phenomenon (causation or **personal identity** or whatever); see **common sense** and **thought experiment**.

Further reading: Baker (2008)

THOUGHT EXPERIMENT

Thought experiments are widely used in metaphysics (and other areas of philosophy) as a way of testing theories. To give you a flavour of how they work, consider **John Locke**'s famous case of the cobbler and the prince. We are asked to imagine that, whilst they are asleep, the 'consciousness' of a cobbler is switched with that of a prince. In other words, all of the cobbler's beliefs, desires, personality traits, emotional tendencies and memories are swapped over into the prince's body, and the prince's beliefs, desires, and so on, are similarly swapped over into the cobbler's body. Now comes the crucial question: when the two people wake up, which *person* is the one who went to sleep in the prince's bed last night? Is it the one who wakes up in the cobbler's bed (wondering where all his finery is, where his servants are, and why his bed is so uncomfortable), or is it the one who wakes up in the prince's bed (wondering why he is wearing fur-trimmed pyjamas and why someone has just brought him a fine breakfast on a golden platter)? Locke thinks the answer is obviously the former. To make things more vivid, we could imagine that yesterday the prince did something terrible – murdered one of his courtiers, say. Who do you think is to blame: the one who now has the body of the cobbler or the one who has the body of the prince? Again, Locke thinks the answer is obviously the former.

Locke concludes from this that **bodily continuity** is not required for **personal identity**, since the *person* who previously had the body of a prince now has a completely different body. What is required for personal identity must be whatever it was that was switched from one body into the other, in other words (in Locke's terminology) *consciousness* (see **memory theory of personal identity** and **psychological continuity**).

Thought experiments are often extremely far-fetched – as in the above example. Locke is not suggesting that this consciousness-switch is an operation that can actually be performed, given our current state of knowledge of physiology and neurology and brain surgery techniques. (The thought experiment is far-fetched even by today's standards, and Locke was writing over 300 years ago.) However, this is not, or at least not just by itself, a reason not to take such a thought experiment seriously. The reason is that metaphysical theories normally aim to tell us something about how things *must* be, and not just how they actually *are* (normally because they aim to offer a **conceptual analysis** or a **reductionist** account of some phenomenon). For example, it is a fact about *actual* persons that they are all descended from apes. However, this does not appear to be a *necessary* truth about persons: it does not tell us a condition that something *must* satisfy in order to count as a person. This is particularly clear if we think of person-hood as a necessary condition for **moral responsibility**: nothing that is a non-person can be morally responsible for what they do. It seems perfectly *metaphysically* possible (see **possible worlds**) – and here is another thought experiment – that we could stumble across members of some alien species, not descended from apes, that we would happily regard as persons (they would be morally culpable for destroying the Earth just so that they could build a hyperspace express route, for example). Whether we ever *will* stumble across such a species, or whether it is remotely likely that we will, is irrelevant to the fact (if it is a fact), demonstrated (or not) by this thought experiment, that being descended from an ape is not a necessary condition for being a person.

There are two important qualifications to bear in mind when thinking about thought experiments. One is that not everyone has the same intuitive reactions to the same thought experiment. If you find yourself just not giving the answer you are apparently expected to give when confronted with one (for example, if it seems obvious to you that the person to blame for the murder committed yesterday is the person who wakes up in the prince's bed with the fur-trimmed pyjamas), that does not mean there is something seriously wrong with your powers of judgement. In this case, Locke is trying to justify a particular theory of personal identity by appealing to our judgements in this case. If your judgement differs from Locke's, that does not mean he is right and you are wrong: his intuitions about personhood do not have any privileged status. Of course, there might be all sorts of other reasons to prefer a **psychological continuity** theory of personal identity to a bodily continuity theory. However, if you genuinely do not share Locke's intuition about the prince and the cobbler, then by your lights that thought experiment does not count as one of the reasons to prefer it.

The other important qualification is that even if you do give the intuitive judgement that the presenter of the thought experiment is expecting you to give, that does not necessarily commit you to upholding that judgement come what may. First, it might be that your intuitive judgement about a thought experiment conflicts with other things you believe (for example, some philosophical theory that in other respects has a lot going for it – see **theoretical virtues**). In that case, *something* has to give, or you will end up with inconsistent beliefs. However, it is not always immediately clear which of your judgements you ought to dispense with. Sometimes, for example, philosophers are happy to 'bite the bullet' and accept that their theory delivers counter-intuitive results in some hypothetical scenarios, on the grounds that there is more to being a good philosophical theory than merely matching up with people's intuitive judgements.

Other well-known thought experiments described in this book include **Frankfurt's nefarious neurosurgeon**, **brains in a vat**, and cases of '**fission**' which raise problems for theories of personal identity. Thought experiments need not be outlandish, however (as the ones just mentioned are). For example, in the literature on **causation by absence**, a standard thought experiment involves someone who fails to water his neighbour's plants, which then die. We are then asked (a) whether he caused the plant's death, and (b) whether the US President (or similar) also caused their death because he also failed to water them. This thought experiment raises questions about causation, but does so by using a completely mundane case.

Further reading: Brown (2009)

TIME

A sub-discipline of metaphysics, the philosophy of time has its roots in ancient Greece, for example, in **Zeno**'s puzzles about **infinity**. However, it was not until the early twentieth century, and the work of **J. M. E. McTaggart**, that it came into its stride. McTaggart posed the famous, although not universally respected, argument for the **unreality of time**: the thesis that there is no time, and nothing ever changes.

It was the various responses to McTaggart's argument that focused a lot of the modern debate, on such areas as **tensed and tenseless theories of time** (i.e. whether tensed properties, like *being future* or *being present*, are metaphysically privileged in some way); the **ontology** of other times, and whether times other than the present exist (e.g. whether **presentism**, **eternalism** or the **growing block theory** are true); whether there is a **flow of time**; the **direction of time**; and, spurred on in part by the theory of **relativity** in physics, whether one could go backwards in time (see **backwards causation** and **time travel**). However, the philosophy of time does not just deal with the nature of time itself, it also deals with how time bears on the nature of things within it. For instance, there are questions as to whether or not material objects have **temporal parts** (see **endurantism** and **perdurantism**), or under what conditions they are identical across time (see **identity across time**).

Further reading: Markosian (2009)

TIME TRAVEL

Whether or not time travel is possible is an issue in the **philosophy of time**. A lot of the literature on time travel deals with the so-called *grand-father paradox*. Imagine you travel back in time and try and kill your grandfather before he met your grandmother. If you succeeded, then you would never be born. However, if you were never born, you could never travel back in time and so your grandfather would not be killed. However, we just said he was killed! Hence we have the paradox.

One lesson one might take from this is that backwards causation is impossible, and so does not occur: if the possibility of backwards causation leads to paradox, then backwards causation cannot be a possibility after all. A less hard-line response is to say that, whilst a scenario where you kill your grandfather is impossible, this does not mean *all* scenarios involving backwards causation are impossible. So you *can* time travel, but if you attempt to kill your grandfather you will be thwarted in some fashion. Perhaps your gun misfires; perhaps you kill a man you *thought* (mistakenly, as it turned out) was your grandfather; perhaps in your haste to get to a good vantage point you slip on a banana peel and sprain your ankle (see Lewis 1976 and Smith 1997).

If time travel is possible, there are various implications. For instance, it has been argued that the possibility of time travel is inconsistent with a variety of metaphysical theories. Firstly, **presentism** – the view that only the present moment exists – has a problem, for if there is no past or future, how can one travel there? (see Dainton 2001; Keller and Nelson 2001 for discussions). Secondly, **endurantism** (roughly, the view that an object is wholly present at every moment at which it exists) runs into a variety of problems when it comes to backwards causation, which **perdurantism** (the view that different **temporal parts** of an object exist at different times) looks better suited to answer (Sider 2001). However, some think the exact opposite is true: that it is perdurantism that has these problems (Gilmore 2007). Finally, as time travel always involves cases of **backwards causation**, all of the issues that bear on the possibility of backwards causation bear on the possibility of time travel.

Further reading: Dainton (2001, Chapter 8); Lewis (1976)

TOKEN

See **type and tokens**.

TOKEN-LEVEL CAUSATION

Token-level causation is causation that holds between particular **events, facts**, or whatever (so, 'John's smoking caused him to get cancer' is a token-level causal claim, whereas 'smoking causes cancer' is a type-level causal claim).

Confusingly, token-level causation is sometimes called 'singular causation' not to be confused with '**singularism**', which is a specific thesis about the nature of (token-level) causation. Usually, though, token-level causation is just referred to as 'causation' (as in, for example, the **counterfactual theory of causation**), unless in the context it is being distinguished from **type-level causation**.

TRANSITIVE CLOSURE

See **ancestral relation**.

TRANSITIVE RELATION

A relation R is transitive if and only if it is such that, necessarily, if some object x bears R to y, and some object y bears R to z, it follows that x bears R to z. The relation of *being taller than* is an example of a transitive relation: if John is taller than Mary, and Mary is taller than Freddy, it follows that John is taller than Freddy. By contrast, *is at least six feet away from* is not transitive: if John is at least six feet away from Freddy, then of course Freddy is also at least six feet away from John. However, John is not at least six feet away from himself.

Identity is also a transitive relation: if Clark Kent is identical to Superman, and Superman is identical to Kal-El, it follows that Clark Kent is identical to Kal-El. This fact is important in debates over **personal identity**, as some of the relations that are claimed by philosophers to account for personal identity, such as *remembering the experiences of*, do not seem to be transitive (see **psychological continuity**). Causation is often taken to be a transitive relation (if c causes d and d causes e, then c causes e), though this is controversial.

If we have a relation that is not transitive (such as *remembers the experiences of*, or *causally depends on* where this gets formally defined – see **counterfactual theory of causation**), we can generally define a new transitive relation on the basis of that relation, known as the 'ancestral' of the relation (see **ancestral relation**). This is a technique that is deployed in both the personal identity and causation literature.

TROPE THEORY

Trope theory is a form of **nominalism**, in the sense that it is a view which denies the existence of **universals**: according to nominalists, if two objects resemble each other (e.g. they are both red) this is not because they literally share something (a universal). All entities for the trope theorist are **particulars**. However, trope theory is the form of nominalism that is closest to **realism** about universals, in that it accepts the existence of **properties** as *constituents* of objects. Take the book in front of you. The trope theorist accepts the existence, not only of the book but of the book's characteristics: its hardness, its colour, its shape. However, crucially these characteristics are (unlike universals) 'unrepeatable' particulars. Just as your book and my book are numerically distinct entities, so the hardness of your book and the hardness of my book are numerically distinct entities. Such 'one off' properties are known as 'tropes'.

How then does the trope theorist account for similarity between objects, for my book and your book having 'something in common' in both being hard? The realist about universals takes this phrasing literally: my book and your book both have the universal *hardness* in common. However, trope theorists read talk of having 'something in common' as just a loose way of talking, not to be taken literally. Our books share 'the same property' in the sense that two soldiers wear 'the same uniform', that is, numerically distinct uniforms of the same **type**, rather than the sense in which two brothers have 'the same father', that is, numerically one and the same man (see **identity** for more on this distinction). My book and your book resemble one another because they each have a trope of the same type.

Of course, this merely raises the question: what is it for two tropes, for example, the hardness of my book and the hardness of your book, to be of the same type? Trope theorists believe that the answer is just that the two tropes *resemble* each other. The hardness of my book and the hardness of your book are like identical twins: they are numerically distinct things, and yet they closely, perhaps perfectly, resemble each other. It is in virtue of having resembling tropes that the books resemble one another, and that a single predicate, 'is hard', applies to both of them.

So trope theorists have an explanation of the resemblance of objects in terms of the resemblance of tropes, but nothing deeper explains the resemblance of tropes. The fact that, say, the hardness of your book and the hardness of my book resemble each other is the metaphysical bottom line, and so resemblance is a **primitive** within trope theory. The resemblance between tropes is an *internal relation*, a relation such that the mere existence of the relata necessitates their standing in that relation (for an uncontroversial example of an internal relation consider the relation pink bears to red of *being lighter than*: the mere existence of pink and of red necessitate their standing in this relation to each other).

All this provides materials for the trope theorist to account for resemblance between particular objects, but how does the trope theorist account for talk of properties in general, for example what is the word 'wisdom' in the sentence, 'wisdom is a virtue', supposed to refer to? The realist about universals has a straightforward answer to this question: the word 'wisdom' refers to the universal of wisdom. Obviously, the trope theorist cannot claim that the word 'wisdom' refers to the universal of wisdom, given that they do not believe in such a thing, but nor can they say it refers to a wisdom trope. There is not one wisdom trope, but many – the wisdom of Plato, the wisdom of Socrates, etc. – so which wisdom trope does the word 'wisdom' in the above sentence refer to? It is clear that the word wisdom in this sentence does not refer to any one single wisdom trope; it is supposed to pick out wisdom in general.

It is open to the trope theorist to follow the **austere nominalist** in subscribing to anti-realism about general **properties**, and offer some kind of **paraphrase** for sentences like 'wisdom is a virtue', without using words that refer to general properties. However, it is more common for trope theorists to be **realists** about general properties and offer a reductive analysis of them (see **reductionism**) that is similar to the strategy deployed by the **class nominalist**. The strategy is to identify a property with a *class of resembling tropes*: the word 'wisdom' refers to the class of wisdom tropes, the word 'hardness' refers to the class of hardness tropes. What makes a given trope a wisdom trope as opposed, to say, a hardness trope? Again, here we have reached the metaphysically bottom line: some tropes are wisdom tropes, some tropes and hardness tropes, and this is not to be explained in more basic terms. This account avoids the difficulty the **class nominalist** has with co-extensive properties (see the **class nominalism** entry for an account of this difficulty). Even though everything that has a heart also has kidneys, each *having-a-heart* trope is distinct from each *having-kidneys* trope. Therefore, the class of *having-a-heart* tropes is distinct from the class of *having-kidneys* tropes.

Trope theory can be seen as a nice middle way between realism about universals and more extreme forms of nominalism. It is natural to think that we can perceive not just particular objects, but the properties particular objects have; I can see the colour of the book, feel its hardness. Austere nominalists cannot take this at face value; if there is no such thing as the colour of the book, then I cannot literally be seeing it (the class nominalist also has trouble here, as I am not literally seeing the whole class of objects which the colour of the book is identical to). Trope theorists avoid this counterintuitive aspect of austere nominalism. On the other hand, the trope theorist also avoids the unattractive aspects of realism about universals: worries about the intelligibility and ontological profligacy of universals.

Further reading: Loux (2006, 79–89); Oliver (1996).

TRUMPING

Trumping is a kind of pre-emption: a case of **causation** where (a) if the cause had not happened, the effect still would have, and (b) there is no chain of intervening events linking the cause to the effect. Trumping is particularly challenging for those who uphold a **counterfactual theory of causation** (see **pre-emption** for more).

TRUTH

Truth is a tricky notion in philosophy. On the one hand, we all use the words 'true' and 'false' perfectly happily in everyday life without finding those terms at all problematic. On the other hand, what *is* truth? That is a really hard question to answer.

One reason it is a hard question to answer is that philosophers do not even agree about whether truth is a metaphysically interesting concept in the first place. One way to think of the issue here is to consider whether or not truth is a **property** of sentences (or statements or propositions or beliefs or whatever). At first sight, it seems that truth *must* be a property; after all, '. . . is true' is a predicate, so to say '*p* is true' would seem to be to ascribe a property (truth) to a sentence (*p*), just as to say 'water is wet' is to ascribe a property (wetness) to a substance (water). Moreover, we often seem to directly *refer* to truth (as in 'tell me the truth!'). And once we agree that truth is a property, it looks as though we need to provide a metaphysical account of its nature. However, care is needed here because use of the term 'property' need not commit you believing that such a metaphysical account is needed. For example, the **class nominalist** holds that to have the property F is merely a matter of belonging to the class of Fs – so a class nominalist might hold that there is nothing wrong with thinking of truth as a property, so long as we understand that all we are saying is that a sentence is true merely by virtue of being a member of the class of true sentences. So some philosophers who think that truth is not a metaphysically interesting concept will say that it is not a property at all, whereas others will say that it is a property, but just not a metaphysically interesting one (in particular, it is not a **universal**). We will talk rather loosely about whether truth is a 'substantive' property, meaning the kind of property about which the metaphysician can and should have something interesting to say.

There is a related question of what the 'bearers' of truth are. In what follows, we will take the truthbearers to be sentences; see **truthbearers** for more.

Deflationary views

Some philosophers – those who hold a 'deflationary' view of truth – think that truth is not a substantive property. According to the 'redundancy theory' of truth, 'p is true' just means exactly the same as 'p': to say that 'snow is white' is true, is just to say that snow is white. (So on a redundancy view, truth is not a property at all.) One problem with this view is that it is hard to see how to apply it to more complex cases. For example, the redundancy theory (as just described, although not everyone means the same thing by 'redundancy theory') cannot deal with 'everything the Pope says is true': if you remove 'is true', you just end up with 'everything the Pope says', which of course is not even a sentence and obviously does not mean the same as 'everything the Pope says is true'.

Other deflationists (sometimes called 'minimalists' about truth) accept that the predicate 'is true' cannot simply be defined away in this way, but agree with the redundancy theorist that truth is not a substantive property of sentences (or **propositions** or . . .). Take the sentence 'everything the Pope says is true'. How would we attempt to articulate the thought that is being expressed here, without using the word 'true'? Well, effectively we would have to say something like: 'if the Pope says "God exists", then God exists; if the Pope says "snow is white", then snow is white, . . . ', and so on, for every sentence the Pope might take it upon himself to utter. Obviously we would have to carry on indefinitely, and that would be at worst impossible and at best extremely tedious. Having the predicate 'true' in our language allows us to save ourselves the bother, because we can simply say 'everything the Pope says is true' instead. However, according to the minimalist, saving us the bother is *all* it does; as with the redundancy theory, 'is true' does not pick out a substantive property of any of the sentences the Pope utters.

Truth as a substantive property

Some philosophers think that truth *is* a substantive property and so an account of what that property *is*, called for. Moreover, different accounts of the nature of truth have very different implications – or at any rate have often been thought to have such implications – for the debate between realism and anti-realism (see **realism and anti-realism (global)**). For example, **pragmatism** is often characterised as a theory of truth; as William James put it, 'the true is whatever proves itself to be good in the way of belief'. Another theory of truth that is distinctly anti-realist is the 'coherence theory' of truth. Roughly, the coherence theory says that to be true is to be part of a coherent system of beliefs. So, for example, the reason why it is false that my feet are currently green, is that such a belief would not cohere with many other beliefs I have about the world – for example, the belief that I have not recently painted my feet green, and the belief that people's feet do not just turn green for no reason. It's easy to see how the coherence theory leads one into anti-realist territory by considering the possibility that two people, or perhaps two cultures, might have different but mutually incompatible systems of beliefs (or **conceptual schemes**). So, 'there are witches', say, might cohere with one system of beliefs but not with the other; and according to the coherence theory it would follow that 'there are witches' is true relative to the first system and false relative to the second. Unless the coherence theorist has some way to rule out this kind of possibility, it is committed to a form of **relativism**.

It is often claimed that metaphysical realism – roughly the view that the nature of reality is entirely independent of the way our minds work or what we believe – requires a 'correspondence theory of truth'. The correspondence theory says, as you might expect, that sentence p is true if and only if p corresponds to reality. That by itself is not terribly helpful, of course; but the basic idea is that, say, the sentence 'Jack is a dull boy' is true if and only if there is some portion of reality to which it corresponds: perhaps the **fact** that Jack is a dull boy or **state of affairs** of Jack's being a dull boy.

Many philosophers (not all of them of an anti-realist persuasion) have baulked at this conception of the nature of reality as neatly carved into 'chunks' that correspond to true sentences. The correspondence theory has fallen into disrepute, partly for this reason. Maybe thinking of the world as containing the fact (in this metaphysically substantive sense of a fact as a 'chunk' of reality) that Jack is a dull boy is all right; but what about the facts that are supposed to correspond to the truth of 'there are no unicorns', or 'Mary rarely goes out without an umbrella'? Exactly what chunks of reality might these sentences correspond to? A second worry concerns the mysteriousness of the correspondence relation: what, exactly, is correspondence supposed to be? After all, it surely cannot be some sort of *physical* relation – what physical relation could the sentence 'there are galaxies billions of light years away' bear to those galaxies?

Some contemporary metaphysical realists have sought refuge in **truthmaker** theory: the idea that for every true proposition, there is some entity that *makes* that proposition true. Truthmaker theory is supposedly more promising than (or perhaps is a better version of) the correspondence theory for two reasons. First, 'making-true' is claimed to be a more perspicuous than 'correspondence'; and, second, truthmaker theory is not committed to the claim that for *every* true proposition there is some fact that corresponds to precisely *that* proposition. For example, what makes it true that Mary rarely goes out without an umbrella might be a large collection of particular states of affairs (Mary's going out on Tuesday lunchtime with her umbrella, Mary's going out on Friday morning without her umbrella, and so on), such that there are a lot more states of affairs of the first, umbrella-involving kind than the second, no-umbrella kind. No special fact or state of affairs of *Mary's rarely going out without her umbrella* is needed to make the proposition true. Nonetheless, truthmaker theory is still apparently committed to a lot of facts or states of affairs that might seem metaphysically dubious. (Take 'there are no unicorns'. Exactly what state of affairs makes *that* true?)

Truth, realism and anti-realism

Two notes of caution are needed when considering the relationship between one's theory of truth and one's position with respect to the realism vs anti-realism debate, because this relationship is not as clear as is sometimes assumed. For example, it is perfectly possible for someone to be a correspondence theorist (or truthmaker theorist) about truth and an anti-realist about mind-independent reality. One might hold that true sentences correspond to or are made true by fact-shaped chunks, maintaining that the nature of these fact-shaped chunks is not itself mind- or theory-independent. (Perhaps it is a feature of our **conceptual scheme** that it carves the world up into fact-shaped chunks such as Jack's being a dull boy, and some other possible conceptual scheme carves the world up into completely different fact-shaped chunks, so that according to that scheme there is no chunk that this sentence corresponds to.)

On the other hand, theories of truth such as pragmatism and coherentism definitely *do* have anti-realist implications. One cannot simultaneously hold on the one hand that, say, the *truth* of 'there are witches' is a matter of coherence with one's system of belief, and, on the other, that whether or not *there are any witches* is a matter that is completely independent of one's system of beliefs (as realism demands). This is because of the obvious fact that for any sentence p, 'p' is true if and only if p: 'there are witches' is true if and only if there are, indeed, witches. (This principle, due to Alfred Tarski is sometimes known as the 'T-schema', and any adequate theory of truth must abide by it.) So if it is a belief-independent matter whether or not there are witches, it must also be a belief-independent matter (*contra* the coherence theory) whether or not 'there are witches' is *true*. Otherwise it could turn out that there are witches, yet 'there are witches' is false (or that there are no witches, but 'there are witches' is true). And that violates the T-schema.

Further reading: Kirk (1999, Chapter 2); Glanzberg (2009); David (2009)

TRUTHBEARERS

See also **proposition**.

What are the 'bearers' of truth? That is, the items that have the property of truth (if there is such a thing): are they sentences, or propositions, or utterances, or what? Metaphysicians normally take the answer to be 'propositions', where propositions are thought of as abstract objects that are (sometimes) taken to be the *meanings* of sentences (see **propositions** for why), so that 'snow is white' and 'Schnee ist weiss' 'express the same proposition', and both sentences are true *because* the proposition itself is true. So while sentences and utterances and inscriptions can also be truthbearers, the 'fundamental' truthbearers are propositions.

However, propositions (conceived in this way) are generally viewed by anti-realists (see **realism and anti-realism (global)**) with considerable suspicion, not least because belief in propositions (in the sense just described) might be thought to commit one to thinking that the world somehow 'speaks its own language', as it is sometimes put. After all, the proposition *that snow is white* is not itself supposed to be *in English* (despite appearances!); the proposition that the *sentence* 'snow is white' expresses is not itself a sentence of English, or French, or indeed any actual language. Anti-realists thus tend to think of *sentences* as the ultimate truthbearers, and (following **W. V. Quine**) construe sameness of meaning across different languages as a matter merely of the intertranslatability of sentences, rather than thinking that two sentences have the same meaning because there is literally something (the meaning) that they share (i.e. they express the same proposition) (see also **proposition** and **conceptual scheme**).

TRUTH CONDITIONS

The truth conditions for a sentence are those conditions that must obtain in order for the sentence to be true. For example, the truth condition for 'snow is white' is that snow is white. Admittedly this does not sound terribly illuminating. In metaphysics, truth conditions are normally mentioned in the context of **conceptual analysis**, where providing a conceptual analysis of a term ('cause', say, or 'person') is a matter of stating the truth conditions for the relevant kind of claim ('x caused y', say, or 'x is a person'). Strictly speaking, one would expect a conceptual analysis of a given term to state the *meaning* of the term. Whether or not the meaning of a sentence ('x caused y', say) just *is* the same as its truth conditions is a thorny issue in the philosophy of language (but also crops up directly in some metaphysical disputes, see **tensed and tenseless theories of time**). Some metaphysicians these days shun talk of truth conditions in favour of talk of **truthmakers**.

TRUTHMAKERS

The 'truthmaker principle' (or 'truthmaking principle') tells us that for every true **proposition** there is some existing entity (or entities) that makes that proposition true. (Truthmaker theory is sometimes claimed to be a good replacement for the correspondence theory of **truth**.) The candidate entity seems clear in the case of propositions that claim that something exists: the proposition <Barack Obama exists> is plausibly made true by Barack Obama. It is generally taken to be a necessary condition for an entity e to serve as the (complete) truthmaker for a proposition p that the existence of e necessitates the truth of p. Hence, although it is plausible to think that Barack Obama is the complete truthmaker for the truth <Barack Obama exists>, it seems that Barack Obama could not be the complete truthmaker for the truth <Barak Obama is the President of the United States>, for the truth of this proposition does not seem to be necessitated by the mere existence of Barack Obama (Obama might not have been President). The most commonly offered candidate for the truthmaker of this proposition is the **state of affairs** of Barack Obama's being President of the United States.

The truthmaker principle is often used as a way of arguing against certain philosophical views, which it accuses of 'cheating' by investing in more truths than they have entities to 'pay for'. **Presentism** is often accused of having problems providing truthmakers for truths about the past. If past events and objects no longer exist, then what makes the following proposition true: <there used to be dinosaurs>? **Austere nominalism** is accused of having difficulties providing truthmakers for true propositions that ascribe properties to objects. As we have already noted, the mere existence of Barack Obama does not guarantee that the proposition <Barack Obama is President of the United States> is true. The challenge for the austere nominalist wishing to satisfy the truthmaker principle is to find – in a world containing only particular objects – entities which guarantee the truth of this proposition. Phenomenalism is also sometimes accused of 'cheating' (see **phenomenalism and idealism** for more on this).

The supporters of the truthmaker principle rarely offer much argument for the principle; it is often taken to be supported by a basic realist intuition (see **realism and anti-realism (global)**) that **truth** must be grounded in reality.

Some philosophers hold milder versions of the truthmaker principle, which allow for various exemptions. For example, many philosophers have the intuition that negative existential statements, such as <there are no unicorns>, given that they do not assert the existence of anything, do not need truthmakers. Also, it might be thought that analytic truths (see **analytic vs synthetic truths**) such as <bachelors are unmarried men>, because their meaning is sufficient to ground their truth, do not require truthmakers. However, it is commonly thought that weakening the principle in this way undermines its credibility. First, how are we ever to catch cheaters if the principle can be modified every time a philosophical view turns out not to have enough truthmakers? And second, the principle 'every truth needs a truthmaker' is supposed to be intuitively plausible. However, once we start admitting that there are lots of truths that *do not* need truthmakers, and correspondingly keep adding exclusion clauses, it is not completely clear why we should think that *any* truths need truthmakers, given that so many truths, apparently, can get by quite happily without them.

A closely related, but more moderate, way of cashing out realist intuitions that truth must be grounded in reality is to hold that truth **supervenes** on being: once we have fixed the facts about what entities are contained at a world, we have thereby fixed the facts about which propositions are true at that world. This principle is more moderate in that it does not require that we find positive entities to make negative truths true. All that is required for the truth of the proposition <there are not any unicorns> to supervene on being is for there to be no two worlds containing all and only the same entities such that <there are not any unicorns> is true at one but not the other. Some philosophers hold even more moderate versions of this principle: *truth supervenes on what things there are and how those things are* (a principle more friendly to austere nominalism), or *truth supervenes on what things there are and what things there were* (a presentism-friendly version of the principle). For those attracted to the thesis that truth supervenes on being, the challenge is to decide which of these various principles captures the true relationship between propositions and reality.

Further reading: Armstrong (2004); Beebee and Dodd (2005, Introduction)

TYPE-LEVEL CAUSATION

Causation conceived as a relation between **types** or **properties**, or as a general feature of a population (as in 'smoking causes cancer'). See **probabilistic theories of causation (type-level)**. Type-level causation contrasts with **token-level causation** (often just referred to as 'causation', because it is the kind most metaphysicians worry about).

TYPE AND TOKENS

Consider the sentence, 'war is war'. How many words are there in this sentence? This question is ambiguous until it is specified whether we are interested in word *tokens* or whether we are interested in word *types*. If we are asking how many word types there are in the sentence, the answer is two: the sentence contains the word type 'war' and the word type 'is'. If we are asking how many word tokens there are, the answer is three, as there are two tokens of the word type 'war' and one token of the word type 'is'. We find the same ambiguity when we ask without qualification how many cars the local dealer sells. We might be wondering how many *types* of car the local dealer sells, in which case if she only sells minis, the answer would be that she sells only one car. Alternately we might be interested in how many *tokens* of car she sells, in which case the answer might be that she sells five a week. (Similarly, 'Sam and Jo are wearing *the same* dress' is ambiguous: it might mean that they are wearing the same *type* of dress, or that they are wearing the very same (token) dress; see **identity**.)

In general, the distinction between type and token is the distinction between a general category and its instances. The distinction is useful in philosophy of mind, where we distinguish between type identity theories of mind, which claim that each type of mental state − for example, pain − is identical with a certain type of physical state − for example, c-fibres firing − and token identity theories of mind, which claim that each specific token of a mental state − for example, Smith's pain yesterday morning − is identical to a specific token of a physical state − for example, Smith's c-fibres firing this morning. In metaphysics, the problem of **universals** is sometimes put as a need to account metaphysically for the fact that tokens fall under types.

Further reading: L. Wetzel (2008)

UNIVERSALISM

See **Special Composition Question**.

UNIVERSALS

Common sense tells us that ordinary, particular objects exist: the book in your hands, the chair you are sitting on. However, do the *characteristics* of those objects, their colour, size, shape and weight, exist, as constituents of objects? Some philosophers think they do, some philosophers think they do not. Among those philosophers who do believe that the characteristics of objects − or '**properties**' as philosophers tend to call them − exist as constituents of objects, there is a great divide. One half of this divide believes that numerically one and the same property can be a constituent of more than one object; it might be, for example, that the redness of one chair is one and the same thing as the redness of some other chair. We call properties understood as entities which can be had by more than one object 'universals', and philosophers who believe in them 'realists about universals'. The other half of this divide, defended by '**trope theorists**', denies that one and the same property can be a constituent of more than one object.

Philosophers who deny the existence of universals are known as '**nominalists**'. So trope theorists are nominalists; other brands of nominalist (for example, **class nominalists**), while they may or not be realists about **properties**, all agree that properties are not *constituents* of objects. For example, those class nominalists who accept that properties exist hold that a property (redness, say) is to be identified with a class of **particular** objects (in the case of redness, the class of red things). So a property is not really a *constituent* of an object at all (since in general a **class** is not a constituent of any of its members).

The realists about universals in turn divide into the followers of Plato and the followers of **Aristotle**. The **platonists** believe that universals are **abstract objects** located outside space and time (so it is not really clear that platonists hold that properties are really *constituents* of objects either, in fact). The telephone box, a **concrete** object in space and time, is red in virtue of instantiating the abstract universal *redness*. Aristotelians, in contrast, take properties to be **concrete** entities, wholly located in each of their instantiations. Just as the Catholic saints of legend can be wholly present in more than one location, so – according to the Aristotelian – redness can be wholly present in a phone box in England and at the same time wholly present in a sunset in China.

It is not obvious that **common sense** compels us to believe in the existence of universals, but realists about universals tend to claim that they are required to explain certain facts or phenomena that common sense *does* compel us to believe in. Here are some examples:

Facts about resemblance

The telephone box and the Coke can resemble each other in both being red. Call this fact '*f*'. The realist about universals explains *f* in terms of the fact that the telephone box and the Coke can both instantiate one and the same universal of redness.

There are two ways in which opponents of realists about universals (the nominalists) respond to this. Most nominalists offer some account of *f* which does not involve a commitment to universals, for example, the **class nominalist** explains *f* in terms of the fact that both the telephone box and the Coke can are in the class of red things, and the **trope theorist** explains *f* in terms of the fact that both the telephone box and the Coke can have resembling redness tropes. **Austere nominalists**, in contrast, simply deny that any deeper explanation of *f* can be given; the telephone box and the Coke can are both red and this cannot be explained in more metaphysically fundamental terms.

Sentences with terms that seem to refer to general properties

Philosophers sometimes call this phenomenon 'abstract reference'. Consider the sentence, (S) 'wisdom is a virtue'. It looks like this sentence refers to an entity, that is, *wisdom*, and says of that entity that it is a virtue.

However, what is wisdom? What is the entity that the term 'wisdom' in (S) refers to? Realists about universals claim that the most straightforward and plausible answer to this question is that 'wisdom' refers to the universal *wisdom*, the entity that is instantiated by all and only wise things. It is generally assumed on both sides of these debates that, in order to avoid an **ontological commitment** to universals, the nominalist must either (i) claim that the term 'wisdom' in (S) refers to something which is not a universal, for example, the class of wise things, or the class of wisdom tropes, or (ii) offer a **paraphrase** of (S) which only contains nouns which obviously refer to particular things, for example, 'wise things, in so far as they are wise, are virtuous', such that the nominalist can claim that this paraphrase gives the 'true meaning' of (S). Those who go for (i) are **realists** about **properties**: they think that 'wisdom' really does refer to the property of wisdom (it is just that that property is not a universal); while those who go for (ii) are anti-realists about properties; they hold that there are no such things as properties.

Probably the biggest difficulty with realism about universals is the challenge of giving an account of the relationship between an object and the universals it instantiates which does not involve **Bradley's regress**.

Most contemporary realists about universals do not take *every* property to be a universal. In general, realists take **natural properties** to be universals (this is sometimes put as the view that universals are 'sparse', as opposed to 'abundant'), and hence account for the genuine resemblance of objects which share natural properties in terms of universals, and give a **class nominalist** or even **anti-realist** treatment of the other properties objects have.

Further reading: Armstrong (1989); Loux (2006, Chapter 1); Oliver (1996)

UNREALITY OF TIME

J. M. E. **McTaggart** (1908) came up with a now very well known argument for the unreality of time. McTaggart first distinguishes two types of fact: '*A*-facts', which are tensed ('the Battle of Hastings is in the past'), and '*B*-facts', which are tenseless ('the Battle of Hastings is earlier than the Battle of Waterloo'). See the entry on **tensed and tenseless theories of time** for more on *A*- and *B*-facts. He then argues that for time to exist there must be *A*-facts, but that if there are *A*-facts then a contradiction is entailed. The contradiction comes about because every event is such that it is at some point past, at some point present and at some point future (for example, the

Battle of Hastings was once in the future back in 1065, was present in 1066, and is now past). However, concludes McTaggart, this means that every event is past, present *and* future. Since that is clearly contradictory (for nothing can be past *and* present *and* future) we can prove by *reductio* there can be no *A*-facts. As *A*-facts are necessary for there to be time, time does not exist.

The obvious response is that no event can be past, present and future *at the same time*, but the above argument does not prove *that*, it only proves that an event has those contradictory properties at different times (this is similar to the problem of temporary intrinsics; see **perdurantism**). McTaggart expends much effort trying to show that this response leads to a vicious regress, although his success on that front is debatable. Other ways to resist the argument include ditching *A*-facts but still believing that time exists (a move favoured by tenseless theorists) or ditching the existence of non-present times so that every time has to be present (a move open to **presentists**).

Further reading: Dummett (1960); Lowe (1987)

UNRESTRICTED MEREOLOGICAL COMPOSITION

A synonym for 'universalism'; see **Special Composition Question**.

ZENO

There are two notable ancient Greek philosophers called Zeno. One is Zeno of Citium (344–262 BC), founder of Stoicism. However, in the context of metaphysics you are more likely to be concerned with Zeno of Elea (born around 490 BC, unknown date of death), whose work is only relayed to us through second hand sources such as the works of Aristotle, Plato and Simplicius. Zeno aimed to defend the view of Parmenides: monism, the view that there is but one thing (see **simple**). As part of that programme, he deployed his famous paradoxes. It is Simplicius' commentary on Aristotle that contains the most forthright arguments for there being but one thing (the 'paradoxes of plurality'). However, the more commonly discussed paradoxes are the ones of motion, focused on by Aristotle in his *Physics*. These paradoxes were aimed less at demonstrating monism was true, and more directly at demonstrating that nothing ever moves.

There are a few such paradoxes. We will consider only one. The *dichotomy* has a simple set-up. Imagine a runner tries to run 10 yards. To do so, she would have to first run 5 yards, but to do that she must run 2½ yards, and to do that she must run 1¼ yards, etc. So, says Zeno, this process can continue forever. However, at every stage the distance that must be covered is finite, so that means that there are an infinite number of (finite) distances that must be covered. Since nobody can ever travel an infinite number of finite distances, Zeno concludes that nothing ever moves. Zeno's other three paradoxes of motion are the paradox of Achilles and the tortoise, the paradox of the arrow, and the paradox of the stadium (the latter is often taken to demonstrate that space, if it exists, must be infinitely divisible) (see also **infinity** and **supertask**).

BIBLIOGRAPHY

Adams, R. M. (1979) 'Primitive thisness and primitive identity', *Journal of Philosophy*, 76: 5–26.

Ahmed, A. (2007) *Saul Kripke*, London: Continuum.

Allaire, E. (1963) 'Bare particulars', *Philosophical Studies*, 14: 1–8; reprinted in Laurence, S. and Macdonald, C. (eds) (1998) *Contemporary Readings in the Foundations of Metaphysics*, Oxford: Blackwell.

Anscombe, G. E. M. (1971) *Causality and Determination*, London: Cambridge University Press; relevant sections reprinted in Sosa and Tooley 1993.

Armstrong, D. (1980) 'Against "austere" nominalism: a reply to Michael Devitt', *Pacific Philosophical Quarterly*, 61: 440–9; reprinted in Beebee and Dodd 2006.

Armstrong, D. (1983) *What Is a Law of Nature?*, Cambridge: Cambridge University Press.

Armstrong, D. (1989) *Universals: An Opinionated Introduction*, Boulder, CO: Westview Press.

Armstrong, D. (1997). *A World of States of Affairs*, Cambridge: Cambridge University Press.

Armstrong, D. (2004) *Truth and Truthmakers*, Cambridge: Cambridge University Press.

Ayer, A. J. (1954) 'The identity of indiscernibles', in A. J. Ayer (ed.), *Philosophical Essays*, London: St. Martin's Press, 1965.

Baker, A. (2008) 'Simplicity', in E. N. Zalta (ed.), *The Stanford Encyclopedia of Philosophy*, Fall 2008 edn. Online. Available at: http://plato.stanford.edu/archives/fall2008/entries/simplicity.

Balaguer, M. (2008) 'Fictionalism in the philosophy of mathematics', in E. N. Zalta (ed.), *The Stanford Encyclopedia of Philosophy*, Fall 2008 edn. *Online. Available at:* http://plato.stanford.edu/archives/fall2008/entries/fictionalism-mathematics.

Balaguer, M. (2009) 'Platonism in metaphysics', in E. N. Zalta (ed.), *The Stanford Encyclopedia of Philosophy*, Summer 2009 edn. Online. Available at: http://plato.stanford.edu/archives/sum2009/entries/platonism.

Balashov, Y. (1999) 'Relativistic objects', *Noûs*, 33: 644–62.

Barnes, J. (1992) *Aristotle*, Oxford: Oxford University Press.

Beebee, H. (1998) 'Do causes raise the chances of effects?', *Analysis*, 58: 182–90.

Beebee, H. (2000) 'The non-governing conception of laws of nature', *Philosophy and Phenomenological Research*, 61: 571–94.

Beebee, H. (2004) 'Causing and nothingness', in J. Collins, E. J. Hall and L. A. Paul (eds), *Causation and Counterfactuals*, pp. 291–308, Cambridge, MA: MIT Press.

Beebee, H. and Dodd, J. (eds) (2005) *Truthmakers: The Contemporary Debate*, Oxford: Oxford University Press.

Beebee, H. and Dodd, J. (eds) (2006) *Reading Metaphysics*, Oxford: Blackwell.

Beebee, H. and Mele, A. R. (2001) 'Humean compatibilism', *Mind*, 111: 201–24.

Berkeley, G. (1710) *A Treatise Concerning the Principles of Human Knowledge Understanding*. Available in many editions and freely available online. A 'translation' into contemporary English can be found on Jonathan Bennett's Early Modern Texts website. Available at: http://www.earlymoderntexts.com/f_berkeley.html.

Bird, A. (2007) *Nature's Metaphysics: Laws and Properties*, Oxford: Oxford University Press.

Bird, A. and Tobin, E. (2008) 'Natural kinds', in E. N. Zalta (ed.), *The Stanford Encyclopedia of Philosophy*, Spring 2009 edn. Online. Available at: http://plato.stanford.edu/entries/natural-kinds.

Black, M. (1956) 'Why cannot an effect precede its cause', *Analysis*, 16: 49–58.

Blackburn, S. (1999) *Think!*, Oxford: Oxford University Press.

Bourne, C. (2002). 'When am I? A tense time for some tense theorists?', *Australasian Journal of Philosophy*, 80: 359–71.

Bourne, C. (2006) *A Future for Presentism*, Oxford: Oxford University Press.

Bradley, F. H. (1930) *Appearance and Reality*, 9th edn, Oxford: Oxford University Press.

Braun, D. (2008) 'Indexicals', in E. N. Zalta (ed.), *The Stanford Encyclopedia of Philosophy*, Fall 2008 edn. Online. Available at: http://plato.stanford.edu/archives/fall2008/entries/indexicals.

Brock, S. (2002) 'Fictionalism about fictional characters', *Noûs*, 36: 1–21.

Brown, J. R. (2009) 'Thought experiments', in E. N. Zalta (ed.), *The Stanford Encyclopedia of Philosophy*, Fall 2009 edn. Online. Available at: http://plato.stanford.edu/archives/fall2009/entries/thought-experiment.

Brueckner, T. (2008) 'Brains in a vat', in E. N. Zalta (ed.), *The Stanford Encyclopedia of Philosophy*, Fall 2008 edn. Online. Available at: http://plato.stanford.edu/archives/fall2008/entries/brain-vat.

Bunzl, M. (1979) 'Causal overdetermination', *The Journal of Philosophy*, 76: 134–50.

Burke, M. (1992) 'Copper statues and pieces of copper: a challenge to the standard account', *Analysis*, 52: 12–17.

Burke, M. (1994) 'Dion and Theon: an essentialist solution to an ancient puzzle', *Journal of Philosophy*, 91: 129–39.

Butler, J. (1736) 'Of personal identity', in *First Dissertation to the Analogy of Religion*; reprinted in Flew, A. (ed.) (1964) *Body, Mind and Death*, New York: Macmillan and Perry, J. (ed.) (1975) *Personal Identity*, Berkley and Los Angeles: University of California Press.

Button, T. (2006) 'There's no time like the present', *Analysis*, 66: 130–5.

Cameron, R. (2009) 'Intrinsic and extrinsic properties', in R. Le Poidevin, P. Simons, A. McGonigal and R. Cameron (eds), pp. 265–75, *The Routledge Companion to Metaphysics*, London: Routledge.

Carroll, J. and Markosian, N. (2010) *An Introduction to Metaphysics*, New York: Cambridge University Press.

Casati, R. and Varzi, A. (1994) *Holes and Other Superficialities*, Cambridge, MA: MIT Press.

Casati, R. and Varzi, A. (2009) 'Holes', in E. N. Zalta (ed.), *The Stanford Encyclopedia of Philosophy*, Spring 2009 edn. Online. Available at: http://plato.stanford.edu/archives/spr2009/entries/holes.

Casati, R. and Varzi, A. (2010) 'Events', in E. N. Zalta (ed.), *The Stanford Encyclopedia of Philosophy*, Spring 2010 edn. Online. Available at: http://plato.stanford.edu/archives/spr2010/entries/events.

Chalmers, D. J. (undated) 'The Matrix as metaphysics'. Online. Available at: http://consc.net/papers/matrix.html (accessed 1 February, 2010).

Chalmers, D. J., Manley, D. and Wasserman, R. (2009) *Metametaphysics: New Essays on the Foundations of Ontology*, Oxford: Oxford University Press.

Clarke, R. (1993) 'Toward a credible agent-causal account of free will', *Noûs*, 27: 191–203.

Clarke, R. (2008) 'Incompatibilist (nondeterministic) theories of free will', in E. N. Zalta (ed.), *The Stanford Encyclopedia of Philosophy*, Fall 2008 edn. Online. Available at: http://plato.stanford.edu/archives/fall2008/entries/incompatibilism-theories.

Collins, J., Hall, E. J. and Paul, L. A. (eds) (2004) *Causation and Counterfactuals*, Cambridge, MA: MIT Press.

Collins, S. (1982) *Selfless Persons*, Cambridge: Cambridge University Press.

Conee, E. and Sider, T. (2007) *Riddles of Existence*, Oxford: Oxford University Press.

Crisp, T. (2003) 'Presentism', in M. Loux and D. Zimmerman (eds), *The Oxford Handbook of Metaphysics*, Oxford: Oxford University Press.

Crisp, T. (2004a) 'On presentism and triviality', *Oxford Studies in Metaphysics*, 1: 15–20.

Crisp, T. (2004b) 'Reply to Ludlow', *Oxford Studies in Metaphysics*, 1: 37–46.

Dainton, B. (2001) *Time and Space*, Chesham: Acumen.

Daly, C. (2009) 'To be', in R. Le Poidevin, P. Simons, A. McGonigal and R. Cameron (eds), pp. 225–33, *The Routledge Companion to Metaphysics*, London: Routledge.

Dancy, J. (1985) *Introduction to Contemporary Epistemology*, Oxford: Blackwell.

David, M. (2009) 'The correspondence theory of truth', in E. N. Zalta (ed.), *The Stanford Encyclopedia of Philosophy*, Fall 2009 edn. Online. Available at: http://plato.stanford.edu/archives/fall2009/entries/truth-correspondence.

Davidson, D. (1967) 'The logical form of action sentences', in N. Rescher (ed.), *The Logic of Decision and Action*, Pittsburgh: University of Pittsburgh Press; reprinted in Davidson 1980.

Davidson, D. (1969) 'The individuation of events', in N. Rescher (ed.) *Essays in Honor of Carl G. Hempel*, Dordrecht: D. Reidel; reprinted in Davidson 1980.

Davidson, D. (1974) 'On the very idea of a conceptual scheme', *Proceedings and Addresses of the American Philosophical Association*, 47: 5–20; reprinted in Davidson, D. (2001) *Inquiries into Truth and Interpretation*, 2nd edn, Oxford: Clarendon Press. An abridged version is reprinted in Beebee and Dodd 2006.

Davidson, D. (1980) *Essays on Actions and Events*, Oxford: Clarendon Press.

Dennett, D. (1984) *Elbow Room: The Varieties of Free Will Worth Wanting*, Cambridge, MA: Bradford Books.

Descartes, R. (1641) *Meditations on First Philosophy* (available in many editions and freely available online).

Devitt, M. (1980) '"Austere nominalism" or "mirage realism"?', *Pacific Philosophical Quarterly*, 61: 433–9; reprinted in Beebee and Dodd 2006.

Diekemper, J. (2005) 'Presentism and ontological symmetry', *Australasian Journal of Philosophy*, 83: 223–40.

Divers, J. (2002) *Possible Worlds*, London: Routledge.

Divers, J. (2009) 'Possible worlds and possibilia', in R. Le Poidevin, P. Simons, A. McGonigal and R. Cameron (eds), pp. 335–45, *The Routledge Companion to Metaphysics*, London: Routledge.

Dowe, P. (2000) *Physical Causation*, Cambridge: Cambridge University Press.

Dowe, P. (2008) 'Causal processes', in E. N. Zalta (ed.), *The Stanford Encyclopedia of Philosophy*, Fall 2008 Edition. Online. Available at: http://plato.stanford.edu/archives/fall2008/entries/causation-process.

Dretske, F. (1977) 'Laws of nature', *Philosophy of Science*, 39: 69–71.

Dummett, M. (1960) 'A defense of McTaggart's proof of the unreality of time', *The Philosophical Review*, 69: 497–504.

Dummett, M. (1964) 'Bringing about the past', *The Philosophical Review*, 73: 338–59.

Dummett, M. (1991) *The Logical Basis of Metaphysics*, London: Duckworth.

Dupré, J. (1993) *The Disorder of Things: Metaphysical Foundations of the Disunity of Science*, Cambridge, MA: Harvard University Press.

Eagleton, T. (1996) *The Illusions of Postmodernism*, Oxford: Blackwell.

Earman, J. (1986) *A Primer on Determinism*, Dordrecht: Reidel.

Effingham, N. (2009) 'Composition, persistence and identity', in R. Le Poidevin, P. Simons, A. McGonigal and R. Cameron (eds), pp. 296–309, *The Routledge Companion to Metaphysics*, London: Routledge.

Eklund, M. (2009) 'Fictionalism', in E. N. Zalta (ed.), *The Stanford Encyclopedia of Philosophy*, Spring 2009 edn. Online. Available at: http://plato.stanford.edu/archives/spr2009/entries/fictionalism.

Ellis, B. (2001) *Scientific Essentialism*, Cambridge: Cambridge University Press.

Eschleman, A. (2009) 'Moral responsibility', in E. N. Zalta (ed.), *The Stanford Encyclopedia of Philosophy*, Winter 2009 edn. Online. Available at: http://plato.stanford.edu/archives/win2009/entries/moral-responsibility.

Fara, M. (2009) 'Dispositions', in E. N. Zalta (ed.), *The Stanford Encyclopedia of Philosophy*, Summer 2009 edn. Online. Available at: http://plato.stanford.edu/archives/sum2009/entries/dispositions.

Faye, J. (2010) 'Backward causation', in E. N. Zalta (ed.), *The Stanford Encyclopedia of Philosophy*, Spring 2010 edn. Online. Available at: http://plato.stanford.edu/archives/spr2010/entries/causation-backwards.

Field, H. (1980) *Science without Numbers: A Defence of Nominalism*, Oxford: Blackwell.

Fischer, J. M. (1995) *The Metaphysics of Free Will*, Oxford: Blackwell.

Fischer, J. M. (1999) 'Recent work on moral responsibility', *Ethics*, 110: 93–139.

Fischer, J. M. (2007) 'Compatibilism', in J. M. Fischer, R. Kane, D. Pereboom and M. Vargas, *Four Views on Free Will*, Malden, MA: Blackwell.

Forrest, P. (2004). 'The real but dead past: a reply to Braddon-Mitchell', *Analysis*, 64: 358–62.

Forrest, P. (2009) 'The identity of indiscernibles', in E. N. Zalta (ed.), *The Stanford Encyclopedia of Philosophy*, Summer 2009 edn. Online. Available at: http://plato.stanford.edu/archives/sum2009/entries/identity-indiscernible.

Frankfurt, H. (1969). 'Alternate possibilities and moral responsibility', *The Journal of Philosophy*, 66: 829–39.

Frankfurt, H. (1971) 'Freedom of the will and the concept of a person', *Journal of Philosophy*, 68: 5–20; reprinted in Watson 1982.

Gallois, A. (2009) 'Identity over time', in E. N. Zalta (ed.), *The Stanford Encyclopedia of Philosophy*, Winter 2009 edn. Online. Available at: http://plato.stanford.edu/archives/win2009/entries/identity-time.

Geach, P. (1968) 'What actually exists', *Proceedings of the Aristotelian Society*, Suppl. Vol. 42: 7–16.

Geach, P. (1979) *Truth, Love and Immortality: An Introduction to McTaggart's Philosophy*, London: Hutchinson.

Gibbard, A. (1975) 'Contingent identity', *Journal of Philosophical Logic*, 4: 187–221.

Gibson, I. and Pooley, O. (2006) 'Relativistic persistence', *Philosophical Perspectives*, 20: 157–98.

Gillies, D. (2000) *Philosophical Theories of Probability*, London: Routledge.

Gilmore, C. (2006) 'Where in the relativistic world are we?', *Philosophical Perspectives*, 20: 199–236.

Gilmore, C. (2007) 'Time travel, coincidence and persistence', *Oxford Studies in Metaphysics*, 3: 177–98.

Glanzberg, M. (2009) 'Truth', in E. N. Zalta (ed.), *The Stanford Encyclopedia of Philosophy*, Spring 2009 edn. Online. Available at: http://plato.stanford.edu/archives/spr2009/entries/truth.

Grandy, R. E. (2008) 'Sortals', in E. N. Zalta (ed.), *The Stanford Encyclopedia of Philosophy*, Fall 2008 edn. Online. Available at: http://plato.stanford.edu/archives/fall2008/entries/sortals.

Grice, H. P. and Strawson, P. F. (1957) 'In defense of a dogma', *The Philosophical Review*, 65: 141–58.

Hájek, A. (2010) 'Interpretations of probability', in E. N. Zalta (ed.), *The Stanford Encyclopedia of Philosophy*, Spring 2010 edn. Online. Available at: http://plato.stanford.edu/archives/spr2010/entries/probability-interpret.

Hall, E. J. (2010) 'David Lewis's metaphysics', in E. N. Zalta (ed.), *The Stanford Encyclopedia of Philosophy*, Spring 2010 edn. Online. Available at: http://plato.stanford.edu/archives/spr2010/entries/lewis-metaphysics.

Hawley, K. (2009) 'Metaphysics and relativity', in R. Le Poidevin, P. Simons, A. McGonigal and R. Cameron (eds), pp. 507–16, *The Routledge Companion to Metaphysics*, London: Routledge.

Hirsch, E. (2005) 'Physical-objects ontology, verbal disputes and common sense', *Australasian Journal of Philosophy*, 70: 67–97.

Hitchcock, C. (2008) 'Probabilistic causation', in E. N. Zalta (ed.), *The Stanford Encyclopedia of Philosophy*, Fall 2008 edn. Online. Available at: http://plato.stanford.edu/archives/fall2008/entries/causation-probabilistic.

Hoefer, C. (2008) 'Causal determinism', in E. N. Zalta (ed.), *Stanford Encyclopedia of Philosophy*, Fall 2008 edn. Online. Available at: http://plato.stanford.edu/archives/fall2008/entries/determinism-causal.

Hookway, C. (2010) 'Pragmatism', in E. N. Zalta (ed.), *The Stanford Encyclopedia of Philosophy*, Spring 2010 edn. Online. Available at: http://plato.stanford.edu/archives/spr2010/entries/pragmatism.

Horsten, L. (2008) 'Philosophy of mathematics', in E. N. Zalta (ed.), *The Stanford Encyclopedia of Philosophy*, Fall 2008 edn. Online. Available at: http://plato.stanford.edu/archives/fall2008/entries/philosophy-mathematics.

Hudson, H. (2007) 'Simples and gunk', *Philosophy Compass*, 2: 291–302.

Hume, D. (1739–40) *A Treatise of Human Nature*; reprinted in L. A. Selby-Bigge (ed.) (1978), Oxford: Clarendon Press.

Hume, D. (1748/51) *Enquiries Concerning Human Understanding and Concerning the Principles of Morals*; reprinted in L. A. Selby-Bigge (ed.) (1975), 3rd edn, Oxford: Clarendon Press.

James, W. (1975) *Pragmatism and the Meaning of Truth*, Cambridge, MA: Harvard University Press.

Jech, T. (2009) 'Set theory', in E. N. Zalta (ed.), *The Stanford Encyclopedia of Philosophy*, Spring 2009 edn. Online. Available at: http://plato.stanford.edu/archives/spr2009/entries/set-theory.

Joyce, R. (2009) 'Moral anti-realism', in E. N. Zalta (ed.), *The Stanford Encyclopedia of Philosophy*, Summer 2009 edn. Online. Available at: http://plato.stanford.edu/archives/sum2009/entries/moral-anti-realism.

Kane, R. (1999) 'Responsibility, luck, and chance: reflections on free will and indeterminism', *Journal of Philosophy*, 96: 217–40.

Kania, A. (2008) 'The methodology of musical ontology: descriptivism and its implications', *British Journal of Aesthetics*, 48: 426–44.

Kant, I. (1781) *Critique of Pure Reason*; reprinted in N. K. Smith (ed.) (2003), Basingstoke: Palgrave MacMillan. (Many other editions and translations are available, including free online versions.)

Kant, I. (1783) *Prolegomena to Any Future Metaphysics*; reprinted in P. Carus (ed.) (1997), La Salle, IL: Open Court. (Many other editions and translations are available, including free online versions.)

Keller, S. (2004) 'Presentism and truthmaking', *Oxford Studies in Metaphysics*, 1: 83–104.

Keller, S. and Nelson, M. (2001) 'Presentists should believe in time travel', *Australasian Journal of Philosophy*, 79: 333–45.

Kim, J. (1971) 'Causes and events: Mackie on causation', *Journal of Philosophy*, 68: 426–41; reprinted in Sosa and Tooley 1993.

Kim, J. (1973) 'Causation, nomic subsumption, and the concept of event', *Journal of Philosophy*, 70: 217–36.

Kim, J. (ed.) (1993) *Supervenience and Mind: Selected Philosophical Essays,* Cambridge: Cambridge University Press.

Kirk, R. (1999) *Relativism and Realism*, London: Routledge.

Knobe, J. and Nichols, S. (eds) (2008) *Experimental Philosophy*, New York: Oxford University Press.

Kripke, S. (1980) *Naming and Necessity*, Malden, MA: Blackwell.

Kroon, F. (2001) 'Parts and pretense', *Philosophy and Phenomenological Research*, 63: 543–60.

Kuhn, T. S. (1962) *The Structure of Scientific Revolutions*, Chicago: Chicago University Press.

Ladyman, J., Ross, D., Spurrett D. and Collier, J. (2007) *Everything Must Go*, Oxford: Oxford University Press.

Le Poidevin, R. (2003) *Travels in Four Dimensions*, Oxford: Oxford University Press.

Le Poidevin, R. (2009) 'The experience and perception of time', in E. N. Zalta (ed.), *The Stanford Encyclopedia of Philosophy*, Winter 2009 edn. Online. Available at: http://plato.stanford.edu/archives/win2009/entries/time-experience.

Le Poidevin, R., Simons, P., McGonigal, A. and Cameron, R. (eds) (2009). *The Routledge Companion to Metaphysics*, London: Routledge.

Lewis, D. K. (1973a) 'Causation', *Journal of Philosophy*, 70: 556–67; reprinted in Lewis 1986b.

Lewis, D. K. (1973b) *Counterfactuals*, Oxford: Blackwell.

Lewis, D. K. (1976) 'The paradoxes of time travel', *American Philosophical Quarterly*, 13: 145–52; reprinted in Lewis 1986b.

Lewis, D. K. (1983a) 'New work for a theory of universals', *Australasian Journal of Philosophy*, 61: 343–77; reprinted in Lewis, D. K. (1999) *Papers in Metaphysics and Epistemology*, Cambridge: Cambridge University Press.

Lewis, D. K. (1983b) *Philosophical Papers, Vol. I*, Oxford: Blackwell.

Lewis, D. K. (1986a) *On the Plurality of Worlds*, Oxford: Blackwell.

Lewis, D. K. (1986b) *Philosophical Papers, Vol. II*, Oxford: Blackwell.

Lewis, D. K. (1986c) 'Events', in D. K. Lewis, *Philosophical Papers, Vol. II*, pp. 262–9, Oxford: Blackwell.

Lewis, D. K. (2000) 'Causation as influence', *Journal of Philosophy*, 97: 182–97; reprinted in Collins, Hall and Paul 2004.

Lewis, D. K. (2004) 'Void and object', in J. Collins, E. J. Hall and L. A. Paul (eds), *Causation and Counterfactuals*, Cambridge, MA: MIT Press.

Lewis, D. K. (2008) 'Ramseyan humility', in D. Braddon-Mitchell and R. Nola (eds), *Conceptual Analysis and Philosophical Naturalism*, Cambridge, MA: MIT Press.

Lewis, D. K. and Lewis, S. (1970) 'Holes', *Australasian Journal of Philosophy*, 48: 206–12.

Libet, B. (1999) 'Do we have free will?', *Journal of Consciousness Studies*, 6: 47–57.

Locke, J. (1690) *An Essay Concerning Human Understanding*. Available in many editions; also freely available online. A 'translation' into contemporary English can be found on Jonathan Bennett's Early Modern Texts website. Available at: http://www.earlymoderntexts.com/f_locke.html.

Loux, M. (2006) *Metaphysics: A Contemporary Introduction*, 3rd edn, London: Routledge.

Loux, M. and Zimmerman, D. (eds) (2003) *The Oxford Handbook of Metaphysics*, Oxford: Oxford University Press.

Lowe, E. J. (1987) 'The indexical fallacy in McTaggart's proof of the unreality of time', *Mind*, 96: 62–70.

Lowe, E. J. (2002) *A Survey of Metaphysics*, Oxford: Oxford University Press.

Ludlow, P. (2004) 'Presentism, triviality, and the varieties of tensism', *Oxford Studies in Metaphysics*, 1: 21–36.

McDaniel, K. (2009) 'Ways of being', in D. J. Chalmers, D. Manley and R. Wasserman (eds), *Metametaphysics: New Essays on the Foundations of Ontology*, Oxford: Oxford University Press.

Macdonald, C. (2005) *Varieties of Things*, Oxford: Blackwell.

McGrath, M. (2007) 'Propositions', in E. N. Zalta (ed.), *The Stanford Encyclopedia of Philosophy,* Fall 2008 edn. Online. Available at: http://plato.stanford.edu/archives/fall2008/entries/propositions.

McGrath, S. (2005) 'Causation by omission: a dilemma', *Philosophical Studies*, 123: 125–48.

McKenna, M. (2009) 'Compatibilism', in E. N. Zalta (ed.), *The Stanford Encyclopedia of Philosophy*, Winter 2009 edn. Online. Available at: http://plato.stanford.edu/archives/win2009/entries/compatibilism.

Mackie, J. L. (1965) 'Causes and conditions', *American Philosophical Quarterly*, 2: 245–54; reprinted in Sosa and Tooley 1993.

Mackie, P. (2006) *How Things Might Have Been*, Oxford: Clarendon Press.

McLaughlin, B. and Bennett, K. (2008) 'Supervenience', in E. N. Zalta (ed.), *The Stanford Encyclopedia of Philosophy,* Fall 2008 edn. Online. Available at: http://plato.stanford.edu/archives/fall2008/entries/supervenience.

McTaggart, J. M. E. (1908) 'The unreality of time', *Mind*, 17: 457–74; reprinted in Le Poidevin, R. and MacBeath, M. (eds) (1993) *The Philosophy of Time*, Oxford: Oxford University Press.

Margolis, E. and Laurence, S. (2008) 'Concepts', in E. N. Zalta (ed.), *The Stanford Encyclopedia of Philosophy*, Fall 2008 edn. Online. Available at: http://plato.stanford.edu/archives/fall2008/entries/concepts.

Markosian, N. (1993) 'How fast does time pass?', *Philosophy and Phenomenological Research*, 53: 829–44.

Markosian, N. (1999) 'A compatibilist version of the theory of agent causation', *Pacific Philosophical Quarterly*, 80: 257–77.

Markosian, N. (2004) 'A defense of presentism', *Oxford Studies in Metaphysics*, 1: 47–82.

Markosian, N. (2008) 'Restricted composition', in T. Sider, J. Hawthorne and D. Zimmerman (eds), *Contemporary Debates in Metaphysics*, Oxford: Blackwell.

Markosian, N. (2009) 'Time', in E. N. Zalta (ed.), *The Stanford Encyclopedia of Philosophy*, Fall 2009 edn. Online. Available at: http://plato.stanford. edu/archives/fall2009/entries/time.

Martin, C. B. (1980) 'Substance substantiated', *Australasian Journal of Philosophy*, 58: 3–10.

Mele, A. R. (2004) 'Bad news for free will', *New Humanist*, 119. Online. Available at: http://newhumanist.org.uk/698/bad-news-for-free-will (accessed 1 February, 2010).

Mele, A. R. (2006) *Free Will and Luck*, New York: Oxford University Press.

Mele, A. R. (2008) 'Free will and science', *American Philosophical Quarterly*, 45: 107–30.

Melia, J. (2003) *Modality*, Chesham: Acumen.

Mellor, D. H. (1971) *The Matter of Chance*, Cambridge: Cambridge University Press.

Mellor, D. H. (1995) *The Facts of Causation*, London: Routledge.

Mellor, D. H. (1998) *Real Time II*, London: Routledge.

Mellor, D. H. (2005) *Probability: A Philosophical Introduction*, London: Routledge.

Menzies, P. (1989) 'A unified account of causal relata', *Australasian Journal of Philosophy*, 67: 59–83.

Menzies, P. (1996) 'Probabilistic causation and the preemption problem', *Mind*, 85: 105–17.

Menzies, P. (2008) 'Counterfactual theories of causation', in E. N. Zalta (ed.), *The Stanford Encyclopedia of Philosophy*, Winter 2008 edn. Online. Available at: http://plato.stanford.edu/entries/causation-counterfactual.

Merricks, T. (1998) 'There are no criteria of identity over time', *Noûs*, 32: 106–24.

Merricks, T. (1999) 'Endurance, psychological continuity and the importance of personal identity', *Philosophy and Phenomenological Research*, 59: 983–97.

Merricks, T. (2001) *Objects and Persons*, Oxford: Oxford University Press.

Merricks, T. (2006) 'Goodbye growing block', *Oxford Studies in Metaphysics*, 2: 103–10.

Merricks, T. (2007) *Truth and Ontology*, Oxford: Clarendon Press.

Miller, A. (2008) 'Realism', in E. N. Zalta (ed.), *The Stanford Encyclopedia of Philosophy*, Fall 2008 edn. Online. Available at: http://plato.stanford. edu/archives/fall2008/entries/realism.

Moore, A. W. (2001) *The Infinite*, 2nd edn, London: Routledge.

Moore, G. E. (1925) 'A defence of common sense', in J. H. Muirhead (ed.), *Contemporary British Philosophy* (2nd series), London: George Allen and Unwin; reprinted in Moore, G. E. (1959) *Philosophical Papers*, London: George Allen and Unwin and Baldwin, T. (ed.) (1993) *G. E. Moore: Selected Writings*, London: Routledge, pp. 106–33.

Moore, G. E. (1939) 'Proof of an external world', *Proceedings of the British Academy*, 25: 273–300; reprinted in Baldwin, T. (ed.) (1993) *G. E. Moore: Selected Writings,* London: Routledge.

Moore, M. (2009). 'Introduction: the nature of singularist theories of causation', *The Monist*, 92: 3–22.

Mumford, S. (2007) *David Armstrong*, Chesham: Acumen.

Nagel, T. (1986) *The View From Nowhere*, New York: Oxford University Press.

Nichols, S. and Knobe, J. (2007) 'Moral responsibility and determinism: the cognitive science of folk intuitions', *Noûs*, 41: 663–85.

Nolan, D. (2005) *David Lewis*, Chesham: Acumen.

Nolan, D. (2008) 'Modal fictionalism', in E. N. Zalta (ed.), *The Stanford Encyclopedia of Philosophy*, Fall 2008 edn. Online. Available at: http://plato.stanford.edu/archives/fall2008/entries/fictionalism-modal.

Noonan, H. (1989) *Personal Identity*, London and New York: Routledge.

Noonan, H. (2003) 'A flawed argument for perdurance', *Analysis*, 63: 213–15.

Noonan, H. (2009) 'Identity', in E. N. Zalta (ed.), *The Stanford Encyclopedia of Philosophy*, Winter 2009 edn. Online. Available at: http://plato.stanford.edu/archives/win2009/entries/identity.

O'Connor, T. (2008) 'Free will', in E. N. Zalta (ed.), *The Stanford Encyclopedia of Philosophy*, Fall 2008 edn. Online. Available at: http://plato.stanford.edu/archives/fall2008/entries/freewill.

O'Leary-Hawthorne, J. and Cortens, A. (1995) 'Towards ontological nihilism', *Philosophical Studies*, 79: 143–65.

Oliver, A. (1996) 'The metaphysics of properties', *Mind*, 105: 1–80.

Olson, E. (1996) 'Composition and coincidence', *Pacific Philosophical Quarterly*, 77: 374–403.

Olson, E. (1997) *The Human Animal: Personal Identity Without Psychology*, Oxford: Oxford University Press.

Olson, E. (2008) 'Personal identity', in E. N. Zalta (ed.) *The Stanford Encyclopedia of Philosophy*, Winter 2008 edn. Online. Available at: http://plato.stanford.edu/archives/win2008/entries/identity-personal.

Orenstein, A. (2002) *W. V. Quine*, Chesham: Acumen.

Parfit, D. (1971) 'Personal identity', *The Philosophical Review*, 80: 3–27. An abridged version is reprinted, with commentary, in Beebee and Dodd 2006.

Parfit, D. (1984) *Reasons and Persons*, Oxford: Clarendon Press.

Penrose, R. (1989) *The Emperor's New Mind*, Oxford: Oxford University Press.

Pereboom, D. (1995) 'Determinism al dente', *Noûs*, 29: 21–45.

Pereboom, D. (2001) *Living Without Free Will*, Cambridge: Cambridge University Press.

Priest, G. (2005) *Towards Non-Being*, Oxford: Oxford University Press.

Priest, G. (2009) 'Not to be', in R. Le Poidevin, P. Simons, A. McGonigal and R. Cameron (eds), pp. 234–45, *The Routledge Companion to Metaphysics*, London: Routledge.

Prior, A. N. (1959) 'Thank goodness that's over', *Philosophy*, 34: 12–17.

Psillos, S. (2002) *Causation and Explanation*, Chesham: Acumen.

Putnam, H. (1981) *Reason, Truth and History*, Cambridge: Cambridge University Press.

Quine, W. V. (1948) 'On what there is', *Review of Metaphysics*, 2: 21–38; reprinted in Loux M. (ed.) (2001) *Metaphysics: Contemporary Readings*, London: Routledge and in Quine 1980.

Quine, W. V. (1951) 'Two dogmas of empiricism', *The Philosophical Review*, 60, 1: 20–43; reprinted in Quine 1980.

Quine, W. V. (1980) *From a Logical Point of View*, 2nd edn, Cambridge, MA: Harvard University Press.

Ramsey, F. P. (1928) 'Universals of law and of fact', reprinted as 'Law and causality: A Universals of law and of fact', in D. H. Mellor (ed.), *F. P. Ramsey: Foundations: Essays in Philosophy, Logic, Mathematics and Economics*, London: Routledge & Kegan Paul, 1978.

Rea, M. (2003) 'Four-dimensionalism', in M. Loux and D. Zimmerman (eds), *The Oxford Handbook of Metaphysics*, Oxford: Oxford University Press.

Reicher, M. (2008) 'Nonexistent objects', in E. N. Zalta (ed.), *The Stanford Encyclopedia of Philosophy*, Fall 2008 edn. Online. Available at: http://plato.stanford.edu/archives/fall2008/entries/nonexistent-objects.

Robinson, H. (2009) 'Substance', in E. N. Zalta (ed.), *The Stanford Encyclopedia of Philosophy*, Winter 2009 edn. Online. Available at: http://plato.stanford.edu/archives/win2009/entries/substance.

Rorty, R. (1989) *Contingency, Irony and Solidarity*, Cambridge: Cambridge University Press.

Rosen, G. (1990) 'Modal fictionalism', *Mind*, 99: 327–54.

Rosen, G. and Dorr, C. (2002) 'Composition as fiction', in R. Gale (ed.), *The Blackwell Guide to Metaphysics*, Oxford: Blackwell.

Rosenkrantz, G. (1995) 'Concrete/abstract', in J. Kim (ed.), *A Companion to Metaphysics*, Oxford: Blackwell.

Russell, B. (1905) 'On denoting', *Mind*, 14: 479–93 (and freely available from many websites).

Salmon, W. C. (1998) *Causality and Explanation*, New York: Oxford University Press.

Sanford, D. H. (2008) 'Determinates vs. determinables', in E. N. Zalta (ed.), *The Stanford Encyclopedia of Philosophy*, Winter 2008 edn. Online. Available at: http://plato.stanford.edu/archives/win2008/entries/determinate-determinables.

Schaffer, J. (2000) 'Trumping preemption', *Journal of Philosophy*, 97: 165–81.

Schaffer, J. (2001) 'Causation, influence, and effluence', *Analysis*, 61: 11–19.

Schaffer, J. (2003) 'Overdetermining causes', *Philosophical Studies*, 114: 23–45.

Schaffer, J. (2007) 'From nihilism to monism', *Australasian Journal of Philosophy*, 85: 175–91.

Schaffer, J. (2008) 'The metaphysics of causation', in E. N. Zalta (ed.), *The Stanford Encyclopedia of Philosophy*, Fall 2008 edn. Online. Available at: http://plato.stanford.edu/archives/fall2008/entries/causation-metaphysics.

Schaffer, J. (2009) 'On what grounds what', in D. J. Chalmers, D. Manley and R. Wasserman (eds), *Metametaphysics: New Essays on the Foundations of Ontology*, Oxford: Oxford University Press.

Schechtman, M. (1990) 'Personhood and personal identity', *The Journal of Philosophy* 87: 71–92; reprinted in Beebee and Dodd 2006.

Scruton, R. (2001) *Kant: A Very Short Introduction*, Oxford: Oxford University Press.

Shoemaker, S. (1970) 'Persons and their pasts', *American Philosophical Quarterly* 7: 269–85.

Sider, T. (2001) *Four-Dimensionalism*, Oxford: Oxford University Press.

Sider, T., Hawthorne, J. and Zimmerman, D. (eds) (2008) *Contemporary Debates in Metaphysics*, Oxford: Blackwell.

Simons, P. (2003) 'Events', in M. Loux and D. Zimmerman (eds), *The Oxford Handbook of Metaphysics*, Oxford: Oxford University Press.

Sklar, L. (1992) *Philosophy of Physics*, Oxford: Oxford University Press.

Smart, J. (1961) 'Free will, praise and blame', *Mind*, 70: 291–306.

Smart, J. (1964) *Problems of Space and Time*, London: Macmillan.

Smilansky, S. (2000) *Free Will and Illusion*, Oxford: Oxford University Press.

Smith, N. (1997) 'Bananas enough for time travel?', *British Journal for the Philosophy of Science*, 48: 363–89.

Snowdon, P. F. (1991) 'Personal identity and brain transplants', in D. Cockburn (ed.), *Human Beings*, Cambridge: Cambridge University Press.

Sosa, E. and Tooley, M. (eds) (1993) *Causation*, Oxford: Oxford University Press.

Strawson, P. F. (1959) *Individuals: An Essay in Descriptive Metaphysics*, London: Methuen.

Strawson, P. F. (1962) 'Freedom and resentment', *Proceedings of the British Academy*, 48: 1–25; reprinted in Watson 1982 and several other collections.

Stroud, B. (1984) *The Significance of Philosophical Scepticism*, Oxford: Oxford University Press.

Swinburne, R. (1984) 'Personal identity: the dualist theory', in S. Shoemaker and R. Swinburne (eds), *Personal Identity*, Oxford: Blackwell.

Swoyer, C. (2008) 'Abstract entities', in T. Sider, J. Hawthorne and D. Zimmerman (eds), *Contemporary Debates in Metaphysics*, Oxford: Blackwell.

Thomasson, A. (2008) 'Existence questions', *Philosophical Studies*, 141: 63–78.

Thomasson, A. (2009) 'Categories', in E. N. Zalta (ed.), *The Stanford Encyclopedia of Philosophy*, Spring 2009 edn. Online. Available at: http://plato.stanford.edu/entries/categories.

Thomson, J. (1983) 'Parthood and identity across time', *Journal of Philosophy*, 80: 201–20.

Tooley, M. (1977) 'The nature of laws', *Canadian Journal of Philosophy*, 7: 667–98.

Tooley, M. (1987) *Causation: A Realist Approach*, Oxford: Clarendon Press.

Tooley, M. (1997) *Time, Tense and Causation*, Oxford: Oxford University Press.

van Inwagen, P. (1975) 'The incompatibility of free will and determinism', *Philosophical Studies*, 27: 185–99; reprinted in Watson 1982 and Beebee and Dodd 2006.

van Inwagen, P. (1981) 'The doctrine of arbitrary undetached parts', *Pacific Philosophical Quarterly*, 61: 123–37.

van Inwagen, P. (1990) *Material Beings*, New York: Cornell University Press.

van Inwagen, P. (1998) 'Metaontology', *Erkenntnis*, 48: 233–50.

Varzi, A. (2009) 'Mereology', in E. N. Zalta (ed.), *The Stanford Encyclopedia of Philosophy*, Summer 2009 edn. Online. Available at: http://plato.stanford.edu/archives/sum2009/entries/mereology.

Vihvelin, K. (2008) 'Arguments for incompatibilism', in E. N. Zalta (ed.), *The Stanford Encyclopedia of Philosophy*, Fall 2008 edn. Online. Available at: http://plato.stanford.edu/archives/fall2008/entries/incompatibilism-arguments.

Wasserman, R. (2002) 'The standard objection to the standard account', *Philosophical Studies*, 111: 197–216.

Watson, G. (ed.) (1982) *Free Will*, Oxford: Oxford University Press.

Weatherson, B. (2008) 'Intrinsic vs. extrinsic properties', in E. N. Zalta (ed.), *The Stanford Encyclopedia of Philosophy*, Fall 2008 edn. Online. Available at: http://plato.stanford.edu/archives/fall2008/entries/intrinsic-extrinsic.

Weatherson, B. (2010), 'David Lewis', in E. N. Zalta (ed.), *The Stanford Encyclopedia of Philosophy*, Spring 2010 edn. Online. Available at: http://plato.stanford.edu/archives/spr2010/entries/david-lewis.

Wegner, D. (2002) *The Illusion of Conscious Will*, Cambridge, MA: MIT Press.

Wetzel, L. (2008) 'Types and tokens', in E. N. Zalta (ed.), *The Stanford Encyclopedia of Philosophy*, Winter 2008 edn. Online. Available at: http://plato.stanford.edu/archives/win2008/entries/types-tokens.

Wetzel, T. (2008) 'States of affairs', in E. N. Zalta (ed.), *The Stanford Encyclopedia of Philosophy*, Fall 2008 edn. Online. Available at: http://plato.stanford.edu/archives/fall2008/entries/states-of-affairs.

Wiggens, D. (1967) *Identity and Spatio-temporal Continuity*, Oxford: Blackwell.

Williams, B. (1970) 'The self and the future', *The Philosophical Review*, 79: 161–80; reprinted in Williams, B. (ed.) (1973) *Problems of the Self*, Cambridge: Cambridge University Press.

Williams, D. C. (1953) 'On the elements of being: II', *The Review of Metaphysics*, 7: 171–92.

Wright, C. (1992) *Truth and Objectivity*, Cambridge, MA: Harvard University Press.

Zimmerman, D. (2008) 'The privileged present: defending an "*A*-theory" of time', in T. Sider, J. Hawthorne and D. Zimmerman (eds), *Contemporary Debates in Metaphysics*, Oxford: Blackwell.

INDEX

Philosophy: The Basics

Fourth Edition

Nigel Warburton

Philosophy: The Basics gently eases the reader into the world of philosophy. Each chapter considers a key area of philosophy, explaining and exploring the basic ideas and themes including:

- Can you prove God exists?
- How do we know right from wrong?
- How should we define freedom of speech?
- Do you know how science works?
- Is your mind different from your body?
- Can you define art?

For the fourth edition of this best-selling book, Nigel Warburton has added new sections to several chapters, revised others and brought the further reading sections up to date, If you've ever asked 'what is philosophy?', or wondered whether the world is really the way you think it is, this is the book for you.

ISBN13: 978–0–415–32773–2 (pbk)

Available at all good bookshops
For ordering and further information please visit
www.routledge.com

Eastern Philosophy: Key Readings

Oliver Leaman

Eastern Philosophy: Key Readings draws together extracts from a wide range of primary and secondary sources, which cover the many branches of Eastern philosophy and religion. Quotations are arranged under concept headings, and open up the debates on topics such as zen, yin-yang and Daoism, as well as offering an overview of Eastern philosophical perspectives on subjects such as happiness, war and imagination.

Material is drawn not only from such cornerstone texts as the *Bhagavad Gita* and the *I Ching*, but also from modern writings on Eastern philosophy and religion. Extracts are prefaced by Oliver Lealman's succinct introductions, and supplemented by a glossary of terms, all of which make this a unique and accessible way into a fascinating discipline.

ISBN13: 978–0–415–17358–2 (pbk)

Available at all good bookshops
For ordering and further information please visit
www.routledge.com

Logic: The Basics

Jc Beall

Logic: The Basics is a hands-on introduction to the philosophically alive field of logical inquiry. Covering both classical and non-classical theories, it presents some of the core notions of logic such as validity, basic connectives, identity, 'free logic' and more. This book:

- introduces some basic ideas of logic from a semantic and philosophical perspective
- uses logical consequence as the focal concept throughout
- considers some of the controversies and rival logics that make for such a lively field.

This accessible guide includes chapter summaries and suggestions for further reading as well as exercises and sample answers throughout. It is an ideal introduction for those new to the study of logic as well as those seeking to gain the competence and skills needed to move to more advanced work in logic.

ISBN13: 978–0–415–77499–4 (pbk)

Available at all good bookshops
For ordering and further information please visit
www.routledge.com

Philosophy of Education: The Key Concepts

Second Edition

Christopher Winch and John Gingell

This new edition of *Philosophy of Education: The Key Concepts* is an easy to use A–Z guide summarizing all the key terms, ideas and issues central to the study of educational theory today. Fully updated, the book is cross-referenced throughout and contains pointers to further reading, as well as new entries on such topics as:

- Citizenship and Civic Education
- Liberalism
- Capability
- Well-being
- Patriotism
- Globalisation
- Open-mindedness
- Creationism and Intelligent Design.

Comprehensive and authoritative this highly accessible guide provides all that a student, teacher or policy-maker needs to know about the latest thinking on education in the 21st century.

ISBN13: 978–0–415–42893–4 (pbk)

Available at all good bookshops
For ordering and further information please visit
www.routledge.com